Invisible
Exile

Invisible Exile

The Travel Writing of Displacement

Kimberley Kinder

UNIVERSITY OF MINNESOTA PRESS
MINNEAPOLIS
LONDON

This project was made possible by a grant from
The University of Michigan Office of the Vice
President for Research (OVPR) and the Taubman
College of Architecture and Urban Planning at
the University of Michigan.

Published by the University of Minnesota Press
111 Third Avenue South, Suite 290
Minneapolis, MN 55401-2520
http://www.upress.umn.edu

ISBN 978-1-5179-1946-7 (hc)
ISBN 978-1-5179-1947-4 (pb)

A Cataloging-in-Publication record for this book is
available from the Library of Congress.

Printed in the United States of America on
acid-free paper

The University of Minnesota is an equal-opportunity
educator and employer.

UMP BmB 2025

To C & C, and our adventures on Fruitless Mountain

.

Contents

Introduction

Travel writing is an old practice connected to identity and governance. During the medieval era, fictional accounts like Chaucer's *Canterbury Tales* and Dante's *Divine Comedy* offered instruction about morality and the social order. During the Enlightenment era, empirical travelogues by philosophers like Francis Bacon and John Locke revolutionized the scientific imagination and shaped colonial worldviews. Similarly, today, gap-year backpackers and heritage seekers write memoirs about visiting distant lands and returning with new understandings about who they are and how they wish to live.[1]

In other words, travel—including the act of writing about it— is constructive. Travelers use movement through space to explore personal identity and social norms. Then, by organizing those experiences into cohesive narratives, they deepen and solidify their perspectives in conversation with others.

However, because construction is an act of power, not all narratives get told. The travel-writing genre contains many historical biases. It favors privileged authors traveling for personal edification or even self-indulgence, as opposed to migrant workers, domestic servants, or war refugees traveling for work or for survival.[2] It favors extended, dramatic, once-in-a-lifetime adventures to faraway and supposedly primitive places,[3] rather than shorter trips to well-trodden destinations closer to home. A third limitation is that society affords men and young adults greater license to roam than women, mothers, and seniors who are pressured to stay home, receive protection, and provide caretaking.[4] Additionally, the genre favors triumphal and appreciative journeys with clear benchmarks of personal growth and development,[5] as opposed to journeys taken in sadness or ending with despair. Cumulatively, because of these biases, many travelers and their narratives are preemptively discounted for reasons like age, gender, class, ability, race, and citizenship.

Despite these long-standing silences, recent trends create important new opportunities to reassess whose voices are valued and how the concept of *journey* is defined. One trend, which other scholars likewise observe, is the rise of digital self-publishing that partially bypasses market barriers to dissemination. Tweets, posts, podcasts, online diaries, and travel blogs now influence where travelers go and how readers perceive distant locations. These sources also provide new evidence for how travelers—including those in diverse and vulnerable contexts—connect geographic mobility with projects of self-development.[6]

A second trend, and one awaiting further analysis, involves the explosion over the past two decades of life history writing not only through online blogging but also through commercial publishing. The publishing world has taken a multicultural turn in recent decades, for instance through the increased visibility of Black and Brown authors, feminist perspectives, and queer-themed literature. Similarly, the boom in autobiographical publishing since the 1990s includes not only elite narratives—the political biographies and celebrity memoirs of the rich and famous—but also a good deal of "previously unknown writers" who are "not celebrities or political figures" and whose work, by airing "a dissenting voice," has "allowed important stories to come to light."[7] This memoir-writing boom is likewise connected with the general rise of "trauma talk" where people tell "their painful stories, not only in the therapist's office and in other private spaces," but also by "publicly broadcasting and disseminating [those stories] as never before."[8] As a result, commercial life history writing now includes many voices and experiences that were previously underrepresented within literary culture.

The authors contributing to this publishing boom use personal narrative to explore shared human experiences, especially experiences of self-change. At its core, memoir writing is about "epiphanies—remembered moments perceived to have significantly impacted the trajectory of a person's life, times of existential crises that forced a person to attend to and analyze lived experience, and events after which life does not seem quite the same."[9] This focus on human experience also includes experiences of space and place. Within autobiography, cultural geography "provides not so much an explanation but the reality background in which [authors] are, more or less, anchored."[10] In response to this anchoring, memoirists often—and intentionally— develop thick descriptions of the dynamic spatial and social landscapes linking their place in the world with their sense of self.

Importantly, even when life history writing is not overtly marketed as travel writing—for instance, as stories about a dramatic, once-in-a-lifetime journey to remote and isolated villages on the opposite side of the globe—many narratives nevertheless engage with mobility themes. Life history writing often contains rich and detailed evidence of people using spatial mobility to reinvent their identities and transform their life circumstances—or, conversely, of mobility barriers preventing such undertakings. This acute interest in movement, anchors, and self-change makes memoirs a potentially rich source of primary data for understanding the interaction between place and identity. Analyzing these emerging sources—including the narratives that defy the historical biases of the travel-writing canon— could potentially move the field beyond its long-standing exclusions to instead establish new parameters for what counts as travel and who gets to write about it.

To this end, when researching this book, instead of starting with the aforementioned preconceived notions about what travel is *supposed* to look like, I started from the proposition that *one goal of travel writing is to explain how movement through space facilitates self-reinvention.* Using this filter, autobiographical travel writing still includes stories of gap-year backpackers and heritage seekers traversing the Global South.[11] But, alongside these staples, this redefined genre can now also accommodate a greater range of travelers and more diverse journeys.

For instance, this alternative metric makes space to include stories of religious exiles journeying from Hasidic Brooklyn to secular Manhattan.[12] It makes space for narratives written by adult adoptees touring prisons in search of their racial roots.[13] It makes space for the experiences of young adults traveling from the impoverished corn fields to the urban ivory towers.[14] It makes space for stories about the girl who knows he's a boy,[15] the Asian kid raised to pretend she is white,[16] the differently abled child instructed to conceal her condition,[17] and the traumatized child whose abuse is ignored[18]—and, specifically, for *the spatial journeys* these authors take on their roads to healing. Some healing journeys involve thousands of miles,[19] while other travelers move only to the other side of town,[20] a seemingly small physical distance that may nevertheless be socially profound.

Regardless of distance, in my assessment, what makes these narratives a form of travel writing is the way authors combine movement through space with the reinvention of self. Although many such narratives have long been—and continue to be—overlooked within travel-writing scholarship, travel is central to the way these narratives unfold.[21] These spatial journeys are deeply transformative, and the corresponding narrations shed important light on cultural geographical theories of place-self relationships.

By bringing previously discounted voices and experiences into the conversation, this book diversifies scholarly understandings about what counts as travel, who gets to participate, and how it shapes identity. Society is diverse. People have opportunities to encounter radically different social worlds without crossing continents or international borders. Travel is often an act of desperation rather than one of privilege. And dozens of repetitive short trips can be just as momentous as one extended trek. By highlighting these other mobility-related experiences, this book reframes travel and travel writing as an important *everyday* tool for identity construction in contexts of *repression and resistance.*

Shining a Light on Invisible Exile

In particular, this book's analysis of diverse, contemporary travel writing focuses on one specific travel archetype—the archetype of *invisible exile.* During the last two decades, stories of invisible exile—my name for an intersectional and ubiquitous but largely unacknowledged form of displacement born of class, gender, sexuality, religion, race, ability, and trauma—have revolutionized life history writing. Instead of only being offered the biographies of the rich and famous, the public now devours tales of ordinary people whose harrowing life circumstances set them on the road to escape oppression and construct new homes. This book is based on forty such life history narratives that, in my view, illustrate the pervasiveness of invisible exile, as well as its costliness and its social power. The authors writing these narratives travel to socially foreign worlds to be safe, and although invisible exile is not a new phenomenon, their journeys to unfamiliar soil are habitually erased.

Diversifying travel writing to include invisible exile challenges expectations about what exile looks like and who experiences it. Research on exile typically focuses on ousted political leaders or activist dissidents who, to avoid imprisonment or execution, are either banished or flee from their countries of origin. These studies emphasize ruptured citizenship. "Indeed," as exile scholars note, "the interplay between nationalism and exile is like Hegel's dialectic of servant and master, opposites forming and constituting each other."[22] It is no surprise, then, that many stories of invisible exile intersect with these themes.[23]

Although citizenship is one measure of belonging, exile does not always involve international borders. In the past, anti-colonial revolutionaries exiled from India sought refuge not by moving abroad but by sheltering within the Francophone enclaves nestled within their British-controlled homeland.[24] Similarly, today, many "Palestinians in Israel . . . live as 'exiles at home.'"[25] In the United Kingdom, women fleeing domestic violence often isolate from known friends, resources, and employers, and so experience "exile even within one's own country, and via journeys of relatively short distance."[26] The notion of exile is likewise salient within U.S. histories of racial passing where African Americans integrating into white communities experienced the "exile" of "leaving behind families, friends, and communities without any available avenue for return."[27]

Building on this racial identity framework, unlike other forms of *passing*, which are temporary and preserve community ties, *passing* becomes *exile* when it becomes indefinite, marked by a lasting break with prior identities and a durable forsaking of belonging. It's not that travelers present different faces in different places. It's that society—the community of origin, the host community, or both—disavows dual citizenship. People are expected to stay on one side of the race line—or the lines demarcating class, gender, sexuality, religion, ability, and trauma—and they are punished if they try to cross those borders. For travelers who make those unsanctioned journeys anyway, the punitive cost is often the stripping away of prior identities and group affinities, as well as lost access to the cultural and economic landscapes that once supported them.

In this book, exile takes many forms. Some exiles, as expected, are formal refugees crossing international borders. Other exiles, however, are neither so formal nor so visible. Invisible exile includes people escaping religious cults,[28] people made homeless through forced displacement,[29] and other travelers who, for various reasons, find themselves cut off from their roots and plunged into strange new worlds sometimes mere blocks from their former homes.[30] Invisible exile includes self-exiled pilgrims embarking on nomadic quests to heal from homophobia, illness, abuse, and rape.[31] It includes people relocating to shed inaccurate gender assignments or escape ableist stigmatization.[32] Some people are born into exile—for instance, born poor or born Black—and then preemptively excluded from larger group memberships.[33] Other exiles are adopted into spaces of privilege only to find they are still marked as Other and inhabit shared spaces without full acceptance.[34]

In all these scenarios, life history writing sheds light on spatial processes of exclusion. It also sheds light on the journeys taken in search of new belonging.

Importantly, in terms of outcomes, these journeys produce mixed results. On the positive side, invisible exile travel writers overwhelmingly report that, by moving through their journeys, they gain at least some degree of personal insight, emotional respite, economic mobility, community support, social validation, or self-fulfillment.

However, their narratives also show that travelers pay a steep price. Exiles lose a lot along the way. There are lost families—lost parents, siblings, spouses, and children—in addition to groupwide ostracization and lost social networks.[35] There are economic losses for travelers who are disowned and whose property is confiscated.[36] There are identity losses through revoked heritage and ruptured personal storylines.[37] The spatial dislocations and broken place attachments are likewise profound.[38] Many invisible exiles do not survive these losses. Or, if they do, they describe feeling that even though their heart still beats, they've endured a form of existential death. Who they were is gone forever, and they face the future as someone else.

The existing scholarship on travel writing—which has historically emphasized the types of journeys that society rewards, rather than ones considered taboo—is ill-equipped to make sense of these losses. This shortcoming must be rectified. Focusing only on what travelers gain silences the pain and trauma of dislocation. Focusing only on gains offers no critique of societies that strip travelers of belonging as punishment for not conforming. Focusing only on gains also says nothing about the nature of the journeys taken through invisible exile, the process of converting furtive motion into self-reinvention, and the places that assist or block these quests. Remaining silent on these matters perpetuates trauma, stigmatization, and alienation—all outcomes that this book resists.

To shed light on these experiences, this hybrid analysis—part social sciences and part humanities—bundles diverse travel experiences together to shed light on a common phenomenon that, until recently, had no name. In naming this phenomenon *invisible exile,* I am also giving it a map—a cartography of starting points, ending points, and stops along the way. By compiling these stories and by plotting their trajectories—literally, through a guided tour of material and symbolic spaces—this book sheds light on the transformative nature of travel and on the normative environments encountered along the way. As such, this book is partly about exilers and hosts, including the forces that frame certain journeys as taboo. Importantly, however, this book is also about the overlooked travelers and the need to bring their erased journeys to light, both to better understand the nature of invisible exile and to help fellow travelers construct common ground.

Invisible Exile Travel Writing Is an Act of Narrative Resistance

In response to social practices that render certain journeys taboo, invisible exile travel writing is an act of *narrative resistance* that disrupts the links connecting space, identity, and social control. *Identity* in this context refers to individual identity in the psychological sense of personality type and life goals, as well as to identity politics in the sociological sense of race, class, and gender. In both meanings of the word, although identity is inherently complex, contradictory, and unfinished, the crux of identity work is to construct a sense of self that feels coherent.[39]

The primary tool for constructing this coherence is narration. Narration can be linguistic, as in the stories people tell and the words they use to interpret experiences.[40] Narration can also be embodied—for instance, expressed through gestures, habits, and accessories.[41] In both cases, identity narration is much like identity itself: fragmented and incomplete, "a kind of trickster" or "ploy by which we disguise the genuine nature of ourselves—as splintered and discontinuous."[42] Despite this discontinuousness, the cornerstone of identity work is to *construct* narrative coherence. Indeed, the capacity to construct a coherent narrative is "the very thing which guarantees us the ability to have a self, at least in the sense of something we perceive as unified and whole."[43]

People construct this sense of unity through dialogue. Dialogue, like identity, is inherently relational. In this "two-way process,"[44] people "project" the identities they seek while simultaneously being "cast" by others into prescribed roles.[45] In this process, environmental "mirroring" plays a crucial role, with some scholars going so far as to assert that "identity narratives can basically only be told to a person by others."[46]

The trouble for invisible exiles, however, is that dialogical interactions can discipline as easily as they validate. In these mirroring processes, "recognition is double-edged: rejection as well as acceptance of the recognized Other is possible."[47] Through selective mirroring, physical and social environments shape and constrain identity development. "Although a community is polyphonic (composed of many voices), the ruling class attempts to create a single hegemonic story to maintain the status quo. This monologic story can be thought of as a master narrative: a dominant discourse that portrays itself as natural, unanimous, and eternal, working to silence alternative narratives."[48]

This silencing marginalizes some narratives and prevents others from emerging. For listeners, narratives that do not conform with preexisting norms may feel inappropriate or irrelevant to the present moment. For speakers, nonconforming narratives may feel "too painful or too distant to put into words."[49] For some people and some topics, society simply does not create appropriate times and places for telling. These disconnects have important consequences. Since "a narrative of identity is a necessary condition for the existence of any notion of agency and subjectivity,"[50] the absence of a community of listeners willing and able to hear and validate certain experiences is "a form of linguistic oppression."[51]

Linguistic oppression produces two kinds of silence, both of which affect invisible exile. The first silence is rooted in privilege and benefits people whose experiences align with social norms. Although a lifestyle lived in harmony with dominant cultural scripts is never worry-free, society rarely demands overt justifications for those experiences. If the idea is that one *should* have a college degree, a white-collar job, a male anatomy, a white complexion, a heterosexual marriage, a house in the suburbs, an able body, and a Christian worldview—and I comply—I am rarely asked to defend my choices. In this context, "being silent" can be "a form of power; by not speaking one is claiming that one need not explain or justify."[52] This silence is normative. Without saying a word, the lack of discussion normalizes the expectation that certain experiences are *the* measure of success, rather than merely one possibility among many.

Alongside the privilege of not needing to speak, a second form of silence involves having the desire to explain but being denied the opportunity to do so. When life does not go according to plan—and especially when unexpected events are negative, rather than positive—people often feel pressure to evaluate what happened. When problems arise, people often feel "the need to gain back power through voice, to justify and explain."[53] In these contexts, "trouble is the engine of narrative and the justification for going public with a story."[54]

Unfortunately, however, many audiences do not wish to hear about certain types of trouble. As just one example, consider sexual assault. "Survivors of sexual violence are implicitly or explicitly told not to talk about their experience."[55] If survivors speak out anyway, they frequently experience "silencing, as in not allowing the speaker to talk, or it can be silencing through refusing to believe, deliberately misunderstanding or re-interpreting the event in ways that do not validate the speaker's experiences, or simply by being distracted and inattentive."[56]

For these reasons, whether a narrative involves sexual assault or other subject matter considered taboo, not everyone has equal access to collective narrative processing. Although co-narration can be a tool to "convert the raw Trouble into a manageable Problem that can be handled with procedural muscle,"[57] when environments refuse to co-narrate, silence predominates, and trouble remains unresolved.

Tales of exile are nothing if not tales of trouble, and the invisibilization of certain forms of exile is a form of linguistic oppression. The travel narratives capturing these experiences are not simply stories of novelty (e.g., of visiting foreign countries and interacting with new cultures) nor are they accounts of normative self-change (e.g., of passing through conventional rites of passage or expected life developments). Instead, tales of invisible exile are tales born from seemingly irreconcilable misalignments between a traveler's sense of self and the life scripts available within their environment. These are tales of journeys and selves that, according to certain dominant ideologies, cannot and should not be made.

Given this refusal to collectively co-narrate certain experiences, telling tales of invisible exile is an act of resistance. Like other acts of "narrative resistance,"[58] these stories have the potential to dismantle the status quo either directly through "overt critiques" of external authority or indirectly through the "posing of an alternative."[59] These acts of narrative resistance produce different historical knowledge about self and society, as well as different ideas about the hoped-for future, thereby "reimagining and transforming our relationship with place, our relationships to others, and our understanding of what behaviors and actions are possible."[60]

From this perspective, I see invisible exile travel writing as a double form of resistance. First, travelers take nonconforming journeys. Second, they defy the normative silence that otherwise keeps such journeys secret. Publicizing these narratives puts invisible exile on the map for others to see. By shining a light on these journeys, fellow travelers can more easily find co-narrative support among peers. Concurrently, this heightened exposure is a resource for revealing diversity, empowering marginalized voices, and moving society as a whole toward greater empathy and inclusion.

Invisible Exile Experiences Are Captured in Cultural Artifacts

In this book, I approach travel-related autobiographies as cultural artifacts. A cultural artifact is an object that provides information about the people and societies creating it. In archaeology, artifacts include the everyday objects and tools that shed light on the relationships, norms, and beliefs prevalent at the time of their use.[61] Similarly, in cultural studies, artifacts from workers' movements or feminist organizing include the newsletters, songs, books, and zines that activists created for educational purposes or to channel outrage, artifacts that, decades later, began appearing as special collections in institutional archives.[62] In all these scenarios, artifacts function as "objects . . . loaded with meaning."[63]

In a similar fashion, literary geographers have long regarded novels, poems, and plays as significant cultural artifacts for three primary reasons. First, these literary depictions "establish powerful images that affect public attitudes about our landscapes and regions," images that "not only describe the world" but also "help shape it."[64] Second, instead of only analyzing empirical and philosophical sources, the inclusion of more diverse literary perspectives enriches the field by "push[ing] toward 'greater multivocality in geographical knowledge.'"[65] Third, literary artifacts serve as "a testing ground in which to confirm and amplify" geographical theories and concepts,[66] which helps geographers "unpack the role of space and place in the dynamics of identity and difference at various scales."[67]

I embrace all three goals in this book. In my analysis of invisible exile, I use literary artifacts to diversify geographical inquiry, to understand how literature shapes the geographical imagination, and to test the state of geographical knowledge.

Additionally, the cultural artifacts examined here were chosen partly because of their ability to challenge conventional biases within the travel-writing genre. Traditionally, travel writing has been narrowly defined as the domain of "independent travelers who distanced themselves from the 'hordes' of tourists by seeking out authentic and never-before-seen sites."[68] These travelers "voluntarily renounce" the "epistemological comforts of home" to instead "consciously seek insecurity through exposing themselves to unconventional travel experiences."[69] These travelers are supposedly driven "not by instrumental reasons, but by sheer 'love of travel,'" by an interest in "global ecumenical consciousness," and by "their interest in social diagnosis."[70]

In short, the term *traveler* is predefined as a position of privilege. "Immigrants, refugees, exiles, nomads, and the homeless also move in and out of these discourses as metaphors, tropes, and symbols but rarely as historically recognized producers of critical discourses themselves."[71] Although many people are on the move, "today, travel writers are still mostly men" traveling for work (e.g., for news agencies, mass media, or diplomatic services) or embarking on risky expeditions with the safety net of class privilege or other forms of "bourgeois security."[72] Moreover, the term *traveler* is explicitly defined in ways that exclude vulnerability. "Travelers with literary ambitions" move "voluntarily and without being subject to any particular economic or political pressure," which means they are "neither exiles nor on the run."[73] Immigrant mobility is likewise dismissed as illegitimate travel based on the assumption that genuine travelers know "not to remain in one place too long" and approach migration as "merely tentative and not intended to be final."[74] This narrow definition pre-empts the "marginal man," the "stranger," and the "newcomer" from counting as a "traveler,"[75] thereby denying these figures a place and voice within travel-writing scholarship.

One partial exception to this pattern is the figure of the flaneur. This romantic street wanderer traverses cities like Paris as "an expression of freedom, a medium for the creation of meaning, and a way of subverting conventional values and world views."[76] Like other travelers, the *flaneur* explores "global ecumene,"[77] but instead of traversing the globe, this traveler finds diversity in the immigrant enclaves nestled within "the marginalized parts" of European cities.[78]

Despite these differences, the flaneur nevertheless still embodies privilege. The flaneur is not the struggling immigrant in Paris. Instead, he—and the flaneur historically "encapsulated a mobile, subjective gaze that was profoundly male"[79]—is the comparably well-off European "endowed with enormous leisure, someone who can take off a morning or afternoon for undirected ambling."[80] Some flaneurs may undertake their ambling with an air of humility, loneliness, and melancholy,[81] rather than the triumphalism of their globe-trotting peers, but the flaneur nevertheless embodies the freedom to pursue "non-conformism"[82] and the privilege of being "embarrassed" not by life's constraints but "by the richness of his or her choices."[83]

I agree that the flaneur's work in broadening the concept of travel to include nearby destinations and to acknowledge the "foreignness within"[84] is a useful first step. However, in my view, this broadening does not go nearly far enough to achieve full inclusion. Why should travel theory overlook the perspective of immigrants, exiles, and people on the run whose experiences, by definition, "cross borders" and "break barriers of thought and experience"?[85] Why prioritize travel from the center to the margins, while "ignor[ing] the journeys of non-European writers in Western countries"?[86] Why assume the grand adventurer is traveling, but discount the possibility that the "travelees" met along the way might be engaged in "various journeys of their own kind"?[87] Similarly, why focus solely on impermanent relocation instead of exploring all "stories about how geographical mobility maps onto social mobility, self-transformation, and possibilities for reinvention," no matter the timeline?[88]

This book challenges all these biases, and it uses nonfictional sources to do so. Other scholars may favor fiction, for instance novels and poems. Fictional sources, which can be realistic, fantastical, or allegorical, are well-studied within the travel-writing field. Nonfictional sources such as guidebooks, field notes, and personal letters are likewise well-established as data sources, especially in studies predating the field's late-twentieth-century humanist turn.

For the purposes of this book, I've chosen to focus on nonfictional sources and, more specifically, on the life histories written by authors who self-consciously attempt not only to record the facts of travel but also to organize their experiences of (im)mobility into narrative frameworks imbued with social meaning. This embrace of nonfiction—far from being an embrace of positivism—emphasizes the intersection between physical travel and identity transformation. It also attends closely to material places, spatial symbolism, and lived experiences, as well as to the physical and social infrastructure supporting identity narration.

Furthermore, the data analyzed here comes almost exclusively from book-length autobiographies. Although I agree that short-form work such as blogs, essays, and short stories are useful artifacts adding diversity to the geographic imagination, the relative brevity of those formats leaves authors somewhat limited in the number of places they can describe and the complexity of meanings they can explore. By comparison, authors writing full-length books have more space to describe—with considerable narrative detail—complex journeys filled with diverse locations, subtle nuances, and contradictory meanings.

I am hardly the first scholar to use memoir-style autobiographies as a source of primary data for social scientific inquiry. Other travel-writing scholars use memoirs to analyze grief and loss,[89] ecological change,[90] Indigenous voices,[91] civil unrest,[92] wartime dynamics,[93] military mutinies,[94] foreign explorations,[95] personal passions,[96] gender norms,[97] sexual anxieties,[98] and anthropological protocols.[99] Similarly, social scientists engaged in nontravel-related analysis use memoirs to study work culture,[100] political struggle,[101] expressive styles,[102] healing ecologies,[103] race and ethnicity,[104] gender and feminism,[105] and mental health.[106] These studies confirm the validity of using life history writing as cultural artifacts for social scientific analysis. Indeed, for literary geographers, "autobiographies, . . . maybe more so than other literary genres, provide opportunities to deepen our understanding of the dynamic links between place, narrative writing and author (or subject)."[107]

Even despite the validity of this approach, life history artifacts remain a relatively underutilized data source within the field of geography. Given the strong focus on place-identity interactions in memoir writing, "it is somewhat surprising that there have been so few geographers who have seriously engaged with autobiographical writing as a genre in which such processes are played out."[108] These trends are changing, however, as scholars diversify the range of literature "deemed worthy of geographical inquiry."[109] Travel-writing scholars and literary geographers are increasingly incorporating autobiographical sources into their work, especially when exploring themes related to equity and diversity.[110] This equity-driven shift in the range of primary material considered relevant for analysis creates important opportunities to rethink the contours of the geographical imagination.

Using this material responsibly, however, requires asking why this material exists and what work it performs. It requires paying attention not only to what the story *is* but also to what the story *does* both for the authors and for society.

Starting with the authors, invisible exile authors embrace life history writing for a variety of reasons. One reason is therapeutic. Exile is traumatic, and writing is a way to process trauma and integrate it into larger life narratives.[111] A second reason involves accountability. Refugees who produce a detailed testimony of exile can transform "something painful into a document which could be used against the perpetrators."[112] A third reason is validation. Trauma and exile are intensely isolating, whereas life history writing "is the act of reaching across the abyss of isolation to share and reflect."[113]

In my assessment, because of this combination of processing, accountability, and validation, invisible exile life history writing is particularly well-suited to narrative inquiry. The goal of "narrative inquiry" is to "sensitize readers to issues of identity politics, to experiences shrouded in silence, and to forms of representation that deepen our capacity to empathize with people who are different from us."[114] The troubled tales of invisible exile align perfectly with these objectives.

This alignment is complicated, however, because nonfictional sources are never mere reflections of reality. A published memoir, like any text, is a "geographical event."[115] These texts are "ideologically *performative*" in that they play a "socializing role,"[116] for instance in the "shaping of our collective sensitivity to differences between 'us' and 'others.'"[117] Indeed, travel-writing scholars have long been aware of "the potentially harmful political implications . . . of travel writing."[118] European narratives of the Global South "contribute to the formation, circulation, and legitimatization of colonial binary images."[119] Detective novels set in the urban slums "[remodel] the way the city is imagined in popular culture."[120] Similarly, the *ruin porn* narratives of urban disinvestment erase the presence of Black bodies and pave the way for white land grabs.[121]

Importantly, the ideological work of travel writing, as with other types of media, tends to *reinforce* dominant ideologies rather than unsettling them. Powerful groups often use the media to suppress political conflict by "shap[ing] the very preferences and desires of the people in such a way that public conflicts against the interests of the powerful do not erupt."[122] Even in work designed to challenge the status quo, for instance by critiquing colonial worldviews, this "symbolic resistance" turns out to be "a very tricky task."[123] Authors engaged in such endeavors often find themselves "working ultimately (albeit perhaps not intentionally) to solidify" the dominant colonial narratives, "ensuring that they travel further and resonate more loudly."[124]

Another factor to consider when analyzing media sources is that, even in nonfictional accounts, narrative is never the same as reality. All narrative is filtered, regardless of whether it comes from news outlets, focus groups, or historical archives. In all these cases, "stories cannot be seen as simply reflecting life as lived, but should be seen as creative constructions or interpretations of the past, generated in specific contexts of the present."[125] Regardless of any ideological goal, for practical reasons, narrative inevitably simplifies the reality it claims to represent. Scholars should therefore assume from the outset that travel writing, like other narrative formats, appears more unified and coherent than the real-time experience of the unfolding events it attempts to capture.

Additionally, compared to less-formal modes of narrative expression—such as scrapbooks, blogs, and everyday chatter—professionally published narratives—such as travel guides, novels, and autobiographies—are relatively polished texts. Like other "display texts," these narratives are "designed not so much for utilitarian purposes to inform as to elaborately display highly tellable circumstances and incidents 'in such a way that the addressee will respond effectively in the intended way, adopt the intended evaluation and interpretation, take pleasure in doing so, and generally find the whole undertaking worth it.'"[126] As part of this polishing, nonfictional autobiographies—like other display texts—may include a great deal of self-justification by authors making moral claims about themselves and their societies.[127]

Cumulatively, although these caveats are important, they are not reasons to exclude autobiographical travel writing from the social sciences as a source of primary data, especially since all narrative is subject to similar simplification, filtering, and posturing. Historians grapple with similar complications when analyzing letters, diaries, eulogies, legal testimonies, and medical records.[128] Data from interviews and focus groups present challenges, as well, since participants often wish to please the researcher, engage in revisionist history, or advance a personal agenda.[129] Similarly, literary geographers analyzing novels, short stories, comic strips, and poetry cannot escape the fact that, although "literature is often referred to as a mirror, reflection, or microcosm of reality," literature is "not . . . reporting."[130] On the contrary, beyond the plausible "degree of isomorphism" required to give a story credibility, an exact and fully accurate description of place "is not the *essence* of literature."[131] Instead, literary texts are valuable "not for their accurate representation of historical or distant places, but as a way to access the 'intricate web of feelings, actions, and interactions of that world.'"[132]

These are important caveats. However, these considerations should not prevent social scientists and literary scholars from including life histories and travel writing in their analyses. In all likelihood, autobiographical travel writing is probably no more and no less suspect than any other commonly used narrative data source. Using this material responsibly simply means remembering that all narrative should be analyzed carefully and with these considerations in mind.

The Data and Analysis Underlying This Book

This book's analysis is based on life history narratives written by authors who experienced various forms of invisible exile. Additionally, although each journey is unique, I purposefully analyze these narratives as part of a collective conversation about place, identity, displacement, and belonging.

To select the primary sources, during the Covid-19 lockdowns when in-person research was abruptly suspended and digital access to publications was temporarily expanded, I used that time and expanded access to evaluate approximately two hundred autobiographies as possible candidates for inclusion in a study about place, identity, and mobility. From there, I filtered the list to focus on accounts that contained an exile resonance.

Although the conventional framing of exile emphasizes displacement across international borders, exile can also include internal banishment from social and cultural worlds even as formal citizenship remains intact. By choice or by force, invisible exiles cross social borders—including the borders of race, class, religion, gender, sexuality, ability, and trauma—in ways that communities of origin, host communities, or both consider taboo. I leave it to other scholars to analyze what it feels like to live on one side of those lines, for instance, to identify as poor, rich, Black, white, male, female, spiritual, secular, or something else entirely. But rare is the book that describes traveling from one side to another, let alone in a context of punitive and durable expulsion.

With this border-crossing dimension in mind, I culled the initial list of approximately two hundred narratives to a final list of forty memoirs written by authors who used physical journeys to cross social borders and remake personal identities. (Additional information about each source is included in the appendix.) This final list includes some formally recognized refugees. Mostly, however, the list includes narratives written by travelers whose exile is generally overlooked and discounted.

Next, rather than dividing these narratives into separate camps—for instance based on whether the travel was domestic or international, whether the journey was short or extended, and whether the motive was related to race, class, ability, or trauma—this book weaves those strands together to construct one shared, multivocal cartography of (im)mobility and identity. One of the goals motivating this study is to diversify the travel-writing canon, but a second goal is to identify experiences that, despite commonly being kept apart, could potentially come together as part of a shared conversation. This multivocal approach refuses to silo authors with race over here, class over there, and gender or sexuality located somewhere else. I agree that each narrative is unique and that author differences must be acknowledged and respected. However, the divide-and-conquer approach common to politics and academia can also marginalize stories by signaling that certain experiences are somehow separate from the larger shared culture. Additionally, such approaches may limit opportunities for knowledge sharing and coalition building, both of which are crucial for contentious politics.

For all these reasons, instead of describing a series of individual journeys or journey subtypes, each isolated from the rest, I read these narratives in close conversation with each other to highlight shared experiences and to analyze them from diverse vantage points. By downplaying the notion of special cases, this technique sheds light on the complex, diverse, and *collective* topography of invisible exile operating within and beyond the United States.

These research goals led to a demographically diverse set of primary data. Of the forty narratives included in this study, six come from authors who fit the classical definition of immigration, which is to say, they were born in countries other than the ones they eventually call home. These accounts come from formal refugees who moved to the United States to escape military conflict (e.g., Abdi Nor Iftin's *Call Me American* and Andrew Pham's *Catfish and Mandala*), as well as unacknowledged refugees moving to escape gendered, sexualized, and class-based violence (e.g., Staceyann Chin's *Other Side of Paradise* and Dan-el Padilla Peralta's *Undocumented*). A seventh narrative comes from a U.S. citizen who spent most of her childhood abroad and then returned to escape religious and sexual abuse (Ruth Wariner's *Sound of Gravel*).

Another ten narratives come from self-identified traveling nomads who spent months or years hiking, cycling, busing, or camping either within the United States or internationally. From my perspective, these narratives qualify for inclusion in this study not because the authors traveled but because they framed their journeys as a form of externally imposed or self-imposed exile (e.g., Raynor Winn's *Salt Path* and Sarah Smarsh's *Heartland*). Additionally, they traveled not—or not only—to escape everyday cares and explore foreign cultures, but also—and primarily—because spatial mobility provided a tool for healing from paternalism, assault, homophobia, illness, ableism, injury, and poverty (e.g., Jillian Keenan's *Sex with Shakespeare* and Jedidiah Jenkins's *To Shake the Sleeping Self*). In these accounts, travel is a mechanism for reinventing identity in a nonnormative, border-crossing manner.

The remaining twenty-three narratives come from authors who neither crossed international borders nor embraced itinerant lifestyles. Instead, these accounts describe moving to different regions within the same country or different neighborhoods within the same city (e.g., Janet Mock's *Redefining Realness* and Shulem Deen's *All Who Go Do Not Return*). What these narratives have in common with the rest, however, is that dislocation was either imposed as punishment for nonconformity or pursued in a quest for safety. Again, in keeping with invisible exile's key themes, these authors experienced exile for reasons of religion, race, gender, sexuality, class, ability, and trauma. Additionally, even when travel involved comparatively short geographic distances, these journeys were nevertheless fateful moments granting access to new environments where travelers could acquire different identities and perform different social roles that were unavailable to them in their environments of origin (e.g., Jenna Miscavige Hill's *Beyond Belief* and Kwame Onwuachi's *Notes from a Young Black Chef*).

Cumulatively, these forty voices represent a demographically diverse cross-section of travelers. Twenty-seven self-identify as female (e.g., Rita Golden Gelman's *Tales of a Female Nomad* and Ayaan Hirsi Ali's *Nomad*), fifteen as queer or trans (e.g., Saeed Jones's *How We Fight for Our Lives* and Katie Rain Hill's *Rethinking Normal*), six as experiencing chronic disability (e.g., Katherine Preston's *Out with It* and Howard Axelrod's *Point of Vanishing*), and thirteen as people of color (e.g., bell hooks's "Kentucky Is My Fate" and Julie Lythcott-Haims's *Real American*). Additionally, nineteen narratives come from people who self-identify as having experienced extreme poverty or homelessness (e.g., Regina Calcaterra's *Etched in Sand* and Liz Murray's *Breaking Night*), nineteen from self-identified survivors of sexual assault or domestic violence (e.g., Aspen Matis's *Girl in the Woods* and Jaquira Díaz's *Ordinary Girls*), and thirteen from people who self-identified as survivors of cults or other forms of religious abuse (e.g., Karen Armstrong's *Spiral Staircase* and Jayanti Tamm's *Cartwheels in a Sari*). Other recurring themes include parental abandonment, adoption, and foster care (e.g., Carlos Eire's *Learning to Die in Miami,* Nicole Chung's *All You Can Ever Know,* and Deborah Jiang-Stein's *Prison Baby*). Additionally, one author writes as a returning citizen (Chris Wilson's *Master Plan*).

Next, in terms of temporality, all forty narratives were published between 1999 and 2020 with seven published in or before 2009, thirteen published between 2010 and 2014, and twenty published in or after 2015. In terms of popularity, as measured by the number of volumes sold, these narratives range from small print runs by independent presses (e.g., Sascha Altman DuBrul's *Maps to the Other Side* and Dorit Sasson's *Accidental Soldier*) to *New York Times* bestsellers turned into Hollywood films (e.g., Jeannette Walls's *Glass Castle* and Garrard Conley's *Boy Erased*). Similarly, some narratives come from authors with no prior or subsequent publications (e.g., Caspar Baldwin's *Not Just a Tomboy*), whereas others come from professional writers and academics who have published many times (e.g., Jennifer Finney Boylan's *She's Not There* and Jeanette Winterson's *Why Be Happy When You Could Be Normal?*). In terms of education, by the time of publication, all forty authors had acquired some professional qualifications and most had one or more college degrees, although eighteen self-identified as first-generation students (e.g., Tara Westover's *Educated* and Deborah Feldman's *Unorthodox*).

To generate this diverse dataset, in addition to making difficult choices about which artifacts to include, I also had to make hard choices about which narratives to temporarily set aside. The more I read, the more I was able to refine my key questions regarding invisible exile and landscapes of power. Focusing on those experiences meant setting aside other narratives that describe what it feels like to be on one side of a major social divide but not what it's like to change allegiance from one side to another. I discarded narratives that favored political conservatism in favor of those advancing social justice. I excluded most celebrity memoirs and political biographies, which are often ghostwritten and frequently designed to court votes or sell other commodities. I set aside memoirs focusing solely on drug addiction, mental illness, and terminal illness—of which there are many—and kept only those where such themes were secondary features alongside the primary theme of social and spatial dislocation. I excluded several gap-year narratives where travel facilitated growth but as part of—rather than deviating from—a socially supported life trajectory. I also discarded memoirs that focused on the impact of other people's journeys (for instance, children writing about the multigenerational consequences of their parents' travel) and kept only first-person accounts written by exiles themselves. Setting aside those books—many of which are excellent and well worth the read—allowed me to sharpen my focus on tales of invisible exile and the places they have in common.

Having culled the possible dataset to a manageable volume of primary source material, I analyzed those narratives as part of a collective. Although each narrative recounts one person's story grounded within a unique personal geography, the authors encountered similar obstacles while moving through similar environments. Reading all forty narratives together allowed me to de-individualize those experiences and de-invisibilize the cartography of exile they shared.

To facilitate this cross-group analysis, my first step was to dissect the key geographical story elements and enter them into a shared database organized around spatial themes such as belonging, becoming, agency, displacement, imagination, liminality, and arrival. Next, I mapped these elements both conceptually and literally—by drawing maps of the actual places, pathways, and boundaries described in each narrative. Within the field of literary geography, "terms like 'mapping' and 'literary cartography' tend to be used literally in human geography and metaphorically in literary studies."[133] Although I love a good spatial metaphor, as a human geographer, I heavily endorse the perspective that a thorough geographical analysis of literary sources must pay close attention to the material, cartographic, and symbolic aspects of actual, tangible space. My literal mapping of invisible exile reflects this commitment.

Moreover, I mapped these journeys using a layering approach, stacking each map on top of the others. This way, instead of seeing each narrative as a separate and isolated experience, I could decipher the spatial landscape these narratives shared. Using this combined spatial topography, I then charted the well-trodden paths of invisible exile, their oscillations and detours, and the spatially grounded systems of support—and erasure—encountered along the way. Finally, I converted this topography back into narrative format, presented here as a cohesive book leading readers on a guided tour through the terrain of invisible exile.

Map of the Book

To spatialize the relationship between place, identity, and mobility, *Invisible Exile* is organized as a piece of travel writing. Like other guidebooks, it unfolds as a tour with each chapter representing a stop along the way. The chapter titles—which name the spatial typologies visited on this tour—come directly from the autobiographies themselves. Additionally, each typology includes a mix of material landscapes with walls, roofs, and street addresses, as well as symbolic elements derived from history, philosophy, and mythology.

This linear presentation belies a messier lived reality. In practice, traveling through invisible exile involves moving back and forth, skipping stops, stalling out, jumping forward, looping in circles, and veering off in unexpected directions. I do not wish to minimize the significance of this meandering, nor do I wish to impose any teleological expectation of stages and progressions. *However, one goal of narration—and of this book—is to organize life's disparate elements into coherent patterns that reveal broader meanings and significance.* With that goal in mind, the map of this book is as follows.

Journeys cannot begin without a departure. Where do invisible exiles come from, and why do their communities interpret travel as treason? To answer those questions, the tour begins with a visit to Plato's Cave (chapter 1) to explore the material underpinnings of group belonging and social control. From there, the next stop is Girl Planet (chapter 2), a place where exiles travel through their imaginations. Through media and fantasy play, authors experiencing dysphoria construct spaces of release and create supportive architecture for alternative self-expression. Next, to intensify these self-actualizing experiences and facilitate co-narration, this book follows travelers to the Bohemian Coast (chapter 3) where travelers use out-and-back scouting trips to explore physical environments organized around alternative worldviews. Although these scouting trips could potentially lead to new life paths, the anxiety surrounding the loss of prior identities, place attachments, and social ties helps explain why travelers often instead choose to return and conform, even when conformity feels oppressive.

From there, the tour arrives at the Void (chapter 4), which is a tipping point where travelers—by choice or by force—are punitively stripped of group membership and enter a space of existential death. Unlike previous imaginative travel and scouting trips, this fateful moment of stripping bare is no longer temporary, and it forecloses the possibility of easy returns. For travelers who survive, the next stop is Bizarro World (chapter 5), or the strange new environments that authors plunge into after exile and without the benefit of prior socialization. Invisible exiles often flounder in this harsh liminal swamp where old selves are lost but replacement identities are not yet within reach. One possible way to escape the associated pain of being neither/nor is to seek spaces of Basic Training (chapter 6) where assimilation could potentially lead to new social integration. In practice, however, rather than finding a warm welcome, invisible exiles often experience considerable gatekeeping in these spaces and encounter new forms of erasure.

In response to these ongoing challenges, the next stop on the itinerary is Footsteps (chapter 7), or places where invisible exiles co-narrate with fellow travelers and at arm's length from judgmental onlookers. These spaces of mutual support and healing can then lead to Sorrowjoy (chapter 8), a landscape where invisible exile often reaches a provisional end. In these spaces, although travelers have achieved some goals, many aspects of their journeys remain incomplete. As a result, like the narratives themselves, this guided tour culminates in an untidy space of both-and oppositions that remain open and unfinished.

Finally, in the conclusion, I step away from this guided tour to offer reflections on these journeys, on the nature of invisible exile, on the connection between travel and writing, and on the geographical implications for belonging. By mapping invisible exile journeys, I hope to shed light on systems of exclusion that often go unrecognized. Healing requires validation, including through supportive environmental reflections. This book provides one such reflection. With it, I hope to spark a shared moment of empathy, reassurance, grief, and joy.

ONE

The Foundations of Belonging

Plato's Cave

Every journey begins with departure. However, most travel writing emphasizes destinations. The genre describes what it's like to dine in Paris, teach English in Africa, or row across the Atlantic. By contrast, exile is driven by the places left behind. It's about environments that, for some people, feel so oppressive or suffocating that it becomes necessary to leave, to go somewhere else—anywhere else—to survive.

Most of this book is about where invisible exiles go, how they get there, and what those journeys signify. However, exile is, by definition, a state of being *pushed,* regardless of whether there are also pulls. Understanding exile, then, requires starting with the point of origin—the departure, rather than the destination—and asking why, or more specifically *how,* those places produce an exile dynamic.

One initial and somewhat counterintuitive element within these dynamics—and one with special relevance to travel writing—involves looking beyond environments that *promote* mobility to instead focus on ones that *resist* it. Spending time in diverse environments can encourage people to reassess taken-for-granted assumptions. Many social groups value this creative rethinking, but some do not. In contexts where change is seen as threatening, one common—albeit repressive—strategy for perpetuating the status quo is to limit the flow of people and ideas across social borders. Because travel promotes transformation, restricting movement closes off important avenues for change.

Exiles, in other words, are perhaps especially likely to come not from places that embrace movement but from places that don't. Invisible exile life history writing is filled with rich descriptions of anchors, boundaries, and borders that, prior to exile, restrict sociospatial mobility. Some authors grew up in separatist communities where social withdrawal was intentional. Others had socio-spatial containment imposed on them by more powerful groups living elsewhere. A third subset came of age in environments where the vast cultural and territorial authority of dominant institutions created few opportunities to casually encounter other perspectives.

The influence of these environmental barriers in reproducing existing and inequitable social relations cannot be overstated. Even so, no environment is fully enclosed. A defining feature of place, as well as identity, is its inherent openness. There is always the potential for places, like people, to change, including in response to border-crossing events that convey evidence of other places and worldviews.

This inherent permeability, however, explains a second—and similarly repressive—key strategy for perpetuating the status quo: socializing people to travel through culturally foreign spaces without meaningful engagement. Cross-border travel that cannot be prevented might make diversity visible, but years of socialization through dismissiveness, stigmatization, and punishment can encourage people to avert their eyes. Instead of seeing mobility as an opportunity for growth, new places and information are instead cast as irrelevant or threatening.

In short, precisely because travel encourages transformation, social prohibitions against travel and against meaningful engagement while traveling are powerful techniques of social control. To explain these dynamics, in this chapter I start by providing detailed examples from invisible exile travel writing to convey the experience of living in bounded, polarized spaces. Next, I provide a theory-informed analysis of the intentional construction of socio-spatial borders, and I identify three subtypes of environments that limit opportunities for travel-related interactions. Then, I summarize theories about the transformative nature of encounter, I outline three common cross-border pathways that could potentially promote social change, and I review common practices that preemptively minimize encounter-based social questioning.

Before proceeding, one note of clarification is in order. Some readers might find this initial focus on borders and boundaries surprising. What is the twenty-first century, after all, if not a time when borders are transgressed, erased, and reconceived on a daily basis? I agree that, although institutions may attempt to freeze society in place, this freezing is always contestable. At their core, invisible exile narratives are about defying boundaries, navigating ambiguity, and exploring hybridization.

I do not agree, however, that this inherent openness means that attempts to freeze social relationships into a prescribed order are therefore irrelevant or innocuous. On the contrary, invisible exile narratives emphasize not only that change is possible but also—and just as importantly—that self-reinvention is extremely difficult, comes with severe social sanctions, and involves considerable gatekeeping both from the community of origin and from the communities travelers hope to join. To lose belonging for reasons of sexuality, gender, religion, race, class, ability, and trauma is harsh. To lose that belonging only to then live without easy access to a replacement home is similarly harsh.

The harshness of these border-crossing journeys explains my frustration when colleagues learning about invisible exile sometimes respond by saying, *Oh no, dear, you must be mistaken in your focus on borders and boundaries, because the world is so fluid and open and hybrid these days, don't you think?* I agree that research on ludic hybridity is currently popular. However, the assumption that these themes are the only themes—or the most important themes—for analyzing place and identity feels like a slap in the face to anyone not privileged enough to be given clear and equal access to spaces of mobility for reflexive self-construction.

The pervasiveness of this dismissive response, along with its hurtfulness, is a key reason I am motivated to write this book. For readers who are interested *solely* in the ludic spaces of postmodernity, many cultural geography studies exist on these themes. This book, however, asks readers to at least consider the continuing impact of borders and boundaries, of fixity and stuckness, and of external constraints and social control. These constraints exist alongside the ludic hybrids and liminal in-betweens that, yes, I will discuss later in this book. Rather than devaluing mobility, analyzing its inequitable distribution only highlights the preciousness of this resource, as well as its centrality to conversations about social justice.

"Be Killed Rather than Transgress"

Starting first with detailed examples as recounted within invisible exile travel writing, on the same day baby Tziri first opened her eyes,

Tziri's father Shulem Deen made himself temporarily blind. As explained in his memoir *All Who Go Do Not Return,* Deen was a young newlywed "living in New Square, a village thirty miles north of New York City inhabited entirely by Hasidic Jews of one particular sect: the Skverers."[1] In this insular village, no one spoke English and, except in the strictest circumstances, outside influences were forbidden.

Although New Square residents rarely left their village, Deen made an exception for the birth of his first child. When the labor pains started, he and his wife splurged on the hourlong cab ride to Mount Sinai Hospital in East Harlem. Leaving New Square was not entirely comfortable—the Harlem hospital had no Kosher food, and the other expectant fathers gawked at him, "whispering: '*It's one of those Hasidics*'"[2]—but Deen waited patiently and said nothing.

After the relief of a safe birth, Deen left mother and child to recuperate only to then encounter new trouble. To get home, he planned to take a taxi from East Harlem to Midtown where he could transfer to the Skverer-owned, gender-segregated commuter bus serving the ultra-Orthodox villages to the north. "The men all sat on one side of the bus with a curtain drawn down the aisle."[3] The ticket for the Skverer bus—a gift from his father-in-law—was already in his pocket. However, on checking his wallet, Deen realized he could not pay for the connecting cab ride. As a Hasid, he had no credit cards or bank accounts, and he was short on cash. "I stood at the curb in front of the hospital, gripped with panic."[4]

Deen panicked because the only other option was to ride the city bus, which felt inconceivable. "I thought of the words of the old rebbe, admonishing his Hasidim never to ride New York City's public transit system. '*Be killed rather than transgress,*' the old rebbe had said, declaring it a cardinal sin."[5] The problem, he'd been told, was that city buses were full of foreign people and foreign influences. In this secular, gender-mixed environment, Deen feared that even the accidental glimpse of a woman's pinky finger could derail his spiritual purity. Moreover, within his Hasidic community, people engaging in forbidden activities—like watching television, reading novels, or playing baseball—could be berated, beaten, and shunned.

Deen rode the city bus that day. There was no alternative. However, before boarding the bus, he took the most important precaution he could think of. "Mournfully, I removed my thick plastic-framed eyeglasses, the world around me turning into a blur of indistinct shapes and colors . . . and kept my eyes downcast."[6] By preventing himself from seeing the diversity outside his village, Deen hoped to pass through it without truly interacting with it and with minimal chance of being affected by it. In short, by temporarily blinding himself, he hedged against travel's tendency to spark transformation.

Welcome to Plato's Cave, a Place of Polarizing Socio-spatial Control

Shulem Deen did not give his village a metaphorical name, but Chris Wilson did. Like Deen, Wilson was acutely aware of the spatial and social boundaries associated with his identity, and he understood those boundaries in a new way after reading his favorite childhood book, "an illustrated version of Plato's 'The Allegory of the Cave.'"[7] As summarized in Wilson's memoir *The Master Plan,* in the allegory, "a group of people live chained together in a cave" where they see shadows flickering across the walls, and "since they've never seen anything else, the people think the screen is the world and the shadows are real."[8] From their perspective, the cave and its shadows constitute the entire known universe.

One day, however, the cave's boundaries are breached when one among them accidentally gets loose and stumbles outside. As the traveler nears the cave's entrance, his first impulse is to turn back, to retreat from the painfully bright lights that hurt his eyes and the disorienting sights that confuse his mind. But eventually, his eyes adjust, his mind adapts, and he marvels at the newly discovered world of vibrant colors and three dimensions. This is the moment when the proverbial scales fall from the traveler's eyes. "There was another world outside, bigger and more beautiful than those poor chained people could imagine. They just weren't allowed to go there."[9]

Wilson uses this allegory to describe his experience growing up in a disinvested, segregated neighborhood on the Black side of America's color line. "Even at eight years old, I knew the story was about me, because I was living in that cave . . . and most kids never left that cave."[10]

Unlike his peers, Wilson did leave, at least for a time. During the years when his mother was healthy and working, he visited her in the suburbs on weekends. Her house was only a thirty-minute drive away, but for Wilson it represented "a different world."[11] In this space of green lawns, fresh produce, and racial mixing, "I was out of the cave."[12]

Unfortunately, however, the temporary escape in Plato's allegory does not lead to personal liberation or social transformation. Instead, it leads to trouble. Excited by his beyond-the-cave discovery, Plato's traveler rushes back to tell his peers about that other world. On re-entry, however, his eyes are no longer adjusted to the darkness. He stumbles while walking, and he cannot detect the sacrosanct shadow-play. On observing these changes, the onlookers conclude that the trip to the surface has driven him mad and that the outside world is dangerous and must be avoided. Instead of becoming a liberating hero, the traveler is cast as a cautionary tale warning others not to stray.

For Chris Wilson, the allegory of Plato's Cave captures what it feels like to live in a cordoned-off world. Similarly, Shulem Deen and other invisible exiles reflecting back on their journeys frequently describe coming of age in environments that were—by design—intensely polarized by race, religion, and other divides. That spatial partitioning made it difficult to explore alternative life paths.

These barriers are significant. However, as in Plato's allegory, border crossing is always possible, even when it is discouraged. This inherent openness helps explain the role of fear and denigration in discouraging travelers from exploring. It's not that people cannot leave, or that gray areas do not exist, or that encounters with difference never occur. Rather, it's that, by creating physical and cultural impediments to socio-spatial mobility, travel becomes more difficult. When this occurs, the "good" characteristics that define place attachment—such as "local roots, community ties, and strong emotional bonds"—may instead be replaced by the "potentially bad" characteristics of "parochialism and restricted opportunities."[13] In short, place, instead of only providing belonging, can also create suffocation.

Living Without the Freedom to Choose

Narratives like Chris Wilson's account of racial segregation and Shulem Deen's account of religious isolationism challenge the notion that people are generally free to choose their own identities, select their own life paths, and decide for themselves how to present to the world. I make this claim even though, by many measures, invisible exiles *do* remake their identities. They leave religions, rework racializations, transition genders, and cross class divides. However, in my assessment, invisible exiles who succeed with this self-reinvention are the lucky ones because their narratives speak far more about the *constraints*—the boundaries, sanctions, and gatekeeping involved—than about some mythical freedom to choose. Far from exemplifying fluid self-construction, these narratives highlight ongoing—if often underacknowledged—systems of repression and control.

All the travel narratives included in this study come from authors who grew up in today's era of global multiculturalism, which is to say, an era dominated by discussions of borderless worlds, flexible cultures, and malleable selves. In this context, unlike the *structural* systems of the past where society "interpellated" subjects by "hailing" people at birth and "inculcating" them with externally prescribed cultural frames,[14] *postmodern* systems are supposedly less deterministic. "While earlier generations are said to have relied upon an identity explanation that was offered to them externally (by authorities such as tradition, the village common good, or the powers of religion), for contemporary generations identity and life-story explications have become an internal affair."[15] These theories suggest that, when it comes to identity, including "the clothes one wears, the job one gets, the music one listens to, the people one socializes with, . . . [and] the choice to go traveling," contemporary society allows—and even requires—individual decision-making.[16] "The removal of any authoritative guidelines" on "how to lead one's life" gives people a "proliferation of choice."[17]

Arguments like these suggest that people are free to shape their own identities with minimal social constraints. I agree that today's global flows of capital, people, and ideas create unprecedented opportunities for cultural borrowing and hybridization. I agree that "porous borders, multiple loyalties, and free mobility are absolutely central" to "neoliberal economic conditions"[18] and that "the global circulation of goods and persons" creates "difficulties" in "defining home."[19] I agree that many people experience "modernity as a peculiar form of 'permanent liminality,'"[20] that "mobility is endemic to life, society, and space,"[21] and that "mobility today is often the rule rather than the exception."[22] I also support scholarship that moves away from ideas of "fixity" to instead "consider more closely the movement of and between categories."[23]

This recognition of fluidity does not, however, mean that fluidity is therefore the only—or the most important—identity debate requiring scholarly attention. Instead, I side with feminists and postcolonialists who challenge the meanings and limits of these imagined freedoms, for instance by highlighting the ongoing significance of race, class, gender, and religion in structuring identities and life paths.[24] I also side with mobility scholars who call attention not only to "the (arguable) withering away of established notions of 'societies' and 'nations'"[25] but also to "the importance of immobilities marked by spatial fixity and territorial attachment."[26] Within liberal democracies, "control over mobility is a form of power with deep historical roots," and it remains true today that "differential mobilities . . . are fundamental to forms of power that make classed, racial, sexual, ablebodied, gendered, citizen and noncitizen subjects, as well as to forms of resistance and countermoves."[27]

As will become clear throughout this book, when invisible exiles choose clothing, friends, music, jobs, and travel in defiance of authoritative guidelines, these assertions of individual autonomy are risky because ensuing sanctions may jeopardize social relationships, economic resources, and personal safety. For authors who make these choices anyway and are successful enough to write books about it, yes, I agree they rework their identities and use geographic mobility to facilitate those transformations. But make no mistake, there is nothing *free* about it. If anything, tales of invisible exile demonstrate the opposite: that for many people, authoritative guidelines remain alive and well, despite being soul-crushingly oppressive.

Every author included in this study describes living, at some point in their lives, in environments that hailed subjects, inculcated identity, and limited exposure to competing perspectives. Moreover, since encounters with difference could not be wholly avoided—especially in today's globally interconnected context—authors also describe being socialized to preemptively discount mobile encounters with people, ideas, and objects that eluded territorial gatekeeping. As a result, even when authors traveled, as when Shulem Deen visited the hospital in Harlem, travelers often acted, almost without conscious thought, in ways that thwarted the transformational potential of those journeys.

Constructing Environments of Territorial Belonging

Most of this book is about leaving Plato's Cave. It's about journeys into and partially through exile and the places that assist or thwart these quests. However, before exploring the process of *leaving*, it helps to understand the condition of *being in*. How do people find themselves inside Plato's Cave? Then, from within that world, how do travelers begin to question whether its socio-spatial framework rings true? Plato's protagonist stumbles outside by accident and then quickly arrives at a new understanding of the world. Real life, however, is rarely so simple. To understand how encounters become possible, including encounters that challenge taken-for-granted assumptions, it helps to start not with post-exile arrival but by analyzing where and how pre-exile journeys begin.

In my assessment, one of the most striking features of invisible exile travel writing is the extent to which authors frame their stories using the language of insides and outsides. There is nothing inevitable about these dualisms. On the contrary, there are several possible ways to organize socio-spatial relationships. One option is the dichotomous "'me'/'us' and 'them'" variant reflected in Plato's Cave, which discursively homogenizes *us* while also flattening and vilifying *them*.[28] Another option is the somewhat more diverse "'me'/'us' and the many 'others,'" which acknowledges external diversity among *them* even as it insists on internal homogeneity among *us*.[29] A third option is "'me' and the transversal 'us,'" which, by emphasizing diverse, multinodal attachments throughout the entire social system, is more inclusive.[30]

I heartily support moving away from reductive dualisms and embracing internal diversity. I also agree that just because "others are not 'for' us does not imply that they are 'against' us" and that "there is no inherent tendency of intergroup differences to turn antagonistic."[31]

Even so, the presence and pain of binary systems is a recurring theme within invisible exile travel writing. Authors describe feeling pressed against a boundary and compelled to make a choice either to stop journeying to remain with *us* or to continue traveling and risk being exiled with *them*. The frequency of these experiences is not a defense of those systems but rather a rebuttal of scholarly narratives that trivialize the ongoing role of external authorities in constructing us/them divides.

When constructing these divides, territory plays a crucial role. Unlike diverse or transversal landscapes, us/them divides often involve "architectures of enmity" that reinforce the supposed hostility between self and Other.[32] "Stories about who we are, where we come from, and where we are going are embedded within the symbols, structures, and normative practices in public spaces," and these "setting narratives are powerful symbolic resources . . . with the ability to oppress or liberate."[33] When organized around enmity, setting narratives use socio-spatial "framing" to display group norms and to exclude competing perspectives, which reinforces the illusion of internal unity and coherence.[34] The territorial borders and barriers framing this coherence serve many purposes. As a protective feature, they may "enclose us within the safety of familiar territory," but these barriers "can also become prisons" for anyone framed as illegitimate, and these territories "are often defended beyond reason or necessity."[35]

Setting narratives mediate belonging. "Belonging" is "a personal, intimate feeling of being 'at home' in a place," as well as "a discursive resource which constructs, claims, justifies, or resists forms of socio-spatial inclusion/exclusion."[36] In theory, rather than being a binary condition, belonging can reflect a matrix of factors including personal memories, family structures, cultural norms, economic experiences, and legal status. At its most extreme, however, belonging may manifest as a felt sense of "existential insideness" rooted in "a total, unselfconscious immersion in place."[37] In practice, this image of complete, uncomplicated belonging is usually unobtainable. Regardless, for many people and communities, the imagined ideal of existential insideness holds deep emotional resonance and becomes an orienting life goal.[38]

Importantly, like place and identity, belonging is inherently contestable. Nonbelonging can take many forms, including "exclusion," as well as "isolation, alienation, loneliness, displacement, uprootedness, disconnection, disenfranchisement or marginalization."[39] Nonbelonging can also be agentic, for instance when people make conscious choices to engage in exploratory self-questioning,[40] critical nay-saying,[41] defiant intransigence,[42] or figurative rebirth.[43] Nevertheless, in the spectrum of belonging, if existential insiders mark one end of the spectrum, the other end includes "existential outsiders" who, due to limited alignment around various identity markers, may experience "a feeling of homelessness and not belonging."[44] Moreover, feelings of nonbelonging often spike with nearness, rather than distance. "Non-belonging, like belonging itself, is generated through proximity" where, instead of leading to mutual recognition, "closeness generates a sense of unassailable, unconnectable difference, a lack of sameness with what is on the other side."[45]

Without wishing to invalidate the yearning for belonging, I agree with the concern that extreme forms of inside-ness and outside-ness are troubling. As other scholars show, demanding homogeneity as a precondition for acceptance "denies and represses social difference," and it "validates and reinforces the fear and aversion some social groups exhibit towards others."[46] Moreover, reality is rarely dichotomous and, when it is, something has usually gone terribly wrong, for instance due to war or apartheid. From this perspective, although "bounded, exclusionary forms of 'community'" can be ideologically powerful, they can also be an "expensive and sometimes violent and dangerous illusion."[47]

I agree with all of these concerns. However, my opposition to hurtful and exclusionary practices does not prevent other people from embracing them, nor does it prevent the harm they cause, including to invisible exiles.

Belonging and nonbelonging are key themes within invisible exile travel writing. A surging sense of nonbelonging is what Shulem Deen experienced at the Harlem hospital where his clothing and foodways set him apart from other expectant fathers. Similarly, the risk of losing belonging within his Hasidic village explains why he removed his glasses before boarding the public bus. Given the fate of Plato's protagonist—of encountering a new environment, being changed by it, and losing belonging as a result—it makes sense that Deen would close his eyes rather than risk a similar fate. That is the power of Plato's Cave. As a binary architecture of enmity, belonging is predicated on seeing the world through *our* eyes only, and belonging is jeopardized by gazing at the world through the eyes of *Others*.

Touring Three Versions of Plato's Cave

Throughout this book, I use the term *Plato's Cave* to refer to any landscape organized around dualistic systems of supposed insides and outsides. Within invisible exile life history writing, I identified three common subtypes of Plato's Cave, which I call the *self-constructed insular compound*, the *externally imposed containment zone*, and the *really big normative bubble*. This list is not all-inclusive, but it is diverse enough to demonstrate some variety in the way architectures of enmity are structured, as well as the range of places involved. These subtypes exist across the United States and around the globe, and they draw borders along the lines of race, class, gender, sexuality, religion, ability, and trauma. Despite their variations, however, the common theme linking these subtypes is that they demand, as a precondition for belonging, a considerable degree of homogeneity among *us,* as well as a shared sense of antagonism toward *Others.*

As a caveat before proceeding, because invisible exiles experience these environments as hurtful, many quotes in this chapter—and throughout this book—reflect their pain. From my perspective, I do not intend for these critical tones to serve as blanket condemnations of the places and communities discussed. Instead, I use these quotes to highlight two key points. The first is that constructing situations where difference is punished remains a prevalent—and hurtful—social practice. The second is that, for many people, even despite claims of a fluid, hybrid world, external authorities continue to exert considerable influence over identity formation, including what people wear, where they work, what media they consume, who they interact with, and whether they can travel.

Self-Constructed Insular Compounds

One subtype of Plato's Cave—and the one captured in Shulem Deen's description of his ultra-Orthodox village—is what I call the *self-constructed insular compound.* When a group feels threatened by other cultures, some among them might choose to opt out of mixed environments by constructing a separatist space for *us* and defending it against *them.* This subtype is especially common in invisible exile memoirs with religious themes, including major world religions, as well as smaller cults.

Despite the ideological diversity of these sects, insular compounds have several common traits. First, in terms of population size, these groups are proportionally small compared to the dominant culture. Second, the groups generally endorse the belief that their identities and practices are—and ought to remain—distinct from other cultures, which they see as incommensurable and threatening. Third, these opt-out communities build environmental barriers around themselves by claiming turf, marking it as *ours,* and isolating it both from the imagined mainstream and from other minority groups. Fourth, once constructed, participants are expected to live most if not all of their lives within these bounded spaces, to conduct themselves as one of *us,* and to eschew the places and practices associated with *them.*

Religious sects build self-contained insular compounds in both rural and urban contexts. In rural settings, physical distance reinforces social isolation. For instance, distance was central to Shulem Deen's description of New Square, which he says was founded when a rebbe "set out to build his own village" away from New York City where, sheltered by distance, residents could practice "our ultraconservative and insular lifestyle" without disruption from "hostile neighbors."[48]

To enforce isolation, opt-out groups often combine distance with other physical and symbolic practices, such as fortification and identity marking. One author, for example, grew up in Colonia LeBaron, an enclave of Christian fundamentalists who left the United States to evade anti-polygamy laws. To construct this enclave, its founders moved to a remote section of northern Mexico, built clusters of housing and other community infrastructure, and surrounded it with barbed wire and electric fencing. The group also marked its turf with a symbol of group identity. "On the tallest of the hillsides . . . jagged rocks and round stones had been assembled to create a giant letter *L*. Painted white, it was always visible."[49]

Self-contained insular compounds exist in urban areas, as well, as was the case for an author who grew up in a Scientology compound called Pacific Area Command. Like Colonia LeBaron, the compound was "comprised of many buildings within walking distance of each other," and it was marked by a public display of the Scientology name and logo on a seven-story building, "lit up and visible for blocks."[50] However, unlike Colonia LeBaron, Pacific Area Command was embedded within the heart of Los Angeles.

This urban example challenges the common assumption that people living in cities inherently inhabit environments of "thrown-togetherness" where difference is unavoidable.[51] On the contrary, invisible exile life history writing suggests that insular compounds are possible—and even common—within diverse urban settings.

Maintaining insularity when embedded within a metropolis, however, raises questions about how this separateness is reinforced in urban contexts that inherently pull in other directions. Part of the answer, it seems, is through social norms regarding time, fear, and secrecy.

Starting with time, scheduling was a central theme for an author who grew up in a series of meeting rooms and apartment buildings occupied exclusively by members of a Hindu-inspired cult (her word). Although the buildings were scattered throughout the New York metropolitan area, the hyper-regimented worship schedule prevented members from interacting with nonaffiliated neighbors. For example, as a child, other neighborhood kids sometimes invited her to play, and she desperately wanted to say yes, but "there was no chance. Every weekend, like every evening, was spent in Queens with Guru."[52]

Alongside controlling time, a second strategy for maintaining insularity involves cultivating fear. Fear is why another author growing up in New York City never explored the racially and ethnically diverse areas located mere blocks from her home. She'd been told since childhood that "there is nothing more dangerous than a goy."[53] According to an ex-Muslim author, fear is also the reason why many immigrants from her home country choose to "insulate themselves in ghettos of their own making" and homeschool female children to keep them "culturally illiterate."[54]

Next, when time and fear cannot prevent social mixing, a third tool for constructing insularity involves codes of secrecy. Scientology children, for example, are frequently drilled in their "*shore story*, which was what we were supposed to tell Wogs [non-Scientologists] if they asked us questions about what we were up to. . . . Rather than saying we were Cadets training to be in the Sea Org, our shore story was supposed to be we were going to a private school."[55]

Codes of secrecy are common in mainstream religions, as well. For instance, some orders within the Roman Catholic Church expect their nuns to remain "wholly isolated from the outside world."[56] Even when convents are embedded in cities, the novitiate are prohibited from seeing or writing to friends and family more than a few times per year. Even then, "we were never allowed to speak of what happened inside the convent."[57]

In summary, self-constructed insular compounds are a variant of Plato's Cave that uses spatial attributes like distance, fortification, and symbolism, as well as social control over time, fear, and secrecy, to construct architectures of enmity. The resulting barriers restrict cross-group idea exchange even when other people live nearby. Opt-out groups construct difference in other ways, as well, for instance through language, dress, education, money, and foodways, which I explore in later chapters. However, territoriality, or the act of physically claiming turf and marking it as *ours*—as a space that only *we* have access to and that *we* defend against *them*—is a common, intentional, and impactful strategy of social control. Occasional mixing remains possible, but social norms reduce meaningful engagement and reproduce separateness.

Externally Imposed Containment Zones

A second subtype of Plato's Cave—and the one reflected in Chris Wilson's description of life on the Black side of America's racial divide—is the *externally imposed containment zone*. These zones are constructed when the ruling culture preemptively designates one or more social groups as supposedly inferior, constructs an environment that limits life opportunities, and imposes that environment onto anyone born into those predefined subject positions. Within invisible exile life history writing, externally imposed containment zones are especially common in discussions about race and class.

Although containment zones have some similarities with insular compounds, the key difference in my assessment is choice. At an individual level, neither Shulem Deen nor Chris Wilson chose their circumstances of birth. However, at the collective level, insular compounds are produced by groups who *elect* to self-isolate, whereas containment zones are *imposed* on people—for instance, low-income communities and people of color—by richer, whiter people living elsewhere.

Externally imposed containment zones can take two possible forms. One form traps people in place, which is what Wilson describes in his account of growing up in a racially segregated neighborhood plagued by economic disinvestment, discriminatory policing, and violent crime. By virtue of growing up in this socially constructed space of deprivation, Wilson's life chances were limited from day one.

A second and related containment zone, however, is the traveling containment zone that denies full belonging for people seen to be *escaping* from fixed spaces of oppression. Another author of color describes this traveling containment zone in her account of moving through white, upper middle-class environments as a person of mixed racial heritage. As a child at the grocery store, "the eyes of the clerk tell me I cannot possibly belong to my own mother."[58] As a college student, other applicants implied that "I was stealing an admissions slot with my Blackness."[59] Similarly, when scuba diving with her white fiancé's family, the boat owner verbally accosted her as a supposed party crasher and stowaway.[60] In these ways, although she did not live in a disinvested inner city, her environment nevertheless imposed significant constraints on her, constraints that did not apply to her white neighbors and relatives.

Containment zones operate through many venues. However, for invisible exiles writing about class divides, educational environments appear to be particularly significant. One author's teacher introduced her on the first day of class as "a foster child" who will be "welcome . . . for the time she's here, and she'll start in the lowest reading and math groups."[61] Another author's classmates followed her home after school shouting, "Garbage! You live in garbage 'cause you *are* garbage!"[62] Experiences like these explain why a third author started skipping school, rather than enduring cruel "jokes about my messed-up clothing," as well as why she hid in the bushes before and after school events to "avoid the humiliation" of being seen alongside her mother's thrift-store dresses, mullet haircuts, and yellowed toenails.[63]

These discriminatory environmental reflections reproduce the containment zone. In educational spaces of potential social and economic mobility, poor kids are told they do not belong.

Whether containment zones emphasize class or race, the defining characteristic is the systematic reduction of choice. Lacking options is not the same as lacking agency. On the contrary, in Chris Wilson's narrative about race in America, he adamantly takes personal responsibility for his behavior, including the decisions that landed him in prison. "The government . . . didn't make me acquire a gun or force me to pull the trigger. I made those decisions, and I took responsibility."[64] However, although everyone has agency, containment zones present severely limited options. "Society didn't put me in prison. . . . But society created the cave. Society put obstacles in the way of black people—slavery, lynchings, redlining, job discrimination, voter discrimination, and all manner of segregation, official and otherwise—then criticized us when we didn't rise above it."[65]

Another author makes similar observations about the limited options in spaces of poverty. Wealth inequity means that people "live in different Americas" depending on their circumstances of birth, "and thus have different understandings" about their place in the world and their life potential.[66] These circumstances do not define individual identity. "You would have been born on one side of that perceived divide, but that wouldn't have predicted anything about the core of you. Not your politics and most definitely not your character."[67] However, in terms of social identity, containment zones present nearly insurmountable obstacles regarding life trajectory. "Study after study" has "plainly said in hard numbers that, if you were poor, you are likely to stay poor, no matter how hard you work."[68] Although all children have potential, environments influence their fate. "Or, to put it in my first language: The crop depends on the weather, dudnit? A good seed'll do 'er job 'n' sprout, but come hail 'n' yer plumb otta luck regardless."[69]

In examples like these, privileged groups use isolation, disinvestment, and denigration to construct social divides that corral vulnerable groups into environments littered with structural barriers and with few resources to overcome them. These constructed environments deter socio-spatial mobility in low-income communities and communities of color. The social stigmas attached to these identities then impose nonbelonging on anyone perceived to be escaping by traveling within spaces of privilege.

Really Big Normative Bubbles

A third subtype of Plato's Cave—and one with especially elusive edge conditions—is the *really big normative bubble.* The cultural beliefs within these environments can appear so taken for granted that people may forget there is even a choice to be made.

This taken-for-granted-ness is aptly captured in one author's description of growing up in Nashville. "Nashville in the nineties was a tricky place to be gay. Evangelical Christianity was the dominant culture, although it was so insular and convinced of its rightness that it didn't see itself as a culture. It saw itself as normal, the way things were."[70] This normative framework—including the way Evangelical Christian norms shaped institutional settings and everyday practices—helps explain his long-term struggle to make sense of his sexuality. "I knew my desires were weird, but I didn't know they were gay. I didn't know the word."[71]

This variant of Plato's Cave has some similarities with insular compounds and containment zones. Like other variants, really big normative bubbles emphasize internal homogeneity—this time regarding sexuality, gender, ability, and trauma—as well as collective refusals to validate supposedly nonconforming experiences. However, unlike insular compounds, which operate at the scale of small opt-out groups, really big normative bubbles often feel as though they encompass the whole world. Additionally, unlike containment zones, where nonbelonging is imposed at birth along the lines of class and race, within really big normative bubbles, nonbelonging often becomes apparent later in life, for instance during puberty or following trauma.

In my assessment, the key social dynamic constructing really big normative bubbles is the silence emanating from the dominant culture's moral stance. A "moral stance" is "a disposition towards what is good or valuable and how one ought to live in the world."[72] These dispositions guide people toward prescribed identities, and they "deflect narratives" away from other possibilities by making it "difficult to confront community and institutional ideologies and sensibilities about what should not be told."[73] For anyone experiencing a nagging sense of nonbelonging—for instance, because of a nonbinary gender or an atypical neurology—this silencing makes it hard to articulate those experiences and explore alternative perspectives.

In invisible exile travel writing, really big normative bubbles are most visible in narratives about gender, sexuality, ability, and trauma. Normative bubbles exert social control in these areas both by presenting a prescribed identity and by refusing to validate so-called deviations from those prescriptions.

Starting with sexuality, setting narratives "carry implications for 'who we are' (or 'who we claim to be')," implications that then limit the social imagination.[74] For a queer author, "the librarians at the . . . public library never, ever, recommended books . . . about queer girls . . . like me. I didn't even know those books existed."[75] Similarly for a kinky author, "like everyone else, kinky kids grow up with questions about our emerging sexualities. The difference is that, unlike people who grow up with normative sexual orientations, we can't turn to pop culture for answers."[76]

These silences can trap people in spaces of confusion and pain. Using gender as an example, "by the time I was nine and entering fourth grade, I was fully aware that I was a girl trapped in a boy's body. I didn't know that transgenderism existed, though, so all that knowledge meant to me was that I was doomed."[77] The moral stance within really big normative bubbles promotes such ignorance. "I was taught absolutely nothing" about transgender identity "in school or out, and my knowledge of it was limited to a 'rare deviation' that you could and should laugh at."[78]

This silence stigmatizes people whose experiences do not conform. For example, in ableist contexts, people whose bodies, speech, or neurology differ from perceived norms are often treated as deviant.

"'Emotional indulgence. Exhibitionism. . . . Weakness of will.' I knew the list almost by heart."[79] Moreover, whether the issue is epilepsy, stuttering, or autism, the few environmental reflections that do exist often reinforce stigma, for instance in Hollywood films where such differences provide "a visual cue to symbolize everything from insanity and abuse . . . to personal weakness, ineptitude, and violent moral corruption."[80] Experiences like these are important reminders of how easily society silences diversity through accusations of mental illness.

Alongside sexuality, gender, and ability, really big normative bubbles often stigmatize trauma as well—for instance, sexual assault. Invisible exiles molested as children sometimes received medical care, but since these exams came without narrative explanations, the only conclusion one author could draw was that "I had driven Ma crazy."[81] Similarly, when rape survivors advocate for themselves, they are often told "to stay quiet. . . . What [the rapist] had done . . . was invisible, something people around me simply didn't want to discuss."[82] Survivors who speak out anyway often suffer further consequences. This was the case for one author when college leaders removed her—rather than her rapist—from the college dorms. "My new room was my cave among strange, stranger-students' caves: all shadowed and dank, a motel for hiding in darkness."[83]

Through this narrative silencing, normative bubbles construct boundaries that discursively separate prescribed identity traits from those deemed deviant or taboo. Because normative bubbles are so geographically extensive and influence so many aspects of institutional and informal culture, the people living in these spaces may rarely encounter evidence that these norms are elective, rather than foregone conclusions. Although this silencing does not create actual homogeneity, it appears to be highly effective in marking some experiences as Other and in signaling that people sharing those experiences do not belong.

Encounters with Difference May or May Not Lead to Transformation

As described previously, a defining feature of Plato's Cave is the way these environments limit exposure to diverse worldviews. Next, a second key element involves conditioning people to preemptively discount counternarratives that elude territorial gatekeeping. This social conditioning increases the likelihood that, if cross-border encounters cannot be avoided, they either have no impact or they reinforce—rather than disrupt—dualistic thinking.

Within the field of geography, space is understood to be inherently permeable and dialogically produced through multiauthored endeavors,[84] and in this regard Plato's Cave is no exception. Religious extremism, white privilege, and transphobic silencing construct barriers, but no hermetic seals. On the contrary, invisible exile life histories are filled with moments, both big and small, when perimeters are breached, giving way to opportunities for cross-group encounters.

Encounter is a loaded concept within the social sciences. Instead of referring only to a meeting of strangers, "encounter" describes "a meeting of opposites" where "a lack of commonality is assumed."[85] In other words, encounters are meetings between *us* and *them*. During these meetings, participants may not understand the other party's perspective and may feel threatened by implicit challenges to their worldviews.

One possible outcome of encounter is transformation. A cornerstone of encounter theory is that exposure to difference can undermine the status quo. "Words such as 'rupture,' 'surprise,' 'shock' and 'animation' are common to descriptions of encounter and describe a moment or instance in which something is unexpectedly broken open."[86] In theory, these cracks can destabilize entrenched ways of thinking. When faced with new and unexpected information, the "break in cultural continuity" can "force" people "to re-create meaning" around "certain routines and taken for granted situations."[87] These reassessments make encounter a potentially important tool for social transformation.

Travel-writing scholarship generally embraces this transformational theme. Travel "brings people into a world of unpredictable possibilities."[88] This unpredictability promotes growth and development because "having constantly to negotiate between the familiar and the unknown" compels travelers to "acquire experiences and undergo transformations."[89] The stories that travelers then develop to explain these encounters function as "witnessing narratives" that capture "the profound experiences they underwent while traveling."[90] These witnessing narratives "implicitly and explicitly express how travel contributes to . . . self-development."[91]

I agree that encounter *can* lead to transformation. However, that outcome is not guaranteed. "Proximity alone does not necessarily equate to a change in values or behaviour."[92] On the contrary, social scientists use the term "social tectonics" to describe scenarios where different groups coexist within shared spaces but "[move] past each other . . . with little contact."[93] In tectonic situations, people with different religious beliefs, class positions, or gender identities might see each other in grocery stores and classrooms but still avoid the type of "contact that actually changes values and translates . . . into a more general positive respect for—rather than merely tolerance of—others."[94] By passing without truly interacting—as when Shulem Deen removed his eyeglasses before boarding the city bus—social tectonics blunt the transformative potential of travel-related encounters.

Furthermore, even when changes occur, those changes are not necessarily progressive. "Encounters with difference . . . outside what we already know . . . are necessarily confrontational since we tend not to welcome difference, transformation, and change into the habitation of our habits."[95] One way to quickly minimize the discomfort of confrontation is to reassert the status quo. This is why, when an encounter is "read as threatening—as some form of security breach"— the resulting "anxiety, fear, resentment or violence . . . can harden prejudice, affirm and (re)produce binary logics, aggravate existing conflicts or re-enact unequal power relations."[96]

This hardened binary is what Plato describes in his allegory of the cave. "Plato looks at travel as a source of civic danger and moral pollution because it exposes unprepared travelers . . . to all kinds of confusing impressions and alien mores."[97] Similarly for Shulem Deen, the fear of being seen as changed when returning to his Hasidic village explains why he removed his eyeglasses. Despite attempts to staunch the borders, no cave is impregnable, but socializing people to carry Plato's Cave within them through their embodied mannerisms, even when traveling, can thwart the transformational power of encounter-inducing mobility.

Three Versions of Beyond-the-Cave Encounters

Despite prohibitions against mobility, encounters are always possible. When analyzing invisible exile narratives, I identified three common pathways for beyond-the-cave encounters. These pathways include *our* trips *out*, *their* trips *in*, and the dawning recognition of diversity among *us*. Each pathway can—but does not necessarily—prompt people to reassess taken-for-granted worldviews.

Starting with *our* trips *out,* despite expectations that residents will live most of their lives within Plato's Cave, most authors ventured out occasionally, as when Shulem Deen visited the hospital in Harlem. Chris Wilson ventured out as well, when visiting his mom in the suburbs. At least for a time, "I was the kid who got out of his chains."[98]

There are many reasons why, prior to exile, invisible exiles spend at least some time outside Plato's Cave. Religious kids from insular compounds sometimes attended public school. "Guru didn't want us going to school at all, but . . . to avoid legal troubles, he reluctantly agreed that we could venture to the outside world to avoid breaking the law."[99] Queer kids from normative bubbles sometimes traveled as well, for instance during a family vacation to New York City that just happened to coincide with NYC Pride.[100] These trips created opportunities to encounter difference.

Second, alongside *our* trips *out,* encounters occur when *they* venture *in.* This is how a Black kid in a homeless shelter met his first mentor, a white volunteer who also taught at an exclusive private school.[101] This is also how another author found opportunities to observe non-Hasidic city employees. On religious holidays when her community lit bonfires, "the fire department sends trucks to every corner to monitor the fires and the firemen stand outside, leaning casually against the truck sides, watching the goings-on."[102] Their presence symbolized the existence of other worlds, which prompted the author to wonder about those off-limits spaces.

Third, alongside *our* trips *out* and *their* trips *in,* encounters occur when people discover diversity *among us.* Dualistic social systems may emphasize homogeneity, but suppressing diversity does not actually eliminate it. On the contrary, in my assessment, people living in Plato's Cave experience *among us* encounters in one of two ways. The first is by observing diversity among peers, for instance when a friend is discovered in a same-sex hookup,[103] a fellow congregant speaks out against a religious leader,[104] or a sibling defies class norms by pursuing higher education.[105] The second way invisible exiles experience *among us* encounters is by becoming aware of misalignments between themselves and the group, for instance when an author realized he was not a girl,[106] another realized she no longer thought in Yiddish,[107] and a third realized she could no longer conceal her stutter.[108] In situations like these, whether difference manifests externally through a peer or internally within the self, invisible exiles prior to exile have opportunities to consider that *we* may not be so homogeneous after all.

All three encounter pathways create opportunities for people living in Plato's Cave to observe information that does not conform with group expectations. Whether *we* venture *out, they* venture *in,* or diversity arises *among us,* these encounters provide evidence that life could be lived otherwise.

People respond to this evidence in many ways. Some express surprise. "Did you see that? . . . There was a man dressed as a woman!"[109] Others experience pain. "What could have been a moment of possibility—a glimpse of another way of living . . .—instead felt like a sting."[110] Some observers are curious. "I feel a strong and desperate longing to bridge the chasm that lies between us."[111] Others are smug. "I felt sorry that the entire student body was being deprived of a real education."[112] In some cases, encounters lead to new opportunities, such as a scholarship-funded acceptance into prep school.[113] In other cases, encounters harden prejudice. "'Shkutzim!' Vermin. Non-Jewish hoodlums. . . . Within moments, the call reverberated through the streets."[114]

Whatever the outcome, these pathways for beyond-the-cave encounters confirm that no environment, no matter how fiercely policed, is fully enclosed. People breach the borders for many reasons, sometimes on purpose, sometimes by accident, and sometimes as a mere practicality. Regardless of how or why encounters occur, narratives of invisible exile show that some people some of the time will inevitably have opportunities to observe other places and other ways of being, which could potentially unsettle group norms.

Policing the Boundaries of Plato's Cave

Encounters are inevitable, but embracing them can be risky. Some risks come from gatekeeping outside Plato's Cave, which I explore in later chapters. However, Plato's allegory focuses on a different danger, and one that is prolific within narratives of invisible exile. For Plato's protagonist, although the bright sunlight is initially painful, no one outside the cave threatens him or tries to stop his explorations. Instead, the social danger of exploring arises not from *them out there* but from *us in here.* When the traveler returns to the cave and shares his stories, he is rejected. Instead of reassessing their worldviews, his peers "work hard, and violently if need be, to put the troublemaking philosopher back in his place (seated and bound amongst the others). Should this fail they will more than likely resort to more violent measures and ultimately seek to put the troublemaking philosopher to death."[115]

No wonder Shulem Deen removed his glasses before boarding the city bus. That tectonic response makes perfect sense in places where acceptance and survival are predicated on conformity.

Within Plato's Cave, people use trivialization, disparagement, surveillance, and punishment to instill tectonic habits. Starting with trivialization, this is what one author experienced when she begged to wear dresses to daycare, and her mom replied, "Oh, Luke, you're just being silly."[116] Another author experienced it when she told her white mother about the racial slurs she heard at school, and mom "heaves a sigh like I've forced her to talk about my race again. . . . 'But you're just one of us, dear, and we love you.'"[117] Trivialization also occurred when a kid in a cult begged to attend a secular birthday party, and her dad "seemed baffled as to why anyone would even want to."[118]

These trivializing responses do not have trivial effects. On the contrary, trivialization discredits the implication that existing environments are failing to adequately reflect all *our* identities or adequately provide for all *our* needs.

Alongside trivialization, another form of policing involves denigration. Denigration includes the stereotypical image of the "'tranny hooker' . . . subject to pain and punch lines."[119] It includes the "bigotry" of "pantomime: limp wrists and exaggerated sashays from mocking church members."[120] It also includes news coverage, for instance about the murderous "lesbian mother and her 'lesbian lover.' I heard this so often, in so many different ways, . . . that after a while it seemed as though being a lesbian was part of the crime."[121] This denigration discourages people from exploring such identities for fear that they will be stigmatized as well.

Alongside trivialization and denigration, a third form of policing involves surveillance. External threats are one concern, but internal monitoring operates on the premise that potential "enemies" could be found "anywhere . . . including domestic territory."[122] This internal monitoring makes it difficult for people to explore encounters without risking sanctions.

Internal surveillance takes passive and active forms. By passive surveillance, I mean the diffuse power that encourages conformity because of the possibility of being observed, even if no one is currently watching.[123] For example, even though the internet offers a potential escape from normative bubbles, that option may not be viable when "the only Internet connected device in the house was the family computer, which sat in plain view against the wall in the dividing space between our open-plan living/dining rooms."[124] Similarly, in insular compounds where young adults are often prohibited from living alone, their shared houses and dormitories ensure that other people are always around to notice potential rulebreaking.[125]

Alongside passive surveillance, active surveillance is when people go looking for evidence of nonconformity. Examples include inspecting trans people's undergarments,[126] reading queer children's diaries,[127] and monitoring congregants' phone calls.[128] For authors reflecting back on these pre-exile experiences, growing up in such environments meant living in a world of informants[129] where parents paid neighbors to act as spies[130] and where locked cabinets were frequently invaded by prying eyes.[131]

Importantly, although some surveillance involves authority figures, surveillance by peers is equally significant. In religious communities, children often "watch each other closely, ever ready to point out someone's spiritual or physical failing."[132] Indeed, "virtually all of the chits [demerits] issued had nothing to do with an adult observing bad behavior, but rather another kid in the group reporting it."[133] Since everyone was a potential spy, authors felt pressured to perform compliance even when encounters could have led to new opportunities.

When nonconformity persisted despite trivialization, denigration, and surveillance, authors faced a fourth form of policing: punishment. Invisible exiles prior to exile were lectured, teased, and mocked.[134] They endured racial slurs,[135] homophobic slurs,[136] morality chants,[137] class-based insults,[138] and other forms of organized public shaming.[139] They were pathologized and subjected to inappropriate medical interventions.[140] They had their possessions stolen and burned,[141] their hair forcibly cut,[142] and their clothing forcibly removed.[143] They were pelted with rocks,[144] shoved through doors,[145] and attacked by dogs.[146] Invisible exiles were beaten and whipped.[147] They were sexually assaulted and threatened with gang rape.[148] They received death threats, knew of others who had been murdered for similar transgressions, and were instructed to commit suicide.[149]

Importantly, what invisible exiles rarely experienced was arrest. Legally, in the eyes of the state, they had done nothing wrong. But the state did not come to their aid either, and oftentimes the state was complicit.[150]

When unleashing this arsenal of pain, the disciplining parties usually framed their behavior as morally justified. Like the cave-dwellers who accused Plato's protagonist of dangerous behavior, invisible exiles were accused of doing something "forbidden,"[151] committing "High Crimes,"[152] and engaging in "capital offenses,"[153] like Shulem Deen's "cardinal sin" of riding public transit.[154] As a consequence, these derogatory and punitive practices harden the boundaries of Plato's Cave both by signaling the limits of a group's moral stance and by encouraging travelers to defer to those norms even when traveling through other social worlds.

The Caves We Carry Within Us

Policing the borders of Plato's Cave produces silence and shame, both of which undermine the capacity to challenge group norms. This silence is clearly visible within invisible exile travel writing, which helps explain why authors so often kept quiet about their nonbinary genders, racial ambiguities, sexual assaults, physical ailments, homelessness status, and physical abuse. "I never mentioned to my mother that my father abused me because I didn't know he had. I thought that it was normal to have to wear sweaters in summer to hide the bruises."[155] These situations were not prevented simply because society refused to discuss them. Instead, the internalized sense that having such experiences was shameful and grounds for expulsion pushed these experiences deep underground.

For authors experiencing nonnormative identities, this collective silence often limits self-knowledge and delays the start of transformational journeys. Using transgender identities as an example, because "it is not safe to say such things, . . . some trans children will not truly, not for a long time, be able to maintain a crystal clear fix on what it is that is troubling them about the way they are presented to the world."[156] Statements like these are common within invisible exile travel writing. These accounts describe the long-standing feeling that something is not adding up, but when faced with a swirl of disconnected and unnarrated sensations, travelers struggle to reach firm conclusions. Instead of clarity, "it will be like a mental gnawing sensation or an itch or a throb that is set off every time gender is specifically mentioned."[157]

This narrative silence instills shame in authors who recognize that something about them feels different but who have not been empowered to articulate what precisely is happening or how they might respond. Within the containment zone of poverty, for example, the "lack of acknowledgment" of class barriers "at once invalidated what we were experiencing and shamed us if we tried to express it."[158] Similarly, within the insular compounds of closed religions, "as much as I wanted to tell them the truth, I was hesitant . . . because I was terrified that the problem wasn't with the [compound], but with me."[159]

This internalized sense of shame can transform people into their own jailers. Surveillance and punishment play a role, as well, but children socialized into Plato's Cave often self-perpetuate their own oppression. This is why, even when one author's family member went public as transgender, he refused to consider taking similar action. "I simply did not want to be one of those people, to become a joke, a deviant, a member of such a stigmatized minority group."[160] It's why, even when another author realized he was queer, "it was such a private embarrassment, such a shadow I was afraid to examine, that I truly didn't."[161] This sense of shame is also why, even when a third author came face-to-face with the racialized words that could have helped her think differently about her identity, rather than exploring those words, "my usual lockdown took over," and the words faded away.[162]

In short, invisible exiles prior to exile internalized systems of self-repression. "In this story I'm telling you I'm the illegal aliens *and* the border patrol. I police myself the way I was taught."[163] Or, as another author phrased it, "the biggest thing choking me was me. I'd been force-fed stigma for so long, I had lost the gag reflex to resist it."[164]

This urge to self-police helps explain why, even when authors found opportunities to explore new environments, they often turned away, as when Shulem Deen removed his eyeglasses. When traveling outside Plato's Cave, travelers often abided by the "custody of the eyes, the quaintly named monastic habit of keeping one's gaze fixed on the ground."[165] Similarly, when new people or competing information entered Plato's Cave, instead of exploring, "I figured I would stay away, because I didn't want to go crazy."[166]

In situations where authors could not turn away, for instance because the competing information emerged from within themselves, invisible exiles often tried to mask that knowledge through self-effacing performances. For an author with a stutter, "I was ashamed of acting like the mute class clown, but it was the only exit route I could think of. . . . If I didn't speak, I didn't stutter. When I was silent, I was normal again."[167] Similarly for an author concerned about his "gay" mannerisms, "I beat them to the punch. I made fun of myself. I mocked my own voice. I exaggerated my silliness to show that I did it on purpose."[168] In examples like these, by masking difference, authors hoped to defend against allegations that they did not belong.

In conclusion, these practices increased the likelihood that, in the event of exposure to a beyond-the-cave worldview, those encounters would remain tectonic and not lead to meaningful change. All the travel narratives discussed in this book come from authors who grew up in a global, diverse, hybrid world, and most grew up in urban settings. However, those traits do not mean authors were free either to travel or to self-reflexively fashion their own identities. On the contrary, external authorities introduced many constraints. The territorial project of constructing us/them environments based on homogeneity, isolation, and exclusion could not eliminate all encounters, but social surveillance and vilification blunted the impact of encounters that eluded territorial gatekeeping.

For invisible exiles prior to exile, the resulting reluctance to meaningfully explore alternative self-expression could persist for decades. At the same time, however, this constant sense of avoidance implicitly signaled that other options were possible. From within Plato's Cave, it was difficult to jump directly into those alternative places and selves. However, small encounters created opportunities for subtle questioning that then laid the groundwork for imaginative travel, which is the subject of the next chapter.

TWO

The Power of Imagination

Girl Planet

Bookstores and libraries draw clear lines between fact and fiction, suggesting narratives should fit neatly on one side of the line and not cross over. However, invisible exile travel writing is filled with nonfictional accounts of fictional journeys. In these accounts, people travel through their imaginations, and these journeys shape future identities and travel paths. These outcomes suggest that, when it comes to travel, fiction and nonfiction might not be separate and instead are often mutually reinforcing.

This interplay between fact and fiction is a key area of interest among literary geographers. When thinking about text shaping the geographical imagination, even the most empirical sounding descriptions expressed "in the language of men who have seen it" are inevitably *situated* and therefore inherently "contingent, contested and linked to questions of power."[1] Conversely, the vibrant environmental details of fictional stories set in real locations make it easy to forget that the literary rendition of these settings is "drawn from a reality that," for the purpose of the story, "was deliberately altered."[2] Consequently, within literary geography, "not only is the distinction between fiction and reality somewhat suspended, but the analysis actually focuses on the symbolic and semantic dialogical transfers between literary discourse and [geographic] imaginaries, and on the referential blurring that ensues."[3]

Given these dynamics, the pivotal question from my perspective is not whether a spatial representation is empirical or fictionalized, but rather, what happens politically, economically, and culturally when people are invited to experience places—including places that diverge from Plato's Cave—through representations? How do these portrayals reshape understandings of identity, relationships, and possible futures? Moreover, what protections, if any, does literature provide when it comes to nonnormative exploration?

When considering the real-world implications of literary geography, one notable factor is the way stories influence physical travel through subsequent tourism and lifestyle migration, which I explore in later chapters. However, physical travel is not always possible, which is why another important—and perhaps more prolific—form of travel occurs through the imagination. What are books and films if not vehicles for projecting oneself into other times and places? In their life history narratives, invisible exiles looking back on pre-exile experiences often describe imaginative travel through media and fantasy play as one of their first self-directed mechanisms for exploring identities that, at the time, felt impossible or taboo. These imaginative voyages are pivotal moments helping travelers cope with alienation by offering glimpses of more affirming worlds, glimpses that, through spatial representations, anchor alternative modes of self-expression within supportive architectural frameworks.

To be clear, imaginative travel is not perfect. Among its limitations, imaginative travel is partial and temporary. It provides no immediate road map for social transformation. It sometimes ends in punishment when, in the eyes of observers, travelers take their fantasies too far. Imaginative travel can also be painful. It hurts to find fleeting release only to continually slam back into a suffocating reality, and it can feel shameful to compulsively seek that which is deemed taboo. To reduce these discomforts, rather than delving deeper into unsettling spaces, many authors do the opposite by intensifying self-repression and limiting repeat trips. Cumulatively, these limitations confirm that imaginative travel is neither flawless nor risk free.

Despite these risks, in a pre-exile context, imaginative travel often plays an important role in the quest to find belonging. For people unable or unwilling to check normative boxes, imaginative travel makes space for enhanced agency, authenticity, and co-narration. Additionally, compared to physical travel, imaginative journeys—which are fleeting and often camouflaged—are a comparatively safer way to explore encounters with difference. Because imaginative travel is *just* a story, *just* a game, or *just* a fantasy, travelers have more latitude to break with group norms. Furthermore, imaginative travel is often the only travel option available to children or other people who, due to age, class, gender, ability, or citizenship, may be unable to physically relocate.

In short, imaginative travel is a valuable way to play with social convention and bring alternative worlds to life. To explain these dynamics, I begin this chapter with examples of imaginative travel as depicted within invisible exile travel writing. Next, I provide a theory-informed explanation of the importance of imaginative travel, including the way imaginative travel constructs an alternative supportive architecture that grounds other places and other selves in enabling environmental frameworks. Then, using daydreams and fantasy play as examples, I analyze the content of imaginative journeys, the places that support them, the props that enhance them, and the techniques for incorporating co-narration. Last, I evaluate these journeys' consequences, including their costs and benefits. Cumulatively, this analysis suggests that imaginative travel can be a crucial step in invisible exile journeys, that it often occurs prior to the fateful moment of expulsion, and that it plays an important role in the overall transformational experience.

"Mary Did *Not* Have Black Hair"

Starting with detailed examples of imaginative travel captured within invisible exile life history narratives, the moment Nicole Chung's kindergarten teacher invited her to play make-believe was the same moment her classmates clipped her wings. As explained in her memoir *All You Can Ever Know*, Chung's Catholic school teacher was casting the children for roles in the annual Christmas pageant, but when the teacher considered Chung for the coveted role of Mary, another five-year-old protested, "Mary did *not* have black hair!"[4]

This quibble might seem surprising given that the entire pageant was make-believe. The children were not really angels, they could not perform actual miracles, nor were they really bringing peace on earth. However, despite embracing so much pretense, the strength of Plato's Cave meant that, at only five years old, the children had already internalized the message that some fantasies were socially acceptable while others—including the ones that unsettled racial privilege—were unacceptable, even when that unsettling occurred only in the imagination.

This curtailing of imaginary possibilities is significant not only because of the racism involved but also because, as a child, Chung relied on her imagination to cope with her ill-defined racialization. Chung had a white mother, white father, lived in a white town, and attended a white school. "And perhaps I never would have felt differently—perhaps I, too, would have thought of myself as *almost* white—but for all the people who never indulged this fantasy beyond my home, my family, the reach of my parents' eyes."[5] Chung was adopted and of Korean descent. Her family rarely acknowledged this fact, but "once my parents and I left our little house . . . we were bound to turn heads."[6] Chung received questioning looks at the store, heard racial slurs on the playground, and observed endless confusion over her then-Hungarian surname. These experiences constructed a gap between Chung's inner sense of self and the identity reflected back by her environment. "Sometimes it was shocking to catch a glimpse of my face in the mirror" and to know that what others "saw was so at odds with the person I believed I was."[7]

Tormented by feelings of nonbelonging, Chung imagined situations where her identity and environment aligned. Initially, she imagined transforming herself to match the space. "If I were a heroine in a fairy tale . . . and a fairy godmother offered to grant me wishes, I would ask for peaches-and-cream skin, eyes like deep blue pools, hair like spun gold instead of blackest ink."[8] In other words, she imagined being turned white.

Eventually, however, Chung encountered new information that cast her identity in a different light. Some encounters came through mass media. "At nine, I turned on the television one night to discover Kristi Yamaguchi, my first Asian American childhood hero, being cheered by crowds and adored in a way I did not think people who looked like me could."[9] Other encounters involved physical travel, for instance during a family vacation to Seattle, a city with a large Asian American population. "Here, finally, I was inconspicuous. . . . It was novel, exhilarating, to be one among so many; it was a glimpse of the world as it could be."[10]

These beyond-the-cave encounters influenced Chung's imaginative journeys. "I wrote stories, dozens of them, about other people, other lives I craved."[11] In these stories, Chung replaced her earlier fantasy of being turned white with "stories featuring some of my first Asian American characters."[12] Creating these characters served several functions, but "the most important thing my expanding creative life gave me . . . was the permission to imagine a world I simply could not see in my white hometown."[13] Chung's protagonists were not children trapped in someone else's reality, but rather were adults determining their own fates. "I let my own characters grow up . . . and I put them in hilltop houses and glamorous apartments in mostly un-named cities" surrounded by "people of varying backgrounds . . . who saw and understood them."[14]

Through imaginative travel to these fictional cities, Chung finally had regular access to a space of authenticity and validation. "Only on the page could I build and live in a world that felt better, felt *right*."[15] For Chung, these imagined stories were a starting point for rethinking the borders of race, nationality, and kinship. They were also an important starting point in her eventual journey out of her externally imposed racialized containment zone. "I wanted to escape. And escape I did."[16] Chung's escape, with its many exile resonances, would involve a complex journey lasting several decades and requiring more than just her imagination, but these early imaginative forays were nevertheless crucial, formative, and empowering stepping stones along the way.

Welcome to Girl Planet, a Place Where Imaginative Travel Is More than Just Make-Believe

Chung did not give her fictional worlds a name, but Jennifer Boylan did. Like Chung, Boylan experienced a profound misalignment between her internal sense of self and the identity her environment reflected back. In Boylan's case, the disconnect wasn't race but gender. Living as a boy but knowing she was a girl, Boylan imagined her way out of this predicament not through imaginary hilltop cities but by landing in a place she called Girl Planet.

Boylan describes these childhood trips to Girl Planet in her memoir *She's Not There*. "Sometimes I played a game in the woods called 'girl planet.' In it, I was an astronaut who had crashed on an uninhabited world."[17] On Girl Planet, being female was simple, uncontestable, and automatic. "The thing was . . . that anybody who breathed the air on this planet turned into a girl. There was nothing you could do about it, it just happened."[18] This gender-transforming atmosphere not only provided a space where Boylan could express her girlness; it also provided a justification—even a mandate—for this expression. "My clothes turned into a girl's clothes, too, which should give an indication of exactly how powerful the atmosphere was. *It changed your clothes!*"[19] This imagined transformation of material objects, including the highly symbolic ones associated with gender expression, implied that her body and identity could transform as well.

To visit Girl Planet, Boylan needed more than just the pretense of an imagined world. She also needed a location in real life that could serve as a portal. She found that portal in a space of social abandonment. "In the center of the forest" near her home "was the elaborate, destroyed mansion of Pennsylvania's former governor. . . . The burned-out house stood on the banks of a lake where sometimes I went fishing by myself."[20] In these seemingly empty woods, at arm's length from authority figures and with formal infrastructure in a literal state of decay, Boylan found the gateway she was looking for. This liminal space granted access to a different reality, a place where her identity snapped into a more authentic resolution. This alternative alignment of place, body, and identity then persisted for as long as she remained within this Girl Planet world.

Imaginative Travel Creates a Space to Ask Questions

In examples like these, whether fantasy landscapes take the form of racially diverse hilltop cities or gender-transforming cosmic worlds, invisible exiles prior to exile use imaginative travel to cope with dysphoria. "Dysphoria" is "an experience of discomfort and sense of dissonance that can exist between one's gender, body and space, essentially a kind of placelessness within oneself."[21] Along with other contributing factors, "the built environment produces this kind of placelessness" when "certain bodies are spotlighted, misrecognized, and rendered deviant through spatial practices."[22] As discussed in the previous chapter, these spatial practices include the construction of insular compounds, containment zones, and normative bubbles, as well as the stigma and silence they enable.

In my assessment, although the scholarship on dysphoria generally focuses on gender, the concept of misalignment resonates with other contexts, as well. Nicole Chung's description of racial placelessness and of feeling shocked by her own reflection illustrates a similar misalignment between her sense of self, her physical features, and the identity her environment reflected back. This dissonance left Chung feeling out of place in her body and her world. Similarly, the life history narratives written by rape survivors, first-generation students, cult survivors, and queer Christians often include comparable descriptions of misalignments between bodies, identities, and space.

Social constructs surrounding race, class, gender, sexuality, religion, ability, and trauma produce these misalignments, and the resulting dysphoric placelessness can propel travelers toward exile or signal that, in many ways, they are already there.

When dysphoric misrecognition occurs—which is to say, when the body-space-identity triad is misaligned—one way to find relief is to change the environment, for instance by making existing spaces more inclusive or by traveling to other more validating locations. Children, however, have limited capacity to pursue either option. They might encounter social difference while traveling with caretakers, and caretakers might advocate for environmental reforms on their behalf, but the choice of whether to travel and what to change belongs to someone else. These constraints help explain why invisible exiles so often escape—at least initially, and especially as children—not through physical travel or social activism but via a third option: imaginative travel through media and fantasy play.

These practices connect invisible exile to the mobility paradigm of imaginative travel. Imaginative travel is similar to physical travel except that, instead of the body moving through space, the mind is "transported elsewhere through the images of places and peoples encountered in the media."[23] During imaginative travel, invisible exiles prior to exile are like the flaneur, guided by "caprice or curiosity" in explorations that are "disorganized and fragmented" yet "endlessly absorbing."[24] Media plays an important role in these explorations because, although travelers can and do invent their own destinations, media provides opportunities to step into the ready-made worlds, cultures, and personas captured in preexisting representations of real places from long ago, fantasy places existing only in fiction, and here-and-now places recast in a different light. Media also showcases environments that travelers may not have thought to invent on their own.

As with other forms of media consumption, imaginative travel via the ideas contained in text and film is an active process. Ideas are inherently mobile. They "'travel' to other times and situations," sometimes "los[ing] some of their original power and rebelliousness" along the way, whereas other times the idea "flames out, so to speak, restates and reaffirms its own inherent tensions."[25] In either scenario, representations "are never inert, nor do they deliver monolithic and unidirectional messages."[26] Instead of passively absorbing an

THE POWER OF IMAGINATION 59

intended meaning, people bring these circulating ideas into conversation with their own life experiences and then co-construct the moral implications and key takeaways. This co-construction occurs individually, as well as collaboratively with peers.

Whether exploring ideas solo or in groups, imaginative travel creates opportunities to consider aspects of the human experience that may push against social convention. It creates a place where Nicole Chung can play with racial inclusivity without her classmates objecting. It constructs a world where Jennifer Boylan can manifest girlness with minimal risk of social reprimand. To be clear, as discussed earlier in this book, media often reinforces—rather than destabilizes—dominant ideologies, and narrative resistance is tricky. However, the life histories of invisible exiles support the assertion that media is nevertheless a potentially powerful way to "open up oneself to experiences beyond the boundaries normally set by society."[27]

In other words, literature and media function as a space to explore difference. Furthermore, since representations circulate more easily than people—for instance, as pages and bytes that do not need to eat or sleep, nurture family ties, or maintain gainful employment—people living in Plato's Cave are perhaps more likely to encounter difference through media-based absent others than through living, breathing bodies strolling down the street. To be sure, media does not circulate with absolute freedom, as paywalls and banned books attest. However, given media's relative ease of circulation, as well as its potential to provoke, it is perhaps no surprise that invisible exiles reflecting back on the early parts of their journeys often describe books and movies as crucial spaces of encounter prompting them to begin asking questions.

Invisible exile life history writing is filled with examples of media exposure leading to social questioning. It was through *The Muppet Show* and *Little House on the Prairie* that one imaginative traveler got her "first glimpse at how another family interacted" outside her cult. "What? No guru? I asked my father why there was no guru on the show."[28]

It was through sitcoms like *Will & Grace* that another author encountered his first positive queer role models. "The characters on TV were not like anyone I knew. They showed me options that didn't seem to exist in my surroundings."[29]

Similarly, it was through a "transgressive" book that a third author first realized that people outside his sect might see sexuality as natural and healthy rather than shameful.[30] After reading that book, "I wondered . . . why I was beginning to feel a strange stirring whenever this rabbi's daughter, a pale, thin girl with a long dark braid sitting across the aisle, glanced my way."[31]

In examples like these, imaginative journeys bring travelers into different social worlds. The resulting shift in "ways of seeing" challenges implicit understandings about "what is deemed possible or banished to the realm of the impossible."[32] This shift in perspective is a central feature of travel-related exploration where, at least according to some scholars, "the 'changing of attitudes'" is "ultimately more important than the changing of 'external circumstances.'"[33] External circumstances can change, however, when returning travelers with new ideas begin asking questions.

This potential to disrupt taken-for-granted norms transforms books and television from mere diversions into avenues of discovery. "Literature . . . isn't a hiding place. It's a finding place."[34] The "ancient promise" of travel writing is that "distance is the land of wishes come true."[35] Through imaginative travel, writers and other media producers "invite their public to join in the spectacle" and to rally around "a hero the reader would like to emulate."[36] This emulation then influences how people see themselves, their world, and their future. Within these fantasy realms, heroines *can* have black hair and gender *can* be fluid. "Yes, the stories are dangerous. . . . A book is a magic carpet that flies you off elsewhere. A book is a door. You open it. You step through. Do you come back?"[37]

Fantasy Grounds Alternative Narration in a Supportive Architecture

Although people can travel through any genre, imaginative travel may work best when approached as fantasy play. Embracing imaginative travel in the spirit of fantasy does not limit travelers to magical, mystical, or alien worlds. Instead, imaginative travelers can approach any environment—including the guru-less landscapes of *Little House on the Prairie* and the queer-positive spaces of *Will & Grace*—as fantasy-like environments that needn't conform to the rules of everyday life. This fantasy approach is useful because, instead of getting caught up in questions of fact versus fiction (or worse, moral versus deviant), the traveler is instead free to defy thinkability and bring seemingly impossible truths vividly to life.

One reason why fantasy feels so freeing is because, as a genre, fantasy defies impossibility. The broader genre of fiction makes space to *question* reality, including by exploring "a range of possible interpretations" of present circumstances,[38] as well as by exploring what *could be* if the world changed in some specific way.[39] The subgenre of fantasy then takes these explorations further by intentionally *breaking free* from prosaic, practical, or functional constraints. In this way, unlike realistic fiction, "fantasy consistently incorporates a radical departure from the real" that "enables us to enter worlds of infinite possibility."[40] The wonderous space of a fantasy world "does not require logic—technological, chemical, or alien—to explain the startling actions or twists of character and plot."[41] Like Chung invoking fairy godmothers and Boylan landing on Girl Planet, startling events "may be explained by magic or not explained at all."[42] Within fantasy spaces, *impossibility* is irrelevant because the fantasy world simply *is*.

This potential to see the world differently gives imaginative travel a political edge. If "political activity is whatever shifts a body from the place assigned to it, . . . makes visible what had no business being seen, . . . and makes understood as discourse what was once only heard as noise"[43]—and that definition works for me—then this shift in thinkability is precisely the political work that imaginative travel performs. Imaginative travel transforms emotional geographies, even when material conditions remain unchanged. It is a tool for exploring "the 'unthought known,' . . . which refers to that which is unconscious and not available to thought, but nevertheless 'known' in the sense of registered somehow within a person's being."[44] By entering "pretend mode" in a space that is "clearly 'marked' as pretence, threatening emotional impulses and unacceptable feelings can be safely activated and dealt with as their connection to reality has been moderated."[45] These shifts in emotional geography then influence the way travelers understand real life. "Far from fleeing reality," fantasy explores "the question of how subjects tie themselves ethically to each other and enter a socially viable world."[46] In all these ways, fantasy exploration through imaginative travel can "feed our capacities for speculation, imagination, and social innovation," all of which can promote social change.[47]

Alongside this speculative capacity to conjure the seemingly impossible, a second invaluable aspect of fantasy travel is that, in addition to breaking with reality, fantasy *grounds replacement realities within an alternative supportive architecture.* To be clear, all social worlds are anchored in and enabled by supportive infrastructure. However, for people whose bodies, identities, and environments align, this supportive architecture is often invisible. "Although human life requires the constant support of complex surroundings, most people" are "like fish that can't see water" and "do not consciously notice" the environment sustaining them.[48] By contrast, for people experiencing dysphoria and other forms of exclusion, the unsupportive and repressive architecture of everyday life is often highly visible. Even if dominant groups are "usually oblivious" to the built environment's normativity, the so-called "pariah groups—whether poor Latino families, young Black men, or elderly homeless white females—read the meaning immediately" in its thwarting of their everyday needs and interests.[49]

By contrast, the supportive architecture of fantasy worlds provides a partial workaround to these dysphoria-inducing environments. It is not only that fantasy *explores* "the anxieties, desires, fetishes of a culture's waking world and dream world"; it's also that, within fantasy spaces, these anxious elements "are resolved into a substantial and systematic architecture" that drives the story forward.[50] In Nicole Chung's stories of racial empowerment, glamorous hilltop cities embody the social and economic success of her racially diverse protagonists. Similarly, in Jennifer Boylan's Girl Planet, the gender-transforming atmosphere not only supports but also compels genderplay. "More than mere background," these substantive environmental frameworks "provide the literal premises for the possibilities and trajectory of narrative action."[51]

Next, alongside defying impossibility and grounding alternatives, a third benefit of approaching imaginative travel with a fantasy mindset is that immersion into fantasy worlds can make imagined places feel more real than real life. This apparent reality can transform imaginative travel into extremely powerful Positive Delusions. The phrase *Positive Delusions* comes from an author who, after being sentenced to life in prison, began collecting pictures from magazines. "A beach. A pretty girl. A nice watch. A slick apartment with a city view."[52] Those images gave him the strength to persevere. "Instead of worrying about the CO tearing up my bunk, I took out my photos and thought, *It's not always going to be like this. . . . This is the life you're going to have.*"[53]

On one level, this author knew it was absurd to hope. As a lifer imprisoned without parole, he had no evidence to support the notion that he would ever again walk free. Nevertheless, he clung to his dreams. "All I knew was that the more time I spent working on my Positive Delusions, the better I felt. And the more convinced I was that I would get there—to that happy life—one day."[54]

The phrase *Positive Delusions* strikes me as an especially apt characterization of the dysphoria-countering sensations of imaginative travel. It highlights the apparent absurdity of mistaking fantasy for reality while affirming that imaginative travel, even in seemingly impossible scenarios, can nevertheless feel real and true. These fantasies—these extremely powerful Positive Delusions—crack open small gaps of hope and give people "something to hold onto" and "a goal to believe in."[55] Moreover, far from being random, Positive Delusions speak to the core of who a person believes she is even if her immediate environment disagrees.

Positive Delusions, like other forms of imaginative travel, allow travelers to inhabit other ways of being. For one author, "I wasn't a little black boy playing pretend in his grandmother's backyard in Memphis. No, I was a Vegas showgirl making her grand entrance in front of a packed house."[56] These alternative selves can feel more authentic than the versions of self reflected back by Plato's Cave. For another author, instead of being trapped in gender dysphoria, "I felt good when I was being Robin Hood or SuperTed" or other male avatars, "like the world made sense, like I made sense. I had a confidence and a pride in myself that felt real and true. It wasn't just acting."[57]

This sense of uncanny realness is a central feature of Girl Planet and one of its greatest strengths. By constructing racially diverse hilltop cities, even if only on paper, and by encountering gender-transforming atmosphere, even if only in the woods, authors travel from *the world that is* to the places and selves that *could be* if only certain characteristics about their bodies or environments changed. These experiences, which Plato's Cave says are not real and cannot or should not become real, are nevertheless made provisionally true through fantasy travel to other worlds. These worlds show travelers something indisputably authentic about themselves, something that in other contexts is silenced and misrecognized. These experiences help travelers cope with dysphoria by providing access to spaces that defy normative limits and that dramatize the possibility of alternative self-narration.

Fantasy Travel Provides Relief from Dysphoria

Misalignments in the body-space-identity triad lead to dysphoric discomfort. One way to temporarily resolve this discomfort is by using
the emotional geographies of fantasy space to change these elements
so that the imagined environment can reveal core truths that are otherwise denied.

Emotional geography is the study of how people experience environments and how emotions define place and space.[58] As a mode
of inquiry that challenges mind/body dualisms, it explores how
landscapes of the mind and of the body come together to shape action potential. Starting with the mind, "the landscape of the mind"
is "a powerful self-narrative tool that allows the person to tell his or
her story, reinforcing and constituting his or her own self-image."[59]
Within these mental landscapes, memories, experiences, and narratives converge to form "affective atmospheres" that "inspire, suggest
or provoke specific kinds of embodied experience . . . that 'prime' bodies to act in certain ways."[60] These imagined atmospheres—like their
real-world counterparts—support "self-building practices" by using
"ordinary everyday activities" to construct "a vital sense of security,
safety and belonging."[61]

This interplay between mind and body then links the emotional
geographies of imaginative travel with the visceral geographies of embodiment. Visceral geography is about what hits one in the gut, what
is felt in one's bones, and what those sensations signify about space
and society.[62] Within visceral geography, embodiment is regarded as
a deeply authentic mode of knowing. "Beneath the biographical, linguistic self we can find another layer, the somatic self, that represents
our relationship with the world in a more direct, unmediated way."[63]
Embodiment scholars use this information to shed light on social
processes by positioning "the body as subject and object of analysis
through which to understand how power acts."[64]

Imaginative travel merges landscapes of the mind with the visceral
geographies of the body to create a space for exploring alternative
selves. Through "the convergence of body, senses, movement, and
change of scene,"[65] invisible exiles imagine ways out of dysphoria
through speculative changes to the body-space-identity triad.

Starting with the body, many invisible exiles prior to exile fantasized about changing their body's physical features to better align

with their sense of self, as when Nicole Chung imagined a fairy god-mother granting her wish for pale skin and blond hair. This desire to alleviate dysphoria by changing the body is likewise why a transgender author spent "daydream after daydream . . . imagining having the power to make these [prepubescent] bumps vanish from my chest."[66]

Similarly for authors experiencing the effects of trauma, given the way trauma lingers in the body, one way to find a temporary reprieve is by projecting oneself into other bodies. This is why, after experiencing rape, one author wrote that "the only time I felt safe . . . was in literature class discussing hypothetical lives, hypothetical sets of events that constructed hypothetical systems of morality."[67] Occupying these other bodies alleviated the dysphoria he otherwise felt within his own skin. "Without realizing it, I had leaped from the body of one avatar to the next."[68]

In examples like these, authors imagine changing their bodies to alleviate the visceral disconnect they feel within the body-space-identity triad. These changes provide a temporary sense of relief from dysphoria even when the changes are only make-believe.

Next, alongside changing bodies, authors struggling with dysphoria often imagine how, if their bodies were located in other places, their identities and relationships would change as well. In the context of racialized poverty, one author projected herself out of the public bus and into the mansions visible through the windows, "only I'd be a different girl, with a different family, and I'd swim in the pool and then go play the grand piano in the living room or watch movies in our personal home theater. The fantasy never got old."[69]

Another author imagined who she might be if, instead of sleeping homeless in the stairwell, she were located on the other side of the apartment doors. "I heard families: children calling out for mothers, husbands speaking their wives' names, sending me reminders of the way love stretched between a handful of people fills a space, transforms it into a home."[70]

Similarly for a third author, instead of being trapped in racial dysphoria, she projected herself through the *National Geographic* into places where her physical features signaled kinship, instead of difference. "I see myself in the Thai children with my same wide smile and lips. I see my summer-darkened self in the complexion of boys from Samoa. My nose is like that of people from the Philippines. Babies wrapped on their mothers' backs in China wear my eyebrows. I see my own feet in the photos of South American girls, their bare feet brown like mine."[71] Somewhere, she thought, her body must fit.

In examples like these, travelers imagined keeping their bodies but locating them in other spaces. This change in environment, they thought, might bring a new self and a different future into being.

Third, alongside changing bodies and places, travelers imagine viscerally enacting other identities by using their bodies in new—if prohibited—ways. In a religious community that forbade romantic relationships, "I pretended I held his hand, experimenting with grips, knitting intricate combinations of fingers, palms, and thumbs."[72] In a homophobic community that forbade same-sex love, a child asked his male friend, "Have you ever seen people having sex on TV? It's like this,"[73] and they then wiggled together on the floor, laughing at the supposed silliness of their game.

In these imagined spaces, changing the body's physical expression was a way to temporarily alleviate the experience of dysphoria. By changing the body, its location, or its enacted expression, travelers both yearned for and speculated about the possibility of finding an alternative sense of home within their own skin.

Physical Portals Provide Access to Fantasy Worlds

These observations raise questions about where people go to make space for imaginative travel, especially when the content is considered taboo. Within the architectural framing of Plato's Cave, even quiet travel through solo reading can be risky, let alone more performative travel through group fantasy play. Despite these risks, no cave is fully enclosed, and invisible exiles prior to exile found or constructed microenvironments that could serve as portals into fantasy worlds. In short, to access imaginative landscapes, the authors needed not only an imagined world to enter but also a tangible launching point embedded within their everyday landscape.

Starting first with solo travel, most invisible exiles launched these journeys in locations where they expected at least some degree of privacy. On the more privileged end of the spectrum, unshared bedrooms were a particular favorite. For an author experiencing ableist dysphoria, "I sit on the bottom bunk of my bed and address our new Labrador puppy. . . . I have never stuttered in a room on my own, and I have never stuttered in front of an animal."[74]

Likewise, for an author experiencing homophobic repression, the space under her mattress became a treasure map to other worlds. "Anybody with a single bed, standard size, and a collection of paperbacks, standard size, will know that seventy-two per layer can be accommodated under the mattress. By degrees my bed began to rise visibly, like the Princess and the Pea, so that soon I was sleeping closer to the ceiling than the floor."[75]

Of course, not everyone has access to private spaces at home, especially during busy daytime hours. Nighttime, however, with its diminished foot traffic and dimmed lighting, can partially overcome these obstacles.

One author used the cover of night while his wife and children slept to covertly listen to the world outside his ultra-Orthodox village. Radios were forbidden, but the kitchen clock had one built in that had never been disabled. "Careful not to make a sound, I moved one of the chairs near the refrigerator, stepped up onto it, and plugged the earphones into the tiny jack."[76] The radio, combined with the nighttime stillness, became a portal into another world. "Listening with one ear to the cackle of static . . . while keeping my other ear tuned for noises from the bedrooms . . . I switched the dial from one station to another, commercials for medical malpractice, car dealerships, and department-store blowout sales filling me with forbidden pleasure."[77]

Nighttime provided a portal for another author, as well, this time for exploring queer sexuality. After finding a pornographic magazine in the woods, he projected himself into the scenes, not as the male chauffeur but as the person pleasuring him. "There is something about being able to study another man's body. No sneaking glances or peeks, no pretending to be looking at something else."[78] The nighttime stillness made space for this exploration. "Mom was in her bedroom on the other side of the apartment, watching television. Every time I heard her footsteps, I would shove the magazine under my pillow and pretend to be asleep until I was sure it was safe."[79] By working within the limits of this partial privacy, "I could stare at the naked chauffeur's body full on and for as long as I wanted."[80]

Alongside unshared bedrooms and nocturnal wanderings, a third common gateway into fantasy worlds involved natural environments, especially ones that looked unused or unmaintained. It's likely no accident that Jennifer Boylan's Girl Planet took shape in the woods. In Western society's dualistic nature-society framework, green spaces that look wild or unkempt are often used in books and film to symbolize gaps in the social order.

Other invisible exiles likewise saw green space as a place for alternative self-expression. One author imagined that, if she lived in the countryside instead of the city, her speech impediment would magically disappear.[81] Another believed that, if only she could find her way to a faraway green patch high in the mountains, she too would become like the mountains: strong, rugged, and free.[82] Similarly, for a third author, "it was in the [unkempt] thickets" and the "mass of overgrown thorn bushes" near his school that he took the bold step of giving himself "a different name," a male name, for the first time, and "out loud."[83]

Portals and Games Make Space for Imaginative Travel with Peers

Although bedrooms, nighttime, and greenery can act as portals for solo travel, another equally important dynamic involves constructing spaces for co-travel with peers. Although co-travelers are often unwitting participants, group fantasy play is nevertheless common within invisible exile travel writing, and peer participation augments the experience by providing an externalized sense of realness and validation.

Within invisible exile narratives, imaginative travelers use games, stages, and vacations to integrate other people into their fantasy journeys. Starting first with informal games, one way to co-travel is by making subtle changes to the games other people are already playing. Playing house, for instance, is a common form of fantasy play that socializes children into normative roles even as it also creates space for covert, nonnormative exploration. In the context of gender dysphoria, "it was during these games" where, by demanding "the coveted role of mom, . . . I had creative license to free my hair from its rubber band . . . and swish my hips as I served my family."[84] Similarly, in the context of kinky sexuality, "I manipulated our scenarios so that whoever was pretending to be the mom or dad that day ended up chasing us around the playhouse with a belt."[85]

In examples like these, playing house not only made space to explore alternative expressions of gender and sexuality; it also brought other people into the fantasy world. Invisible exiles recalling these experiences valued the apparent validation from coconspirators, especially since external validation in nonplayful contexts was so scarce.

Second, alongside informal games, authors used formal programs in the performing arts to recruit co-travelers. Even though imaginative travel on stage meant different things to different participants, for invisible exiles, the presence of co-traveling peers added an enhanced sense of realness. For people experiencing dysphoria, this group dynamic then created an apparent sense of validation.

As examples, in an ableist context, an author's stutter vanished entirely when she stepped onstage. While in character, "I can make my voice reflect all the emotions trapped in my body. . . . I balloon into my new persona until, at the end, I'm breathless and high."[86] In this fantasy space, she saw herself as competent and, for a fleeting but blissful moment, other students and teachers agreed.

In a religious context, the fanaticism that usually separated an author from other kids momentarily disappeared while attending dance class. Although "the other girls rarely spoke to me, . . . I could memorize the movements and, in doing so, step into their minds, lunging when they lunged, reaching my arms upward in time with theirs."[87] In this fantasy space, synchronized movement symbolized belonging.

Next, alongside games and the performing arts, a third option for imaginative co-travel involved finding ways to role-play with people who were unaware a game was afoot. In the context of gender dysphoria, one author called kids from school on the telephone and introduced herself as a visitor named Keisha. "In the guise of my alter ego, I daydreamed out loud about my life as a girl,"[88] including joining the dance squad and shopping for cute outfits. "Talking on the phone was my first bit of storytelling, and Keisha was my heroine."[89]

Another transgender author used a similar strategy during family vacations. "Holidays are about escaping your real life and it would be so easy to let that secret part slip out to people who didn't know me and whom I would never see again."[90] When playing with other vacationing children, he introduced himself as male—as Jake—and received the satisfying environmental response of having that gender accepted.

It was the same for another transgender author who found similar opportunities for imaginative co-travel during moments of general silliness, for instance when joking with friends that she spent her weekend hanging out with the famous cast from *Harry Potter.* Her friends knew she was lying, and she used that knowledge to simultaneously pretend-disclose her transgender status. "'It's true,'" she said about the actors, "'and you want to know something else? . . . I'm not really a boy. . . . I have to wear this boy-mask because my mom wanted a boy. But I'm actually a girl.' . . . Then we all started laughing because it was just so absurd."[91] In examples like these, jokes created a space where travelers could simultaneously speak and hide. "Lying that I knew the cast of Harry Potter and wore a boy-mask made it so my friends didn't know what to believe."[92]

Cumulatively, whether traveling solo in bedrooms and forests or co-traveling through games, role-play, and vacations, invisible exiles found provisional spaces to explore other identities. These cracks in the normative architecture of everyday life were just large enough that authors could prod and stretch them until they became portals into fantasy worlds. In these spaces where Girl Planet overtook Plato's Cave, imaginative travel helped authors cope with dysphoria by providing access to speculative environments that defied impossibility and supported alternative self-narration.

Personas, Props, and Talismans Enhance the Travel Experience

While constructing fantasy worlds, many authors used additional strategies to bring their imaginative travel more vividly to life. Reflecting back on these pre-exile experiences, invisible exiles recalled using media personas as character guides and material props as performance enhancers. They also used magical talismans to set their journeys in motion and to justify, even if only to themselves, why such journeys were necessary and legitimate.

Starting first with role models, many authors based their fantasy identities on the real and fictional people they encountered through the media. They pretended to be Medusa, Eurydice, and "Penelope . . . dreaming of my husband's body."[93] They adopted the mannerisms of "Rambo, the Terminator, and Commando" coming to liberate oppressed communities from civil war.[94] They also impersonated "William Clark and . . . Captain Meriweather Lewis . . . discover[ing] new places no one had ever seen."[95]

Importantly, as potential role models, these personas were not just mildly different from the lifestyles common within Plato's Cave.

Instead, from travelers' perspectives, these personas embodied a radical departure from the norm.

For example, the racial containment zone that is federal prison is perhaps as far away as an impoverished Black man can get from the glamorous lifestyles of the rich white women depicted on *Sex and the City*. Even so, and perhaps precisely for this reason, that television show was one author's ultimate Girl Planet fantasy. "Guys laughed at me so much, . . . but, come on—that show lit me up! . . . It was my Positive Delusions on-screen."[96]

This search for different ways of being explains why another author who felt frustrated with the psychiatric institutions that labeled him as "sick" turned instead to "stories from indigenous cultures" to "imagine a different way"—and a potentially less stigmatizing way—to conceptualize his mental health.[97]

Similarly, for an author who felt trapped by domestic violence, Amelia Earhart symbolized everything her own mother was not. "Amelia was brave and courageous. She didn't let others limit her dreams and she never took no for an answer. . . . And unlike [mom], she wasn't interested in being dependent on a man."[98]

When searching for alternative role models from within Plato's Cave, imaginative travel sometimes felt like the only place where authors could locate images for how to live otherwise. In all these cases, media provided a way to locate these seemingly provocative personas.

Second, when embodying these avatars, travelers used material props to intensify the visceral experience. Some travelers used props to rescript their bodies, for instance by "stuffing a small cuddly toy down the front of my pants . . . to correct myself to the physical form I knew was associated with my gender identity."[99] Others used props to express different cultural identities, for instance when, "with my cap twisted sideways and my pants sagging below my waist, I practiced walking with a ghetto swagger."[100] Travelers also used props to simulate social interactions, for instance by waving "branches like feathered fans . . . before whirling around to peek over my shoulder, making eye contact with one man in the audience as if a spotlight had landed on him."[101]

In these examples, travelers used props to enhance the visceral experience of imagined journeys. By changing their embodied narration, props provided material support for identifying otherwise.

Third, alongside props and personas, travelers used the magical objects described in books and films to set fantasy journeys in motion. "Secretly, I too am waiting to fall down a hole into Wonderland, or pass through the back of a wardrobe into Narnia."[102] For one author, "I cried myself to sleep at night, hoping that some genie would magically appear and all my troubles would be solved."[103] For another author, "I fantasized about" being rescued by "a private eye in a room with thick blinds and hazy smoke."[104] A third author "wished for a Hogwarts letter" that would grant passage to "the hospital wing where Madam Pomfrey would give me some terrible tasting potion to drink, but which I would take gladly and marvel as the bumps" of emerging breast tissue "slowly melted away."[105] A fourth author was likewise half-waiting for "a final draught (draft) that would change me forever, like Alice's bottle, like the tremendous potion in *Dr. Jekyll and Mr. Hyde,* like the mysterious liquid that seals the fate of Tristan and Isolde."[106]

In examples like these, potions, wardrobes, and other magical talismans set journeys in motion. It's not only that magical objects provide an apparent mechanism for making the impossible true; it's also that, in these stories, the arrival of magical objects launches the narrative action. Prior to their arrival, the unsuspecting protagonists had no real plan of escape and no viable means for doing so. But then, when these magical objects appear, the characters are launched on transformative quests whether they want the adventure or not.

For invisible exiles, this sense of an external force enabling and even compelling a journey provides a partial workaround for the self-inhibiting impulses of doubt and shame. Instead of fully acknowledging their desires, which can feel terrifying, especially early in a quest, travelers can simply pretend that, like their fictional avatars, a magical series of events gives them no option but to explore. On Girl Planet, travelers simply become female whether they want it or not. This deference to an externalized authority, even if only in a traveler's mind, can make it easier to explore material that feels risky or taboo.

Plausible Deniability Provides a Measure of Safety

Although fantasy draws its power from defying reality, another key advantage of imaginative travel is that it provides a cover of safety. Plausible deniability is important in contexts where society punishes people for flouting social norms. However, the fictional premise of fantasy gives travelers a ready defense. Nicole Chung's hilltop cities are just made-up stories, and Jennifer Boylan's Girl Planet is just a silly game. By strategically invoking fictionality, travelers can protect themselves from at least some of the punitive consequences of transgressing.

Importantly, although plausible deniability offers many protections, its shield is not absolute. For one thing, fantasy travel cannot last forever. "Fairy tales and fantasy, I understood, were like the training wheels on a child's first two-wheel bike: a forgivable crutch at the outset, but one we are meant to progress beyond needing."[107] For another thing, the freedoms afforded by imaginative travel are not infinite. Although fantasy play is generally considered a natural part of childhood, "injecting fantasy into non-playful interactions is largely constructed as deviant, even amongst young children" who, at a very early age, are expected to "have a developed appreciation of the boundary between fantasy and reality."[108]

Within invisible exile travel writing, one author's story of sexual dysphoria provides a particularly clear example of this context-specific divide. For lack of alternatives, kinky kids often incorporate the corporal punishment scenes from children's literature into their erotic fantasy play. However, although these stories contain potentially sexualized language, children are expected to know those words are not socially acceptable when written in other places, for instance when typed into a Home Depot computer terminal. For a boy who did exactly that, after "the euphoric fog of self-disclosure cleared," he "realized he wasn't alone—a middle-aged man was standing right behind him, wearing an expression that confirmed he'd read [his] confession."[109] The same words that were legitimate in a storybook were taboo at the hardware store. The kid "didn't even bother to delete his words. He just fled the scene of his crime."[110]

These normative boundaries surrounding fantasy play help explain why, even as Nicole Chung's Christmas pageant classmates permitted themselves to impersonate angels, they would not allow an Asian girl to play Mary. The pageant played at a story the children believed was real and good. But at only five years old, these youngsters had internalized the message that decentering white privilege was false and wrong. For these reasons, unprompted, they shut it down, even in their imaginations.

These caveats are important, but in my assessment, fantasy travel is nevertheless an important waystation in journeys through invisible exile. In pre-exile moments, imaginative travel is both a temporary escape and a way to begin constructing an alternative future. "During your escape, books can . . . give you knowledge about the world and your predicament, give you weapons, give you armour: real things you can take back into your prison. Skills and knowledge and tools you can use to escape for real."[111] It's not only that, through imaginative travel, invisible exiles find respite from dysphoria. It's also that, through media role models and fantasy play, the supposed dividing line between fact and fiction blurs.

Fantasy Travel Comes with a Mix of Costs and Benefits

Cumulatively, and even without leading to quick or lasting solutions, invisible exile narratives demonstrate that the supportive architecture of imaginative travel can feel extremely real. However, this apparent reality is double-edged. Although imaginative travel provides much-needed access to spaces of authenticity and validation, it can also spark confusion and shame, expose travelers to social sanctions, and fuel new rounds of self-repression. In short, no journey is risk free, not even when traveling through the mind. Despite these risks, to the extent that imaginative travel casts places and identities in a new light, it supports processes of self-transformation.

Starting first with the benefits of imaginative travel, these journeys can make the impossible feel true in ways that are important and validating. "The one place where, ironically, I could feel well and truly real, was in my imagination."[112] In some cases, the persona initially invented for role-play begins to feel like the author's true self. The alter ego in these instances "was no longer imaginary to me; she was the most authentic thing about me."[113] Imaginative travel does not solve every problem. Gender dysphoria "could not be quelled by rayon" alone, and yet "the nights when I was alone dressed up and 'being female' were always a great relief for me. For a few short hours, I felt as if I didn't have to put on a show."[114]

Alongside relief from dysphoria, imaginative journeys can provide travelers with a much-needed sense of hope and possibility. In a class-based narrative, these glimpses of other worlds "filled me with a longing to build the same; it was inspiring to me."[115] Similarly, in an anti-ableist narrative, "as I put [the co-conspirator puppy] back into her bed, . . . I reassure her that we are heading to a new place, a new beginning."[116] In these ways, imagined journeys held the promise of a potentially happier future.

These hypothetical promises of a better future can provoke strong emotional responses. In a gendered context, through imaginative journeys, a traveler experienced "the thrill of sounding out loud a snippet of a secret thought."[117] In a queer context, the author felt "something like butterflies and fireflies, and the thrill of the roller-coaster drop rushed through me."[118] In a racial context, imagining other lives through "magazines and maps . . . helped settle the crazy inside me."[119]

These positive emotions are important. But imaginative journeys do not last forever, and the magical talismans launching them rarely arrive in real life. The magical wardrobe does not appear, nor does the genie or the private eye. In one case, the imagined army of foreign liberators did arrive, but then the soldiers turned around and "left so fast they didn't even take their stuff."[120]

These observations underscore the hard truth that visiting Girl Planet is not the same as making durable social change. This realization can feel discouraging. "It was a bitter pill to swallow when I realized that no one would ever pick up the glass slipper I left behind."[121] Even as children, invisible exiles realized their fantasies "couldn't go on forever" because, although games and role-play worked for a while, the practicalities of growing up and "paying rent would require something new to focus on."[122] No matter that fantasies felt deeply real, the constraints of real life always seemed to catch up. "My body was a ticking time bomb and every day in the back of my mind was a quiet refrain—tick tock, tick tock, tick tock."[123]

Moreover, when these journeys end, returning travelers often struggle to reconcile their expanded sense of Girl Planet possibilities with the limited discourses available in Plato's Cave. After returning, the journeys that temporarily set travelers free could then fill them with shame. For a transgender author, "I allowed myself to think about being Jake, which segued into acting as though I *was* Jake for a few minutes before I snapped out of it and berated myself. . . . I suddenly felt a bit sick."[124] Similarly, for a kinky traveler, "I . . . lay on my stomach" as though draped across someone's knee "to drink the confusing cocktail of satisfaction and self-loathing that came of that position."[125]

These strong emotions of authenticity coupled with shame help explain why some Girl Planet adventures end not in validation but in fear. After indulging in a fantasy journey, a traveler might "wake from scripture-inspired nightmares—blue cones of flame licking my feet."[126] Nightmares like these reflect the fear that desiring the taboo meant something was wrong. The more a traveler indulged in such fantasies, "the more profoundly I believe I'm a bad girl."[127]

This sense of shame helps explain the secrecy surrounding imaginative travel. "Like any teenage boy trained at reading things he shouldn't be, I looked both ways before opening" queer-themed books, "then got up and grabbed a decoy off the shelf. . . . I kept it open on the second chapter and within reach in case someone I knew came down the aisle and I needed a quick alibi."[128] This shame encouraged secret-keeping. "There was an instinct at work in me, a learned intuition," to keep quiet around authority figures.[129] "Even at that age, we all sensed that there was something shameful about our game. We never played House with adults nearby."[130]

Punishment was one concern. As one author stated, "I felt like I would get in trouble" if anyone "saw me reading this book."[131] However, another concern—and often a much larger one—was that exposure to and censorship by the people in Plato's Cave would pop the precious but fragile Girl Planet bubble. Travelers were "scared" that someone would "find out the truth" about their fantasies, and their Girl Planet alter ego "would be dismissed as a fraud."[132]

In short, even when travelers felt irresistibly pulled toward other modes of self-expression, they understood in no uncertain terms that their societies denounced their yearnings as bad or wrong. They also understood that, to maintain belonging within their current communities, they needed to keep their imagined journeys secret.

Importantly, imaginative travel does not cause this shame. Instead, shame emerges from the internalized sense that the desire for such fantasies is unacceptable. "Shame" is the sense of having transgressed social boundaries in such a way that "your entire person is infected by something inherently bad and potentially contagious."[133] In some cases, shame is "reintegrative" in that it motivates people to recommit to group norms, while in other cases shame ostracizes by labeling entire groups as abnormal or "outcasts."[134] This distinction is important because travelers often respond to the shame invoked by fantasy play by taking self-repressive steps that they hoped will prevent the ostracization that might otherwise follow.

Even then, imaginative travelers risk punishment. Although fantasy play is often tolerated in young children, "if I had been even a couple of years older, . . . I might have earned a slap instead of a sigh."[135] Some travelers *were* slapped,[136] or verbally berated. "I sat in the backseat and listened to my father shout. How could Mother have let me sin so openly?"[137]

In other cases, parents confiscated and destroyed props, both as punishment for imaginative travel and to thwart future journeys. When a transgender author's father discovered her speaking on the telephone as a girl, he dragged her into the bathroom and sheared off her long curly hair.[138] Similarly, when a queer author's mother discovered the erotic library hidden underneath the mattress, she hurled the books out the window, "went into the yard, poured paraffin over the books and set them on fire."[139]

Some travelers respond to these punishments with defiance. One author's parents tolerated his seemingly passive escapes through Hollywood movies in the local theater, but they drew the line when he hung salvaged movie posters on his bedroom walls. In addition to having him whipped, "from this time on, whenever something bad happened, I was blamed for bringing evil to the house."[140] Despite these punishments, the author refused to stop daydreaming. "Even while I was scrubbing [Hollywood] English off my bedroom walls, I was writing new words on the walls of abandoned houses where no one could scold me."[141]

Although defiance is always an option, a more common response, it seems, is to spiral deeper into shame and despair. One author tried to will away her interest in secular culture. "The thought of having so many toys seemed almost selfish, or at least that is what I told myself."[142]

Another author berated herself for fantasizing about forbidden love. "I disgusted myself. Seated before my shrine, I ripped up the one photo . . . that I had smuggled with me, and begged Guru for inner assistance."[143]

A third author spent hours working on a diorama for school, but then, in a fit of rage, "hurled a pillow across the room, smashing the pieces . . . onto the floor."[144] In her narrative, the diorama's broken popsicle-stick picket fence was a powerful symbol of how painful it felt to dream about a happy home in an environment that consistently crushed it.

Many travelers try to stop this pain by stopping their daydreaming. "Meddling with the inevitable can only lead to trouble, even if the meddling takes place only in your mind."[145] As powerful as imaginative journeys might feel, travelers are not delusional. They know that, despite feelings of realness, imaginative travel is a bubble of space that is unlikely to become spontaneously durable.

Knowing imagined alternatives are supposedly impossible does not, however, make it easy to let them go. Instead, despite the pain, travelers often feel compelled to persist, to return, and to explore imagined places and imagined selves until, eventually, something begins to shift. At some point, travelers realize that imaginative travel is changing their sense of who they are and what they want from their future. "The world that opens up to me in that library has no boundaries whatsoever. . . . That boundless expanse calls to me, louder and louder with each passing day."[146] Or, as another author phrased it, "the seed of curiosity had been planted; it needed nothing more than time and boredom to grow."[147]

As part of this growth, imaginative journeys can lead to action. "I resolve to leave . . . one day. . . . I don't know how. . . . But I know, with great certainty, that it will be."[148] Imaginative travel is powerful in its own right, but because it can spark creative rethinking, it need not stop at fantasy. On the contrary, within the overall exile journey, imaginative travel through media and role-play "was just the beginning."[149]

In conclusion, although diving directly into new social worlds often feels jarring, imaginative travel through media and fantasy play allows travelers to begin exploring alternatives that feel simultaneously impossible and authentic. Through imaginative travel, people living with dysphoria construct spaces of release and inhabit environments organized around alternative self-narration. As a fantasy space, Girl Planet provides these suppressed truths with a supportive architecture that helps travelers experience themselves as they *could* exist while simultaneously maintaining some level of safety through plausible deniability. These experiences underscore the importance of imaginative travel within invisible exile journeys. The next step in this pre-exile context is to create opportunities for *physical* travel, which is the subject of the next chapter.

THREE

The Process of Unbecoming

The Bohemian Coast

A common theme in popular culture is *getting out of Dodge* or escaping difficult circumstances by irreverently breaking away from stifling environments and never looking back. In Jack Kerouac's *On the Road,* J. D. Salinger's *Catcher in the Rye,* and Ridley Scott's *Thelma & Louise,* the main characters decide the best way to solve their problems is to leave the places where they feel bored, abused, or misunderstood, and try their luck elsewhere.

By contrast, invisible exiles tell a different tale. Prior to exile, authors feel alienated and other environments look enticing, but instead of trying to leave, they work hard to stay. Indeed, a key theme within invisible exile travel writing is how far authors will go to fit in, comply, and belong. Instead of running away, travelers choose to return and submit to environments that feel oppressive.

This willingness to embrace self-repression reflects the power of place attachment. Even when authors do not feel full acceptance, they nevertheless rely on their environments for food, shelter, protection, employment, identity, and love. Although the fantasy of leaving in search of something better might feel appealing, the actual experience of severing ties—of entering exile—is often unbearable.

In this chapter, I discuss place attachment in the context of people who take short trips to validating environments but who then choose, at least initially, not to stay in those places. I examine the reasons behind those choices, including what authors gain through travel, what they think they will lose by permanently relocating, and how they negotiate these trade-offs.

As discussed in the previous chapter, imaginative travel is a useful way to begin exploring. However, imaginative travelers often yearn for physical travel as well. They yearn for trips to real places where they can embody their most authentic identities more fully. One way to achieve this goal is through scouting trips to places filled with strangers. By traveling to places where nobody knows them, travelers can shed preconceived notions about who they are and how they are supposed to live. This anonymity creates a testing ground where travelers can experiment with new and potentially liberating identities.

Despite these possibilities, scouting trips also present challenges. One challenge is the lingering sense that the experimental identity is an impossible utopia, similar to a vacation that is enjoyable in the short term but not sustainable indefinitely. Another challenge is the struggle between wanting to live differently while simultaneously wanting to preserve existing social connections. These challenges help explain why, even when scouting trips feel freeing, many travelers don't stay and instead choose to return to oppressive environments and resume pretravel roles.

Unfortunately, these returns often go poorly. After experiencing validation and being changed by those experiences, it can feel painful to reenter stifling social worlds. Furthermore, the pressure to hide evolving identities can undermine physical and mental health, social relationships, and daily functioning. Some travelers cope by developing different identities for different places, but this spatial partitioning, instead of granting access to two worlds at once, often leaves travelers feeling like ghosts with shadow selves in two worlds but full selves in neither.

In this chapter, I examine the experiences of invisible exiles who, prior to exile, use short trips to explore alternative identities, as well as the conflicting feelings of freedom and danger those trips ignite. To explore these themes, I first provide detailed examples of scouting trips as recounted within invisible exile travel writing. Next, drawing on theories of place and identity, I explain how travel-related anonymity allows people to temporarily escape social roles and test the potential to live differently. Then, I discuss the idea of place attachment, including the way place attachment can trap people in oppressive situations, as well as the reasons why disrupted attachments—even to repressive places—can feel problematic. Last, I describe how, by taking short trips in secret, travelers attempt to balance the desire for escape with the competing desire for connection. Overall, this analysis highlights the power of place attachment, including its potentially negative effects on people struggling to cope with alienation and dysphoria.

"I'll Be Goddamned If I'm Going to Give up Everything"

Starting with detailed examples recounted within invisible exile travel writing, Jennifer Boylan's memoir *She's Not There* aptly illustrates this pattern of venturing out, having validating experiences, and then returning and recommitting to systems of self-repression. As a child, Boylan could only express her femininity through dress-up and make-believe, but as an adult living alone, she had other options. She still presented as James at work. But after work, "I'd come home and *go female* and pay the bills and write and watch television," until the next morning when "I'd go back to boy mode."[1]

Boylan enjoyed feeling more like herself in private, but she yearned to also venture out as her female self in public. "I waited on this side of the door . . . wondering when, and if, I would ever be able—as a woman—to feel that rain upon my face."[2] Eventually, she stepped outside and drove to the Esso Station to buy a tank of gas. "I thought I was going to perish from fear."[3] She persisted and was pleasantly surprised by the outcome. "I waited in line to pay for the gas, and no one looked at me twice. 'Thank you, ma'am,' said the attendant."[4] The entire trip passed without incident.

Despite this success, Boylan nevertheless remained fearful of being recognized. "I did not want to jeopardize the program" where she worked "or my own professional integrity by risking intrigue."[5] To protect the belonging she already possessed—incomplete though it was—she drove home and recommitted to living publicly as James.

At least, she tried, until she again felt the overwhelming need to travel. Boylan's next trips were bigger, for instance to Nova Scotia, a place where nobody knew her and where the off-season hotel was mostly empty. In this anonymous environment, she put on her bra, combed out her hair, "looked in the mirror and saw a perfectly normal-looking young woman."[6] There she was, out in the world, her true reflection, Jennifer.

The experience felt gratifying, and Boylan considered staying forever. "I thought about settling in one of the little villages around here, just starting life over as a woman."[7] However, this beautiful idea also felt impossible, which is why she instead returned home and went to her "closet with an enormous garbage bag. Into this I put my skirts, my hose, the blue knit top, some underwear, my makeup, some bobby pins, everything. Then I tied up the trash bag and walked out to the curb and left it there."[8] To further cement her conviction to leaving her female identity behind, she got married, became a parent, and re-committed to living exclusively—even in private—as James.

This self-repression worked for a while, but eventually Boylan once again felt the need to travel. This time she crossed an ocean for the privilege of anonymity, and instead of hiding in an empty hotel, she let her female self live fully and in public. In Amsterdam, dressed *en femme*, as she called it, Boylan visited parks, museums, and restaurants where endless strangers responded to her as just another female American tourist. Basking in this acceptance, she felt relaxed, "hovering, weightless, levitated by music above the sorrows of the world."[9]

Once again, however, this weightlessness did not last. After four days in Amsterdam, Boylan returned home and resumed life as James. She didn't want to. She wanted to live full-time as Jennifer. "Of course it's what I want. But that's not the point."[10] The point for her was that living as a woman in a place where people knew her as male meant risking her job, family, and safety, all for a future with no guarantees. She chided herself, "What do you think you're going to do about this now? Have a sex change, at age forty? Abandon all the love that has made your life whole, so that you can enter into a new life, about which you know nothing?"[11] It felt impossible. The cost was too high. "I'll be goddamned if I'm going to give up everything I've always wanted just so I can *fit*."[12]

Welcome to the Bohemian Coast, a Place of Anonymous Temporary Release

Boylan did not give her destinations a conceptual name, but Jillian Keenan did. As explained in her memoir *Sex with Shakespeare*, Keenan also traveled to explore secret aspects of her identity. After enduring a tumultuous childhood, receiving a disabling health diagnosis, and suppressing a stigmatized sexual identity, she yearned to assert independence. "It was time for me to unfreeze."[13]

Like Boylan, Keenan unfroze by traveling. At age seventeen, she dropped out of school and moved to Spain. The anonymity of living abroad where no one knew her gave her the freedom, for the first time, to fully explore her sexuality, not just furtively through books and films but in real life with real partners. By spending time in anonymous places, "I was becoming a more confident, uninhibited version of myself."[14]

Keenan calls this space of release Bohemia. More specifically, she compares her time in Spain to Shakespeare's description of the Bohemian seaside in *The Winter's Tale*. *The Winter's Tale* begins in Italy where a jealous king wrongfully accuses his pregnant wife of infidelity and imprisons her. When their daughter, Perdita, is born, her seemingly illegitimate birth appears to seal the child's fate. Born in disgrace, Perdita is banished to the desolate land of Bohemia where she is left on the coast to die. However, instead of dying, she is discovered by a shepherd's family and, in this way, the "little lost one . . . born in prison" is freed from her sacrificial role and "grows into a confident, self-assured young woman."[15]

For Keenan, "Spain was my Bohemia."[16] Like Perdita's journey, traveling to this new place was both an act of erasure separating her from her past and a moment of possibility enabling the creation of a new identity. Being away from familiar places made it easier to let go of their moral judgments, which then made space to explore the otherwise stigmatized aspects of her sexuality.

This connection between travel and self-transformation is a central theme in travel writing. "In medieval allegory, the development of the inner person is shown in an outer journey, in seemingly physical encounters."[17] In present-day narratives, travel is likewise "seen as a resource in the endeavor of self-realization,"[18] a way "to discover a true 'self'"[19] and an opportunity to "understand the self as much as the foreign."[20] By moving through space, "the traveling individual is through acts and tales expressing a story about who he or she is or wants to be."[21] Like Jennifer Boylan buying gas and visiting museums, these trips are not mere errands. Instead, these journeys are driven by "a meaningful, existential desire" to "endow the individual's identity with a richer and fuller experience of being."[22]

For invisible exiles prior to exile, much of this exploration occurs during scouting trips. In queer geography, "scouting trips" are short out-and-back trips where travelers assess both "a potential place to live" and "the *possibilities* of living life as a gay man,"[23] or a trans woman like Boylan, or a kinky person like Keenan. These scouting trips are exploratory in that they "tended to take place *before*" travelers "disclosed their sexual difference to themselves or others," and they are also formative, with "migration itself (or even the potential for migration)" acting "as a powerful catalyst for coming out."[24]

That is the power of the Bohemian Coast. "*The Winter's Tale's* tonal change, from downbeat to upbeat, seems abrupt. But it's not an accident. Different places bring out different versions of ourselves."[25] The shift from Italy to Bohemia, like Boylan traveling to Amsterdam and Keenan traveling to Spain, creates new possibilities. In all three narratives, the protagonists' identities begin to change, and these changes are made easier through travel to places filled with strangers.

Within invisible exile life history writing, the Bohemian Coast takes many forms. Some authors find it by traveling through Europe, South America, or Asia. Others find it in the cities they already call home, for instance in secular spaces or countercultural neighborhoods, in restaurants, movie theaters, bookstores, and bars. The specific location is less important than the characteristic of finding a space of release that enables exploration.

These exploratory trips build on previous imaginative travel, but instead of minimizing the experience through fantasy and jest, the Bohemian Coast allows travelers to embrace these other selves more fully. In this sense, whereas Girl Planet deals with "the just perceptible, the barely there, the nagging presence of an absence,"[26] the Bohemian Coast is a solid landscape "defined above all in terms of contact, immersion and immediacy" where "enactments of self and landscape" bring both self and place into "sensuous, tactile and experiential being."[27] As a testing ground, scouting trips are about finding safe enough places to experiment with authentic but previously repressed identity traits. Rather than discovering foreign places, these trips are like a "journey to myself" organized around the feeling of "déjà vu" and "the desire to recover an original lost home" that is both real and never was.[28] It is about investigating what a Girl Planet identity might look like in real life and whether society might accept that identity if travelers lived them elsewhere.

Travel Creates Landscapes of Anonymity

One reason physical travel promotes self-change is that exposure to novel environments can encourage rethinking. However, although I agree that novelty is useful, in my assessment, novelty is *not* the Bohemian Coast's defining element. Instead, in my view, its two most important traits are anonymity and impermanence.

Beginning with anonymity, anonymity as a motive for travel challenges the assumption that travel is primarily about novelty. According to some scholars, "travel writers deal primarily with the 'differences' between the traveler's home and the societies to which she travels."[29] If difference were the most important factor, to the extent that globalization creates "an increasingly homogeneous world, travel is senseless because there are no longer any genuine differences between countries and town."[30]

I believe that genuine differences persist and are constantly being created. However, invisible exile travel narratives suggest that these differences are not necessarily the reason why authors travel to the Bohemian Coast. The Bohemian Coast is about anonymity, not novelty. Physical mobility creates "a demarcated time and space" that is "qualitatively different from the rest of the life course."[31] In this liminal zone, "removed from her past personal history by a place where no one yet knows her," the traveler "is free to experiment" with other ways of being.[32] Travel creates a spatial break between a traveler's current self and her potential self. Back home, "my mother has thoughts of me, my father does, my sister does, my ex-wife does, my son does. Everybody does. . . . [But] you get off the plane in Bangkok. Nobody has anything in their minds about you. . . . You can be somebody new, you can be different. And you can change."[33] In this place of anonymity, "all the pressure's off, no one cares," and there is "no need for a mask."[34]

Invisible exiles reflecting back on pre-exile scouting trips express similar sentiments. "Traveling alone, you get to be whoever you want. I don't mean lie. I mean you get to be a blank slate. You can't leave behind your skin color, or your height, or the handsomeness or homeliness of your face. But you can leave your story behind. If you've broken hearts, the new place doesn't know. If you've lost trust in people and yourself, the new place doesn't know. If everyone thinks you love Jesus, but you never really have figured out what you believe, the new place doesn't care."[35]

In short, travel creates opportunities for self-transformation not because travelers encounter foreign cultures—although novelty may help—but rather because this newfound anonymity allows travelers to shed prior roles and experiment with other possible selves. For authors visiting the Bohemian Coast, anonymity, not novelty, is the key to this release.

Anonymous Release Through Travel Is Impermanent

In my assessment, the Bohemian Coast includes any location where anonymity releases people from external expectations and provides validation for repressed selves. However, these visits to the Bohemian Coast are often discontinuous and incomplete. They are, in other words, impermanent. Instead of making a once-and-for-all grand move to a potentially liberating environment, invisible exile journeys, including pre-exile trips to the Bohemian Coast, oscillate between exploration and retrenchment.

One key reason travelers retrench is that the Bohemian Coast can feel like an impossible illusion. In the real world, Bohemia is landlocked, and so by definition it cannot have a seaside. If there is no seaside, how can the fantastical identities attached to it be real?

Some literary critics believe Shakespeare made a geographical error, or that, five hundred years ago, Bohemia had a small coastline that has since disappeared. Jillian Keenan, however, prefers a more allegorical explanation. For her, the Bohemian Coast is neither a mistake nor a place lost to time but rather an "intentionally impossible utopia" or "a kind of never-never land, a perfect place that cannot exist in real life," but that travelers visit regardless and where those visits radically alter the storyline.[36]

This notion of an impossible utopia taking physical form in defiance of facts or conventions is what gives the Bohemian Coast its strength. For Shakespeare's Perdita, traveling from cold Sicilia to the feral seaside is not just about escape; it's also about making the impossible true. In a similar vein, for Jennifer Boylan, the Nova Scotia hotel and the Amsterdam sidewalks provide a reflection of her identity that is not only different from the reflection back home but that, at home, is considered impossible. "By intuition I was certain that the thing I knew to be true was something others would find both impossible and hilarious."[37] By contrast, when traveling to places where nobody knew her, the apparent impossibility of Jennifer did not matter. She simply was. End of discussion.

Although this apparent realness born of anonymity is a strength, the lingering sense that this reality is nevertheless impossible is the Bohemian Coast's biggest weakness. For travelers like Boylan and Keenan, their travel-related reflections felt real in the moment, but like the soothing effect of cold water on a burn, which dissipates the moment the tap is turned off, this sense of possibility vanished when travelers returned home and were once again surrounded by familiar places and people.

In short, venturing out of Plato's Cave allowed travelers to embody other identities temporarily, but those seaside selves were not yet stable enough to leave the Bohemian Coast and persist in less validating environments. Travelers could journey out and back many times, but according to Plato's Cave, the two selves could not coexist.

These dynamics help explain invisible exile's corkscrew travel path. Like Boylan's journey, Keenan's self-exploration was similarly impermanent. She embraced her kinky self in Spain but then abandoned it, at least for a time, after returning to the States. "I reincarcerated myself in my own mind."[38] Like Boylan, Keenan would find other opportunities for out-and-back travel, and like Boylan, she would explore for a long time without fully arriving, and also return home without truly fitting in. As a result, instead of leading to immediate, long-term liberation, traveling to the Bohemian Coast both intensified her sense that an alternate self was possible and led to a painful state of denial and haunting.

Finding the Bohemian Coast in Real Life

Travelers find exploratory release in a variety of places. Although the tourism industry is filled with special packages promising to deliver release through hedonistic adventures to foreign places, within invisible exile travel writing, the Bohemian Coast often takes more mundane forms. In keeping with the spirit of the "short-distance wander," "insofar as we define traveling not just as the conquest of large geographical distances but as an advance into unknown, unsafe terrain," then "depending on who one is and where one is living, even crossing a street can be a journey."[39] In this way, although some authors find exploratory release through foreign travel, others find it through small-scale travel closer to home.

Whatever the location, these journeys can feel thrilling, like discovering Girl Planet in real life. However, alongside exhilaration, travelers also describe confusion and fear. The disappearance of habitual norms can feel disorienting, and it can be dangerous to navigate unfamiliar spaces without prior socialization. For these reasons, the Bohemian Coast simultaneously points toward a possible exit from Plato's Cave and, oftentimes, frightens travelers into returning.

Taking these assertions one step at a time and starting with the question of where travelers go to find anonymity, several invisible exiles found spaces of release by visiting foreign countries. Importantly, however, it was not the foreignness that mattered so much as the anonymity that helped travelers feel empowered to step away from internalized identities and externally prescribed social roles.

As examples, in a gender-themed narrative, during a solo trip to Mexico, "it hits me for the first time" that "I do not need anyone's permission to do what I want to do. I am free to make my own decisions, follow my whims, and take whatever risks I choose."[40]

In an anti-ableist narrative, during a solo trip to Italy, "there was . . . no one I saw on a daily basis, no one for whom I was supposed to play a role. . . . I . . . didn't have to organize myself into a person for anyone's eyes."[41]

Similarly, in a queer-themed narrative, during a solo journey through South America, "I was in a foreign place, far from any watchful eyes, from anyone who knew me. The invisibility. It made me realize how much of decency is built through community, through other eyes."[42]

In these examples, travel releases people from social roles. Importantly, however, this release is not about *withdrawing* from social interaction. Instead, like Jennifer Boylan walking the bustling streets of Amsterdam, the Bohemian Coast is about *interacting* with strangers who have no prior expectation of who the traveler is or how she ought to live. If strangers then validate a traveler's alternative identity, this validation signals that the traveler could, in theory, adopt the new identity full-time.

Although the travel-writing genre favors stories about foreign countries, the life histories of invisible exile show that travelers are just as capable of finding the Bohemian Coast through short trips to nearby destinations. In my assessment, domestic travelers find these destinations both in subcultural contexts and in the imagined mainstream. Then, through repetition, anonymous travel lasting only a few hours can gradually accumulate into self-change.

Starting with subcultural spaces, travelers hoping to escape normative bubbles often find the Bohemian Coast in alternative sections of town. During the twentieth century, many countercultural groups claimed turf in disinvested neighborhoods. Then, through chain migration, so-called outcasts—for instance, gay men, single moms, anarchists, and the homeless—claimed space, marked turf, and created community-specific support services. These neighborhoods then attracted other travelers, migrants, and runaways who either shared those identities or felt drawn to those spaces, even if the implications were not yet clear.[43]

As examples, invisible exiles prior to exile gravitated toward "Kalakaua Avenue . . . where all the older girls, the queens, and the gay guys partied."[44] They "started making excuses to spend time in the Cedar Springs section of Dallas" where, despite being "too young to get into most of the [gay] bars . . . I'd happily walk up and down the street, looking at the men casually holding hands or reading books in the [queer] bookstore."[45] Similarly, when visiting Greenwich Village, travelers saw "freaks, punks, religious fanatics, drag queens, and NYU students" who "stared back at us with our own faces."[46]

In these places, travelers found alternative expressions of gender, sexuality, and class identity. In these countercultural environments, travelers could surreptitiously observe, explore, and eventually test their capacity to identify otherwise.

Alongside alternative neighborhoods, invisible exiles found the Bohemian Coast in mainstream settings, as well. When Jennifer Boylan visited Amsterdam, she did not seek out the local transgender community. Instead, she wanted ordinary people in everyday contexts—hotels, sidewalks, restaurants, parks, and museums—to accept her presentation as female.

Similarly, travelers escaping religious compounds often sought the Bohemian Coast in mainstream settings. An ultra-Orthodox author from Brooklyn, for example, used out-and-back trips to other New York City neighborhoods—the areas her sect usually avoided—to explore secular culture. In these places where no one knew her, she experimented with other lifestyles. "I've started taking my wig off. . . . I take off my long black skirt in the car. I'm wearing my jeans underneath."[47] Through these anonymous journeys, for a few hours each week and in the company of strangers, she tested the idea of becoming secular.

The Dangers of the Quest

Irrespective of the specific destinations, scouting trips to the Bohemian Coast are not the accidental encounters described in chapter 1, nor are they constrained by imagination as in chapter 2. Instead, these visits are intentional—if sometimes fumblingly pursued—forays into anonymous spaces to see whether, in a place where no one knows them, travelers can adopt alternative modes of self-expression. The experience, it seems, is simultaneously thrilling and terrifying.

Starting first with positive emotions, scouting trips can feel exciting. "In this foreign world of the normal, nothing felt remotely normal—it was extraordinary."[48] For a closeted author exploring a gayborhood, "the spectacle of *ordinary* gay men baffled me. . . . [But] I didn't need to fully understand gay culture in order for it to make me feel welcomed."[49]

Similarly, for a religious exile visiting a secular restaurant, "I eat as if having returned from war, victoriously. Lamb spring rolls, beef carpaccio, salmon ceviche, what strange food gentiles eat!"[50]

Alongside excitement, however, scouting trips can also spark negative emotions. One common negative emotion is uncertainty. When departing on out-and-back trips, travelers often do not know where their journeys will lead or what precisely is driving them. Although Jennifer Boylan knew she wanted to feel the rain on her female face, visiting gas stations and museums in skirts was not the same as knowing what those trips might add up to.

Instead, visiting the Bohemian Coast is like departing on a quest. "A quest is not at all that of a search for something already adequately characterized, as miners search for gold or geologists for oil. It is in the course of the quest and only through encountering and coping with the various particular harms, dangers, temptations, and distractions . . . that the goal of the quest is finally to be understood."[51] In a similar manner, for Boylan in Amsterdam and Keenan in Spain, the outcome—and even the goal—of the journey was far from certain.

Alongside uncertainty, another common negative emotion arising through travel is anxiety. It could be the anxiety of seeing a drag queen for the first time in real life. "Her choreography and bravado were so certain she was almost scary, in the way that being in the same room with someone who is overconfident can make you feel shy."[52]

It could also be the anxiety of participating for the first time in a new public setting. "Bars, I had come to learn, were a celebrated institution of Western culture, where humans went to meet other humans . . . But how did it work?"[53] The ultra-Orthodox traveler picked a bar at random and decided to order a drink he'd seen in movies, but then he became self-conscious. "What if 'gin and tonic' was not a drink but an inside joke of some sort . . . like moonshine, something sold in another place and another time, and I'd appear foolish for asking for it?"[54]

These anxieties sometimes escalated into full-blown terror, which is what one author experienced when she visited the cinema. "It's my first movie and I don't quite understand what movies are for yet: if they are . . . true narratives, or if they are mere amusements."[55] Chosen at random, she watched a tale of kidnap and murder, which left her deeply unsettled. "Perhaps they are right about the outside world, I thought at the time. What a nightmarish existence it must be."[56]

Jillian Keenan's trip to Spain likewise involved both empowerment and fear, including one incident that led her to lock herself in her bathroom and hide in her empty bathtub. With the benefit of hindsight, Keenan could see more clearly why being around other kinky people initially felt "overwhelming."[57] The idea of hurting someone—of wanting to cause pain or desiring something that others call abuse—could fuel guilt and shame. When meeting others who shared those desires, "the realization that our fantasies could become realities is the scariest thing of all."[58]

This fear is partly due to the sense of incommensurability between travel and home. For Keenan, how could she be a masochist? "Wasn't I a feminist? And a pacifist, too?"[59] It was not easy to square those values with the kinky ones she explored in Spain.

Other invisible exiles struggled with similar confusion. Even when Plato's Cave did not ring true, "I wasn't equipped, as a child, to make room for arguments . . . that would shatter the foundations of my very existence."[60] Despite realizing the truth of a nonconforming identity, "years of social messages would not let me go."[61] A transgender author could cut his hair and, "for the first time . . . see my reflection as a boy staring back at me,"[62] but seeing this truth did not set him free. On the contrary, "I knew it in my heart that I *had* seen it," but because this reflection still felt impossible, instead of feeling empowered, "this contradiction broke me."[63]

Alongside confusion, it can be dangerous to navigate new social worlds without prior socialization. In Shakespeare's *Winter's Tale*, the foreign messenger delivering the baby to Bohemia lacks environmental awareness and so is killed off by a bear.

Although no invisible exiles included in this study report being mauled by bears, they faced other dangers from environments that could turn similarly menacing. As just one example, for Jillian Keenan, in the absence of structured coming-of-age paths for kinky kids, many young people explore secretly, for instance through online environments where predators also lurk or by arranging hotel hookups with potentially untrustworthy strangers. In time, Keenan came to realize that "I was the safe one. Think about that: I dropped out of high school, moved to a foreign country, and let a drug dealer whip me bloody before I had even learned about safe words—and compared to dozens of other stories I've heard, mine was the 'safe' path."[64]

Moreover, even after navigating these doubts, fears, and dangers, travel to the Bohemian Coast did not always end with acceptance. Although strangers in Amsterdam accepted Boylan's presentation as female, another transgender author had a different experience in Tulsa. Things went well at first. "It felt so good, meeting all these people, making a fresh start in a new environment as . . . a girl, the person I was meant to be."[65] However, when her new peers discovered she was trans, "everyone in the group stopped talking to me."[66]

Many factors influence whether travelers find acceptance. Boylan in Amsterdam was affluent, able-bodied, and white. But if, like other invisible exiles, she'd been Black, had a stutter, was undocumented, was part of a cult, or was homeless, her claim of being just another woman in the crowd might easily have been rejected for reasons unrelated to gender.

For all these reasons, although scouting trips can feel hopeful, another possible outcome is a heightened sense of hopelessness. This hopelessness can arise, for example, when a traveler realizes he is queer while still lacking any practical understanding of what that might imply. "I don't even know what it would look like to be gay."[67]

This hopelessness can arise when a child realizes he is a boy while still knowing nothing about gender dysphoria. "I was not *just* a tomboy, as everyone had repeatedly told me I was. But it was an impossible thing. . . . The bare-faced truth was clear: there was nothing at all to be done about this situation."[68]

This hopelessness can also arise while trying to reconcile religious values with secular ones. "I felt torn in two. . . . I found it well nigh impossible to think logically and accurately in college, where I was encouraged to question everything, and then turn off the critical faculty I was developing when I returned" to the convent "and become a docile young nun."[69]

This sense of impossibility is a key reason why travelers recommit to Plato's Cave. For one author, after plucking up the courage to visit a bar only to feel disoriented by the unknown, "I fled . . . back to my home . . . where I knew the rules."[70]

For another author, after daring to register for a college entrance exam only to be stymied on test day by this strange new thing called a bubble sheet, "I felt ridiculous. Now that I'd seen the other students"—students who not only had formal training in math and English, but who also understood the protocols of test-taking—the dream of pursuing higher education "seemed absurd. . . . That was their world. I stepped into overalls and returned to mine."[71]

Examples like these demonstrate that traveling to the Bohemian Coast can feel double-edged. Travelers feel the pull of possibility, but the abrupt tonal change from one world to another can feel overwhelming. When that happens, instead of embracing the supposed liberation travel provides, travelers often return to Plato's Cave and recommit to its rules. Although those environments feel stifling, their familiarity offers at least some comfort, as well as a partial sense of belonging.

Place Attachment and the Ties That Bind

These challenges point to another phenomenon, which is the internal policing that kicks in as belonging begins slipping away. In invisible exile life history writing, travelers venture out and experience authentic versions of self, but then pull back and shove themselves into less satisfying roles. This pattern raises questions about why people return. Now that travelers have not only glimpsed a fictional alternative but actually experienced it firsthand, why of their own accord do they refuse to go free? Or, as one invisible exile phrased it, "I shut each cage and wonder why the stupid chickens come back to the coops every night."[72]

Although fear is one factor, my sense is that a far more powerful factor is place attachment. Boylan did not abandon Jennifer and recommit to James because she had negative experiences while traveling *en femme*. On the contrary, the strangers she met accepted her as female. Instead, the key factor seems to reside in one key detail that makes Boylan's experience different from Perdita's experience in *The Winter's Tale*, which is that Boylan's story comes with place attachment.

In Shakespeare's narrative, Perdita arrives in Bohemia as an infant with no possessions, no accomplishments, and no social connections. However, because she also has no memories, she can grow into someone new without grieving what she lost.

By contrast, Boylan liked her job, loved her wife, and enjoyed her financial security. Like other invisible exiles, she knew exactly what she could lose if she stayed in Bohemia too long. As freeing as it felt to travel, her attachment to and dependence on the places left behind created a major impediment to moving elsewhere and becoming otherwise full-time.

A key reason why travelers like Boylan turn away from the freedoms they crave and return to environments that feel suffocating is that *the same places that hurt them also provide support.* Since the environments that suffocate are the same ones that travelers rely on for everyday needs, travelers cannot abandon one without also losing the other.

This recognition that place attachment is a mixed bag confirms but also unsettles theories about the relationship between place and belonging. *Place attachment* refers to the "positively experienced bonds, sometimes occurring without awareness, that are developed over time from the behavioural, affective and cognitive ties between individuals and/or groups and their sociophysical environment."[73] Because these attachments are central to identity and belonging, "one of the necessary conditions for meaningful human existence is an attachment to a specific place"—or set of places and mobility patterns—that encourages "growth and development while providing a firm emotional, social and intellectual foundation on which to build."[74] Moreover, alongside place attachment, the concept of *place dependence* goes a step further by positing that, in addition to feeling warmly toward certain places, many people also depend on specific, noninterchangeable environments for life-sustaining resources such as employment, kinship, protection, language, and social standing.[75]

Scholars generally assume that place attachment and place dependence are positive traits as long as those places remain accessible. Scholars also generally agree that the loss of place—whether due to demolition, displacement, or other circumstances—is a major life loss, not just emotionally through broken connections but also practically in terms of the ability to live and thrive.[76] The recent "mobility turn" complicates these assumptions by questioning "the perceived prioritization of more rooted and bounded notions of place as the locus of identity."[77] However, this increased attention to "the dynamic interplay between movement and fixity" does "not mean that mobilities replace fixity as a preferred mode of existence, nor discount the beneficial consequences of having a stable, fixed living place."[78] Place attachment and place dependence remain significant social factors, especially in the context of mobility injustice.[79]

I agree that place attachment can be beneficial. However, a less commonly acknowledged factor is that, as with other forms of belonging, place attachment and place dependence have a darker side. Although nonbelonging is often problematic, the "sticky geography" of place entrapment can be equally problematic.[80] For example, when considering why women in abusive relationships may return to their abusers, one common factor is the perpetrator's dual role as both abuser and protector. Women might detest the abuse, but societies that undermine female economic independence often force women to rely on abusive environments for food, shelter, status, and healthcare. Moreover, if the larger society believes that a woman belongs to a specific environment, then even if she leaves, her community may just send her back. For all these reasons, place attachment and place dependence "could constitute a barrier to women seeking to escape."[81]

This combination of factors—of being attached to and dependent on places that both sustain and oppress—helps explain why travelers return. Jennifer Boylan could travel to Amsterdam for a few days, but she was not a Dutch citizen, did not speak the language, did not have a work visa, and was not entitled to health care. By contrast, in the United States she had an enjoyable job that paid for food, housing, insurance, and retirement, as well as a family that she loved. As much as her home environment did not validate her as Jennifer, it sustained her as James. To permanently escape the harmful aspects of those suffocating places, she risked losing the roles and relationships that gave her life meaning.

This double bind is common within invisible exile narratives. For an author with an abusive boyfriend, "where would I go if I left?"[82] Staying with friends "wouldn't last," and institutional options were even more traumatizing, which meant "I was stuck."[83]

For a queer author, "my parents were paying for more than half of my education, and if I couldn't change who I was, they were going to take this away from me."[84]

Similarly, for a religious exile, "what life will I have as a gentile? A single mother, struggling to raise a son in the most expensive city in the world, without a family to help, . . . without a dollar in a savings account or food stamps in my pocket."[85]

In examples like these, staying felt unbearable, but leaving looked worse. Authors could have families, shelter, and financial resources, or they could embrace alternative identities, but they didn't see an option for both.

Alongside financial and logistical considerations, an even stronger form of place attachment involves love and affection. In stories about bereavement, which is another subgenre of life history writing, authors describe the death of a loved one as a loss of self. Since identities are relational and co-narrated, the "people we love seem to become part of our self" such that, when a loved one dies, "one grieves not only for the dead but also for oneself" and for the relational part of self once held between the two.[86]

Invisible exile narratives are not stories about loved ones dying, but they are stories of bereavement born of severed family ties. As I explain in the next chapter, the primary reason travelers enter exile is because society disowns them. Relatives refuse to join them on their quests or to associate with people undertaking such journeys.

In an attempt to avoid future exile, many travelers try to abandon the Bohemian Coast instead. For one author, "I knew that I couldn't run around the world adventuring, not if I wanted to stay married, which I did."[87] For another, "no rabbinical court will let me leave with my son."[88] For a third, "the thought of abandoning my parents, of joining a community of gay-friendly people and somehow continuing life without them—this seemed even worse than suicide."[89]

Like other forms of bereavement, this scale of loss can become existentially unsettling. One of the great contradictions in identity studies is that, even though identity is always changing, "a central feature of felt identity is its tendency toward continuity, or at least perceived continuity, over time."[90] Since perceived continuity is what gives people the sense of having a self, continuity disruptions are "existentially troubling" and can "introduce doubt at the very basic level of being."[91] As psychologists have shown, when the "psychological thread binding their past, present and future" breaks, people become "particularly vulnerable to the idea of suicide. Without an appreciation of self-continuity, a person's connections to the past are erased and the future holds no meaning."[92]

Place is implicated in these dynamics because of the strong functional relationship between place and identity. Due to place attachment and place dependence, "a major source of identity continuity is the locations or types of locations within which given identities are enacted."[93] Places, like people, are interlocutors in identity narratives, which is why, "when connections to familiar surroundings are severed, when meaningful places and treasured objects become lost or inaccessible, these projected parts of the self are experienced as lost."[94] Just as bereavement breaks relational identity, place loss introduces similar ruptures.[95]

Due to these dynamics, invisible exiles face an impossible choice. Although Shakespeare's Perdita incurs many losses when abandoned in Bohemia, her amnesia softens the blow. By contrast, invisible exiles know precisely what they will lose, and the specter of such losses makes it difficult to willingly choose to go.

Given the high costs of exile, it would be surprising if travelers like Boylan and Keenan did not return to Plato's Cave, no matter the sweet release of feeling temporarily free elsewhere. Indeed, one of the most striking elements of invisible exile travel writing is that they are decidedly *not* stories of getting out of Dodge. On the contrary, authors describe feeling desperate to stay, even despite high levels of oppression.

This desperation explains travelers' determination to return to Plato's Cave. "Anything. I'll do anything to erase this part of me."[96] Even when staying hurts, "to say that I did not want to leave would be an understatement. The very idea . . . filled me with dread."[97] At this point in their journeys, invisible exiles are aware that leaving is possible. "All the ingredients were there," but as long as loved ones, like parents or spouses, remained committed to Plato's Cave, "I couldn't truly contemplate leaving."[98]

This desperation to stay is likewise why Jennifer Boylan balked at her therapist's suggestion that she pursue a gender shift. When he suggested it, "I felt like punching him."[99] The costs were simply too high. "If I do this, I'm going to lose everything, don't you understand that? *Everything.*"[100]

When home, family, and sanity are at stake, this obligation to make a choice—to weigh the pros and cons of different places and different selves—can feel paralyzing. When combined with the apparent impossibility of holding onto the never-never-land of the Bohemian Coast, many authors conclude, for a time, that continuing to travel is irrational. "Isn't it best to stay where you belong, rather than risk trying to insert yourself somewhere else and failing?"[101] Imaginative travel through books and films provided additional reasons for caution. "Tennyson's Lady of Shalott, who for so long had been my alter ego, . . . had tried to break out of her prison, as I had mine, but the effort had destroyed her."[102] Was it wise to follow suit? This trepidation leads many travelers to approach the Bohemian Coast less as a potential home and more like the adventure of *Jack and the Beanstalk*. "We get somewhere we couldn't go otherwise and we profit from the trip, but we can't stay there, it isn't our world, and we shouldn't let that world come crashing down into the one we can inhabit."[103]

For all these reasons, invisible exile travelogues are not at all like Jack Kerouac tales of rebelling against social conventions and escaping on the open road. Far from raring to go, authors are desperate to stay. They feel attached to and dependent on their home environments. Although temporary travel provides much-needed relief, the idea of a permanent, irreversible crossing feels devastating.

Given this impossible choice, no wonder travelers like Jennifer Boylan returned home, disposed of her girl clothes, and recommitted to living as James. Another author likewise threw away her hidden-but-precious items when she got married—in her case, her beloved secular books—so that, if her marriage proved infertile, her mother-in-law could not blame this outcome on her "illicit" reading habits.[104] Similarly, the specter of exile is why a third author repeatedly "recommitted" herself to her spiritual community by trying to convince herself that "the outer world" she craved was illusory and "useless."[105]

In all these ways, after living more openly during scouting trips, invisible exiles then chose to step back into the closet. "No one shoved me back in there. Maybe I'd just been standing in the doorway of that dusty closet, tripped, and somehow fell back inside. It shouldn't have been that easy to un-become myself."[106]

These retrenchments involve more than just lip service. Instead of just pretending to comply, invisible exiles make herculean attempts to actually believe the social constructs that oppress them. This conviction requires considerable denial. "Gradually, I strengthened the protective mental cage around the knowledge of my gender identity. I accepted it but . . . I instigated a total ban on probing thoughts . . . fending off the urge to ask the *forbidden questions*."[107] This denial reflects an attempt to dissociate the core values of Plato's Cave from the authors' experiences of suffocation. "I never connected the dots—in fact I sought to avoid connecting the dots" that linked these value systems to "oppression" and "the lack of free, individual choice."[108]

These denials were painful, but they also felt necessary. "I had to believe everything I was taught, if only to survive."[109] When faced with the impending risk of broken social ties and ruptured place attachment, stopping at the threshold and deciding *not* to keep going can seem eminently reasonable.

The High Costs of Returning Home

Returning, however, produces mixed results. Recommitting to Plato's Cave helps travelers hold onto the belonging they already possess, but the pressure to conform and self-censor is exhausting. As a potential workaround, invisible exiles often use spatial partitioning to present one identity in some locations and a different identity elsewhere. Unfortunately, the results are rarely satisfying. Rather than feeling alive in two worlds, invisible exiles often feel fully alive in neither and instead feel trapped in a state of perpetual haunting.

To understand why travelers in pre-exile contexts so frequently develop spatially splintered selves, it helps to understand both the appeal and the costs of returning home. Starting with the appeal, after the anxiety and disorientation of the Bohemian Coast, "it was a relief to slip back into a world that was known."[110] Feeling grounded is comforting. "You don't want to spin through space without a tether."[111] Conformity can also provide a sense of protection. "I had to admit the new found safety I had gained from the clutches of the Toilet Police was a relief. I was no longer a prime target for bullying."[112]

In examples like these, recommitting to Plato's Cave provides a sense of security. However, despite these short-term gains, recommitting is also painful, and that pain can become overwhelming. No matter how many times Jennifer Boylan tried to abandon her female self, recommitting to her identity as James did not end her suffering. If anything, having seen her female reflection—having embodied that identity and having other people accept it—made it harder to return. Her journeys were brief, but they changed her sense of what felt true, even if that truth still felt impossible. This awareness then twisted the knife when she replaced Jennifer with James.

Within the travel-writing genre, this sense of loss and secrecy is *not* the norm. Usually, travelers expect to be rewarded on their returns.

This expectation of a reward is the second key difference—alongside place attachment—between Shakespeare's *Winter's Tale* and the experience of invisible exile. In Shakespeare's version, when Perdita, now a fully grown woman, returns from Bohemia to Italy, her mother's faithfulness is affirmed, her now-loving father embraces her, her dead mother is miraculously resurrected, and her reinstated royal status means she can now marry her beloved Bohemian prince.

Nonfictional travel writers rarely expect such extravagant rewards, but the genre's norm is nevertheless to frame travel as socially valued. "The adventurous traveler is usually regarded as . . . a person interesting enough to write books and magazines about and to be followed around by a documentary film team."[113] Backpacking trips and heritage quests similarly contribute to "the library of a person's experiences capable of being turned into interesting stories," which returning travelers narrate in college application essays and during job interviews to signal character strength and leadership potential, which helps careers advance.[114]

By contrast, for Jennifer Boylan returning from Amsterdam, Jillian Keenan returning from Spain, and other invisible exiles returning from their Bohemian Coasts, there is no expectation of a social reward. Their communities do not treat their journeys as positive steps in self-development. Instead, from the perspective of Plato's Cave, visiting the Bohemian Coast looks less like the making of an identity and more like its spoiling. Instead of *becoming* (i.e., transitioning toward a desirable state of self-fulfillment), these journeys appear *unbecoming* (i.e., devolving into an unappealing and destabilizing downward spiral).[115]

In short, like other travelers, invisible exiles prior to exile travel for self-transformation, and their journeys provide an arsenal of material for narrating who they wish to be. However, unlike their counterparts whose returns are celebrated, these travelers risk *punishment* on their returns, which compels them to keep their journeys secret.

Keeping travel secret, however, is challenging. One challenge is that exploratory trips expand the distance between the home environment and the evolving inner self, which can make returning increasingly uncomfortable. "I have grown too big to fit back into my old world."[116] "I felt increasingly irritated" with the "strict limitations on all aspects of my daily life—from telling me what sport to play to how to wear my hair."[117] Such irritations arise because, after exploring the Bohemian Coast, "I was never the same again. When I returned, . . . that long-dormant fire of adventure had been rekindled and the glamour of my life turned gray."[118]

Examples like these show that traveling to the Bohemian Coast changes the way travelers see themselves and their life potential. However, given the stigmatized nature of these changes, returnees must constantly monitor themselves to ensure these changes go unnoticed.

This constant monitoring points to a second reason why travelers struggle to keep their journeys secret, which is that secret-keeping is exhausting. Like other secret keepers, returning travelers "must be constantly monitoring for signs that one's behavior may depart from a standard, and then at times actually *alter,* override, or stifle these deviant behavioral impulses."[119] This constant monitoring leads to "'emotional dissonance' or the clash between 'real' feelings and a 'false' display," which creates "an unstable state/psychological tension . . . that over time leads to strain and distress."[120] The negative consequences of emotional dissonance include cognitive, interpersonal, and physical impairments; diminished life satisfaction, emotional regulation, physical stamina, spatial intelligence, and relational intimacy; and increased rates of exhaustion, withdrawal, and depersonalization.[121]

Invisible exile travel writing is filled with examples of such self-censorship and its exhausting consequences. For one author, "I'd spent so much time and energy guarding myself against enjoying books too much, afraid that a compelling narrative might turn me into a heretic."[122]

For another author, when a friend from the Bohemian Coast asked to visit her at home, she felt "something like panic. What if he found the root cellar? What if he discovered the fuel tank?"[123] She feared his discovery of her roots would shatter the fledgling alternative identity she wanted to project.

Similarly, for a third author whose boyfriend shared her laptop, because "my search history felt like a crime scene, . . . I learned to hide my tracks."[124] After erasing her searches and concealing her files, "I exhaled with palpable relief. My secret was safe. It ached to be so grateful for an empty history."[125]

In all these ways, invisible exiles monitor themselves to prevent other people from learning about their journeys. This denial can protect travelers for a while, but like anyone engaged in self-repression, travelers suffer. "A defeatist feeling loomed over me."[126] One author felt "exhausted by the years I have spent pretending to be pious and chastising myself for my faithlessness."[127] Another "wanted a magic cure, and yet the treatment that I had found was making me miserable, inhibiting my emotions, and stifling my conversations."[128] A third author saw herself "living someone else's life . . . in a designer world that has been designed for someone I no longer am."[129] This disconnect felt alienating and unending. "I would stay in this lonely sexual purgatory . . . for the next five years."[130]

These examples underscore how discouraging it can feel to travel to the Bohemian Coast while also keeping that journey secret. Authors felt relief from traveling but exhausted from hiding on their return.

In many cases, travelers considered whether they could stop the pain of return by no longer traveling. However, curtailing travel was likewise difficult. "Speaking to people outside our world made me think too much, and, as we all knew, too much thinking led to problems. Yet I could not resist."[131] Even though it was forbidden to ask questions, "once I started asking them, it was hard to stop."[132] Moreover, these challenges increased over time. "The older I got, the more frequently my mother and I would push each other to the precipice of what we actually needed to say, only to back off just before either of us was forced to get more specific. . . . But this only meant that the unanswered questions became ever more loaded."[133]

The harsh reality, then, is that, prior to exile, travelers face a double bind. Traveling to validating places can feel freeing, but staying there risks social rejection from home. Conversely, returning home is problematic because secrecy is exhausting, but how can travelers permanently walk away from the places and people they love?

The Spatially Segregated Self

In response to this apparent neither/nor situation, one possible work-around, at least in theory, is to spatially compartmentalize different aspects of self. Spatial compartmentalization is similar to the psycho-spatial strategy of "splitting" where, when faced with "conscious and unconscious hurts and anxieties . . . we locate what are felt to be incommensurable feelings in different places."[134] Jennifer Boylan spatially compartmentalized when she implicitly divided the world into zones like Amsterdam that were safe for Jennifer and zones like her workplace, which she reserved for James. Crucially, Boylan was careful to keep those zones separate. In theory, this spatial partitioning could allow travelers to maintain both identities on parallel spatial tracks. In reality, however, instead of having two selves, travelers often found themselves living fully as neither.

Spatial compartmentalization is a common theme within invisible exile travel writing. One author used this strategy when trying to build romantic relationships in contravention of her cult's prohibitions against dating. "I knew that all my hopes for a romantic adventure would end if I got caught and reported to Guru."[135] To avoid detection, she refused to meet potential boyfriends anywhere except Greenwich Village. "If I continued to restrict my dates . . . to areas like Greenwich Village where disciples never went, and if they did, it might be a case where I could end up reporting them, then everything would work smoothly. I convinced myself that having [a boyfriend] wouldn't be a problem if I kept clear boundaries that separated my [boyfriend]-life from my Guru-life—neither would have to know about the other."[136]

Other invisible exiles likewise constructed spatially partitioned identities. One author separated his public housing self from his prep school self. "I was carefully managing which aspects of myself I'd present to the people around me."[137]

Another author concealed her zealous homelife from her new and seemingly mainstream friend. "I couldn't reconcile his world with mine so I separated them."[138]

A third author likewise found herself standing "with one foot in each sphere, drawn to the exotic universe that lay on the other side of the portal," only to be "wrenched back by the warnings that sounded like alarm bells in my mind."[139]

For a time, travelers hoped that this spatial partitioning would solve their problems. "Surely, I think, I can have my cake and eat it too."[140] As one author explained, "I refused to admit that I might have to choose, that I was creating an impossible reality."[141] Another author likewise clung to the hope that "it is possible to make this transition without paying the price of choosing between values."[142] In short, travelers hoped that spatial compartmentalization might resolve their dysphoric struggles without requiring a lasting socio-spatial break.

Maintaining these double lives, however, was often draining. Even in the comparative safety of online environments, "paranoia reigned.

We stuck to our handles, never divulging identifying details. You never knew who was a spy."[143] Even though Jennifer Boylan never wore women's clothing to work, "I lived in constant fear of detection and kept waiting for the chair of the program to call me up and say, *Boylan, we've heard stories. . . .* I knew what the consequences would be."[144]

Spatial partitioning was also lonely. "I needed to reveal my news, to have the pleasure of describing my very own boyfriend aloud," but the only confidants available within Plato's Cave "would have reported me in an instant with glee."[145]

Then, even if travelers could keep the Bohemian Coast a secret from Plato's Cave, they faced the added challenge of keeping Plato's Cave a secret from the Bohemian Coast. For the author who did not want her boyfriend to know she lived in a cult, "I artfully dodged his questions. When he inquired about the origins of my name, I laughed, claiming my parents were eccentrics. When he asked about my childhood, I shrugged, saying I was raised in Connecticut. . . . When he hinted about past relationships, I blushed, stammering that I couldn't remember any."[146] Dating only in Greenwich Village allowed her to explore forbidden relationships, but secret-keeping undermined intimacy, which is one reason the relationship fizzled out.

This dispiriting condition of having a shadow existence in two worlds but a full self in neither can lead to a sense of haunting, or feeling like a ghost. For geographers, ghosts are the "reapparition of the departed."[147] They are entities that were once present, then left, then returned again, but in an incomplete way, leaving the entity trapped in "an endless process of returning, without ever arriving."[148] The reason ghosts cannot fully arrive is because they no longer belong in the places left behind. This nonbelonging makes it impossible to regain a sense of home.

In a similar manner, because the Bohemian Coast changes the traveler's sense of self, those changes make it difficult to fully reintegrate into Plato's Cave. Conversely, just as returning can feel impossible, venturing out also remains incomplete. Travelers go and return, moving closer to out, then pulling back, all without truly arriving at either destination.

This sense of haunting feels unauthentic. "Any joy I managed outside of our home felt, to me, like a form of betrayal. I found I was always hiding."[149] Haunting also imposes limits on future growth. "With each restriction lifted, I find another one lying just behind it. And I can't help but be reminded all the time that there are some things I will never be able to experience."[150] Within this ghostly trap, "I found out the hard way that lingering between the two value systems ... stunts the process of becoming one's own person."[151]

In examples like these, the splintered travel path of invisible exile rarely feels satisfying. Instead of having the best of both worlds, authors cycle between hope and dissolution, "which would in turn give way to hope once again, but dimmer and weaker each time, until I would swing back to confusion and disillusion in an endlessly maddening cycle."[152]

With each new cycle, the chasm between a traveler's two possible selves would grow until, as often occurred, the traveler reached a breaking point. "I could stand with my family, or with the gentiles, on the one side or the other, but there was no foothold in between."[153] Neither side offered a nuanced, fluid, or hybrid alternative. Instead, "both sides seemed to suggest the same efficient solution: cut ties. Either abandon what you've known your entire life and your family, or abandon what you're learning about life and new ideas."[154]

Reaching this breaking point did not mean travelers wanted to leave. On the contrary, travelers often did everything they could to resist it. "I wanted to keep my footing steady between both worlds. Taking the full plunge either way felt too overwhelming."[155] However, this balancing act is hard to sustain.

In conclusion, this effort to stay reinforces the finding that stories of invisible exile are *not* stories of getting out of Dodge. It's true that travelers felt suffocated and that they found empowerment elsewhere, but they also felt anxious about leaving and held tightly to the belonging—incomplete though it was—that they already possessed. Instead of pulling up stakes, travelers doubled down and recommitted, even if it meant enduring staggering levels of self-repression. Some travelers tried to sidestep these challenges by spatially partitioning different aspects of self. However, this haunted existence was often painful and lonely. Eventually, many travelers reached a breaking point where, by choice or by force, one of their two worlds and one of their two selves had to be abandoned. That breaking point is the subject of the next chapter.

FOUR

The Fateful Moment of Exile

The Void

Leaving home is often hard. Moving to a new place to pursue educational or work opportunities might be strategic, but travelers may still feel sad or homesick when separated from the places and people they love. Leaving can be even more painful when, instead of responding only to the pull of new opportunities, travelers feel a push from places that, perhaps because of economic crises or environmental disasters, are no longer able to sustain them. For all these reasons, leaving home is never easy, even in the context of moving to opportunity.

As a substitute for capital punishment and a form of existential death, exile elevates these hardships. Being compelled to abandon the place one is deeply attached to and dependent on—compelled to leave as punishment even without somewhere else to turn—is devastating. Given how suffocating it can feel to live in oppressive environments, and given that many invisible exiles do eventually build more satisfying lives, it is perhaps no surprise that exile is often misread as moving to opportunity. However, I disagree with this reading, and I believe that such mischaracterizations do a disservice to invisible exile by erasing the extreme experience of being ostracized, evicted, stigmatized, and shunned.

As discussed in the previous chapter, invisible exiles often try to avoid this outcome. Instead of raring to go, they work hard to stay. However, many travelers eventually reach a breaking point. For some authors, the mental health strain of living in Plato's Cave reaches a critical, life-threatening threshold. For other authors, threats to their physical safety escalate as peers begin noticing their imaginative travel and scouting trips. For these reasons, although invisible exiles are acutely aware that exile will be painful, at some point, the pain of staying may overtake the pain of leaving, and the existential death of exile may look like the best option.

When it arrives, the moment of exile is emotionally fraught. When possible, travelers try to prepare in advance by making plans, collecting resources, and mentally saying goodbye. Regardless of preparedness, in the first moments after departure, many travelers feel relief at having escaped or feel hopeful about starting fresh. These preparatory actions and optimistic emotions resonate with the moving-to-opportunity script, which perhaps explains some of the confusion.

However, stopping there omits too much of the invisible exile story. As travelers separate from friends, family, homes, belongings, beliefs, identities, and protections, the positive emotions of escape and hope are quickly overshadowed by the devastation of forced displacement. Moreover, unlike other forms of travel, these departures are not temporary, do not involve warm goodbyes, and do not come with an expectation of return. Travelers might hope that, by sacrificing some parts of their identities, other parts might flourish. But that's not why travelers leave. Instead of growth—instead of moving to opportunity—exile is a form of self-death. Yes, something new might arise, perhaps, if travelers are lucky. But the search for something new is not the cause of departure. It's just what comes next, maybe, if exiles survive.

To explore these dynamics, in this chapter, I start by recounting a few departure moments as described within invisible exile travel writing. Next, I provide a theory-informed discussion about exile as a fateful moment, and I analyze the escape plans that travelers develop when they realize it's becoming too dangerous to stay. Then, after analyzing the moment of rupture, I explore the extent to which invisible exile narratives align with the trope of moving to opportunity. Last, I argue against those comparisons by explaining how exile functions as a substitute for capital punishment and how, first and foremost, travelers experience it as self-shattering. Being forced out—being shunned, disowned, reviled, and rejected—is not the same as missing loved ones while seeking new prospects, and the common misrecognition of this key fact is yet another form of painful erasure.

"We Left Ourselves on the Other Side of a Void"

Starting with descriptions of the moment of exile, Raynor Winn was fifty years old when she and her husband lost a multi-year legal battle and were told they had one week to vacate their farm. As explained in her memoir *The Salt Path,* vacating would mean walking away from their home, their livelihood, and the place of their most cherished family memories. One week later, surrounded by boxes and with the bailiff pounding on the door, Winn and her husband hid under the stairs trying to avoid departure. Eventually, however, they had to yield. They stood up, walked outside, got in their car, and drove away.

This departure felt surreal. "Leaving it all behind. It was a dream. Nothing was real. Driving away from twenty years of family life, work life, everything we'd owned, hopes, dreams, the future, the past."[1] This eviction stripped Winn of her property and the foundation for her identity. "I'm a farmer and a farmer's daughter; the land's in my bones."[2] The seasonal cadence of penning sheep, sowing corn, and harvesting grain infused her life with rhythm and order. But now, with neither property nor home, "I'm cut free from that connection, from the meter of my existence. . . . I'd feared I would lose it, that tie to reality, when our land was lost."[3]

After eviction, Winn and her husband had no choice but to try something new. Job prospects were limited for women her age and for men with her husband's health condition. For shelter, they initially stayed with friends, but disliked the idea of imposing, and so, on a whim born of desperation, Winn suggested they pack a tent and take a very, very long walk. She got the idea when, while hiding from the bailiff, she noticed a long-forgotten book—part guidebook, part memoir—about a man who hiked five hundred miles. Seeing it, "I just knew we should walk. And now we had no choice."[4]

To prepare for their nomadic life, Winn purchased two cheap backpacks and a secondhand tent. She then began the difficult task of deciding what to carry. "Packing a rucksack when you're fifty isn't the same as when you're twenty."[5] At fifty, she was unable to carry even small amounts of extra weight, which meant making do with less. Next, on the morning of their departure, Winn reread the guidebook for reassurance. "I . . . told myself again that we could do this."[6] Despite these preparations, it was still jarring when she arrived at the trailhead to start the trek and the unvarnished reality of her altered life circumstances washed over her. "Standing on the side of the road, . . . our rucksacks by our feet, we were finally, truly, homeless. I'd never been homeless before."[7]

Backpacking would give the couple something new to focus on. It would create space to grieve their losses and consider other futures.

But it would not erase their eviction, their lost home, or their lost identity. Hiking would not undo the significant deflection their lives had taken, nor would it make their departure any less imposed, unwanted, or irreversible. Those facts made this trip different from prior travel. "Traveling in the knowledge that you have a point of return gives you the will to keep moving away. There's always a door you can return to and drop your bag, even if the door is the thing you're escaping from. But the feeling that day was entirely different. There was no door."[8]

Winn's old life and her former place in the world had come to a permanent end. "The earth had cracked; we left ourselves on the other side of a void that we could never cross."[9] No matter what happened next, there was no going back. Something new might materialize, but pursuing something new is not why she left. Instead, with the bailiff pounding on the door, there was simply no option but to accept expulsion and step into the Void.

Welcome to the Void, a Place Where Travelers Are Stripped Bare

Winn describes eviction as crossing into a void. Other exiles, like Carlos Eire, use similar language. As explained in his memoir *Learning to Die in Miami,* Eire stepped into the Void at age eleven while being airlifted out of Cuba. "Earlier today, I left behind my parents, my entire family, all of my possessions, and my native land."[10] The scale of this social, spatial, and psychological rupture was so extreme that it posed an existential threat to Eire's sense of being. "In other words, I've just died. I've passed through the burning silence that strips you bare of everything you've ever been."[11] This act of being stripped bare left Eire feeling "totally alone in a dark void."[12] He described this void as an "oppressively vast emptiness" that "felt eternal, and inescapable."[13] Eire would revisit the Void many times in his new American life, especially during moments of anxious dissociation. But the Void was born here, at this moment of exile. It was created during the act of leaving a place so profoundly that it seemed to suck his self right out of him.

In my assessment, the Void is the place travelers enter when they *leave.* This type of leaving differs from previous imaginative travel and scouting trips because those journeys are temporary and community ties persist. By contrast, the departure associated with the Void is profound and irreversible. Travelers are not merely spending time away. Instead, they are breaking associations with places, people, cultures, and selves—or having those breaks imposed on them—with full knowledge that this rupture could make it impossible to return. This type of leaving signals a radical break in identity and marks a profound revocation of belonging. Whether travelers leave by choice or by force—and it's usually a tangled mix of both—the hallmark of the Void is the stripping away, through exile, of place, identity, and connection.

Within invisible exile narratives, travelers use many phrases to describe this moment of rupture. Many say quite simply that they are "leaving" or have "left."[14] These exits are not about running errands or enjoying temporary reprieves but rather are durable breaks with home, family, community, culture, and self. Some travelers reflecting back on these moments say they chose to leave,[15] although, in my assessment, choice is a questionable concept in contexts of structural or interpersonal violence. Other travelers felt coerced into departing and described it as being forcibly removed,[16] "expelled,"[17] thrown out,[18] or permanently "banned"[19] from their homes and communities. In both scenarios, whether leaving felt voluntary or imposed, invisible exiles characterized it as an "escape"[20] where "the strings have been cut"[21] or "I . . . yank myself free,"[22] sometimes sneaking out under the cover of darkness.[23] Other times, like Raynor Winn driving stoically away from her farm, authors left silently and without fanfare, as though, through departing, their bodies, along with the rest of their identities, might simply disappear.

Whatever form these departures took, *leaving* was not merely a change of address. On the contrary, travelers say they "closed the door" on the past[24] and "opened the door" to some unknown future[25] by crossing "a bridge between two places,"[26] a bridge that "exploded in the very moment of its making."[27] This explosion created the sense that their old selves had "died,"[28] were "murdered,"[29] or "cease[d] to exist."[30] Later, in the years that followed (and as discussed in upcoming chapters), travelers realized these separations were more complex because, for better or worse, years of social conditioning do not evaporate without a trace. However, in the moment of exile, travelers mourned the death of their former selves—the girl who uttered "her last words"[31] and the boy who lay buried in "a grave that is at least ten meters deep."[32]

The extremity of this language differentiates the Void from earlier trips to Girl Planet or the Bohemian Coast. These deathly metaphors underscore the profundity of stepping into a stripped-down place of forsaken identity and belonging. On entering exile, travelers are stripped of permission to continue co-identifying with longtime communities, and this rupture shatters the relational selves those ties sustained.

The Void, in other words, is the initial space of exile. Stepping into it involves a spatial dislocation, social rupture, and identity forfeiture that brings travelers to a place where the past ends, prior identities crumble, and taken for granted futures dissolve. In this bleak space, there is hope that a new, more authentic self might emerge. But that hope does not erase the fact of exile. Like Raynor Winn succumbing to the bailiff and Carlos Eire fleeing political unrest, the Void is born not out of a desire to be somewhere else, but out of the collapse of one's place in the world and the self that went with it.

The Fateful Moment of Exile

Stepping into the Void is what sociologists call a fateful moment. "Fateful moments" are "times when events come together in such a way that an individual stands, as it were, at a crossroads in his existence; or when a person learns of information with fateful consequences."[33] Moments become fateful when circumstances change in ways that are profound, irrevocable, and fraught. "Fateful decisions are usually almost by definition difficult to take because of the mixture of the problematic and the consequential that characterizes them."[34] These moments, which often feel urgent but lack complete information, require people to "launch into something new, knowing that a decision made, or a specific course of action followed, has an irreversible quality, or at least that it will be difficult thereafter to revert to the old paths."[35] These fateful moments are risky because, even if the plan is unlikely to "go awry," the "consequential penalties" of missteps are significant.[36]

For invisible exiles, *leaving* is a fateful moment. In us/them environments, breaking with home, community, family, and culture is often deemed unforgivable. Importantly, it is the group's unwillingness to accept diversity—rather than the traveler's interest in exploring novelty—that makes these moments fraught. People try new things all the time, sometimes successfully and sometimes not, and societies develop transitional aids and safety nets to support this growth and development. However, invisible exiles stepping into the

Void receive no such support. In the eyes of their communities, the unbecoming nature of their identity transition merits abandonment, instead of assistance. It is the collective decision to impose exile as a consequence for some perceived violation of social norms that sets fatefulness in motion.

Following such profound ruptures, invisible exiles have no option but to construct near-total replacement lives. As discussed in later chapters, travelers rebuild in many ways, for instance through long-distance hiking like Raynor Winn or by pursuing higher education like Carlos Eire. Other invisible exiles migrate to new cities, join alternative communities, or enlist in the military. These various attempts may or may not work out, and if one plan fails, travelers can try others. However, those endeavors come *after* the fateful moment, rather than defining it. Travelers can experiment with many new lives and many new selves post-exile, but what cannot be undone—the fateful tipping point of no return—is having left or been pushed out.

Make no mistake, this fateful moment of departure is dangerous. Having entire families and communities withdraw emotional support, physical protection, logistical assistance, financial resources, and shared turf means that almost every business-as-usual routine is now uncertain. This shunning also increases the riskiness of future hardships. Life is unpredictable and plans go awry. When people have access to communal safety nets, they can take bigger risks because they have access to resources enabling recovery. In other words, group assistance makes risk-taking less fateful.

By contrast, stripped of everyday support and emergency safety nets alike, invisible exiles are now vulnerable not only to life's big gambles but also to ordinary hardships that might otherwise feel routine. If Raynor Winn twists her ankle during her five-hundred-mile hike, or if Carlos Eire feels lonely while abroad, these travelers cannot seek solace or assistance by returning home. Who they were, how they lived, and where they came from are gone now. This enhanced exposure to risk and vulnerability makes *leaving* fateful, no matter what comes next.

The Pain of Staying the Same

These high stakes raise questions about why travelers step into the Void, rather than remaining in the partial safety of imaginative travel and scouting trips. The answer, it seems, is that, as painful as it is to leave, at some point, that pain is eclipsed by the danger of staying.

This eclipse does not make leaving easy or make the costs less staggering. Nevertheless, travelers sometimes have little choice but to endure those costs either because they are no longer permitted to stay or because the costs of staying become too significant.

The decision to leave often comes at a moment when travelers realize their out-and-back journeys are no longer working and straddling divergent worlds is becoming too dangerous. When travelers anticipate an impending departure, they often try to prepare at least a few things in advance by collecting resources to take with them and exploring possible places to go. But even without this prep work, as the dangers of staying increase, leaving—even without a parachute—can become the safest option.

One author faced these dangers after her scouting trips to queer bookstores and gay bars cast her sexuality in a new light. As she gained confidence in her queer identity, she yearned to be more open, including by telling people about her new girlfriend. "I tell her I would rather die honest than live the deceitful life she has planned for herself."[37] However, living openly attracted the attention of homophobic peers who targeted her for an attempted gang rape. She escaped the worst of the attack through grit and happenstance, but the incident confirmed just how dangerous her situation had become. Living a double life was suffocating, but living openly could get her assaulted or killed. As the risks of staying mounted, she decided it was time to go.

This sense of reaching a tipping point where staying becomes unviable helps explain why travelers accept the risks of entering the Void. Travelers know that leaving will not be easy. However, "the difficulties of change are certainly easier to face, to embrace, when we are exhausted by the difficulties of our current reality."[38] This exhaustion does not erase the pain of leaving. "Even when you are desperate for change, even when you are ready to cling onto any lifeline that comes your way," the process "is never easy."[39] However, when the alternative to leaving is violence, those risks can motivate a person to fight for her life, even if it means living that life elsewhere.

This sense of movement born of desperation—whether in response to internal struggles or external threats—is a recurring theme within invisible exile travel writing. Starting first with internal struggles, invisible exiles reflecting on their experiences often describe a mounting sense of desperation that imaginative travel and scouting trips could no longer soothe.

This suffocation takes many forms. For a queer exile, "I am almost thirty, and I've never touched anyone. Is this my life?"[40] For a religious exile, "if I stay here . . . I'll just do what every other girl does: get married at fifteen. I don't want to do that, and I don't want to be somebody's third wife."[41] Similarly, for an author struggling amid ableist culture, her suffocation was manifest in the growing list of needs and wants that went unfulfilled. From small things like ice cream cones to large things like her journalism career, "it all came tumbling down."[42]

These situations erode mental health. For one author, "I was alone with this pain and that is how it would remain."[43] For another, "I was so repressed I couldn't breathe."[44] For a third, "my soul was afraid of dying . . . from a loss of self."[45] For a fourth, "I felt like a chalk painting dissolving in the rain."[46]

Such suffocation is difficult to endure. "This sad melancholic existence, this sad half-life state I was in, was not a drill, this really was going to be *it* for the rest of my time on Earth. . . . I didn't even feel real."[47] This dissociative hopelessness can feel like living death. "While most of my contemporaries in the outside world were finishing graduate school, getting engaged, buying apartments, eagerly embarking on life's possibilities, I realized I had already died."[48]

Tragically, in response to such anguish, many travelers consider suicide. One author toyed with the idea of letting her body fall off a cliff. "I leaned off the edge of the cliff at a sharp angle, my arms held outward like wings . . . and I thought, *well, all right. . . . Let's do it, then.* Then a huge blast of wind blew me backward, and I landed on the moss."[49]

Another author tried to slash her wrists but the knife was dull, tried to overdose on medication that turned out to be nontoxic, and tried to jump in front of a train only to be pulled back by a stranger.[50]

In some cases, authors saw suicide not only as a possible escape but also as a possible way to reclaim personal agency. When one author was forcibly separated from her fiancé as punishment for losing faith, she used her life as a final bargaining chip. "I had no control over anything, but the prospect of taking my own life was a way to change that. I knew that the Church had great fear about what happened when someone died or committed suicide on their watch."[51] Hanging out an open window, she demanded they release him, or else she would jump.

Situations like this one, where authors are punished for deviating from the rules of Plato's Cave, point to another source of potentially life-threatening danger. Alongside the mental health implications, when beliefs and allegiances shift, other people may respond with anger and violence.

A transgender author from Oklahoma, for example, was increasingly threatened with hate crimes as she moved through puberty. After starting hormone treatments, her friends' parents alleged that her presence at school endangered other children, so "the school then started an investigation to expel me."[52] When that failed, her best friend was told, "if you keep hanging out with that boy, you deserve to be stoned to death."[53] The author's mother worried about potential violence as well. "She told me she imagined me . . . getting jumped, possibly murdered. She imagined someone burning our house down."[54]

It was the same for an ultra-Orthodox author when his peers began noticing his imaginative travel and scouting trips. He was verbally accosted when an acquaintance saw him reading a secular book. "This is heresy, this! . . . HOW CAN YOU READ THIS, HOW? THIS IS FORBIDDEN, THIS!"[55] He also received death threats in response to his anonymous blog about ultra-Orthodox lifestyles. "May the cholera descend upon his limbs, may he be ensnared within the devil's clutches, may he be buried alive, his mendacious tongue skinned, his mad eyes gouged; may he hang, strangle, and choke. May we live to see it speedily and with joy."[56] He took these threats seriously because he knew of others in his community who had their tires slashed, windows broken, bodies beaten, faces shaved, and children taken for lesser spiritual crimes. "What will we do," his frightened wife asked, "if people find out it's you?"[57]

These combined dangers—the mental health crises of unbearable life circumstances and the physical dangers of potentially lethal violence—reinforce the message that, at a certain point and regardless of place attachment, it is no longer safe to stay. Exile might be unwanted, but staying in Plato's Cave risks despair, depression, suicide, bullying, abuse, beatings, rape, and murder. As a result, "I would have no choice but to leave home if I was going to thrive."[58]

Developing an Escape Plan

Deciding to go is not the same as knowing how to manage it. Many invisible exiles do not have the luxury of developing an escape plan.

Some ruptures arrive too quickly, or travelers lack the resources to put plans in motion. Another challenge is that, although travelers rarely understand this at the time, their escape plans often turn out to be woefully insufficient given the scale of dislocation they ultimately face. Regardless, stepping into the Void is a daunting prospect, and travelers often try, in secret, to make at least some preparations.

Preparing can be as simple as setting the intention to leave and allowing time to mentally adjust. This is how one traveler approached his decision to cycle the length of two continents. He was in a deep malaise when he met someone who had cycled from New Jersey to Argentina. "Like the clarity of love at first sight, . . . this idea struck me like Cupid's arrow. *Could I do that?*"[59] He decided on the spot to try something similar, and he randomly selected a departure date two years in the future. This delay created space to adjust to "the bigness of it," which felt overwhelming, "but I had to do it. It felt correct. It felt like a key I'd been looking for."[60]

Alongside adjusting to the idea of leaving, delayed departures create space to research destinations. One author used the time to research the Pacific Crest Trail. "I had many things to determine, and quickly."[61] She googled the route, studied the lingo, and reviewed online blogs. She researched where and when to begin, what to carry, and how to cope without creature comforts. "It seemed like a tremendous leap of faith to forsake the tools I'd always been told I needed. And yet leaving college to walk was such a massive leap of faith already, and nothing I'd ever trusted and believed in seemed true any longer."[62] Having made the decision to go, she still had to wait for the snow to melt, and she used the time to prepare.

Alongside acclimating to the idea of leaving and building a supportive knowledge base, several travelers used prep time to gather money for departure. A pending exile might "freelance all sorts of work for the extra cash,"[63] or sell her computer and books "for enough money to buy the [airplane] ticket."[64] In this process, travelers use the trappings of their former identity to fund their escape. "I bring my diamond ring and some of my old wedding gifts to a jeweler in Westchester, who gives me a pile of cash in exchange."[65]

Heartbreakingly, many invisible exiles begin these preparations as children. One group of siblings created a shared "escape fund" by selling posters, mowing lawns, chopping wood, and babysitting.[66] At one point, they lost their savings when their father smashed their piggy bank and spent the money on alcohol. After that incident, the author bought a change purse, which she wore on her body at all times, and "we started saving again."[67]

These examples of escape funds hidden from prying eyes resonate with another key theme of preparing to leave, which is that travelers make these preparations in secret. Secrecy is essential for travelers who expect to be stopped or punished if discovered. This is why one author kept quiet about his plans to leave the ex-gay conversion program that his parents had pushed him into. "I didn't want to act too quickly, alert the . . . staff to my intentions. I knew they would immediately inform my parents," who would then insist that "I stay longer."[68]

Another invisible exile likewise prepared "in silence. . . . No one, not my brothers or my best friends, knows about my plan to bicycle to Vietnam."[69]

To maintain secrecy, authors sometimes camouflaged their preparations. One author's escape plan involved taking a college class, which was difficult to conceal, but possible to misrepresent. "In order to get Guru's approval of my decision, I knew I'd have to convince him that my actions would ultimately work to serve him."[70] The need for a false facade, however, did not stop travelers from building escape routes, even as they continued performing an outward show of consent. Little by little, they prepared their escapes. "Though it felt too daunting to parachute into the outside world all alone, I pledged to take small steps away . . . moving slowly toward freedom."[71]

Travelers making secret preparations did not always know when they would leave or where they would go. Sometimes the prep work was simply a way to avoid being caught off guard. This desire for emotional closure is why one traveler began approaching each family gathering as though it was "for the last time . . . just in case I do decide to make my exit."[72] She knew her friends and family would see departure as betrayal. For people in her situation, there were no goodbye hugs or holiday reunions. "It's strange to look around the dining room table . . . at the people I call my family—aunts, uncles, cousins, and distant cousins—and think that maybe in a year's time they will have become a faint memory."[73] She approached this existential loss with comparable gravitas. "Subconsciously I have started to say good-bye to the people and objects in my life as if preparing to die."[74]

The Moment of Rupture

Although these preparations are painful, they are only a prelude to the moment of rupture, by which I mean the onset of exile and the decisive step into the Void. No matter how much travelers prepare, the Void usually arrives with jarring, disorienting upheaval. These departures have many possible triggers, including internal shifts and external threats. Regardless of the trigger, due to the social and spatial rupture that follows, invisible exiles are keenly aware that their lives will never again be the same.

Starting with internal triggers, one common trigger is when mental health struggles reach a crisis point that can no longer be hidden or ignored. For one author, this moment came when her mounting distress spiraled into a full-blown breakdown. "At first I could not even contemplate this option" of leaving, "which was surrounded with all the force of a taboo. But the strain took its toll, and . . . I broke down completely. It was now clear to us all that I could not continue."[75]

It was the same for another who woke up "hungover, strung out, and depressed" and decided he had to change or die.[76] "It was as if I had wakened from a dream. It was as if I realized I was drowning."[77] Instead of drowning, he decided to leave. "I left that afternoon with two duffle bags and nothing else."[78]

Alongside internal triggers, a second set of triggers involves external threats to personal safety from other people, threats that escalate from words to actions. The resulting fear can motivate travelers to take the previously unthinkable step of leaving.

For example, although one author endured years of misogyny, something shifted when she was about to be forcibly married to a stranger. At that moment, instead of demurring, "a kind of instinctive desperation prompted me to bolt."[79]

It was the same for another author who, as he neared adulthood, was increasingly likely to be conscripted. "We can either carry guns and kill people," his brother said, "or leave and send money back to our mom and sister."[80] Given those options, he decided to go.

These two travelers became official refugees, which was uncommon within my dataset. However, the experience of *leaving* to avoid escalating danger is otherwise ubiquitous as external threats push unrecognized exiles into action as well.

For one author, it was the ongoing physical abuse she faced at home. After one painful episode, she recalled making "two decisions. The first was that I'd had my last whipping. . . . The second was that . . . I was going to get out."[81]

For another author, it was the moment she learned that the same caretaker who molested her was now molesting her younger brother. "With a certainty that took my breath away, I decided I had to get away . . . and I had to bring my siblings with me."[82] In the middle of the night, with the children ducking from view, her oldest brother drove them out of their compound, never to return.

Alongside internal breakdowns and external threats, a third set of triggers occur when unrelated events make travelers hyper-aware of their own mortality, which can stimulate courage to take decisive action. This was the case for an author whose car crashed during her drive home from the Bohemian Coast. "In the last few seconds, . . . I think it is a just way to end my life, that I should die as I stand on the cusp of freedom."[83] She did not die. Instead, she woke up in her upside-down vehicle and discovered she could pull herself free, both from her car and her religion. "Only now can I truly feel invincible. . . . I am no longer nervous, no longer uncertain."[84]

It was the same for another author when her brother was injured in a motorcycle accident and, rather than driving him home for homeopathic care, she took him to the emergency room. In her family's eyes, inviting Western medicine and institutional oversight into their lives—no matter that it saved her brother's life—marked her as "a traitor, a wolf among sheep."[85] She had been inching toward leaving for months, but this event cemented her exit. "After that night, there was never any question of whether I would go or stay. It was as if we were living in the future, and I was already gone."[86]

Next, a fourth set of triggers pushing travelers to make fateful departures involves the discovery of a viable alternative. This scenario is most common in narratives where travelers have time and space to prepare.

One author explored college as a possible escape route. When an acceptance letter arrived, "I didn't have a conversation . . . about it. . . . It seemed easier to just go, so I packed whatever clothes and shoes I could fit into my car and drove north."[87]

It was the same for another author when she was accepted as a college transfer student. "If you go away, that's it," her foster mother insisted. "That's the start of your own life. . . . If you leave, you will be on your own for good—do you understand? Once you're out, you're out."[88] Like other invisible exiles, she understood and left.

A fifth set of triggers involves being expelled. Several invisible exiles were kicked out of their homes as teenagers, usually as punishment for being queer,[89] showing independence,[90] defying authority,[91] or refusing abuse.[92]

Adults were expelled as well. As rumors spread about one author's atheism, he was called into a meeting and told, "'You must leave the village.' I was being expelled."[93] The author countered that he had a house and a mortgage, and that he needed to consider his children before deciding what to do. "This was America in the twenty-first century. You couldn't force people from their homes unless you were the government, and the bedzin wasn't the government."[94] To force his expulsion, the rabbis wrote an open letter stating that this man was wicked. It was a "call on all God-fearing Jews to dissociate from me in all matters. I was not to be hired as an employee or allowed residence in their homes. . . . My children were to be denied admission to their schools."[95] To protect his family, he packed and left.

Exile Can Lead to New Opportunities

The ex-Orthodox author described above felt angry at being expelled, but he also saw a silver lining. "I no longer belonged here. This was a community of the faithful, and I was no longer one of them."[96] He worried about moving his children away from everyone they'd ever known, but he also wanted a different life. "I wanted no more than a world in which I was not lying and hiding. I wanted the freedom to simply be who I was, without fear or shame."[97] His kids, he felt, deserved the same.

This mix of emotions—of anger and resentment at being forced out, combined with hope for a more palatable future—underscores that, although leaving is often traumatic, it can lead to new opportunities. This observation raises questions about whether the framework of invisible exile can ever sit comfortably alongside the cultural trope of moving to opportunity.

In my assessment, invisible exile life histories show that travelers sometimes see these ruptures as moments of freedom and possibility. However, their narratives also show that stepping into the Void—

a move born from the push of displacement, not the pull of new prospects—gives exile-based narratives a qualitatively different tone.

In recent years, the scholarship on exile has taken a hopeful turn. There's a growing fascination with "romantic exiles" and a prevailing sense that exile has "been transformed . . . into a potent, even enriching, motif of modern culture."[98] To be sure, "the notion that exile can be an opportunity or even a privilege jars with much writing on the topic, which is stereotypically nostalgic and forefronts hardship and loss."[99] Even so, compared to older accounts that "associate exile with dispossession and displacement," newer accounts "suggest that it is a form of liberation; a modern utopian condition full of freedom and possibilities."[100]

I see some potential in this suggestion that exile can be a space of freedom. Some famous writers and artists throughout history used exile to continue producing rebellious work that would have led to imprisonment or execution back home. I also agree that present-day refugees sometimes frame their narratives in upbeat tones. Instead of "dwell[ing] on personal suffering," they "emphasized the greater sacrifice of compatriots languishing in . . . jails or suffering the hardships of . . . guerrilla camps."[101] By contrast, the sturdy housing, safe streets, scholarship programs, medical care, and career opportunities available to refugees living abroad can transform exile into "a time of opportunity and excitement."[102]

Similarly, invisible exile narratives contain some evidence that invisible exile, as a path away from danger and toward a different future, can feel empowering. The marketing material for these memoirs often reinforces this hopefulness, for instance through subtitles like *My Journey from Homeless to Harvard,*[103] *My Climb out of Darkness,*[104] and *My Journey from Life in Prison to a Life with a Purpose.*[105]

Not all invisible exiles can claim such victories. Raynor Winn's account of being evicted from her farm is ultimately a story about sliding down the socioeconomic ladder, rather than climbing up.

Nevertheless, perhaps as a testament to human resilience, or perhaps due to the limited appetite among publishers and readers for narratives devoid of redemptive themes, all of the life narratives I analyzed contained claims that, by moving through exile, travelers gained some degree of personal insight and life satisfaction. For Raynor Winn, despite the losses, "we were free here, battered by the elements, hungry, tired, cold, but free. . . . Not camping out with friends or family, being a burden, becoming an irritation, wearing friendship away to just tolerance. Here we were still in control of our life, of our own outcomes, our own destiny. . . . We chose to walk and seized the freedom that came with that choice."[106]

Moreover, during the moment of exile, travelers often feel a mix of emotions. Alongside negative emotions like anger and fear, they describe feelings of freedom, correctness, possibility, and strength.

Starting with freedom, after having felt suffocated for so long in Plato's Cave, the act of leaving, along with the prospect of living otherwise, can feel euphoric. For Carlos Eire, his first thought when waking up to his first morning in exile was, "I never expected to find this kind of freedom. For the first time in my life I no longer had shadows to fear at every turn, or someone else's baggage to mind or haul."[107]

Similarly, for an author who packed her stuff even while being told she could never return, "I try to identify what I'm feeling: *Anxiety? Fear? Excitement? Uncertainty?* And then I find the word: *Freedom.*"[108]

Second, for several authors, this sense of freedom was accompanied by a sense of correctness. It was the sense of having "initiated my own rite of passage,"[109] or the feeling that "I had to do it"—to leave—"for any chance of a real happy authentic life."[110] This sense of correctness could feel euphoric. "I am intoxicated with a feeling of rightness, a psychological snapping together of mating parts, a lucid moment of geometrical perfection. A liberating bliss."[111] Leaving was risky, but it felt right. "I have to take risks if I want to change any aspect of my life."[112]

Third, this sense of freedom and correctness came with a sense of new possibilities. "I had not asked to be thrown out of my house, but now I was happy to pursue my own dreams."[113] Invisible exiles tried to see this change as "exciting! . . . You can do *anything,* be anything you want to be! Everything is ahead of you!"[114] Whether departure was chosen or imposed, it forced people to make a move, including to "the kind of place where people go when they want to . . . make room for new and better things."[115] As "a fresh start," these moves felt "like the start of some new beginning that was lurking in my subconscious for a while."[116]

Fourth, these feelings of freedom, correctness, and possibility could engender a sense of inner strength. "I felt the seed of something strong sprout something real in me."[117] This author was leaving college to become a "dropout" and a "homeless" person sleeping in the woods while "walking north with my fellow self-exiled desert pilgrims."[118] However, compared to the alternative of withering away in post-traumatic victimhood, exile offered "the promise of escape from myself, the liberation only a huge transformation could grant me."[119]

In short, the first few days of exile often felt euphoric even as travelers stepped into harsh circumstances. Even a newly homeless teenager felt this euphoria after being kicked out and spending her first night in a public park. "We made it," she wrote at the time; "Hey Journal, Sam and I are free."[120]

Exile Is a Form of Self-Death

Based on these descriptions, I agree the first moments of exile can feel giddy and hopeful. However, without wishing to minimize those emotions, this optimism does not make exile the same as moving to opportunity. In my assessment, the trope of moving to opportunity comes with assumptions about individual choice, transitional aid, and ongoing connections that do not apply in the context of exile and that do not adequately capture the trauma of rejection, expulsion, and shunning. Despite some initial hopefulness, exile is, at its core, a form of erasure and a substitute for execution. Instead of pulling travelers toward opportunity, exile is designed to induce existential death.

One key difference between moving to opportunity and stepping into the Void is the compulsory nature of departure. "Exile is not, after all, a matter of choice: you are born into it, or it happens to you."[121] Using Raynor Winn's eviction from her farm as an example, unlike Winn's adult daughter who grew up and left home to build her own life, Winn was pushed out by unwelcome forces. She did not leave because she aspired to become a hiking nomad. She hiked because her former life had been forcibly taken.

This revocation of belonging changes the nature of leaving. "The conventional home-leaving script cannot accommodate an imposed journey."[122] Leaving to pursue educational or employment opportunities is not the same as leaving to escape homophobia, ableism, sexual abuse, or racial violence. "To be expelled was different from leaving voluntarily. To be expelled is to be rejected, and to be rejected is to be disgraced."[123] Disgrace changes the tone of leaving. "Leaving home can only happen because there is a home to leave."[124]

A second relevant factor differentiating invisible exile from moving to opportunity is the lack of transitional support. Other home-leaving scripts involve rites of passage, such as graduations and farewell parties that mark a traveler's departure, as well as housewarming parties and drinks with colleagues that mark a traveler's arrival.

By contrast, the Void offers no such support. Exiles are not waved off with hugs or given helpful advice, nor does any new community stand ready to welcome them or show them the ropes. This lack of transitional support helps explain why Raynor Winn's eviction felt like a journey defined solely by loss: "Not heading for a new beginning, not a fresh start with life opening up before us."[125] Without rites of passage or transitional aids, exile looks less like opportunity and more like a dead end.

A third complicating factor involves broken connections. In most home-leaving scripts, even when travelers know they may be away for a long time, returns are both possible and expected, for instance when adult children return for holidays, weddings, and funerals. Similarly, in today's globally connected world, migration is "an ongoing process which often involves continuing mobility and communication between past and present home countries."[126] Indeed, present-day migrants frequently find employment through "seasonal" or "transnational" work, which allows them to "shuttle back and forth" between different communities.[127]

By contrast, invisible exile comes without an expectation of return. "The pathos of exile" is that "homecoming is out of the question."[128] In Winn's case, once evicted, her home and farm were barred to her as the legal property of another. For authors leaving religious sects, "we do not accept their return, ever. . . . We do not accept the repentance of heretics because we do not believe them. If they appear to have repented, we maintain they have done so fraudulently."[129] Experiences like these reinforce the conclusion that, although all mobility can lead to homesickness and longing, invisible exile comes with a finality and stigma that is less present in other departures.

Fourth, even if exiles find new opportunities, those gains do not negate the pain of being *erased,* which is qualitatively different from the pain of being *apart.* A recent study of racial exile, for instance, opened with the story of a light-skinned Black girl who, as a child, was sent "from Chicago's South Side to Los Angeles to live the rest of her life as a white woman."[130] The girl never saw her parents again, not even decades later as her father lay dying, because she "was a white woman now. There was simply no turning back."[131] Stories of moving to opportunity do not capture this sense of "no longer belonging as a family member and no longer sharing experiences, stories, and memories of times past."[132] This type of leaving—the type that involves being stripped bare of prior identity, heritage, and kinship— often leaves people "heartbroken," no matter the gains.[133] This scale of rupture is simply not well reflected within the moving-to-opportunity script.

This stripping away of identity, kinship, and heritage is even more harsh when it takes a punitive form. Exile by definition is a separation imposed as punishment. It involves a "vested authority" that compels a "prolonged absence" from one's community "as a punitive measure" for offending group norms.[134] As a punishment, it works by "designating an offender [as] an outcast and depriving him of the comfort and protection of his group."[135]

This emphasis on punishment underscores the tight connection between spatial dislocation and physical death. In ancient Rome, citizens could choose exile as an alternative to capital punishment. In colonial England, convicts opting for banishment were informed that returning from the colonies would mean execution. Furthermore, physical displacement is often paired with social erasure. When exiles are labeled "the 'enemy,' the 'subversives,' and the 'terrorists,'" the community left behind is often prohibited even from merely speaking their names.[136]

This social erasure reinforces the sense of lost identity. Because identity narratives demand coherence, any rupture that introduces "disorientation, disembeddedness, rootlessness, routelessness,"[137] for instance by constructing "some physical or chronological distance between the lives individuals once led and the lives they lead now,"[138] undermines the capacity to construct a cohesive sense of self. Exile introduces these ruptures to the extreme. As "a condition legislated . . . to deny an identity to people,"[139] exile functions as a form of "self-death,"[140] a form of "social death,"[141] and as a condition that is "like death but without death's ultimate mercy."[142] To gloss over that fact by mischaracterizing invisible exile as moving to opportunity is therefore yet another form of problematic erasure.

The Shattering of Everything

This discussion of exile as existential erasure sheds light on the full weight of *leaving*. Even when travelers have an escape plan, and even when travelers feel an initial surge of euphoria, they must still endure the moment when their previous lives and former selves shatter beyond repair.

As discussed previously, leaving can spark positive emotions, but it also provokes strong, durable, negative ones. Some invisible exiles experience grief and shame. "I felt, quite simply, sad, and was constantly wracked by a very great regret."[143] Others experience abandonment. "I feel like a lost child. . . . I am alone in the place where I live, which is even harder than being alone in a place where you don't know anyone."[144]

These authors had traveled before, for instance to the Bohemian Coast, but the journey into exile felt more harrowing. "I closed my eyes and felt each pothole and pebble we rolled over during what felt like the longest few minutes of my life."[145] Even though staying was unsafe, departure was also dangerous. "This voyage was even more wrenching than the other journeys I had made, and my heart pounded with the implications of what I was doing and what my father and my clan would do when they discovered that I had run away."[146]

Other negative emotions arise from the grief travelers feel for the things they leave behind. "The jewelry was easy to part with, but the dishes and linens I shopped for so lovingly five years ago, the friends I worked so hard to make, the entire extended family network I was once a part of—those are harder to disengage from."[147]

In terms of possessions, stepping into the Void meant leaving without the material objects that once anchored identity and symbolized social ties. "It feels new and strange to suddenly have to make do with so little, and there is a quiet panic in me at the thought of having so few possessions to tie me down."[148]

Exile also means separating from loved ones. For one author, "I did not speak to my father, not even on the phone."[149] For another, "precisely because my grandmother loved—loves—me, she tightened her grip until it became so painful that I had no choice but to yank myself free."[150] These social breaks felt painful but necessary. "Even if it meant becoming a stranger to my loved ones, . . . I would have a life of my own."[151]

For me, the most heartbreaking accounts of severed ties were not about lost caregivers—although I agree those losses are significant— but rather were about lost access to the people for whom travelers once provided care. One author berated herself for leaving her chronically ill mother behind with an abusive boyfriend. "How could I leave her with him? But how could I stay? I couldn't; not anymore."[152]

It was the same for an author who, after being expelled, lost access to his five children. His former community financed legal petitions accusing him of traumatizing the children by feeding them machine matzah, wearing blue jeans, and owning a television.[153] Their mother also had the children deliver notes, ostensibly written by them, reading, "I am sorry, . . . I can no longer be in contact with you."[154] To protect his children from these conflicts, he chose not to force visitation, even though this outcome was devastating. "I did not lose in court. Instead, I lost my children's hearts, and with them, very nearly, my sanity."[155]

These losses, which often lack social acknowledgment, explain why one author wrote her narrative not as a success story but as a tale of loss. She acknowledged the financial gains that followed her decision to leave, but her memoir was ultimately a way to grapple with the sorrow of losing so much of herself and her community along the way. "There are many complicated reasons why so few people cross a socioeconomic dividing line in a lasting way, but one of the reasons is simple: It is a painful crossing."[156] Despite her upward economic mobility, she mourned the closeness she no longer shared with her mother and grandmother, as well as the daughter she could no longer raise. "If I were to become pregnant from that moment on, it would be a different soul, a different person."[157] That child would not share her traditions or experience her heritage. For better or worse, "a cycle had been broken, and the place it tore was between me and you. . . . I cried to mourn a loss in success."[158]

Leaving Felt like Dying

In my assessment, these extreme ruptures reflect the historic link between exile and death. Invisible exiles do not trade one fate for the other. They do not evade execution in exchange for life elsewhere. Instead, they appear to experience both fates simultaneously.

For a religious exile, when her community was ordered to shun her, even her own brother complied. When they ran into each other on the subway, "he stiffened, turned around to stare past me as if I were a ghost."[159] Only one person, her mother, refused. In retribution, every single tenant in her mother's apartment building—all members of the same religious sect—abruptly moved out, which stripped them not only of friendship but also of income. "Survival, home, and job. . . . In an instant, those, too, were snatched away."[160] Before exile, she had social connections and financial support, but afterward, "I had been erased. Vanished. Jayanti who? . . . The silence chilled me."[161]

Travelers sometimes initiated their own erasure. During one author's gender transition, "I asked my mom to take down all the photos in the house of me as a boy."[162] Her mother cherished the toddler years and wanted to save the photos, even if they were no longer on display, but the author insisted they be destroyed. "I'd been Katie for only a matter of days but was ready to completely excise Luke from my life."[163]

Other authors shared this determination to erase the old and become someone new. "I wasn't looking to improve the conditions of my life. I wanted to change my life out of all recognition."[164] A metamorphosis of this scale felt both momentous and irreversible. "Your life changes in an instant. When it does, it splits into two different lives, with two different timelines, the bridge between Before and After exploded in the very moment of its making."[165]

These descriptions of shattered identities illustrate the connection between exile and death. "Leaving home evoked extreme feeling[s] of abandonment and loss. It was like dying."[166] One author "banished" his former self "to the grave in which he belongs."[167] For another, "I have no past to cling to. . . . My two identities have finally split apart, and I've killed the other one."[168] For a third, "my former self . . . had gone; she had indeed died under the funeral pall."[169] Statements like these reinforce the sense of finality that comes from a type of leaving that doubles as existential erasure. Like death, after exile, "you can't go back to Before."[170]

This sense of impending death is not without its silver lining. To be sure, most invisible exiles describe stepping into the Void as its own form of hell. "To be utterly alone, forever, and to be painfully aware of one's eternal loneliness, this is Hell, at least my Hell, the one I entered that morning for the first of many times."[171] Even so, these descriptions of death also contain references to new life. Travelers killed one self, but saved the other.[172] They died while refusing to rebury themselves.[173] They dug graves for who they once were while giving themselves a new name.[174]

Statements like these reinforce the sense that, within invisible exile, death and rebirth go together. In urban geography, banishment is often framed as sacrifice. "Some life may have to be abandoned, damaged or destroyed in order to protect, save or care for other forms of life."[175] Justifications like these are often used to perpetuate inequity, for instance when Black and Brown lives are sacrificed to advance white interests. Similarly, within invisible exile travelogues, the communities doing the banishing often assert that expelling the traveler is about protecting the group.

A critique of these self-serving, malevolent narratives is certainly warranted, but for the moment, I want to highlight how, within invisible exile travel writing, a similar narrative occurs not only at the collective level but also at the level of the exiled self. Invisible exiles describe themselves both as the life being sacrificed and as the life being protected. Their frequent references to self-death underscore how severely the Void strips away their former identities. This erasure, however, simultaneously frees the traveler's nonconforming parts to potentially grow and prosper elsewhere. For Carlos Eire, as painful as it was to step into the Void, "I couldn't wait to escape. . . . Losing everything, including my family, seemed like a small price to pay. Or so I thought."[176]

Comments like these reflect a core dilemma facing invisible exiles as they consider how to make sense of leaving. By staying, it felt as though some part of them was dying, but to save those parts, Plato's Cave allowed them no option except to sacrifice other aspects of their identities.

From this perspective, stepping into the Void destroys some aspects of self, which is a form of self-death. However, by allowing this death, a new and more authentic self might someday emerge. Maybe. If travelers are lucky. Because rebirth is not guaranteed, and the process of expulsion remains devastating.

In conclusion, entering exile is a fateful moment involving big changes, high stakes, and no easy returns. Invisible exiles make these moves when the dangers of staying outweigh the dangers of leaving. When possible, travelers try to prepare for departure, but often they simply cannot wait. At the moment of departure, travelers might feel a surge of hopefulness or relief, but those positive emotions are often short-lived and quickly replaced by the harsher realities of existential death. As for what to do after death, which is to say, the challenge of building a new identity elsewhere, that is the subject of the next chapter.

FIVE

The Swamp of Harsh Liminality

Bizarro World

The concept of travel as a liminal time-out is a recurring theme in travel writing. The traveler boards a plane, laces up her hiking boots, or mounts her bicycle and is away in a place where, for a little while, she can ignore the demands of home and work. This sense of being away creates space for self-exploration and personal growth. Then, after a while, the traveler returns and resumes her life, perhaps with a fresh perspective, but often much as it was before.

I agree that travel can generate this sense of playful release. However, in my assessment, this soft language of a *temporary reprieve* fails to capture the harsh experience of traveling in the wake of expulsion. Instead of a temporary time-out enabling self-exploration, invisible exiles are far more likely to enter a *harsh liminal swamp* of durable illegibility and protracted nonbelonging.

This harsh liminality catches many invisible exiles by surprise. After years of imaginative travel and scouting trips, many travelers felt at least somewhat prepared to navigate their new, post-exile environments. However, visiting a place for short bursts and select purposes is not the same as living there full time. Moreover, because these newcomers usually arrive without robust socialization, invisible exiles often struggle to make sense of the bewildering array of material practices and social cues in the new space. This inability to anticipate even the most basic everyday norms can lead to a sense of disorientation and crisis.

Moreover, rather than abating over time, the sense of alienation often intensifies. It is natural to misstep when navigating unfamiliar environments. From the traveler's perspective, these blunders—while potentially embarrassing and sometimes dangerous—are important learning opportunities. Through trial and error, travelers receive useful feedback, which enhances their situational awareness going forward. By contrast, the situation often looks different to the people witnessing these blunders. Instead of seeing a newcomer who is undergoing a natural resocialization process, observers see someone who, in their quick assessment, should already possess environmental literacy. From that perspective, blunders look less like learning and more like incompetence or disrespect. This difference in perspective can undermine belonging because the same process that brings travelers into greater functional alignment with new environments can also lead to new rounds of rejection.

All travelers, whether in exile or on vacation, learn about space and society through trial and error. Within the travel-writing genre, learning while doing in response to unexpected situations is a key mechanism enabling personal growth. However, unlike tourists and other travelers who leave home, learn through mistakes, and then return to societies that did not witness their blundering, invisible exiles intend to stay and do not have the luxury of shedding stigma through departure. Instead, rejected from the old but out of step with the new, invisible exiles often find themselves mired in a harsh liminal space where the past—a place travelers thought was dead—persists in ways that thwart easy belonging and render the future uncertain.

The harshness of these liminal experiences contradicts the notion that mobility provides an easy solution to the ongoing problem of dysphoria. This lack of an easy spatial fix defies the expectations of social science colleagues who sometimes ask me, *Aren't these problems solved when everyone just moves to the gayborhood?* I agree that some people—for instance, through queer tourism or lifestyle migration—find environments that more effectively support their identities and satisfy their emotional needs. However, not everyone has this option. Many people lack the financial capacity to relocate solely as a lifestyle preference, especially since lifestyle migration is generally "restricted to those who are materially 'relatively affluent.'"[1] Although runaway communities provide cheaper options, where would one go to find a neighborhood-based community of rape survivors, cult survivors, or folks who used to be homeless? Furthermore, why should people who have endured trauma related to sexuality, ability, race, and gender restrict themselves to enclaves that only exist in a handful of cities and that are being gentrified out?

Travel can accomplish many things. It can provide a reprieve, enable personal growth, and expose travelers to new ideas. However, being expelled from one's home is not the same as finding a replacement community. Moreover, many invisible exiles are not interested in joining new separatist enclaves.

For all these reasons, as a corrective to the usual depiction of travel as a temporary reprieve, in this chapter I explore the harsh liminal landscape of protracted nonbelonging in the context of having no welcoming place to land. To explain these dynamics, I start by providing descriptions of post-exile liminality as recounted within invisible exile life history writing. Next, I provide a theory-informed explanation of liminality as a state of incomplete identity transition where the past ends but without fully releasing its hold. Then, by bringing these theories into conversation with invisible exile narratives, I highlight two common types of post-exile illegibility. Environmental illegibility, including a traveler's struggle to make sense of physical and social cues, can generate feelings of bewilderment and crisis. Subject illegibility, including an observer's inability to understand a traveler's identity and mannerisms, can lead to new rounds of rejection.

Combined, these dual dynamics help explain why, after escaping from the emotional suffocation and structural violence of Plato's Cave, invisible exiles' circumstances often initially get worse, not better. The same resocialization process that could, in theory, lead to a new sense of home often instead leads to a new sense of homelessness and an ongoing sense of despair.

"I Didn't Belong Out Here Either"

Starting with examples from invisible exile narratives, when Karen Armstrong decided to stop being a nun and instead become a full-time English major, she thought the transition would be simple. As explained in her memoir *The Spiral Staircase,* Armstrong had prior experience with secular culture. She had grown up outside the convent and, more recently, had taken classes at a nearby university to prepare for her presumed future as a parochial schoolteacher. These out-and-back trips created a landing zone where, after leaving her faith and shedding her habit, she could begin her life anew. "I could . . . simply move into my college and carry on with my studies as though nothing had happened."[2]

The reality was more jarring. After living apart for so long, Armstrong felt politically illiterate. "I entered the secular world completely ignorant of the problems of our time, and because I lacked basic information, could not make head or tail of the newspapers."[3] Everyday culture felt similarly foreign. She attended concerts and dances, which "was interesting, but had nothing to do with me."[4] The prospect of handling money also felt unsettling. With the convent no longer managing her finances for her, "I had to buy my own food and manage my own budget, and I found this obscurely frightening."[5] Rather than risk mistakes, she decided not to eat.[6]

To complicate matters further, just as Armstrong felt flummoxed by her new environment, her new peers were flummoxed by her. One evening, after arriving late to the college dining hall, "instead of bowing briefly to the principal in mute apology for my lateness, . . . I found to my horror that I had knelt down and kissed the floor."[7] She adopted this penitent posture swiftly and without conscious thought, only to then realize her mistake. "A quick glance" at the other students "who were staring at me incredulously, reminded me that what was normal behavior in the convent was little short of deranged out here."[8]

This confusion, fear, and blundering meant that, instead of gradually beginning to heal from exile, Armstrong's sense of dislocation mounted. On the one hand, she had irrevocably broken ties with her former home. "I was a secular, and the enclosure was barred to me now."[9] On the other hand, leaving the convent did not erase its imprint on her identity. Due to this difference in personal history, "I realized that my reactions were entirely different from those of most of my contemporaries in this strange new world. Perhaps they always would be."[10] As the days passed, instead of growing closer to her classmates, she became increasingly sensitive to their differences. In this space of separation from her old world and alienation from her new one, "I had found, to my considerable sorrow, that even though I no longer belonged in the convent, I didn't belong out here either."[11]

Welcome to Bizarro World, a Place of Harsh Liminal Crisis

Armstrong did not give this neither/nor place a name, but Carlos Eire did. In his memoir *Learning to Die in Miami*, Eire named this place Bizarro World. Eire arrived in Bizarro World after passing through the Void while being airlifted out of Havana and then arriving in the strange new space otherwise known as Miami. Looking back on that experience, Eire describes Miami as a disorienting realm where his most basic assumptions no longer applied and where entirely different logics prevailed. "As I saw it then, Cuba had become some other dimension, far from earth: A parallel universe not unlike that of Bizarro World in the Superman comic books, where everything was the opposite of what one might expect on earth."[12]

A key characteristic of Bizarro World is that strangeness cuts both ways. From Eire's perspective, Miami was odd. Its single-serve cereal boxes, processed meat on white bread, and candy-filled vending machines provided "proof positive that we'd entered the Twilight Zone, some sort of dimension where you could never get your bearings because everything was so weird, so mind-blowingly and unpredictably strange."[13]

Conversely, to Eire's new classmates, the environment was normal and only Eire looked strange. Although his pale skin and blond hair did not stand out, his history was etched into his appearance in other ways. "My eyeglasses were utterly ridiculous on this side of the Florida Straits: the ugliest possible proof of my alien status that I could have asked for."[14] His accented speech betrayed him as well. "I was branded on my face as well as my tongue."[15]

This bidirectional sense of place-self misalignment indicates that Eire's identity transition remained incomplete. Although he was now legally an American, culturally he felt out of place. Cuba was gone to him, and with it went his parents, possessions, language, foodways, and even his original name. Despite this separation, to Eire's new schoolmates, he remained Cuban to his core. To them, Cuba wasn't the place Eire left; it was the identity he still embodied, and they rejected him for it.

This rejection stung. "All of my life I'd longed to be *here* in the United States of America. . . . I'd been seeing images of this place, playing with its toys, and consuming its goods and entertainment since the day I was born."[16] This imaginative travel made a mark, but as a socialization tool, it was not nearly robust enough to prepare Eire for the reality of living in his confusing and unwelcoming new home.

Like other invisible exiles, Carlos Eire and Karen Armstrong both struggled to navigate their post-exile environment. For Armstrong, the disorientation left her feeling in "exile" not from her home country but "from everything that made sense."[17] She had only moved a few miles down the road, but the social distance felt immense, and she felt "lost in a universe that has suddenly become alien."[18] Similarly for Eire, "I imagine a squadron of flying saucers hovering nearby. That would be so great. But there aren't any spacecraft. . . . There are no aliens here, save for ourselves."[19]

Other invisible exiles likewise struggled both to understand their new situations and to find a suitable vocabulary for describing their disorientation. Entering Bizarro World was like entering the "unknown,"[20] crossing to "the other side,"[21] moving to "the outside world,"[22] entering "limbo,"[23] and crossing into "unknown territory."[24] On crossing these social borders, travelers felt like "a fish out of water,"[25] "a caveman dropped into the modern world,"[26] or "like something out of a cartoon."[27]

Moreover, it wasn't just the travelers who felt baffled. Invisible exiles quickly realized that the people they met in Bizarro World were similarly baffled by them. "People stared at us as if Area 51 had released its aliens."[28] Some travelers, like Karen Armstrong and Carlos Eire, appeared white, straight, cisgendered, and able-bodied, which helped them blend in for a while. But they also embodied other characteristics that eventually marked them as different. Like Armstrong bending down to kiss the floor or Eire speaking with a Cuban accent, years of socialization into certain ways of speaking, walking, dressing, eating, and thinking left its mark. These traits confused new peers who, instead of responding with curiosity and empathy, often seemed aghast and highly judgmental. In this space of being simultaneously separated from the old and alienated from the new, many authors began to doubt whether exile could indeed lead to new beginnings.

Soft Liminality Provides a Cathartic Time-Out

Tourists, backpackers, heritage seekers, and travelers of other types often feel disoriented in new environments. For many globetrotting adventurers, "liminal notions" of "margins" and "danger" add "excitement" to the journey.[29] Moreover, as discussed in previous chapters, stepping away from habitual landscapes can enable self-exploration and personal growth.

I agree with the above. However, when theorizing travel as a liminal space, I prefer to make an additional distinction between the *soft liminality* of a temporary reprieve and the *harsh liminality* of protracted nonbelonging. In both scenarios, travel exposes people to new environments and facilitates social release. However, "the underside of freedom" is "an unprecedented level of insecurity."[30] In my assessment, as the relative level of insecurity increases—for instance, as the focus shifts from tourists on vacation to refugees in exile—the nature of liminality shifts as well. For invisible exiles, in the wake of fateful departures, insecurity rather than freedom dominates the story. This insecurity, combined with the expectation of no easy returns, shifts travel-related liminality from a space of exploratory release into a landscape of protracted crisis. This harsh liminality might eventually lead to post-liminal growth, but it can also act as quicksand and lead to long-term stalling out.

Within the social sciences, *liminality* is associated with transitional thresholds and marginalized in-betweens. Early twentieth-century studies of rites of passage defined liminality as the second stage of a three-stage model of identity transition. The first stage, "separation," is "characterized by symbols of detachment" from the prior identity.[31] Next comes "liminality, in which the ritual subject or 'liminar' is ambiguous and passes through a realm that has few or none of the attributes of the 'before' and 'after' states."[32] The process then concludes, at least in theory, with "aggregation," at which point "the liminar has reached a new identity position" and is "expected to adopt certain norms."[33] Within this process, the middle *liminal* stage is conceptualized as being neither/nor. In this "unstructured state in-between two structured states,"[34] the old identity is suspended, but a replacement identity has not yet arrived.

Although contemporary scholars agree that ambiguity is central to liminality, they challenge the assumption that identity transformations unfold in a straightforward manner. A transition may follow a prescribed path, for instance "boy to man" and "girl to bride,"[35] but transitions can also take unexpected turns or remain incomplete. Agreeing that "liminality has to do with transitions . . . does not mean that all transitions go smoothly. They do in fact not."[36] Instead of following "a linear path between one state and another," some liminars end up "straddling the line" or occupying "a permanent place of modulation."[37] Other times, through circuitous turns and unexpected twists, the identity ultimately reached is quite different from the one initially imagined.

Geographers are especially likely to associate liminality not with easy shifts to well-ordered spaces but with environments that feel marginalized, hybrid, and indeterminant. Liminal geographies en-capsulate a "deviance from a norm," "an uncertain socio-spatial encounter with otherness," and a "temporary eruption of radical emancipatory possibility."[38] These liminal landscapes are not neutral vacuums in between well-defined spaces. Instead, they form a "critical threshold" that exists "outside ordinary time," a threshold laden with "the sense that things could be otherwise."[39]

Travel-writing scholars generally cast these liminal landscapes in an empowering light. In response to capitalist alienation, "traveling entails the temporary disconnection from the profane world of the division of labor which is replaced by a state of enhanced freedom in a new time-space continuum."[40] In response to sexism, traveling frees women not only "from geographical constraints, but also from the ideological constraints of their assigned role in patriarchal society."[41] In both scenarios, freedom from "clock-time" and from the "duties or obligations of the home culture" leaves "the individual backpacker . . . to a greater extent than elsewhere left in solitude to structure both her time and her action."[42]

This sense of liminality as a space of release that enables self-actualization is a recurring theme within travel writing.[43] In this temporary, in-between context, travelers can live otherwise, self-directed, and free.

Harsh Liminality Is a State of Protracted Paralysis

I agree that travel generates liminal effects. However, in my assess-ment, the above portrayal overemphasizes liminality's softer forms. *Soft liminality,* in my use of the phrase, is characterized by a reprieve from ordinary roles and burdens. Soft liminality often arises from the decision to temporarily opt out of workaday life, explore more ful-filling alternatives, and then "reenter"[44] everyday routines through "reassimilation"[45] back into the collective.

By contrast, invisible exiles rarely describe post-exile liminality as a space of temporary reprieve, nor do their experiences readily give way to a new normal or a resumed status quo. Instead, invisible exiles appear far more likely to feel *mired* "betwixt and between" and *bogged down* in places where "they are neither one thing nor the other."[46] For this reason, although I agree soft liminality plays a role, especially during pre-exile imaginative travel and scouting trips, stopping there would omit the deepening uncertainty and protracted anguish that comes from long-term ambiguity.

Invisible exiles often struggle with this uncertainty. At times, they embody the figure of the "existential outsider" who, rather than being "intimately joined by bonds of familiarity, attachment and at-homeness," instead lack "a knowledge of how to orient," lack "a feeling for the hidden dimensions of particular [new] places," and lack "a sense of personal and interpersonal history in relation to [the new] place."[47] In contrast to the conventional description of *the traveler* as someone who is "not at home" but feels "at home everywhere,"[48] invisible exiles in Bizarro World often feel like "a social and moral untouchable."[49] This is the nature of exile. Just as "you can't go back to some earlier . . . condition of being at home, . . . you [also] can never fully arrive, be at one with your new home or situation."[50]

I wish I could soften this language by adding complexity and nuance, which would satisfy my personal desire to see the world as rich with ambiguous edges and hybrid in-betweens. However, in the context of invisible exile, my professional sense is that this starker framework is both a more accurate representation of the initial post-exile experience and an important counterweight to the postmodern tendency to overemphasize fluidity and to under-acknowledge the structural and embodied barriers to mobility.

One key challenge that helps explain these harsh dynamics is the problem of incommensurability. Classical theories of identity aggregation define end states in relation to prespecified starting points. In general, I am skeptical of these approaches. I acknowledge that, at their core, stories of invisible exile are all about unconventional transitions and unexpected travel paths. However, invisible exiles who survive, thrive, and get their stories published show that, even though diverse pathways are always possible, these pathways come with real and often insurmountable barriers. Instead of transitioning from childhood to adulthood or from being single to being married—two states that are defined reciprocally—invisible exile is more like an apple trying to become a shoe or a tadpole trying to become a butterfly. No one else in Armstrong's English department arrives by way of the convent, and no one else in Eire's elementary school arrives by way of communist revolution.

Given the apparent incommensurability of what existed before with what comes after, travelers struggle to construct a liminal hinge that might help them exit the former and enter the latter. Instead of fluidity or hybridity, this apparent incommensurability reinforces the sense of being neither/nor.

Alongside incommensurability, a second key challenge involves deep, existential insecurity. Tourism often takes people outside their comfort zones, but it rarely turns entire worlds and value systems upside down. Invisible exile, however, does precisely that. "When everything you've ever known is suddenly up for question, what are the values you retain and what do you discard?"[51] After passing through the Void, invisible exiles grapple with "questions about the very nature of what is real, what is important, and what is worth living for."[52] Attempting to answer these questions in Bizarro World requires significant and lasting changes in practical behaviors and moral philosophies. "Tearing myself away . . . opened up a huge world of freedom, but it also forced me to think about new kinds of limitations to freedom: health insurance, taxes, rent or mortgage payments. I had to have priorities."[53]

Asking questions about who to be and how to live is not the same as finding answers. "Just because I can't go any further as a man doesn't mean I can just pick up and start on the road to being female. I don't know how to do that."[54] For one author, "just because I take action to live a more traditional lifestyle doesn't mean the unrest in my spirit settles."[55] For another, "without the attachments, she is a woman in limbo. . . . Away from those roles and alone, she is someone she doesn't know."[56] Far from a temporary reprieve creating space for self-reflection, statements like these illustrate the profound disorientation of harsh liminality as a potential space of existential unraveling.

Taken together, when incommensurability and insecurity, rather than growth and reprieve, are the dominant organizing logics, travelers appear less likely to describe liminality as a soft space of spontaneity. Instead, they use harsher terms indicating fear, confusion, and foreboding. For them, having crossed the threshold of the known world and made the decision to keep going—to let themselves fully arrive in this strange new world—the outcome is not playful. Instead, it feels "risky and forbidden."[57] Travelers are "bewildered, insecure, confused."[58] In Bizarro World, travelers feel "terrified"[59] or "scared silly"[60] as they feel themselves "floating lost and unrooted."[61]

In essence, rather than experiencing *mobility*, Bizarro World is a place where travelers experience *stuckness*. In any society, "mobility is riven with power-geometries" where some groups "are more in charge of it than others; some initiate flows and movement; some are more on the receiving end of it than others; some are effectively imprisoned by it."[62] Having power over mobility enables "social navigation" through "the assessment of the dangers and possibilities of one's present position, as well as the process of plotting and attempting to actualise routes into an uncertain and changeable future."[63] When external forces block social navigation, people experience "stuckness," which "hinders their ability to undertake future-orientated actions and, subsequently, their ability to plan for and control the course of their own lives."[64]

Unlike more privileged travelers, other tourists, or even their new peers who give the appearance, at least, of being able to come and go at will, invisible exiles often feel immobilized. Given the incommensurability of before and after states, as well as the insecurity of having no clear exit route, travelers in Bizarro World experience a liminality where growth can easily give way to paralysis. "The space I inhabited in that moment"—a place of homelessness and destitution—"was the safest, securest place I had, and I didn't want to move."[65]

Environmental Illegibility Leads to Feelings of Crisis

The paralysis evoked by such bewildering environmental change is a stark illustration of the harshness of invisible exile's liminal state. After exile, travelers relocate to the places they yearned to join, but this change of address does not make those places feel like home nor does it automatically translate into the capacity to design one's future. One challenge is that, because travelers lack the socialization required to decode their new environments, they often experience them as spaces of crisis. A second challenge is that the people in these new spaces frequently lack the level of socialization required to understand the lingering pre-exile traits that travelers embody, which leaves travelers vulnerable to stigmatization. Taken together, this mutual illegibility often traps invisible exiles, at least initially, in a protracted state of liminal placelessness.

Starting first with *environmental legibility,* I use this phrase to refer to a person's capacity to make sense of her social and spatial environment, as well as to anticipate how that environment functions in everyday contexts. People acquire environmental legibility through socialization. "The purpose of socialization is to provide knowledge of expected behaviors and the ability to perform in society in accordance with societal norms."[66] This process includes mastering social dynamics, such as learning to interpret group hierarchies and behavioral cues. It also includes mastering material culture, such as learning the practical uses of various objects and the symbolic meanings of places and artifacts.

Although socialization is a lifelong process, it usually begins at birth and, by certain ages or milestones, people are expected to achieve certain levels of competency. For people who are well-socialized into an environment, its objects and routines usually fade into the background. "There is . . . a regularity of events: for instance, eating out at the same corner-house once a month" or "walking the same way between home and work each day."[67] Rather than requiring conscious decision-making, "habit underlies these events," and they unfold almost "without question."[68] This condition of "ontological security . . . enables most people, most of the time, to take for granted—to trust—that our ordinary, everyday worlds are reliable and dependable."[69]

Lifestyles, however, are context specific, and the values, beliefs, and behaviors reinforced through socialization can vary widely from place to place. This variation helps explain why immigrants socialized into one environment may find that their assumptions do not hold in their new homes. Furthermore, even for authors like Karen Armstrong whose move from the convent to the college only spanned a few miles, travelers exiting Plato's Cave were often "socialized into behavior and norms quite different from what the 'outside world' accepted."[70] This lack of context-specific socialization can make it difficult for travelers—even those who ostensibly remain local—to anticipate how their new environments will function.

Importantly, this confusion is evident even in narratives where, prior to exile, travelers felt relatively confident in their ability to live elsewhere. One author, for example, thought he understood the outside world. "I had watched hundreds of movies, read dozens of books, devoured thousands of newspaper and magazine articles. I imagined that the language and the cultural nuances and the behavioral peculiarities of non-Hasidim would come to me like a second skin, once I shed my old one."[71] It wasn't until after his expulsion that he realized his mistake. Imaginative travel is a useful stepping stone, but "one does not become a homicide detective from reading crime novels, or a trial lawyer from watching courtroom dramas. All the movies in the world could not adequately prepare me for living in this new world."[72]

In short, despite imaginative travel and scouting trips, invisible exiles are unprepared. "As expectation meets reality, migrants come face to face with the limits of their knowledge of the local setting and way of life."[73] Invisible exiles may feel an affinity toward the social groups they hope to join, but those "strong positive value-statements about distant peoples and places" are based on "a minimum of knowledge about them," rather than deep familiarity.[74] The resulting liminality "is not only the result of being caught between two cultures, but reflects the tension between reality and imagination."[75] Travelers' preconceived ideas, which are often based on novels, films, or brief tourism, do not align with reality and do not encompass everything they need to know to navigate those environments effectively.

This post-exile environmental illiteracy, which is a recurring theme within invisible exile travel writing, is reflected in stories about clothing, walking, eating, and budgeting. Starting with clothing, even when a religious exile knew where to buy secular apparel, its symbolic aspects eluded him. "I found that I could make little sense of contemporary fashions."[76] From books and films, he knew professionals often wore ties and sweaters to work, so he bought some. But instead of blending in, he felt called out when a coworker said his new sweater was preppy. "I was left to wonder: Was preppy good? Was preppy bad? I turned to the Internet, but the answers were elusive. Preppy. Urban. Sporty. Business casual. So many terms, but how did one know what was what? What style suitable for whom, and for what occasion?"[77]

Just as clothing proved confusing, so too did the practice of walking. One author felt disconcerted when walking in public after removing her full body veil. "Every woman who has worn such a veil for years and then taken it off will attest that it is difficult to walk at first. It is as if, uncovered, your legs do not work the same way."[78]

Another author felt unnerved when, as part of her gender transition, she began walking outdoors in skirts. "I felt raw and vulnerable. . . . There were a number of occasions when I wished I still had that male shield standing between me and the harshness of the world."[79]

A third author likewise felt disoriented while trying to walk down stairs after experiencing physical trauma. "I could see each stair clearly enough, but couldn't gauge the drop between them. . . . They looked like a suggestion of stairs, a possibility of stairs, but nothing I could trust."[80]

In examples like these, walking, like clothing, had seemed self-explanatory prior to exile. But in Bizarro World these everyday elements were anything but ordinary.

Next, once travelers were dressed and walking, another Bizarro World challenge involved unpredictable foodscapes, for instance, the shapeshifting nature of chicken. In one narrative, the author was eagerly looking forward to Lima's famous cuisine until he was served his first meal: a bowl of soup containing a protruding chicken's foot. "The sight devastated me."[81] He ate potato chips and Oreos instead.

Another author was similarly eager to connect to local foodways until a new acquaintance offered him the delicacy of swallowing a still-beating chicken's heart. "They seek generously to share their world with me, never realizing that their diverting marvels are my wounding horrors."[82]

Similarly, for Carlos Eire arriving in Miami, although he was thrilled to become an American, his first American meal—a chicken sandwich—perplexed him. "It's so orderly, so controlled, so geometrical, so colorless, this plate of food. Two triangles that form a square, inside a circle, laid out on a larger square. . . . Who dismembered this lumpy, clucking creature and turned it into a geometry lesson?"[83] Nearly retching, he forced himself to swallow, disguising his gagging as hiccups.

Alongside clothing, walking, and eating, another common area of befuddlement involves money. Social groups develop distinctive cultural norms related to money, spending, and debt, which explains why, even though one author was struggling to pay rent, she recoiled at the suggestion of accepting student aid. "I don't believe in Government Grants," she said, because she'd always been told that "to accept one was to indebt yourself to the Illuminati. 'That's how they get you.'"[84]

Another author had a similar response when, as part of her refugee support package, she was offered a government loan. "I was disturbed at the idea of owing a debt to an infidel. That would surely mean I would have to pay interest, which is un-Islamic and wicked. This was certainly an infidel trick."[85]

Cultural norms around money also explain why, even though a third author was struggling to afford food and diapers, his wife resisted his plan to pursue cash-paying work. "Has it not occurred to you that we'll lose our food stamps?"[86] Working informally for Hasid vouchers had come with no such concerns.

Much of this anxiety surrounding money, clothing, and foodways exists by design. Within Plato's Cave, withholding information about other environments is a common strategy for preserving the status quo. "All my father's stories were about our mountain, our valley, our jagged little patch of Idaho. He never told me what to do if I left the mountain, if I crossed oceans and continents and found myself in strange terrain."[87] This lack of awareness creates barriers when invisible exiles try to navigate new social worlds. Travelers who are "not taught how to gradually manage the challenges of independence" are often "wholly unprepared for the bewildering range of opportunities and obligations" they encounter after leaving.[88]

Given travelers' limited familiarity with the objects, concepts, and protocols of Bizarro World, it's no surprise that they blunder. One author trying to navigate her new college campus made one mistake after another, enrolling in the wrong classes, boarding the wrong buses, and failing her first exam. "The morning of the exam . . . I barely had time to wonder what a blue book was before everyone produced one from their bags. The motion was fluid, synchronized, as if they had practiced it. I was the only dancer on the stage who seemed to have missed rehearsal."[89]

After failing the test, she asked a classmate for advice, and the classmate suggested focusing less on the lecture notes and more on the textbook. "'What textbook?' I said. '*The* textbook,' [she] said. She laughed as if I were being funny. I tensed because I wasn't."[90] Until that moment when her classmate literally held up the book and pointed to the page numbers printed on the syllabus, she had not realized her courses had textbooks, let alone that the point was to read them.

Examples like these demonstrate that, after exile, many travelers simply do not know how to decode their new environments. This illiteracy, far from being merely inconvenient, transforms liminality into a space of crisis.

One key characteristic of crisis is unpredictability. "The severing . . . of the links between past, present, and future" creates "the inability to anticipate the future," which then casts the reproduction of everyday life into doubt.[91] Landscapes are complicit in these dynamics because, far from being dull and ordinary, their supportive architecture plays a crucial role in the successful completion of everyday tasks.

A second key characteristic of crisis is hyper-awareness. Hyper-awareness occurs because, during a crisis, "we become aware of the present that ordinarily slips out of consciousness, and it becomes something viscerally present, a point hovering between past and future."[92] This heightened awareness—which, for invisible exiles, is born of the inability to predict what will happen next—then signals that, although travelers have separated from former places and selves, their larger process of identity transition remains incomplete.

This sense of crisis is different from the sense of novelty or foreignness. Within the travel-writing genre, many travelers voluntarily renounce the "tactical domain of everyday life"[93] by eschewing the "familiar streets, foods and dialects that enable us each day to accept without question the fallacy that things ought to be the way they are, because that is the way they are."[94] Indeed, for many people, a key goal of travel is to experience something new.[95] However, although the thrill of an adventure can produce an adrenaline rush, facing actual and long-standing danger is a far more menacing prospect.

As examples, for an author who did not anticipate that indigenous bathrooms would be outdoors and communal, because she packed only pants and no skirts, she had to expose herself daily to the gaze of luring men.[96] For another author, because she severely underestimated how much food and water she needed to carry to survive in the desert, she nearly perished several times during her cross-continental trek.[97] Likewise, because a third author was ignorant of the basic safety symbols embedded within her new environment, she took a leisurely walk through a lovely mountain meadow filled with active landmines.[98]

Examples like these demonstrate that imaginative travel and scouting trips do not provide the level of socialization required to truly understand and successfully navigate the spaces outside Plato's Cave. Having the idea to leave is one thing, but "to cross the threshold is to enter another world . . . and we can never be really sure what is on the other side of the door until we open it."[99] Travelers know what they are separating from, but that does not mean they know where they are headed or how that place will function. "I learned that it is one thing to say farewell to tribal life; it is quite another to practice the life of a citizen."[100] Although travelers like her "yearned for freedom," because they were unprepared for it, "once they found it, they were bewildered and broken by it."[101] Instead of finding new growth, travelers mired in liminality felt the sense of being on the verge of something new that was nevertheless slipping farther away.

In sum, at this point in their journeys, invisible exiles have clearly separated from their previous communities and entered a space of liminal transition. However, their journeys do not flow seamlessly from separation through liminality to aggregation. Instead, travelers' lack of context-specific knowledge often leaves them unable to make sense of their new environments. The surprises and errors that then ensue show travelers just how far they stand from finding a new sense of belonging.

Subject Illegibility Leads to Renewed Rejection

Alongside the challenges of environmental literacy, a second challenge involves finding acceptance among peers. As with other new arrivals, "the traveler not only makes observations, but is also himself observed, examined and grilled by his potential hosts."[102] Although invisible exiles undergo a natural resocialization process, the people observing them are usually unaware that this process is occurring and are therefore unsympathetic to its associated difficulties. As a result, when travelers blunder, instead of seeing someone who is learning and who, through trial and error, is closing the gaps between them, observers often see only failing, and they often respond with stigma and exclusion.

This rejection arises not so much because travelers struggle to decode new environments but because observers struggle to decode travelers. I use the phrase *subject legibility* to indicate the extent to which observers within an environment accurately comprehend the values, motivations, and experiences of other people. Mutual subject legibility may come easily for people who have "a shared history, shared language, human connections, and agreement with the particular norms of the 'world.'"[103] However, invisible exiles often come from different social worlds, and their embodied traits are easily "caught in between the classificatory systems that define societies."[104] As neither one thing nor the other, they exist somewhere in between, caught in a place of limbo.

This subject illegibility is a defining feature of liminality. Liminality is about detachment and erasure, rather than inscription. Karen

Armstrong is no longer a nun, and Carlos Eire is no longer in Cuba, but the question of who and what they will become remains unclear. Neither they nor their new peers have a meaningful sense of their identities. "The liminar is socially if not physically invisible. Their ambiguity means that they are outside definition."[105] Armstrong and Eire exist, but they feel unseen and ill defined, even to themselves.

This neither/nor condition interferes with the narration required for identity work. Using refugees as an example, the scale of refugee losses and the severity of violence endured means that refugees often have no language to make themselves understood in other contexts. Because they have "no ready-made cultural 'script' for their experiences, they must remake their stories as they go, telling of illnesses and social breakdowns for which ordinary metaphors are profoundly unsuited."[106] This inability to effectively co-narrate means that, unlike the classical model of identity transition, which points like an arrow from separation through liminality to aggregation, refugee narratives are usually crafted "in the midst of the story" and so focus on "uncertainty and liminality, rather than progression and conclusion."[107]

Being caught in this protracted liminal state can have several negative consequences. One consequence, as mentioned previously, is social invisibility. In the post-exile landscape, the liminar exists as "the unseen seeing," or as a "specter" that watches with hyper-alertness while remaining invisible to those it observes.[108]

A second consequence is stigmatization. In addition to being "structurally 'dead,'" the liminar is also "regarded as unclean with contact being prohibited or curtailed during liminality lest they should 'pollute' those who have not been 'inoculated' against them."[109] In other words, it's not only that the liminar is unintelligible to observers; it's also that, because the liminar appears to violate social conventions, her presence is cast in a negative light. These dynamics can leave exiles feeling like "a leper"[110] and can stimulate feelings of alienation and jealousy toward their new peers. "*They* belong in their surroundings, you feel, whereas an exile is always out of place."[111]

Taken together, invisibility and stigmatization impede aggregation. Unlike other tourists and travelers, invisible exiles cannot escape liminality by returning home and resuming everyday routines. On the contrary, with no past to return to and no apparent future within reach, invisible exiles enter a harsh liminal space, which functions as "a non-place, an antechamber suspended between the living and the dead."[112]

Moreover, rather than abating over time, these harsh feelings of nonbelonging usually intensify. With the benefit of hindsight, invisible exiles reflecting back on exile describe being initially unaware of just how far they stood from aggregation. It was only as travelers repeatedly tried—and repeatedly failed—to navigate their new social worlds that the immensity of their nonbelonging became clear, both to themselves and to others.

Unfortunately for invisible exiles, inadvertent blundering is a major obstacle to new belonging. This outcome is somewhat unexpected because blunders create opportunities for learning. By making mistakes and receiving feedback, travelers become more adept at performing in accordance with new expectations. However, the people observing these blunders and providing this feedback often have the opposite reaction. Instead of seeing blundering as learning, they interpret errors as evidence of incompetence and justification for exclusion.

One author, for example, arrived on a new college campus where she initially tried to conceal her history of family abandonment. "When people ask why my parents never visit, my answers are vague."[113] Her peers did not like this vagueness. "The less I say, the more questions people ask."[114] In response to their growing frustration, she overcorrected and began sharing too much. "Finally, one day when my roommate asks me why I'm so secretive about everything, I blurt out, 'Well, Cynthia, I guess it's because my mother says that this Chinaman in Montego Bay is my father, and he told me he never did the nasty with my mother. So I'm not really sure which penis exactly is responsible for my existence.'"[115] This oversharing monologue continues for several more sentences, after which the roommate "never asks me anything again."[116]

This sense of navigating a Bizarro World tightrope without knowing how far is too far versus not far enough is a common theme within invisible exile travel writing. "My attempts to strike up conversation . . . felt awkward and strained; it seemed as if their sentences carried a subtext I could not decipher."[117] Invisible exiles craved acceptance. "All I wanted was to be liked and respected, and instead, in this moment, I felt wholly misunderstood. I felt stuck in a limbo between not wanting to be known as the goofy American and holding back so much that I wasn't allowing myself to be seen or understood."[118] In cases like these, instead of finding common ground, "I felt like I was talking to an alien."[119]

In theory, these meetings of opposites could potentially lead to mutual learning.[120] One author, for example, moved to a liberal college town where her new peers were surprised to learn that she "had grown up with conservative ideas about government and Catholic doctrine against abortion."[121] Conversely, she was stunned to realize that they "didn't know where their food came from"[122] or "what it feels like to pee in a cup to qualify for public benefits to feed your children."[123] In theory, encounters like these could lead to mutual learning.

Invisible exile narratives, however, suggest that mutual learning during encounters is rare. Far more often, when differences arise, observers do not question their own beliefs and instead see invisible exiles as solely responsible for any divergences. This finding aligns with other work in literary geography where, "for the insider, the newcomer sometimes seems naive and stupid, behaving and acting in an improper manner yet largely unaware of his profound ignorance of place."[124] This assumption that the fault lies with the traveler diminishes the likelihood that the observer will engage in the self-reflection required for mutual learning.

One author's story about an incident during her freshman year history class aptly captures this dynamic. Partway into the lecture, she raised her hand and said, "'I don't know this word. . . . What does it mean?' There was silence. . . . The professor's lips tightened."[125] When the lecture resumed without a response, the author could sense she'd done something wrong. "Whenever I looked up, there was always someone staring at me as if I was a freak. Of course I *was* a freak, and I knew it, but I didn't understand how *they* knew it."[126] When class ended, a classmate said, "'You shouldn't make fun of that. It's not a joke'. . . . I went straight to the computer lab to look up the word 'Holocaust.'"[127] Only then did she realize the significance of her question and the reason why asking it had appeared so offensive. She kept quiet after that. "I didn't raise my hand for the rest of the semester."[128]

Stigmatization is a common Bizarro World experience. It arose when an author disclosed her homelessness to the family of hikers who, until that moment, had welcomed her over a shared cup of tea. "The man reached out and pulled his child toward him and the wife winced and looked away."[129] Stigmatization also arose when an author declined a Sunday movie invitation out of habit, and her roommate "rolled her eyes" whispering, "she's *very* devout."[130] For other invisible exiles, it was the way local kids were "trailing us, laughing and talking too fast to be understood."[131] It was "the hungry, curious way people gawk at me."[132] It was that "speaking in the soft black southern vernacular that was our everyday speech made me the subject of unwanted attention."[133] It was discovering that people with her background were perceived as "pushy, offensive, and unhygienic."[134] It was that, "until now I was proud of my English," but because people "kept correcting my mistakes and laughing at my accent, . . . I felt humiliated and different."[135] This stigmatization explains why, in Bizarro World, "I spend most of my time without company."[136]

These rejections stung, not only because they conveyed nonbelonging but also because they coincided with a learning process that, in other circumstances, could have moved invisible exiles from liminality to aggregation. The author who initially signed up for the wrong classes, boarded the wrong buses, and misunderstood the textbook eventually started figuring things out. Despite failing the first exam, "on the next exam I scored a B, and by the end of the semester I was pulling A's."[137] When she received her first high score, she looked around for her friend—the one who told her how to use the textbook—so they could celebrate together. "Then I remembered," after the Holocaust debacle, "she didn't sit with me anymore."[138]

These experiences of stigmatization challenge the theory that liminality arises through separation and the *erasure* of former traits, as opposed to persisting because of the way old traits *linger* out of context. Although invisible exiles have separated from their former homes, "I could not shake the feeling that I still carried the aura of a Hasid, emitting vibrations of alienness to all around me."[139] Another religious exile would likewise "walk on the street dressed like a gentile and it would seem as if everyone was staring at me, that they could tell I was different. . . . I was wearing the right clothes and I had grown out my hair long and full, but what if it was in my face on my forehead, written for all to see?"[140]

Experiences like these do not undo the fact that travelers are in exile, but it raises questions about how much *separation* has truly occurred. One author felt too Vietnamese in the United States, but "in this Vietnamese muck, I am too American."[141] Another tried to leave her rural southern roots behind only to realize that, "living away from my native place, I became more consciously Kentuckian than I was when I lived at home. This is what the experience of exile can do."[142] Similarly, fifteen years into exile, a third author was "only beginning to truly understand . . . how difficult it is to sever all ties with the culture and religion in which you are born."[143]

Due to these experiences, many invisible exiles wondered whether, because of the way their past lingered, they could ever *aggregate* otherwise. Instead, it seemed that, even "if you went, no matter where you ended up, like every immigrant you'd still feel the invisible dirt of your motherland on the soles of your feet."[144]

As a result, in Bizarro World, instead of feeling connected to new social groups, invisible exiles often felt even more strongly defined by their former identities. Those experiences intensified the feeling of being an outsider. "Watching the natural interactions of students and faculty, I was jealous of their seeming unity. They shared a background and culture of American normality."[145] By contrast, this author felt like a disoriented stranger who did not understand how to navigate mainstream culture. Then, when she finally discovered a group of students who seemed to share her experiences, they did not accept her. "Queens College had a large percentage of immigrants enrolled, eager to begin their American experience, and it was with this group of students that I felt the most in common. However, my Connecticut accent didn't convince others that I too was a newly arrived foreigner."[146]

It was the same for another invisible exile when she began her post-rural life. "There was no language for whatever I represented on campus. Scholarships and student organizations existed to boost kids from disadvantaged groups such as racial minorities, international students, and the LGBTQ community. I was none of those things."[147] However, not occupying a pre-articulated form of diversity did not erase her sense of difference. "Professors and other students often assumed from looking at me or hearing me speak that I was a middle-class kid with parents sending me money."[148] Although she knew those assumptions were incorrect, she didn't have the words to explain who she was or what she was experiencing. "I didn't know the term 'first-generation student' and didn't grasp yet that I had in fact 'grown up poor' and was still very much 'living in poverty.'"[149] Lacking this narrative, she felt physically present but socially unseen.

Many invisible exiles struggle with this lack of a ready-made language for self-expression. "Unformed words clustered in my throat," but they "were stillborn, caught in the long delivery between me and the outside world."[150] It wasn't that he had nothing to say, but rather that he had no confidence in being heard. To communicate is to share a perspective, which did not feel possible in this liminal space. "To have a perspective you needed to be seeing from somewhere, to be located, and I didn't feel located at all. I didn't belong to any place."[151]

Unfortunately, when it comes to overcoming these disconnects, invisible exiles rarely receive much support. As Karen Armstrong explains in her memoir about leaving her convent and enrolling in college, "what I needed was a crash course in the current political scene, but this was not available, and I felt so ashamed of my ignorance that I did not dare to ask questions that would have revealed its abysmal depths."[152] She saw activists who would probably have helped if asked. "But the ringleaders looked absolutely terrifying to me—unapproachable in their righteous rage. I would as soon have approached a charging bull as expose my political naïveté to them."[153]

Other invisible exiles felt similarly judged, for instance when asking for directions after arriving in Japan. "According to one [information booth] supervisor, foreigners have been seen toting touring bicycles out of baggage claim but no one has tried to ride out directly from the airport. I am about to be the first fool to try."[154] As he made his way toward the city—not knowing whether it was legal to ride in the street but unable to locate anything resembling an American sidewalk—he saw another cyclist and called out for help. "I chase after him, shouting questions in my bad Japanese: *How do I get out of this airport? Where can I find inexpensive lodging? Where is the public rest room?* He looks at me the way people look at dogs foaming at the mouth."[155]

These examples explain why, instead of asking for help, travelers often try to conceal their differences and insecurities. As one author explained, the worst part of Bizarro World wasn't the blunders but rather the way people constantly misunderstood. "I *looked* normal. I couldn't tell the story every time I crashed, couldn't just crash into people with my story, too. The story felt too emotional, too strange to put into words."[156] As a result, rather than explaining, "my instinct was just the opposite—to keep my blindness invisible."[157]

These experiences underscore that the end of one self does not automatically lead to a soft, playful exploration of open-ended possibilities culminating with the aggregation of a tidy replacement self. Instead, harsh liminality is like a swamp where travelers get stuck. Like Karen Armstrong arriving late to dinner and penitently kissing the floor, blunders are a primary way that invisible exiles learn to decipher and adhere to new social codes. Having made that mistake once and noticed the incredulous responses, Armstrong never again repeats it. In short, she becomes more like the people around her. However, the public nature of these learning moments—realized through the shocked and judgmental responses of peers—undermines the increased acceptance that could have otherwise emerged, leaving her instead in social limbo.

This catch-22 means that, from the perspective of invisible exiles, each blunder—however humiliating—moves them one step closer to fitting in. But instead of seeing learning, observers see transgression. In Armstrong's case, they see a young woman who, until that moment, appeared normal. However, cast in this new light with her lips pressed to the floor, she looks eccentric, perhaps dangerous, and certainly deranged. The most common response—disapproval followed by avoidance—then perpetuates liminality by withdrawing social support for a new place to call home.

Are You Happy Now?

In the years after exile, one author occasionally ran into former acquaintances who inevitably asked, "So, are you happy now?"[158] This question probably seemed reasonable to the people doing the asking. After all, wasn't unhappiness the reason he'd left, and wasn't happiness the outcome he'd hoped to achieve? That might be true. But, at least initially, invisible exile does not work that way. Instead of blossoming into a new self with a new life in a new place, protracted liminality can become increasingly painful.

The deepening pain of Bizarro World is a recurring theme within invisible exile travel writing. As liminality persisted, "the charm of being in the wilderness was completely gone."[159] With each new rejection, "self-consciousness crept in. I was no longer as carefree."[160] Instead of finding a new sense of connection, "I find . . . the black-hollow desperation of a runaway."[161]

These experiences of intensifying malaise can make liminality feel like a space of wasting away. This wasting away can be metaphorical, for instance through the alienation that leaves travelers feeling unseen. It can also be literal, for instance among invisible exiles whose disorientation is so profound that they struggle even to eat. As Karen Armstrong observed when reflecting back on the first years of her post-convent life, "I was just not making it out here as a secular. . . . What was the point of feeding my body when my mind and heart had been irreparably broken?"[162]

The combined experience of environmental illegibility and social stigmatization often leads to increasing—rather than decreasing— feelings of nonbelonging. "As weeks churned into slow months, I felt more isolated."[163] One author "constantly felt like an unwanted outsider."[164] For another, "now that I'm here, I feel so adrift."[165] In cases like these, "months passed, and I found myself with a kind of loneliness I had not anticipated."[166] This loneliness felt like erasure. In Bizarro World, "I no longer knew who I was."[167]

At this point in their journeys, the quest to leave Plato's Cave feels difficult and painful. Instead of embarking on a quixotic grand escape, "I felt rootless, lost. To be a nomad, always wandering, had always sounded romantic. In practice, to be homeless and living out of a suitcase was a little foretaste of hell."[168]

Moreover, as this hell stretched from days and weeks into months and years, invisible exiles felt increasingly discouraged. At the start of the exile journey, "everything had been new. My search was underway. The great epiphany felt possible, close at hand."[169] But as time dragged on, as liminality set in and aggregation did not follow, "I wondered if my search was nothing but . . . an enormous white flag in disguise."[170] This liminality no longer felt like a temporary reprieve. It was "not a miracle in slow motion, but a slow-motion death."[171]

Thinking about harsh liminality not as a playful reprieve enabling growth but as a space of slow-motion decay helps explain why the question *Are you happy now?* can feel like twisting the knife. Such questions might be appropriate for soft liminality where travelers temporarily step away from the strain and drudgery of everyday burdens, but harsh liminality casts the question in a different light. Harsh liminality is born of a painful separation, and it persists in part due to the social withholding of somewhere new to arrive.

From this perspective, asking about happiness makes no sense. "When I look back" on the moment of exile, "it feels like I was at the borders of common sense, and the sensible thing to do would have been to keep quiet, keep going, learn to lie better and leave later."[172]

But that's not what she did. Waiting felt impossible. She had to risk it. "And here is the shock—when you risk it, when you do the right thing, when you arrive at the borders of common sense and cross into unknown territory, . . . you do not experience great joy and huge energy. You are unhappy. Things get worse. It is a time of mourning. Loss. Fear."[173]

Comments like these reinforce the conclusion that harsh liminality is not an ascent into happiness and instead can quickly become a downward spiral. However, just because things get worse does not mean exile was the wrong choice. On the contrary, "however disorienting my transition, I knew that I had chosen the right path."[174] From this perspective, the obstacles of Bizarro World are rescripted "as some kind of Herculean challenge that I must endure in order to become a new woman. . . . In shedding my skin, I am being reborn."[175] Despite the pain and loneliness, "I am on this bike, on my spirit quest, in the desert wilderness. . . . This is where I must learn."[176] Like Carlos Eire choking down his first chicken sandwich, gagging was "my very first step toward becoming an American, my first successful attempt at being someone other than myself."[177]

Although these experiences can feel unpleasant, travelers hope they will lead to new beginnings. This hope is the latent promise of Bizarro World. "It's wild here, a corner where tides, winds and tectonic plates collide in a roar of elemental confusion. . . . Something's changing. Something's forming. I can't see it yet, but I can feel it coming."[178]

In conclusion, after being stripped of prior belonging by passing through the Void, travelers enter a confusing and disorienting liminal state where their past selves are gone but their future selves remain uncertain. Many travelers tried to prepare for exile through imaginative travel and scouting trips, but those preparations fall short of the socialization required to effectively navigate new social worlds. Even travelers who felt well-prepared still found themselves stumbling. For invisible exiles, these blunders are learning opportunities that bring them into closer alignment with the new environment. For onlookers, however, those blunders call attention to travelers' differences, which leads to stigmatization and avoidance. As a result, although liminality is a common theme within the travel-writing genre, the *soft* liminal framework of a playful reprieve rarely does justice to the *harsh* liminal experience of getting stuck in the nonplaces between the living and the dead.

One possible way out of harsh liminality is aggregation, for instance by constructing new identities that are more legible to peers. Those endeavors, including the questionable notion that one might find aggregation through assimilation, are the subject of the next chapter.

SIX

The Project of Strategic Assimilation

Basic Training

Social scientists generally see assimilation as an outdated concept. Although scholars once described it as a desirable way to integrate minority groups into a dominant culture, this framework may now feel problematic because of the way it normalizes an imagined mainstream, ignores complex identities, and devalues cultural diversity.

Despite scholarly claims that assimilation has fallen out of favor, assimilation strategies are a ubiquitous feature within invisible exile travel writing. At least during certain moments, travelers set assimilation goals for themselves, goals they pursue by participating in structured retraining programs. By changing their clothing, language, knowledge base, employment, bodies, values, and lifestyles to match the group they wish to join, invisible exiles hope assimilation will bring an end to liminality.

In societies that endorse us/them systems of belonging, assimilation is often imposed as a prerequisite to group membership. In practice, however, even when travelers gleefully embrace an assimilation project, these endeavors rarely lead to full acceptance.

This breakdown occurs not because invisible exiles do not aspire to assimilate—they do—or because U.S. culture does not reward assimilation—it does—but rather because society encourages assimilation while simultaneously impeding it through three forms of gatekeeping. First, the so-called host group restricts access to the resources needed to begin assimilation work. Next, assimilation is not only about acquiring new skills but also about submitting to new and sometimes unwanted discipline. Then, even if invisible exiles clear those hurdles, other factors—like age, race, gender, and ability—splinter assimilation into different paths, some of which are upwardly mobile while others lead to dead ends. For these reasons, even in societies that reward assimilation, embracing this goal rarely leads to exile's end.

To better understand the complicated embrace of—and subsequent disenchantment with—assimilation, I begin this chapter with examples of assimilation endeavors as described in invisible exile narratives. Next, I provide a theory-informed evaluation of assimilation's supposed fall from grace. I then demonstrate that the lived experience of invisible exile provides a powerful counternarrative by displaying a generally optimistic embrace of assimilation strategies, at least in certain contexts. I review these strategies to explain how travelers go about these endeavors and what they hope to gain. I then analyze the gatekeeping practices that either impede assimilation or steer it in restrictive directions. In response to this limited acceptance, many invisible exiles subsequently conclude that, instead of prioritizing assimilation, which favors host goals over travelers' needs, travelers might be better served by constructing other paths to more self-directed futures.

"My Fingerprints Vanished . . . like a Serial Killer Trying to Escape the Law"

Starting with examples from invisible exile travel writing, when Kwame Onwuachi arrived at the Culinary Institute of America, it felt as though he had arrived in the magical world of Hogwarts. As explained in his memoir *Notes from a Young Black Chef,* this stimulating environment with its "smart uniforms" and "volumes full of spells" promised to "magically transform whoever walks through the gates of the campus from a muggle into a chef."[1]

Onwuachi wanted to be transformed. After waking up strung out in trashed apartments one too many times, he was tired of the powerless role he'd been assigned since birth. "If I had followed the rules, the guidelines and parameters that had been set for me—as a young black man in America—would have ground me down."[2] Onwuachi wanted something different. "I never wanted to be seen as a failure again. . . . I never wanted to feel powerless again."[3] As an alternative, he decided to reinvent himself as a different self with a different future. "I resolved that I would become someone not to be messed with, not through fear but through talent."[4]

Onwuachi's tool for self-transformation was the Culinary Institute of America, a place where he would accept training in the skill and art of French cuisine. Gaining entrance to this environment, however, was challenging. At $33,000 per year, tuition was a significant barrier. "I wanted to be there; they wanted me there; but between us stood the Grand Canyon of insufficient funds."[5] With family help, a payment plan, and constant outside employment, he cobbled together enough cash to eke through. The stress, however, took a toll. It left "me crying over my knife roll" at night.[6]

Next, once tuition was paid, Onwuachi spent thousands of hours allowing his body, mannerisms, and instincts to be reshaped. Like a soldier handling a rifle, he clung to his knives and was drilled daily in their use. "We burned through hundreds of pounds of produce, dicing until the correct dimensions and physical knowledge were in our bones."[7] This training made Onwuachi functionally interchangeable with other professional chefs. "My fingerprints vanished. I looked like a serial killer trying to escape the law."[8]

Alongside acquiring technical skills, this metamorphosis required Onwuachi to submit to a new system of discipline. French kitchens generally follow "the *brigade de cuisine* system," which was devised by a French military chef in the late nineteenth century and "is structured as you'd expect from a soldier."[9] The brigade's foundation "is an iron-clad chain of command. Like the military, a kitchen is set up to function as one brain with many hands."[10] Also like the military, the brigade's system of authority often shades into abuse. When Onwuachi was subjected to this abuse, for instance being verbally berated for minor mistakes, he coped by reminding himself that the verbal onslaught was just part of the script. "I was playing a role. . . . He yelled, and I was yelled at. Simple, really."[11]

Later, as a Culinary Institute graduate, Onwuachi's career began to thrive. He found good work, made plans to open his own restaurant, and received a much-coveted invitation to appear on the reality television show *Top Chef*—all signs of a successful self-reinvention.

By other measures, however, Onwuachi's metamorphosis remained incomplete, most notably because French chefs are overwhelmingly white. It is perhaps no surprise that he found himself in such a white world given that his goal was to break with the places and rules established for Black men and embrace different rules and opportunities—the ones established for other people in other places with other skin colors. Nevertheless, no matter how far Onwuachi's skills advanced, only he among his colleagues was expected to keep "paying dues," and only he was targeted by traffic cops while driving home after late-night shifts.[12]

Even the invitation to appear on *Top Chef* did not remain uncolored. Despite Onwuachi's credentials from a top culinary school, and although the producer agreed his French cooking "was amazing, absolutely amazing, . . . The problem is, Kwame, and I hate to say it, but America isn't ready for a black chef who makes this kind of food. . . . Fine dining: velouté. What the world wants to see is a black chef making black food, you know. Fried chicken and cornbread and collards."[13]

Onwuachi had to make a choice. He could refuse to pander to racial stereotypes and miss his television debut, or he could swallow his pride and use the show's publicity to advance his other goals. His new restaurant was opening soon. Since "*Top Chef* would hugely boost my exposure," to help the restaurant succeed, "I agreed."[14] The experience, however, was a clear reminder that, even though he could chop and sear identically with other chefs, full acceptance remained incomplete.

Welcome to Basic Training, a Place to Become like Everybody Else

Although the Culinary Institute had a formal name, Onwuachi gave it a second, metaphorical name as well. He called it Basic Training. "Basic training," he explains, operates "in the 'break you down to build you up' kind of way."[15] In a military context, "a fresh-eyed, soft-bellied grunt heads to Camp Lejeune or Fort Benning and emerges as a hard-bodied, steel-willed soldier."[16]

Far from being a passive or gradual process, the spaces of Basic Training are intense and grueling, and not everyone who enlists succeeds. "In the military, basic training is meant to weed out the weak from the strong, those who cave under pressure from those who rise to the challenge."[17]

Additionally, instead of accommodating individuality, Basic Training transforms people into interchangeable cogs who perform prescribed roles to perfection. In other words, the landscape of Basic Training is about conformity. It does not value ludic ambiguity or cultural hybridization. It is about complete and utter compliance with the norms of the group that trainees hope to join.

This description of Basic Training resonates with descriptions from other invisible exiles who, instead of enrolling in culinary school, enrolled in actual military boot camps. As Jaquira Díaz explains in her memoir *Ordinary Girls*, while growing up in an unstable family in Puerto Rico, she, like Onwuachi, initially followed the subservient script imposed on her as a poor woman of color, in her case by dropping out of school and becoming romantically involved with abusive men. Then, also like Onwuachi, Díaz made the decision to exile herself from that externally imposed containment zone by pursuing a type of redemption she felt was only possible through complete metamorphosis.

Díaz's tool of metamorphosis was the U.S. Navy. "In the navy, I became a completely different girl."[18] Like Onwuachi's experience in culinary school, Díaz's acceptance into this new world was conditional on her mastering new skills, which required considerable dedication. "I worked hard—harder than I'd worked my whole life."[19] Also like Onwuachi, thriving in the navy meant consenting to discipline. "I took orders. I followed the rules."[20] Through this process, Díaz reinvented herself. No longer the high school dropout, "I aced my safety classes, personnel inspections, physical fitness tests. I aced the firefighter training, the gas chamber, weapons training. I felt like I was a fucking superstar."[21]

Despite these successes, as was the case for Onwuachi, becoming a boot camp superstar did not translate into total belonging. For Díaz, the barrier was not race but sexuality. One evening while riding an emotional high after accomplishing a grueling task, Díaz shared her first ever kiss with a woman. "For the first time in my life I finally felt like myself, like the woman I was supposed to be."[22] Military gatekeepers, however, did not see it that way. Instead of seeing Díaz's queer liaison as a sign of personal growth, they saw it as the end of her military career. After the hookup, she endured weeks of harassment and was eventually hounded out of the navy. "I had loved boot camp. . . . But I would eventually run."[23] Once again, mastering skills and following orders was not enough to secure full belonging.

For the purpose of this chapter, Basic Training includes any location where travelers undergo systematic retraining to adapt themselves to new environments. Crucially, as illustrated by Onwuachi's and Díaz's experiences, a defining characteristic of Basic

Training environments is that, although the quest to escape liminality can take many forms, the version available in Basic Training is not self-directed. These are not stories about discovering inner truths and becoming unique snowflakes. Instead, Basic Training is about learning to conform with someone else's agenda. Whether in the military or in the kitchen, these structured reeducation programs link belonging with compliance.

Moreover, even when trainees triumph as celebrity chefs and boot camp superstars, liminality often persists. Basic Training provides one possible route toward social integration, but it comes with no guarantees, especially for people whose race, class, gender, sexuality, religion, ability, and trauma are seen as nonconforming.

Like Onwuachi and Díaz, many invisible exiles describe going through periods when they fiercely committed to assimilationist endeavors. To pursue this goal, travelers searched for places offering structured support for self-reprogramming. Then, while in Basic Training, authors worked themselves to the bone—physically and emotionally—to make themselves fit a prescribed mold. They gained skills and accepted discipline until they could perform the new identity interchangeably with peers, only then to realize that, even post-assimilation, their exile remained ongoing.

In invisible exile travelogues, Basic Training takes many forms. Onwuachi chose culinary school and Díaz chose the navy, but invisible exiles found structured spaces for resocialization in many places. Some travelers found it in educational settings, including language courses, cultural programs, study abroad opportunities, alternative high schools, community colleges, and four-year universities.[24] Other travelers participated in workforce training programs[25] or various military boot camps.[26] A few travelers found Basic Training through religious institutions[27] or medical facilities.[28] As supplements, travelers often used libraries, bookstores, and video streaming services to augment their learning process.[29] Travelers learned from the school of hard knocks, as well, while living on the road,[30] hiking over mountains,[31] and cycling across continents.[32]

Regardless of the exact location, the key characteristic of a Basic Training environment is that it provides a crash course on how to live otherwise. For invisible exiles, entering Basic Training is about embracing rigorous resocialization with the goal of becoming interchangeable within a larger group. It is about trying to gain acceptance by acquiring the traits of one group and by erasing lingering markers of ever having identified otherwise.

That is the goal, anyway, but invisible exile life history writing suggests that assimilation—even when rigorously pursued—is rarely as magical as it may initially appear. Even despite an eagerness to fit in, travelers often encounter considerable gatekeeping. In this chapter, I divide gatekeeping into three analytical subtypes: front-end gatekeeping (such as Onwuachi's Grand Canyon of insufficient funds), which prevents easy entry into Basic Training environments; mid-phase gatekeeping (such as the French kitchen's system of abusive discipline), which weeds people out as they move through the process; and end-phase gatekeeping (such as the racialized invitation to appear on *Top Chef*), which limits full acceptance for reasons unrelated to technical or symbolic mastery. Because of these gatekeeping practices, assimilation alone rarely provides invisible exiles with the full acceptance they desire.

Is Assimilation a Dirty Word?

A key tension of this chapter is that, even though assimilation theory is widely criticized within academia, self-initiated assimilation strategies are nevertheless a recurring theme within invisible exile travel writing. I agree with my critical scholarly peers that demanding assimilation as a precondition of acceptance is exclusionary. However, for travelers experiencing traumatic displacement and liminal ostracization, the idea of finding a new tribe is understandably alluring. The trauma of harsh liminality—of being stuck as neither/nor—can motivate travelers to embrace the idea that, by letting go of old identity markers and embracing new social norms, they might finally find acceptance. However, regardless of what travelers might gain, this chapter also shows that assimilation rarely leads out of exile, no matter that travelers may wish it so.

In sociology, assimilation means to become like the dominant group. In early twentieth-century immigration studies, "the assimilationist perspective defines the situation of immigrants as involving a clash between conflicting cultural values" with immigrants on one side and hosts on the other.[33] To resolve these clashes, immigrants were expected to let go of conflicting values and replace them with the values of the dominant group. In short, assimilation is about "unlearning" the norms and traits previously acquired in other places "to successfully learn the new way of life necessary for full acceptance" elsewhere.[34]

To the extent that assimilation actually occurs, scholars generally agree that it involves acquiring both technical and cultural knowledge. *Technical knowledge,* sometimes referred to as "instrumental culture," involves "the skills, competencies, and social behaviors necessary to make a living and contribute to society."[35] In Kwame Onwuachi's culinary narrative, instrumental culture involved learning how to negotiate a payment plan and mastering the precise techniques for chopping vegetables.

Alongside technical knowledge, *symbolic knowledge,* sometimes referred to as "expressive culture," involves "the values, worldviews, and patterning of interpersonal relations and sensibilities that give meaning and sustain the sense of self."[36] In Onwuachi's case, expressive culture included compliance with workplace discipline and deference to racialized foodways.

Taken together, mastering instrumental and expressive culture should, in theory, grant access to group membership. By becoming fluent in these "shared meanings and understandings," as well as by reducing "linguistic and cultural discontinuities," assimilation can potentially promote "a sense of belonging."[37]

Although social scientists generally agree that technical and symbolic knowledge plays a role in assimilation, scholars disagree about why and how immigrants acquire this knowledge. Classical scholarship frames assimilation as natural and spontaneous. "Assimilation occurs by the diffusion of values and norms from core to periphery. By osmosis, as it were, these new cultural forms are gradually absorbed by immigrants, bringing them closer to the majority."[38]

Other scholars disagree. For them, assimilation is not inevitable and is instead a strategic choice. "Assimilation strategy occurs when the individual decides not to maintain his or her cultural identity by seeking contact in his/her daily interaction with the dominant group."[39] Even if immigrants cherish their previous identities, beliefs, and customs, in societies that penalize difference and reward conformity, choosing to adapt can be pragmatic. As a conscious choice, this adaptation is neither passive nor the spontaneous outcome of osmosis.

In this debate, evidence from invisible exile narratives aligns with the critics. While osmosis certainly plays a role in Onwuachi's culinary training and Díaz's military boot camp, the reason they enrolled in structured retraining programs was to gain *explicit* training in instrumental and expressive culture. Moreover, given the fierce gatekeeping involved—for instance, the physical and financial hurdles—it seems unlikely that this resocialization would have occurred by osmosis alone. Instead, invisible exiles consciously chose to embark on a journey of self-transformation, including by working to overcome the gatekeeping obstacles obstructing their path.

Another point of disagreement among scholars is that, even if an assimilation strategy is possible, scholars disagree about whether it is the only way—or even the best way—to achieve belonging. On the one hand, for over a century, "assimilation" has been "the most frequently used concept for immigrant groups' integration with American society, and it is closely monitored and often measured by academic studies using a variety of indices."[40] These indices measure success according to the extent to which each successive generation moves "a step closer to more complete assimilation" and "a further step away from ethnic 'ground zero.'"[41] The underlying assumption is that increased levels of assimilation translate into upward economic and social mobility.

I agree that U.S. culture often rewards conformity and punishes difference. However, a new wave of scholarship pushes back against the idea that this state of affairs is either natural or desirable, as well as against the assumption that assimilation is the best and only path to success. This new research challenges the assumption that assimilation was ever the dominant immigrant experience; that adaptive processes are linear; that previous traits are inferior; that new traits are better; that everything from the past must be abandoned; that immigrants change but hosts do not; that cultural hybridization is rare; that there is such a thing as the mainstream; that immigrants assimilate into the mainstream instead of into other subcultures; and that assimilation leads to upward mobility.[42] This research also suggests that, even among lifestyle migrants who are determined to embrace new norms, "reality bites once they have settled into life in the destination" and can observe firsthand all the ways that the new environment may not align with their prior expectations.[43]

I agree with each of these criticisms. However, despite the abundant empirical evidence and moral sway supporting these critiques, invisible exile life histories demonstrate that, at some point during their journeys, travelers frequently initiate explicit projects of letting go of old identity traits and acquiring the new ones they associate with an imagined mainstream. To be clear, these assimilation endeavors do not negate the above critiques even as they shed light on the lingering influence and alure of assimilation myths. Exploring these dynamics also sheds light on the intensity of gatekeeping that persists even in this so-called era of global mobility and hybridization.

Invisible Exiles Purposefully Embrace Assimilation Strategies

Starting with questions of intentionality, one key claim of this chapter is that, at certain moments within invisible exile travel narratives, many authors endorse assimilation as an explicit goal. Like other exiles stuck in a harsh liminal swamp, "you can spend a lot of time regretting what you lost," or "you can become a beginner in your circumstances."[44] Given the "urgent need to reconstitute their broken lives,"[45] many refugees replace the "fatalism" of succumbing to liminality with the intention "to become someone else by instantly and forcefully adopting allegedly Western habits."[46] The hope is that assimilation will lead to new belonging. This hope makes sense given that, in U.S. culture, the exiles heralded as "marvels of adjustment" are usually those who "seem, on the surface at least, to have contributed their talents entirely to their adopted country."[47]

Although all migrants might consider an assimilation strategy, this option may hold special allure for invisible exiles. As explained in previous chapters, invisible exiles often entered or were pushed into exile precisely because they felt drawn to the identities and lifestyles outside Plato's Cave. It makes sense, then, that after exile, travelers would try to acquire those norms and values through explicit resocialization.

This explicit desire to pursue assimilation is a ubiquitous theme within invisible exile life history writing. "I wanted to fit in, not stand out in any way. I was hell-bent on becoming an American."[48] For one author, "I'm supposed to build roots in this foreign land" by "doing something that makes me feel like an Israeli rather than an immigrant."[49] For another author, making the decision to embrace education and self-discipline—two values he associated with the white middle-class—was a way to "prove I belonged."[50]

To prove belonging, travelers remade themselves both through external identity markers and through internal thought patterns. One common method involves self-conscious attempts to master new styles of communication. From a technical perspective, this might mean learning a new language, which is why, when an ex-Orthodox author entered exile with her son, "the first thing I do is teach [him] English. We read books together and watch *Sesame Street*."[51] From a symbolic perspective, it means mastering verbal and nonverbal social cues, which is why another author bought a copy of *Job Interviews for Dummies*. Without explicit retraining, the fear was that "I would say the wrong thing, or look the wrong way, and it would only confirm what everyone knew: just another Hasid, freakishly stuck in a medieval world, unable or unwilling to make the necessary accommodations to modern living."[52]

Alongside speech patterns, invisible exiles also embraced other identity markers, such as clothing, accessories, and foodways. One author embraced all three. In lieu of traditional clothing, "I bought a pair of jeans . . . and a T-shirt with the American flag."[53] He went to a barbershop where "you could choose your hairstyle from the [photos of] celebrities on the walls," and he chose a style associated with American rap music.[54] Next, he added accessories. "I bought a necklace, a wristband, and some sneakers. I was sure no one looked more American than me."[55] Finally, dressed in his new attire, he and his brother went to a restaurant to celebrate his American future. "The menu was confusing . . . but burgers seemed like the most American dish, so we both ordered one."[56]

In such examples, travelers embrace assimilation as an intentional choice by consciously remaking themselves in the image of the group they hope to join, even if they do not yet fully understand the cultural nuances involved. These statements of intentionality are ubiquitous within invisible exile travel writing. "I decided I had to begin. Somewhere. With something. These new steps were all mine."[57] Instead of languishing in liminal ambiguity, "at least if we made that first step we had somewhere to go, we had a purpose."[58] Finding this purpose was about taking charge of the invisible exile experience. "Life before had happened to me as childhood happens to everyone. The mark of adulthood is when we happen to life."[59] By embracing an assimilationist undertaking, travelers hope to end liminality and find belonging.

Travelers Reinvent Themselves Through Structured Intervention, Not Passive Osmosis

Alongside the will to be remade, another key claim of this chapter is that, at least during certain moments, invisible exiles pursued this goal by embracing intensive, structured programs of assimilation-style resocialization. Socialization generally involves both active and passive processes. On the active side, social institutions like schools and churches provide explicit instruction, but passive socialization plays a role as well. In keeping with the Foucauldian-inspired interest in diffuse rather than disciplinary power, for people born into a community, "more often than not, we were not taught the rules of our lives, we simply absorbed them."[60] Similarly, in immigration research, it was long assumed that assimilation would unfold primarily through osmosis.

While acknowledging the important role of passive socialization, my sense based on invisible exile narratives is that few exiles, while trapped in a harsh liminal state, actually believed that passive osmosis would resolve their situation. Instead, travelers overwhelmingly opted for more structured, intensive retraining. This focus on explicit retraining differentiates invisible exiles—at least at this point in their journeys—from other travel writers, including those "aimless strollers" engaged in "highly individualized" and "nonpurposive" travel organized around "disconnection," "freedom," and "caprice."[61]

Invisible exiles, by contrast, often pursued self-initiated retraining with the intensity of a drill sergeant. One author gave himself a study schedule. "I read for ninety minutes, then took an hour break, often to watch *Seinfeld,* then read another ninety."[62] He used physical discipline to reinforce his learning. "If I didn't get the problem right, I had to . . . get on the floor for twenty-five push-ups."[63] He then stuck with this routine regardless of whether he enjoyed it. "That's a skill everyone needs: the determination to finish disappointing tasks."[64]

Another author who endured months of Bizarro World blundering decided to remake herself in the image of her new college roommate—someone who, in her mind, embodied mainstream culture. To achieve this goal, she bought clothes from Walmart in the style she thought her roommate might wear, even though wearing those items—even only in the privacy of her bedroom—felt uncomfortable. "I took them off immediately, feeling that somehow they were immodest."[65] She tried again the following evening, "and was again shocked by the sight of myself."[66] She repeated this ritual every night for a month until the clothes—like the persona they seemed to symbolize—began to feel like a second skin. This daily ritual was part of her Basic Training.

Jaquira Díaz, the navy bootcamp superstar, had a similar experience when, after getting hounded out of the navy, she committed to another project of intentional retraining, this time by enrolling in a college writing program. "I looked at the concentrations. . . . I put an X next to Creative Writing. And then I circled it, twice, just to make sure there was no confusion."[67] For Díaz, this decision was a declaration. Instead of absorbing a storyteller's identity through osmosis, she would claim that identity through explicit retraining. "My whole life, I'd always known. But the x, the two circles, they made it feel real. Now other people would know, too. And I would do whatever I had to do, but I would be a writer."[68]

To be sure, these assimilation projects were rarely quick or easy. On the contrary, depending on the context, the ability to blend in might require years of clothing refinements, hormone therapy, and medical appointments with therapists, voice specialists, and surgeons.[69] In many cases, it involved imprinting a new identity onto the contours of the body and withstanding the pain of that process. "I belong here, and the work I'm doing now proves it. By the end of the first day, my knees are shaking and I've got splinters in my hands. My clothes are sticking to my body."[70] The process could be difficult. However, "on the days that feel dark and endless, I make myself a simple promise: I'll get out of bed in the morning. Then I'll head up the hill to class. If I put one foot in front of the other, day by day, I'll move closer to the light at the end of all this struggle."[71]

Despite these challenges, invisible exiles were often deeply committed to the idea of Basic Training. "For me, this was no summer vacation. . . . I needed this. . . . For the first time, I was making my daily life fit into a bigger purpose: climbing out of the place I'd been born into."[72] By embracing Basic Training, invisible exiles made progress, little by little, toward a potential escape from Bizarro World. These incremental gains then reinforced their belief that, by committing to active resocialization, rather than relying on passive osmosis, travelers could more effectively find their way to a place where they belonged.

The Quest to Become Just like Everyone Else

Alongside committing to structured resocialization, another key point of this chapter is that, at least while in Basic Training, invisible exiles measure success based on the extent to which they appear to match their new peers. Even among travelers who eventually lose faith in assimilation myths, the primary goal of entering Basic Training is to gain acceptance by shedding old identity markers and perfecting the ability to blend in with new spaces.

To be clear, Basic Training is not simply about reinvention, a process that could lead to many possible outcomes. On the contrary, Basic Training is about a subtype of reinvention where the goal is to mold travelers completely and perfectly to fit a prespecified environment by making them functionally identical to and interchangeable with the people around them.

For a religious exile, this meant "wearing jeans and a V-neck" and letting her hair grow "long and straight. . . . I must look just like everyone else here. . . . Finally, the blessed feeling of anonymity, of belonging; are they not the same?"[73]

For a transgender author, it meant "being seen as . . . just an average girl, no identity politics or medicalized body complications."[74] In her eyes, "it was this passing . . . that mattered the most."[75]

Similarly, for an international refugee, it meant perfecting his written English. "No accent there, on paper; I own those words completely. . . . They get me to where I want to go, without anyone asking dumb questions or giving me funny looks."[76] His conviction that assimilation was the path to belonging explains why he felt such delight when his teacher praised his writing. After receiving that feedback, "I know for sure that I can be an American, that not only can I pass for one, but be one, for real."[77]

Importantly, another subtheme within these quests is that travelers often measure success not only by acquiring the norms and values of their new environment but also by erasing the traits they associate with Plato's Cave. A key assumption within classical assimilation theory is that immigrants must abandon the old to embrace the new. Although I agree with critiques of this theory—that many immigrants prefer their pretravel cultures and that cultural mixing is common—invisible exile travel writing nevertheless suggests that, at least while in Basic Training, travelers often embrace erasure, sometimes as a practical matter and sometimes with considerable glee.

One author, for example, felt that achieving a new sense of cultural belonging could only happen if she let go of the values associated with her former world. "If one is to succeed in modern society, one must unlearn anachronistic, out-of-place attitudes. This unlearning applies to money as much as it applies to sex."[78]

Another author likewise believed that he needed to let go of his past spirituality to make space for new, queer-positive thinking. "This trip would . . . pry my fingers from the parts of myself that had to go. I was holding tight to the narratives of my youth like treasure. But with hands full, I couldn't receive anything new."[79]

Similarly, for a third author, abandoning her former ideas about so-called healthy eating allowed her to embrace new foodways, like *chicharrón,* which is "fried pigskin that's been boiled for hours in a vat of lard."[80] Precisely because this dish contradicted her previous identity so thoroughly—"I can't remember when I last had bacon in my house"—"my experience of *chicharrón* is a different kind of affirmation. It suggests that I have let go of the old and given myself permission to move on."[81]

To be sure, as discussed in previous chapters, letting go can feel painful. However, while in Basic Training, invisible exiles are less likely to dwell on those losses and more likely to frame them as evidence of forward motion. One author, for example, contrasted the painful erasure of the Void with his far more jubilant self-erasure via assimilation. "This is such an enjoyable death. Or should I call it murder? . . . What English word do you use when you kill yourself and become a new *you*?"[82] Far from mourning his lost culture and lost identity, he approached those losses with glee. "Yes, Carlos [his former name] got self-squashed. . . . Squashed flat, like a cockroach in the kitchen sink."[83]

Through this exuberant self-squashing, travelers hoped to gain access to the life opportunities available to their new peers. This determination to become like the supposed mainstream explains why one author joined school sports and took college entrance exams even though her high school guidance counselor said foster kids like her could not succeed. By taking those steps despite his objections, "I'm fully aware that this is another step toward mainstreaming—doing what my peers are doing, regardless of how different my background has been from theirs."[84]

As these examples demonstrate, many invisible exiles go through periods when they feel eager to reinvent themselves to match their new environment. During those moments, authors often define success based on the extent to which they shed their past cultural traits and made themselves appear interchangeable with everybody else.

Assimilation Strategies Are Quests for Safety and Belonging

In exchange for assimilating, invisible exiles hope to receive several benefits. After passing through the Void and getting bogged down in Bizarro World, exiles often feel trapped in a place where they belong nowhere and possess little agency. By contrast, by embracing assimilation, travelers hope to gain acceptance, control, and security.

Starting with acceptance, invisible exiles pursuing assimilation often yearn for an emotional belonging that transcends technical membership. At this point in their journey, invisible exiles often possess "de jure citizenship,"[85] for instance, by having formal refugee status—or, in Kwame Onwuachi's case, by holding a formal degree from the Culinary Institute of America. However, "cultural citizenship,"[86] or the ability to use technical and symbolic mastery to claim belonging and have that claim validated, involves a level of emotional belonging that runs deeper than "formal structures of inclusion."[87] Indeed, this gap between formal and emotional belonging is a recurring theme in immigration studies where, regardless of legal status, immigrants and refugees sometimes struggle "to feel 'at home'" in new settings.[88]

In a similar manner, a key reason why invisible exiles embrace assimilation is their yearning to experience emotional acceptance. One author, for example, had trouble befriending the villagers who all seemed to hide from her whenever she approached until a local woman offered her a set of non-Western clothing. Adopting the vernacular style felt strange because her U.S. body had a different shape. "I am already feeling like a hippopotamus."[89] The social effect, however, was instantaneous. "Suddenly, I am not so strange. My eyes, my hair, my skin are the same; but now I am wearing the traditional clothes of the village. They are willing to accept me. From that point on, I am one of them."[90]

Another author, a mixed-race woman hoping to find acceptance within affluent white society, similarly yearned for emotional belonging, and she used consumerism, spirituality, and marriage as tools in this quest. Shopping was relevant because consumption signifies class identity. "I plunk that credit card down time after time after time at these expensive stores, spending more than I can afford to try to buy the certainty that I belonged."[91] Spirituality was likewise significant because certain religious traditions are associated with whiteness. "I learn how to pray to a God who discriminated against Black men."[92] She took a similar approach when deciding who to marry. "A white boy, a white *husband* was the route to the destination I desperately craved without even knowing it: belonging in America."[93]

As these examples show, regardless of legal standing, travelers often see assimilation as a primary pathway to cultural and emotional acceptance. With this acceptance, travelers hope to gain greater control over their lives.

This search for control is why one author mastered the technical skills and symbolic cues of family law not only to gain middle-class acceptance but also to reduce her vulnerability to other people's agendas. As a teenager, she had broken free from her mother's abuse, but her younger sister was not so lucky. Time and again, ignorant social workers took her sister away from the author's protective care and returned her to the abusive home. "My only hopes of ever rescuing [her] lay in my understanding of how the system works and getting respect from the people who work in it."[94]

Similarly, the link between cultural mastery and self-determination explains another author's commitment to reading books he disagreed with. This included a bestseller promoting "a real Machiavellian worldview, where every action is about getting ahead. You have to break others . . . using real strength, but also lies and misdirection."[95] He opposed that moral code. "That's not me. I believe in honesty."[96] However, he nevertheless saw value in mastering those concepts. "Life is a hustle, . . . and [that book] helped me understand the game. . . . Once I understood their methods, I understood their priorities, and I could combat them. Even though I was playing the game straight, that gave me power."[97]

For many invisible exiles, gaining acceptance and control through assimilation looked like a way to achieve a third benefit, which was an enhanced sense of security. Marginalized groups often use performances of assimilation to protect themselves from harm. Women of color, for example, often have no choice except to travel between social worlds while completing their daily rounds, and "their adjustment to the 'world' around them" is "a necessity" for economic and physical safety.[98] Similarly, for women escaping religious cults, assimilating into the dominant culture can help reduce revictimization. "Although education and work history were unimportant inside the cult, they are necessary in order for these women to have any level of financial security in mainstream society."[99]

For similar reasons, invisible exiles experiencing harsh liminality often embrace assimilation in the hope it will enhance acceptance, control, and security. To be clear, this recurring faith in assimilation is both pragmatic and worrying. "Whilst it is not and nor should it have to be the aim of every trans person to 'pass,' the fact is that, in the twenty-first century, those who wish to pass have the best opportunity to succeed."[100] Due to discrimination, which persists despite claims of living in a globally cosmopolitan world, for many invisible exiles, assimilation—or the perceived lack thereof—continues to influence economic and social well-being.

Three Types of Host Gatekeeping

Shifting gears, in the remainder of this chapter, I focus less on invisible exiles' assimilation strategies and more on the gatekeeping that blocks their path. Even in societies that reward assimilation, not all travelers are afforded the same opportunities to acculturate. On the contrary, some travelers have easier access to assimilation-supporting resources. Additionally, even when travelers achieve identical levels of cultural mastery, dominant groups use other barriers—like race and gender—either to block inclusion or to allow it but only on inequitable terms. These barriers apply as much to invisible exiles as to other social groups.

These outcomes reflect negotiations between invisible exiles and the groups they hope to join, a negotiation between so-called travelers and hosts. *Travelers* in this context are new arrivals to a social space, and *hosts* are existing members who may or may not welcome the newcomers into their midst. To be clear, a host is not someone with stronger legal claims to belonging. On the contrary, in Onwuachi's culinary narrative and Díaz's description of military boot camp, both authors are full legal citizens, just like their peers.

Rather, from my perspective, the language of newcomers and hosts more accurately reflects a power disparity. In the case of invisible exile, travelers assert belonging in new spaces. In response, more powerful groups claim the privilege of granting or denying that belonging.

In us/them social contexts, assimilation is often framed as the ticket to acceptance. "The 'requisites' for one person to belong mean that s/he has to assimilate to the language, culture, values, behavior and religion of the dominant group."[101] In reality, however, "the processes of belonging are always tainted with deep insecurities about the possibility of truly fitting in, of even getting in."[102] Instead of automatic acceptance, "everyday life becomes a constant negotiation whereby the migrants seek to reconcile their experiences with their hopes and dreams."[103] In this negotiation, powerful groups use gatekeeping to regulate access.

In invisible exile narratives, gatekeeping occurs at many points. Front-end gatekeeping, as I call it, involves blocking access to the resources needed to begin an assimilation endeavor. Midpoint gatekeeping involves requiring submission to new discipline as travelers move through the resocialization process. Endpoint gatekeeping involves denying full membership to certain people regardless of their legal identity or their level of technical and symbolic mastery. Cumulatively, in invisible exile travel narratives, more powerful groups use all three practices to police the boundaries of belonging.

Gatekeepers Block Access to Assimilation-Enabling Resources

Starting with front-end gatekeeping, one way to control who can achieve mastery over instrumental and expressive culture is to regulate who has access to the educational resources enabling this mastery. Examples from history include prohibiting slaves from learning to read and discouraging women from reading newspapers. By blocking literacy and restricting knowledge, these practices limited who in society had the capacity to wield economic and political power.[104]

Invisible exile narratives are filled with examples of front-end gatekeeping. The groups that travelers hope to join often require formal documents, prior knowledge, financial resources, and schedule compliance as preconditions to access socialization resources. However, not all exiles can meet these prerequisites, which undermines their capacity to fully participate within the new environment.

Starting with documentation, citizenship is one form of front-end gatekeeping, and the inability to prove citizenship can impede access to assimilation-enabling resources. One author encountered this gatekeeping when applying to college. "My classmates all had the security of being U.S. citizens! How would a college admit me without *papeles*?"[105]

Another author won the right to apply for a green card, but he needed official documents to get his application processed. In this catch-22, "I needed to produce civil records to escape a country so broken that we had no civil records."[106]

A third author similarly found that, despite her undisputed citizenship status, she could not enroll in school without a birth certificate. Acquiring this document was difficult because she was born at home, her birth was never registered, and her family disagreed about her birthdate. When a Delayed Certificate of Birth finally arrived, "it felt oddly dispossessing, being handed this first legal proof of my personhood: until that moment, it had never occurred to me that proof was required."[107]

Next, even when legal status is clear, invisible exiles often have to prove prior knowledge before they can access even the most basic educational and job training programs. One author needed to present a high school diploma, which he did not have, or pass a series of English and mathematics tests, which many invisible exiles with his background cannot do.[108] These requirements create barriers for people who grow up in communities that do not provide access to standardized education.

Alongside content-based barriers, front-end gatekeeping also operates through an uneven awareness of how educational systems operate. "Little by little, a new realization began to sink in: Most everyone else in my class had a leg up on me without being aware of it. They had knowledgeable parents, SAT tutors, awareness of how the system worked."[109] This difference in implicit knowledge can make test taking difficult regardless of test content.

Then, even when invisible exiles test well and begin receiving college brochures in the mail, they may not know how to evaluate schools or navigate admissions. "I had no idea how to process any of them,"[110] and no one she knew could offer advice. "They knew even less about the process than I did."[111]

Next, even if travelers overcome these hurdles, class status creates an additional barrier. Transgender folks, for example, often require medical intervention to fully embody their authentic gender, but "not all trans people come of age in supportive middle- and upper-middle-class homes, where parents have resources and access to knowledgeable and affordable health care that can cover expensive hormone-blocking medications and necessary surgeries."[112] The desperate desire to overcome these financial barriers explains why one author became a teenage sex worker. "Without money of my own, I had no doctors, no hormones, no surgeries. . . . So we used the resources we had—our bodies"—to pay for medical care, even though it meant risking "HIV/AIDS, criminalization, and violence."[113]

Class status creates barriers for other travelers as well. Earning acceptance to a prestigious university does not mean invisible exiles can afford to matriculate. "I was frantically emailing a department head, explaining my 'financial situation' and begging for help," but the conversation "eventually hit a brick wall with the financial aid department."[114] Even in situations that come with financial aid, this aid is often only available to applicants whose parents are willing to disclose their federal tax returns. "I wasn't even sure my parents filed taxes, but if they did, I knew Dad wouldn't give them to me if he knew why I wanted them."[115]

These financial realities introduce considerable hurdles to using educational settings—a primary site of socialization—as a resource for assimilating into the imagined mainstream. "I started my college career needing something I didn't get because the need went unacknowledged on a form that didn't ask the right questions. Most people who write laws weren't raised by their grandparents due to economic hardship, and the federal aid formula is based on the assumption that parents help pay for college."[116]

Then, even if invisible exiles have documents, knowledge, and financing, they often encounter a fourth front-end barrier: scheduling. An author pushed into early motherhood prior to invisible exile, for example, had trouble accessing educational resources after exile, at least until discovering "adult programs—easier for a mom like me to work with than a traditional undergraduate environment."[117]

Scheduling barriers negatively impact transgender authors as well. This includes "the frankly unbelievable waiting times" for intake appointments, as well as a second protracted wait time before doctors will agree to perform surgery.[118] In the meantime, the author was living his life and engaging in other activities, including ones that would require him to relocate for work, before the drawn-out process of gender transition was complete, which would mean restarting the process all over again with a new provider. In other words, even after committing to gender transition, because of these scheduling barriers, "I was going to be stuck in this hideous limbo ... for years."[119]

Assimilation Requires Submission to New Systems of Discipline

After overcoming front-end gatekeeping, many invisible exiles run into mid-phase gatekeeping, which, in my terminology, occurs after travelers gain enough access to begin a structured assimilation project but before the process is complete. For invisible exiles, one of the most significant types of mid-phase gatekeeping involves submission to new systems of discipline. Whether someone is born into a culture or assimilates into it, membership is often predicated on compliance with group norms, which is why, even when travelers disagree with some norms, they may choose to submit rather than risk exclusion.

As discussed earlier in this book, systems of belonging involve both empowerment and control. Conformity can grant access to resources, but that access is predicated on submitting to group norms. Within immigration studies, "migrants enter a society and an economy within which rules and rituals produce consent,"[120] and acceptance within these systems "depends on how one is constituted as a subject who exercises or submits to power relations."[121] Assimilation in these situations involves not only acquiring cultural competency but also consenting to new systems of hierarchy and discipline.

For invisible exiles, assimilating into preexisting, externally defined subject positions usually involves acquiring some traits they desire, along with others they may oppose. This was Kwame Onwuachi's experience when he submitted to the head chef's verbal abuse while training to become a French chef. Although being yelled at was unpleasant, the legitimacy of his claim that he belonged in a professional kitchen hinged as much on his deference to authority as his ability to sauté.

As I explore later in this book, many authors like Onwuachi eventually push back. Rather than adopting "a second blind nature" reminiscent of Plato's Cave,[122] travelers eventually challenge the new norms that feel unethical or undesirable. However, that resistance usually comes later, after travelers feel confident enough in their new identities to risk breaking some of its rules. By contrast, in the early stages of self-reinvention, the tenuous claim to belonging often inhibits protestation, even to practices that feel unsavory.

This quest to find belonging helps explain why one transgender author embraced normative gender traits, including ones that felt oppressive. In claiming femininity, "all of the cruel expectations that society puts upon women . . . were now falling on my shoulders."[123] In response, she began obsessing about her weight, became overly apologetic, and began speaking in uncertain tones. "It was exactly the kind of madness that I found least appealing in the lives of the women I knew," and yet, despite these moral objections, "what I wanted was to *belong*. If being female—to others, at any rate—seemed to include self-doubt, insecurity, and anorexia, then some part of me felt, *Okay, well, let's do all that, then*."[124] At this point in her journey, complying with gender norms—even harmful ones—felt necessary to exit liminality and aggregate into womanhood.

Invisible exile travel narratives are filled with similar examples of deference to assimilation-based discipline regardless of whether authors felt actual agreement. In one instance, when filling out immigration paperwork, "I had to choose between being African, African American, Hispanic, or Caucasian. This threw me at first because I had never thought of myself as African. In Somalia we identified ourselves by our tribes."[125] He checked a box anyway, even though it did not feel correct, just to keep the process moving.

As a second example, "up until the day I set foot in Everglades Elementary School, I'd had two last names, each equally significant. . . . But everything changed in an instant at that school in Miami. 'Only one surname per customer,' the assistant principal said."[126] This author, like the previous one, felt disconcerted by this change in how he was permitted to self-identify. However, also like the previous author, he selected from the pregiven options rather than risk being jettisoned from Basic Training.

Alongside these externally imposed labels regulating identity, assimilation also requires adhering to lifestyle norms. For one author, this meant embracing the limits—and not just the perks—of her new middle-class identity. "Even after I cleaned up and changed my lifestyle, my new world brought a different kind of entrapment—overwork and a search for perfection, for happiness targets, and goals like excessive workouts at the gym, the drive for more money, more property, more acceptance by my peers."[127]

Another author felt similarly coerced into a normative lifestyle because of his need for medical care. To afford health care, he needed insurance, which "means having a job. It means staying in one place, so it means being stable."[128] These requirements felt unappealing to this anti-establishment sojourner who would have preferred to be hopping freight trains.

As part of this discipline, invisible exiles often feel policed even in what they are permitted to think. One author became a religious exile because she wanted the freedom to think for herself. Later, as an aspiring literary scholar who was also epileptic, she felt drawn to the work of Alfred Tennyson, a fellow epileptic. His "walled up" characters "resonated with the hallucinatory visitations that kept me imprisoned in my own inner world."[129] She wrote her doctoral dissertation on this largely unacknowledged theme within Tennyson's writing. However, the ableist professor assigned to review her thesis rejected the premise that scholars should spend time analyzing such "odd passages" and "weird seizures," which he deemed "unsuitable for a doctorate."[130] Based on his belief that academia should not make space for such nonconforming embodiments, she was denied her degree.

Taken together, these descriptions of external discipline illustrate the range of mid-phase gatekeeping that invisible exiles face while in Basic Training. This mid-phase gatekeeping can lead both to empowerment and to discomfort. For a transgender author, "I grew very quickly to enjoy this newfound respect and power" of being seen as male; "I did not however enjoy the way it made me appear a threat to girls who stood at the bus stop."[131] Even so, because invisible exiles often defined success based on their ability to appear the same as everyone else, travelers often, at least initially, saw no option except to comply.

Assimilation Often Follows Segmented Pathways

The above examples demonstrate the challenges arising from front-end and mid-phase gatekeeping. After clearing those hurdles, many invisible exiles face a third set of barriers. End-phase gatekeeping, in my use of the phrase, involves discriminatory practices that bifurcate assimilation into different paths. "Even assuming that one person is willing to assimilate, there might always remain other dimensions (e.g., place of birth or skin color) which would prevent full sameness and, therefore, expose that person to discourses and practices of socio-spatial exclusion."[132] A condition of "segmented assimilation" exists when society rewards privileged immigrants with upward mobility while giving less-privileged immigrants a negative reception.[133] White immigrants from Europe, for example, are welcomed as white-collar professionals while Black and Brown immigrants are redirected to strawberry fields and slaughterhouses. These experiences are an important reminder that, even given identical levels of technical and symbolic mastery, "not every form of belonging is possible, as 'people are not free to choose their belongings outside of the bounds of power.'"[134]

Within invisible exile narratives, assimilation often takes segmented forms, for instance, bifurcated by gender. One transgender author was accepted as female once she changed her physical appearance. However, this led to subservient treatment. Now that people saw her as female, male coworkers felt uncomfortable socializing with her after work, car salesmen began offering her inferior financing, and strangers began sexually harassing her in dark parking lots.[135]

Another invisible exile who initially felt eager to embed herself within traditional cultures likewise began to feel differently when she realized her acceptance depended on her submission to gender subordination. During a special community meal, the group seated around the table began to sing and she joined in, but the women around her told her to stop. "'We can sing when we are by ourselves, but not when the men are present.' And suddenly, for me, the magic, the joy, the spirituality—and the bonding—is gone."[136]

Another author experienced a similar second-class welcome when she joined the ranks of long-distance thru-hikers, a group overwhelmingly composed of men. As part of the thru-hiking culture, hikers leave notes for each other in spiral bound notebooks distributed across the trail. These "trail registers had become my only link to other hikers, my way of communicating with my north-drifting community."[137] She initially enjoyed reading these notes and adding her own, until she "saw something horrifying."[138] Several of the male hikers were entertaining themselves by describing her in sexually derogatory terms. As a female hiker, she was vulnerable to "Pink Blazing—the act of following female hikers they wanted—tracking."[139] In other words, even though she had mastered the technical and symbolic knowledge of the thru-hiking community, due to her gender, many members of that community would only accept her on terms that felt objectifying and menacing.

Alongside gender, another form of end-phase gatekeeping involves race and ethnicity. Despite one traveler's eager embrace of American culture, he experienced frequent discrimination because of his Cuban background. "I'm not allowed to join the crossing guard patrol," "my bike gets torn apart," and a boy from school "loves to call me a spic."[140] These experiences complicated his previous understanding of Plato's Cave. Plato, he writes, focused exclusively on the cave dwellers who exerted control among themselves, but Plato said nothing about the policing that might arise from people outside the cave. "He . . . said nothing about those in the real world who would have to contend with the refugees from the world of illusion. What crazy bastards, those cave dwellers," he imagined them saying.[141] That's what his teachers and fellow students seemed to be saying about him.

Other authors—especially authors of color—experienced similar hostility in response to their attempts to assimilate into upwardly mobile socioeconomic positions. One author spent years refining his ability to perform in accordance with white middle-class norms, which eventually made him eligible for parole. However, instead of celebrating this accomplishment, prison administrators "threw their efforts against me. . . . They even changed their own rules so they were no longer required to give me a hearing for placement in the halfway house, since there was no way, with my record, they could legitimately deny me."[142] He eventually gained access to the halfway house where, during his free time, he enrolled in college. But again, his caseworker objected. "'You're a convict,' she said. She used that word as an insult. 'You got to lower your standards. You can get a job at a gas station. Maybe. If you're lucky.'"[143] When he defied her expectations by earning straight A's, she retaliated by reducing his privileges. When that didn't deter him, she ordered his reincarceration. "You have to accept that you are at the bottom of society, and you always will be."[144]

Examples like these demonstrate that, even after passing through Basic Training, some invisible exiles receive limited acceptance into the social worlds of their choosing not because they lack technical and symbolic mastery but because the culture in question is exclusionary. These exclusions undermine the appeal of assimilation work. "As any real exile will confirm, once you leave your home, you cannot simply take up life wherever you end up and become just another citizen of the new place. Or if you do, there is a good deal of awkwardness involved in the effort, which scarcely seems worth it."[145] Then, even for people who embrace assimilation, it requires considerable effort to overcome these cumulative forms of gatekeeping. As one author phrased it, "this wasn't going to be as simple as my childhood fantasy character play or my occasional outings as Jake," his imagined avatar; "actually *transitioning* . . . *was* going to involve a lot of the pain I had subconsciously feared."[146] Identity transition was a theoretical possibility, but society introduced many barriers, and not everyone could or wanted to pay that price.

In conclusion, invisible exile travel writing provides ample evidence that many authors eagerly embrace assimilation strategies. At least during certain moments in their journeys, travelers explicitly try to master the technical and symbolic knowledge that, they hope, will bring them into alignment with other members of the groups they hope to join. Although osmosis plays a role, these self-initiated assimilation projects are usually intentional, rigorous, and highly structured. Moreover, instead of hybridity or individuality, these projects are about learning to fit into a homogeneous and externally defined mold. However, the hoped-for rewards of acceptance, control, and security do not always materialize. Even despite a traveler's eagerness to assimilate, gatekeepers frequently block the assimilation path. The resulting disenchantment then leads many invisible exiles to search for alternative escapes from Bizarro World liminality, for instance by co-narrating a little less with the dominant group and a lot more with fellow travelers, which is the subject of the next chapter.

SEVEN

The Healing Potential of Co-narration

Footsteps

Storytelling is a potent tool for promoting health and wellness. Employees commiserate over the proverbial watercooler. Doctors listen to tales of woe while administering to the sick and injured. People broadcast deeply personal and painful experiences over daytime television and social media. Likewise, in the realm of trauma recovery, putting words to distressing events is an important part of the healing process.

Sharing stories is especially healing when speakers have access to empathetic audiences willing to listen and provide supportive feedback. Empathy, however, cannot be assumed. Even in today's culture of trauma talk, speaking out—whether about workplace issues, sexual assault, or racial discrimination—can lead to serious consequences like lost jobs, smear campaigns, and defamation lawsuits. Even in lower-stake settings, cultural norms often signal that some people's stories and some types of suffering are seen as not normal, not credible, or not important.

Earlier in this book, I highlighted the significance of silencing prior to exile. Moving away from Plato's Cave, however, does not necessarily free authors from cultures of silence and shame. On the contrary, *narrative asymmetry* is a central theme in invisible exile travel writing even after leaving. I use the term *narrative asymmetry* to describe situations where travelers adapt their speech and storylines to conform with new norms but where those efforts at mutual intelligibility are not reciprocated. In these situations, travelers become linguistically and culturally multilingual, which enables them to engage with topics important to host communities. Host groups, however, often remain unfamiliar with the narratives travelers need to tell. This situation creates a persistent lack of mutual understanding concerning the shape and meaning of life events.

In invisible exile travel writing, this narrative asymmetry manifests in three distinct ways. The first is limited imagination. Hosts often lack direct experience with exilic dysphoria, displacement, and liminality, and so they often respond to travelers' stories of exile with confusion or disbelief. A second asymmetry involves selective attention. When interacting with travelers, hosts tend to focus on the aspects of stories that align with their agendas, rather than prioritizing the storyteller's perspective, which distorts the narrative process. A third asymmetry involves moral stance. Hosts frequently pass judgment on the meaning and significance of exile experiences, whether they are knowledgeable about the experiences or not, which often leads to stigmatization.

In all these ways, and often without conscious or malignant intent, the narrative resources available after exile are often a poor fit for travelers' storytelling needs. This mismatch creates imbalanced communication and social silencing, rather than mutual recognition. This silencing is problematic because putting words to difficult experiences is a crucial tool for trauma recovery and identity work.

As an alternative, many invisible exiles seek—and greatly value—opportunities to co-narrate with fellow travelers, particularly in spaces where hosts are absent. In these *places of our own,* invisible exiles find a more authentic and supportive self-reflection in the eyes of other people walking similar paths. In addition to providing emotional and logistical assistance, these filtered spaces can function as safe havens where travelers can receive empathy, experience catharsis, and engage in identity work. To be clear, these environments are not perfect and may, at times, feel triggering or exclusionary. However, in these filtered gathering spaces, invisible exiles often feel a sense of release from the constant demand to adapt, self-censor, or justify.

This chapter is about where travelers go to find these validating reflections and narrative supports. To explain these dynamics, I start with examples of the challenges and opportunities related to conarration as recounted in invisible exile travel writing. Next, I review the theoretical links between co-narration and identity work in the context of trauma. I then provide examples of narrative asymmetry to show how limited imagination, selective attention, and moral stance often lead to stigma. Next, I explain how travelers construct filtered places of convergence where, at arm's length from other observers, invisible exiles can co-narrate with fellow travelers. Last, even while acknowledging these spaces' imperfections, I conclude by reiterating the value of shared but sheltered spaces for co-narration and recovery.

"A Safe Place Where We Could Openly Be Ourselves"

Starting with detailed examples of co-narration as recounted within invisible exile travel writing, when Janet Mock moved from Honolulu to New York City, she was eager to blend in. As explained in her memoir *Redefining Realness,* "it was the first time in my young life when I was able to be just another twenty-two-year-old living in the big city, shedding the image that my hometown had assigned me."[1] After years of transphobic bullying, the opportunity to be silent about her gender felt like a precious resource. Instead of being "forced . . . every day to combat preconceived ideas and stereotypes," this chance to be unremarkably female created the "freedom to declare who I was" and to independently "discover who I wanted to be."[2]

Alongside wanting to blend in, however, Mock also wanted to feel truly seen. These competing desires explained her anxiety when falling in love. For Mock, the rambling conversations that usually build intimacy between lovers felt asymmetric. Her potential new boyfriend seemed at ease. He "spoke effortlessly about the details of his life," including his childhood, hobbies, and work.[3] He "seemed available to the world because he knew, somewhere deep within himself, that the world was available to him."[4] Mock, however, had a different perspective. She wanted to share her stories and life experiences, but intimacy seemed risky given her history of rejection. "If he knew me, then this would end."[5]

In short, Mock faced a paradox. Keeping silent about her transgender history freed her from other people's judgments, but it also erased large portions of her identity. Living without this full self-reflection—without the opportunity "to see your life reflected in someone who speaks directly to whom you know yourself to be"—was "an utterly lonely place to be."[6]

One potential alternative to either staying silent or risking rejection is to seek support from people walking a similar path. For example, years before, as a high school student in Honolulu, Mock participated in a transgender support group called Chrysalis, "a safe place where we could openly be ourselves without the commentary of the outside world."[7] In this filtered space, the teens could discuss gender issues if they wanted. Or, away from cisgender judgment, they could temporarily forget about gender and instead simply be, talking and laughing with ease. The support group also hosted visiting guest speakers who showed Mock "that having an everyday life out in the world in the daylight was a possibility."[8] In short, within this filtered co-narrative space, Mock found acknowledgment, acceptance, and hope.

Although Mock valued peer support, as she got older, she stopped attending Chrysalis and even began avoiding her transgender friends when in public. "Some of us were considered 'passable,' while others were not."[9] Mock's hormone treatments, clothing choices, and makeup techniques made it increasingly likely that strangers would accept her as female. But "I grew self-conscious when I hung out in large packs of trans girls because the risk of being read as trans heightened."[10] If Mock was with them and they weren't *passing,* strangers were more likely to question her as well. "So I began stealthily separating myself from the group."[11]

Going solo in New York allowed Mock to reap the benefits of conformity, but it also came with trade-offs. On the one hand, it gave her greater freedom to define her own identity. On the other hand, when making friends and falling in love, she shared a version of herself that felt "distorted."[12] Blending in meant keeping secrets, and secrets "trap you, and you become so wound up" in secret-keeping that "the self you know, the you deep inside, is obscured by a stack of untold stories."[13]

To help herself heal from this erasure, Mock decided to narrate her story not just with her potential new boyfriend—who did struggle to accept her—but also by returning to places like Chrysalis, this time as the adult guest speaker holding up the mirror for the next generation. "When a girl with tears in her eyes embraces me and tells me 'I want to be like you when I grow up,' or 'Reading your story has given me hope' or 'You're my hero,' I understand the gravity of her statements."[14] Self-disclosure was not Mock's initial goal when leaving Honolulu, but making the decision to rejoin support groups and embrace opportunities for sheltered, collective reflection then facilitated her healing.

Welcome to Footsteps, a Sheltered Space for Co-narration

Janet Mock found self-reflection at Chrysalis. For Shulem Deen, it was Footsteps. As explained in his memoir *All Who Go Do Not Return,* Footsteps is the name of a New York City nonprofit created by and for people leaving the ultra-Orthodox community. Since Deen had

already adjusted to many aspects of secular life by the time he discovered Footsteps, he did not need the organization's basic services.
"Education night. GED tutoring. Résumé writing. Assistance with
college applications. I didn't need those things."[15] Nevertheless, he
felt compelled to return. "I realized that I needed the people."[16]

Deen had other people in his life, including the acquaintances he
met through work and night school. However, the social gulf separating his perspective from theirs made it difficult to build deeper
intimacies. To cope with his loneliness, Deen wandered the streets
in the evenings searching for somewhere to belong, which is how he
stumbled across Alcoholics Anonymous. "I was not an alcoholic, but I
felt a kinship with these people, each in his or her own way suffering,"
yet "determined to go on."[17]

Deen found a more durable community through Footsteps. "The
peer support, I learned, was valuable even to those who felt as though
they'd 'made it,' who already held degrees and jobs and had lovers
and closets full of secular clothes and years of secular experiences."[18]
Disowned by their families, Footsteppers attended each other's graduations, weddings, and holiday dinners. They could discuss religion
and exile if they wanted, but Footsteps was also a place to feel implicitly understood. Without requiring any explanation, the group knew
the broad outlines of everyone's story, and no one cared that some
among them still struggled with "basic concepts about the outside
world: how to buy clothes, what to do on a date, where to buy a Hal-
loween costume."[19]

In short, Footsteps was a place to find people walking a similar
path. It was an environment where fellow travelers could talk through
their troubles, or just relax in a space that did not require self-
distortion to blend in or an explanation for why one did not.

Although Shulem Deen's version of Footsteps is located in Manhattan, and Janet Mock's version, Chrysalis, is located in Honolulu,
Footsteps-like spaces include anywhere travelers cross paths and
co-narrate with each other and at arm's length from other groups.
Unlike Basic Training, which is all about trying to become indis-
tinguishable from an imagined mainstream, Footsteps is *a place of
our own*.[20] In the filtered company of fellow travelers and away from
uninformed, judgmental observers, invisible exiles see their identity
reflected in the eyes of the group. Instead of being the odd one out—
the one who must either keep secrets or self-justify—Footsteps is a

space where invisible exile is the default experience shared by most people present.

Travelers find or create Footsteps in many locations. Formal support groups were important for travelers like Mock and Deen. Other travelers likewise visited Ujamaa (Stanford University's Black Community Services Center)[21] and the Little Blue House where the University of Tulsa's human rights clubs would meet.[22] Other gathering spaces were less formal, for instance the subcultural communities coalescing around radical bookstores[23] and queer house parties.[24] Invisible exiles found each other in nondedicated spaces, as well, such as certain restaurants, bus stops, and campgrounds where, for logistical reasons, travelers were likely to congregate.[25] Moreover, in situations where physical gathering was not possible, travelers came together through online chat rooms and telephone hotlines,[26] or they used books, films, and artwork to co-narrate at a distance.[27]

In whatever form Footsteps takes, its defining feature is that it provides space for disclosure, witnessing, and validation, all of which are crucial for identity work and trauma recovery. "We don't heal by forming a secret society of one."[28]

Despite the strong links between co-narration and recovery, few invisible exiles find empathic reflections in non-exile-specific spaces. Janet Mock made friends in New York City, and Shulem Deen met people through his night classes, but neither author felt comfortable being entirely open with those peers about their past. On the contrary, being open risked misunderstanding and rejection.

By contrast, when travelers find each other in places like Footsteps—places where a greater degree of commonality can be assumed, and where anti-trans, anti-Orthodox, and other phobic aggressors are mostly absent—instead of feeling silenced, these sheltered spaces of mutual recognition make it easier to speak. These environments show travelers they are not alone, which makes space for camaraderie and conversation. These spaces are not perfect since visiting can, at times, feel triggering or exclusionary. However, having a filtered space of convergence often facilitates healing.

Co-narration for Trauma Recovery

To understand these dynamics, it helps to first revisit the significance of co-narration in identity work in the context of trauma recovery. A fundamental principle of identity theory is that "narrative is the natural mode through which human beings make sense of their lives."[29] Collaborative co-narration is crucial to that process because identity work is a negotiation between self and society. The narratives supporting this identity work "emerge in social interactions, in which certain events, and especially certain interpretations and evaluations of events, will be validated."[30]

Receiving this validating response is a valuable tool in addressing oppression. People experiencing hardship or trauma "need a witness who ascertains their status" as an oppressed, injured, or displaced person.[31] These witnessing narratives acknowledge and label the social dynamics underlying their suffering. This labeling process is important because "facts don't speak for themselves, not even the facts of raw suffering."[32] Instead, cultural categories define what counts as normal, questionable, or violent.

Moreover, when it comes to trauma, many facts do not speak at all. "All trauma is preverbal"[33] in that the "memories of such experiences are not recalled at will in the form of a complete, coherent memory" and instead "intrud[e] into consciousness in the form of fragmented visual, auditory, olfactory or tactile sensory memories."[34] This preverbal and fragmented situation interferes with co-narration because, to people unfamiliar with trauma symptoms, survivors' accounts often come across as "nonlinear" and "unreliable."[35]

These dynamics explain why a crucial aspect of recovery involves putting words to traumatic experiences. Building "the capacity to bring unconscious processes or barely articulable and deeply troubling feelings into a symbolic register" is "pressed forward as that which can heal the survivor of trauma."[36] People can undertake this work independently, for instance through journaling or other forms of therapeutic writing. However, this narrative processing can be even more powerful as a collaborative undertaking. In clinical contexts, therapists provide "a particular kind of relationship dedicated to this task."[37] In public culture, books, photographs, and films can disrupt the silence surrounding trauma while also providing survivors with comfort and inspiration.[38] In all these scenarios, the goal is to find "an empathic mirror" in the eyes of others, a mirror that "generates a secondary representation, a symbolic representation, . . . that contains and soothes an otherwise powerful and destructive feeling."[39]

The problem for invisible exiles, however, is that these mirroring dynamics are only useful when they are validating, and validation is uncommon when speakers and listeners lack a common frame of reference. "People do not tell stories in a vacuum."[40] Instead, the narrative resources available to speakers are shaped by cultural and institutional contexts that come with "an ideological slant."[41] These narrative resources shape assumptions about who gets to speak, what stories can be told, what goals are permitted, which losses are grievable, and which narratives will be discounted as implausible.[42]

These observations raise the important question, "What happens to the testimonies and stories which fail to conform?"[43] This question is important because narrative resources are "a relational pact" in that speakers can tell a story, but the audience decides whether to recognize it as valid.[44] This need for recognition makes some stories risky. "Risky stories" are stories that could potentially harm the tellers when "taken into the public sphere" and "circulate[d] beyond the storyteller's control" regarding "who can use those stories, and to what end."[45]

These risks create problems for invisible exiles, especially when exile is combined with trauma. When trauma remains unnarrated, survivors often remain "mired in a quandary between the desire to organize emotionally significant events and the inability or fear of doing so."[46] Without a narrative framework, traumatic memories live on as flashbacks, "but are not narrativized into a coherent sequence of events and reflections associated with a past self."[47] These ongoing symptoms then disrupt everyday functioning because this lack of symbolic integration "threatens or shatters the construction of a vigorous and self-sufficient self-image."[48]

Narrative Asymmetry Between Travelers and Hosts

Despite the importance of co-narration, one key claim of this chapter is that assimilation culture encourages narrative asymmetry. By narrative asymmetry, I mean that, even though travelers become familiar with other groups' norms, those groups generally remain less aware of travelers' experiences. One possible response to this asymmetry is to stop discussing things that feel surprising or out of place. When Janet Mock moved to New York, and when Shulem Deen left his ultra-Orthodox village, they were determined to move forward, leave that past behind, and embed themselves within new social worlds. However, although blending in can feel freeing, the resulting silence surrounding dysphoria, exile, and liminality leaves many travelers unable to make sense of the lingering impacts of their journeys.

One lingering impact is contrapuntal awareness. The word *contrapuntal* refers to the simultaneous awareness of multiple selves and multiple worlds. Many travelers—including invisible exiles—learn how to blend in with new environments, but blending in is not the same as forgetting. On the contrary, in many ways, the past lingers. "For an exile, the habits of life, expression, or activity in the new environment inevitably occur against the memory of these things in another environment."[49] In this assimilated yet contrapuntal state, travelers are aware of new social norms while also being aware of the "submerged but crucial presence" of "other histories."[50] Moreover, thought patterns and identity traits often persist long into exile, and they often exhibit a stubborn recalcitrance to refashioning. This stickiness of thought, memory, and embodiment helps explain why, for many exiles, "both the new and the old environments are vivid, actual, occurring together contrapuntally."[51]

This contrapuntal awareness can feel isolating. "Most people are principally aware of one culture, one setting, one home," but "exiles are aware of at least two."[52] This difference in perspective where plurality is vividly apparent to travelers while being nearly invisible to the people around them helps explain the comfort of places like Footsteps. Fellow travelers know, without being told, that regardless of how well assimilated anyone appears, other histories and experiences remain present, even if unexpressed and unacknowledged in other contexts.

Alongside contrapuntal awareness, a second environmental mirroring that is rare in other environments but common in Footsteps involves the trauma of exile. Exile is traumatic, even in situations where it leads to new opportunities. Moreover, although I agree that moving is often stressful even without forced displacement, the imperative to break with one's community to find safety casts exile in a different light, and one that non-exile observers are rarely familiar with. Invisible exiles have often endured other traumas, as well, such as sexual abuse, homelessness, or physical violence, and they may choose to co-narrate those experiences in other settings. However, those support spaces usually leave the additional trauma of exile unacknowledged.

Because of these key differences in lived experience, host communities often fail to provide adequate narrative support for post-exile healing. Instead of arriving at their journey's end and in a new place of belonging, travelers are more likely to describe feeling stuck at yet another plateau where their old self is not fully jettisoned and where assimilation culture does not make space to collaboratively process their dual awareness and traumatic losses. These disconnects lead listeners to dismiss and stigmatize the stories travelers need to tell. As a result, even after a seemingly successful assimilation endeavor, the silence required to *pass* can replicate the silence previously endured in Plato's Cave.

Silencing Through Limited Imagination

In my assessment, the narrative asymmetry preventing collaborative co-narration manifests in three key areas: limited imagination, selective attention, and moral stance. Starting with limited imagination, life experiences shape the way people understand the world—what is normal, possible, or incomprehensible. For anyone who has never experienced invisible exile, it can be difficult to make sense of travelers' descriptions of those events.

This disconnect is evident in refugee studies where the limited imagination of clinicians interferes with mental health work. "Understanding stories of suffering and healing depends on a shared world of assumptions, ideas, values and motivations."[53] Often, however, the stories that refugees need to tell "involve life circumstances that are outside the bounds of the clinician's experience," including descriptions of brutality, dispossession, and injustice that "are, in some ways, difficult to imagine" by anyone who hasn't experienced it firsthand.[54] This inability to imagine—let alone help fill in the gaps—becomes even more challenging in the context of trauma where narrative access to personal experiences is compromised.

Although one possible response to unexpected stories is to diversify taken-for-granted worldviews, less empathic responses are also common. For mental health practitioners, "when stories deviate from our expectations for plausibility, intelligibility, order and coherence, we have several options: we can expand our vision of the possible; we can interpret the narratives as defective, indicating cognitive dysfunction or some other form of psychopathology; or we can question the motives and credibility of the narrator."[55] Unfortunately, clinicians often greet unexpected narratives with suspicion. Then, although these misunderstandings arise from the listener's inability to make sense of new information, the resulting blame for narrative misalignment is usually assigned solely to the vulnerable speaker. This limited capacity to understand other worldviews can then leave travelers feeling "perpetually haunted and alone in an uncomprehending society" where they are "lost in the present without a tellable history."[56]

Invisible exile travel narratives are filled with examples of non-exile audiences that appear unable or unwilling to understand the stories that invisible exiles need to tell. In clinical settings, one author sought counseling to help herself, as a Black woman raised in the rural South, to cope with the emotional challenges of living among affluent white urban Californians. However, "in those early years therapy did not help. I could not find a therapist who would acknowledge the power of geographical location, of ancestral imprints, of racialized identity. . . . And certainly in my early college years I lacked an adequate language to name all that had shaped and formed me."[57] Instead of finding empathy and guidance, the clinician's inability to imagine other worlds replicated the problems therapy was supposed to resolve.

Another author had a similar experience when struggling to adjust to secular culture. She also sought therapy, but again, "it simply did not work."[58] Her psychiatrist flat-out refused to discuss the traumatic aspects of convent life, insisting instead that her descriptions were untrustworthy. For him, "the religious life was like the secret gardens or lost domains of literature. He saw serene processions of beautiful nuns gliding down sunlit cloisters, and imagined the convent as an enclave of sisterly peace and concord. . . . Indeed, he clung to this idyllic vision so persistently . . . that I sometimes wondered what psychological significance this fiction held for *him*."[59] Whatever the answer, the limited imagination of this mental health professional blocked his ability to co-narrate even before deep exploration began.

This problem of limited imagination occurs in nonclinical contexts as well. For instance, one author tried to use a college writing class to help himself heal from physical and sexual trauma. "I believed that I could control any story I told. If something happened, I could write about it, own it, resolve it. Simple."[60] Feverishly, he wrote draft after draft of a short story until he captured the event as he'd experienced it. "But when it was time to discuss my story in the workshop, my classmates were mostly baffled. The assignment had been to write a nonfiction essay so how could the narrator—presumably me—die at the end?"[61] His peers did not have the life experience required to understand how trauma can function as a form of self-death, which left the author without a co-narrative reflection. Instead of helping process the trauma, this failed attempt left his restigmatized emotions "roiling, half contained, like a dam waiting to burst."[62]

In examples like these, travelers do the work of putting their experiences into words, but their audiences of clinicians and peers lack the imaginative capacity to comprehend the truth of their statements. In response to this limited imagination, listeners rarely question their own assumptions. Instead, they appear far more likely to dismiss travelers' stories by concluding that nothing is wrong with the listener's worldview and that the problem lays exclusively with the teller.

Silencing Through Selective Attention

Alongside this first challenge of limited imagination, a second reason co-narration falls short involves selective attention. Oftentimes, even when audiences could understand an exile story if they wanted, listeners instead prefer to hear versions of the story that prioritize their own interests.

For example, a study of Zimbabwean refugees attending university in Britain found that British activists frequently recruited refugees to publicly share their stories. The Brits especially liked hearing stories of "heroic 'great escapes' and 'clandestine, hurried departure in conditions of real danger.'"[63] In reality, however, becoming a refugee was often less dramatic, more drawn out, and heavily bureaucratic. Additionally, many refugees felt happy in Britain and were not pining for their country of origin. However, because British audiences were disinterested in stories of bureaucratic paperwork and contented resettlement, when refugees did speak publicly, the audience usually reframed their stories as "an uplifting 'morality play' that denigrated the regime and established the moral and physical courage of the hero."[64]

This example shows how, even in situations where exiles are encouraged to speak and where audiences are eager to listen, co-narration often remains partial and biased. The listener's selective attention creates space for storytelling, but only according to the listener's priorities. This selective attention encourages speech while simultaneously foreclosing opportunities to develop fuller, more complex, and more authentic accounts of the actual exile experience.

Invisible exile travel narratives are filled with similar examples of selective attention generating silence, rather than speech. One author, for example, was frequently asked to explain himself after his expulsion from the ultra-Orthodox community. Bank tellers, bartenders, officers, pharmacists, or other strangers who asked to see his photo ID saw the picture of someone in a head covering and with side curls, then tried to square it with the "bareheaded, beardless man in secular garb" standing in front of them.[65] These strangers would then "ask, casually, the way you notice a stain on someone's shirt, or a bruised chin, or a bad haircut: 'What happened?'"[66]

The question was short and casual, but the answer was not. The author sometimes imagined how he might respond: how he might tell the bank teller or cop or bartender about ancient Israelites, lost kingdoms, duplicate narratives, arranged marriages, lost children, mentally ill parents, forbidden books, secret blogs, and agonizingly slow losses of faith. "I would imagine these conversations, but I would not have them. *That's not what they want to hear.* . . . They want to hear what *happened.* What was the incident? The moment that changed it all. But there was no moment, no solid line across time to which I could point and say: *That's* when I became a nonbeliever."[67] In such situations, audiences ask travelers to narrate, but they do little to co-construct appropriate times and spaces for telling, which makes answering difficult.

It was the same for another author who was often introduced at social events with references to her religious past, which invariably led to naive and triggering questions. In response, another acquaintance—also a religious exile—asked friends to stop mentioning her past in front of strangers. "But that didn't seem right either. I didn't want to make those years a dark secret."[68] However, deciding not to keep this secret did not resolve the question of how best to disclose it, because "neither did I want to get unduly heavy and ruin the party."[69] As a partial workaround, she began telling snippets of her story in a highly stylized manner. "It was really easier to fob my guests off with a couple of funny stories and leave it at that."[70] This strategy satisfied people's curiosity even as the larger realities—the ones her new community could not comprehend and were unwilling to accept—remained tucked away.

Moments like these are common within invisible exile narratives. At certain moments, some small detail about the traveler's past slips out and pricks curiosity, but this curiosity remains incomplete. People ask for explanations, but without doing the work to allow adequate time for co-narration, create appropriate spaces for telling, or establish the level of trust required for openness. As a result, instead of facilitating speech, these questions reinforce silence. When the bank teller or cop or bartender asked, "'What happened?' . . . I would offer a curt smile. 'Life.' Or, 'Long story.' What else could I say?"[71] Then, as these scenes replay over and over with a series of new people all behaving in the same manner, each successive nontelling hardens travelers' internalized sense that their experiences are beyond the frame of social understanding.

Silencing Through Moral Stance

Alongside limited imagination and selective attention, a third barrier to co-narration involves moral stance. A moral stance is a normative judgment about what is and is not acceptable to say, think, do, or be. When it comes to co-narrating unexpected experiences, "a critical dimension is whether the deviation from the culturally dominant narrative can be heard when it is voiced."[72] A fundamental tenet of subaltern studies is that not all stories are heard when spoken.[73] Cultural and institutional norms designate some topics as taboo—a form of silencing that heaps shame and blame on "deviations" that are perceived as "so threatening to the dominant narrative that they simply cannot be heard" even when expressed, "and so continue to be silenced."[74]

This silencing does not mean stories remain untold, but, if tellers persist in sharing risky stories, they may experience recrimination. Overt discipline could, in theory, create space for negotiation—for airing claims and counterclaims—which could raise awareness about disagreements. By contrast, sometimes the harshest response is not retribution but silence, or the refusal to even acknowledge that a speech act has occurred. "Talk does not always imply voice. . . . By being silent, one can impose silence on others."[75]

Invisible exile travel writing contains many examples of the chilling silence arising from a host's moral stance. The moral stance of secular culture explains why one author kept her Hasidic past a secret. "I discovered quickly the true opinions of outsiders"—which was that they saw the ultra-Orthodox community as dirty and backward—after which "I was too horrified to tell anyone where I came from."[76] Disclosure, she learned, led to ridicule, not acceptance.

The moral stance of mainstream psychiatry explains why another author concealed his mental health experiences. In his view, the heavily stigmatized manner in which Western psychiatry viewed natural variations in emotional and cognitive functioning discouraged openness. "There were so many people in the punk community struggling with mental health issues and not having comfortable language to describe what they were going through."[77] Without a nonstigmatizing and culturally appropriate narrative framework, invisible exiles struggling with trauma and other challenges often internalized the message that it was better not to speak.

Similarly, for a third author, the prudish moral stance surrounding sexuality helped explain why people who claimed to love Shakespeare nevertheless refused to explore the violent sexual appetites depicted in his plays, including some appetites she shared. "We tend to skim over Shakespeare's most challenging scenes, . . . or play them for absurd laughs, because otherwise they're too hard to digest."[78] Instead of interrogating these taboos, this moral stance encouraged people to pretend those topics—and the identities they represented—were simply not present.

In all these examples, travelers learn that, due to the moral judgments of their new communities, self-disclosure after exile often leads to renewed rejection. Without a nonstigmatized way to narrate past identities and ongoing exile experiences, the silence of feigned assimilation may feel like the only safe option.

Silence Through Nonspeaking, and Through Distorted Speaking

Cumulatively, the limited imagination, selective attention, and moral stance of the new community make it difficult for travelers to co-narrate exile-related experiences. The result is a repressive form of silence that can involve both nonspeaking and distorted speaking.

Starting with nonspeaking, deciding to remain silent is common in situations where invisible exiles feel their narratives will be belittled, dismissed, or are simply too complicated or challenging to hear. This nonspeaking is what Janet Mock experienced in New York when, at least initially, she withheld her transgender experiences from her potential new boyfriend. It's also what Shulem Deen experienced when he shrugged off the question, *What happened?*

Invisible exile travel writing is filled with similar examples. One author felt pressured by ableist culture to conceal her epilepsy. "My doctors warned me that even though we lived in an enlightened age, the condition still carried a stigma, and that epileptics often found it difficult to gain employment."[79]

Another author felt pressured by classism to conceal his excitement when visiting college campuses with his high school debate team. "I worried that if I expressed so much as the most fleeting hint of emotion, I would only open myself up to the teasing of my teammates. *They* had parents and siblings and cousins who'd gone to Ivy League schools; Princeton was just some typical shit to them."[80]

A third author felt similarly pressured by racism and classism to keep silent about her southern roots. "In a short period of time I learned to change my way of speaking, to keep the sounds and cadences of Kentucky secret."[81]

In examples like these, post-exile environments pressured travelers to keep quiet. Openness risked ridicule, and silence provided safety, albeit a version of safety that came with the cost of self-censorship.

Next, alongside this pressure to keep quiet, a second form of silencing occurs not when stories remain untold but when they are only told in a fragmented, incomplete, or distorted manner. Distorted tellings have the benefit of airing some version of the truth, but the ongoing need to self-censor can nevertheless reinforce a sense of stigma and nonbelonging.[82]

As examples, one author felt pressured to tell distorted truths when asked by fellow hikers why she and her husband had time to take such an extended trek. When she answered truthfully about being homeless, "people recoiled. . . . So we had invented a lie that was more palatable."[83] Instead of saying they lost their home, she began saying they sold it. "What was the difference between the two stories? Only one word, but one word that in the public perception meant everything: 'sold.' We could be homeless, having sold our home and put money in the bank, and be inspirational. Or we could be homeless, having lost our home and become penniless, and be social pariahs. We chose the former."[84]

This pressure to speak but only in a distorted manner explains why another author developed similarly partial narratives about her rural past. After extensive liminal blundering on her new college campus, she welcomed opportunities to spend time in different environments where she could present a more assimilated front. As part of her new self-presentation, she shared stories about her upbringing, but only the parts her peers found entertaining. Using this approach,

"I became a popular dinner guest, with my stories of hunting and horses, of scrapping and fighting mountain fires."[85] In hindsight, she acknowledged this self-presentation "wasn't the truth exactly" because it concealed the most painful—and most formative—aspects of her history.[86] However, it was a version of self her peers found palatable and were willing to reward with friendship.

In situations where travelers feel compelled to speak but are punished for speaking the full truth, distorted narratives can help travelers navigate these interactions with minimal negative consequences. However, regardless of whether stories remain untold or are distortedly told, the experience is often invalidating.

This sense of invalidation is what a transgender author experienced when concealing her gender history from her new college friends. "When you're close to people, you want to feel like you can share all of yourself, that you shouldn't have to hide just because something about you is different or unexpected."[87] Openness, however, risked isolation. "Honestly, I was scared. I had no idea if they would be cool or if they would reject me, and if it were the latter, I didn't want to find out."[88] Moving away from Oklahoma was supposed to set her free, but instead self-censorship followed her, even into exile.

To summarize, because of the narrative asymmetry surrounding limited imagination, selective attention, and moral stance, invisible exiles after exile often struggle to find co-narrative support. Travelers may yearn to share their stories and develop deeper intimacies, but they also feel compelled to withhold key aspects of their identities, especially the parts that are frequently misunderstood or disparaged. As a result, even if listeners accept a traveler's assimilation performance, the silence required to fit, to blend in, and to *pass* can replicate the suffocation that motivated travelers to enter exile in the first place.

Co-narrating in a Place of Our Own

This ongoing silencing explains the value of having places where travelers can co-narrate with fellow travelers and away from other observers. This enhanced sense of connection in exile-oriented spaces emerges in part because "trauma acts as a social glue, connecting victims of different events through similar stories."[89] This sense of shared understanding is crucial because storytelling only aids recovery when speakers feel "safe to disclose," for instance because the environment feels "nurturing" and the audience is "willing to listen."[90] These filtered spaces then become "safe havens,"[91] "affective sanctuaries,"[92] and spaces "of physical and emotional retreat, where one feels safe to process big or difficult emotions without judgment."[93] These havens may comprise only a handful of points on a map, but where they occur, the collective reflection of shared experiences "acts as a powerful mechanism for defence against guilt and shame"[94] and creates "a potential public space for retelling."[95]

Importantly, however, these collective gathering places are rarely based on nostalgia. Other immigrants often come together to celebrate and preserve cultural heritage. Some immigrants make "a fetish of exile" by trying to "*impress* their experience on others,"[96] or they engage in "dark tourism" by transforming their "'difficult' heritage into viable tourist attractions."[97] Nostalgia can be a resource in these contexts. For people separated from their roots—for instance, due to immigration, neighborhood demolition, natural disaster, or civil war—the yearning to revisit those places either physically or through imaginative travel can become a unifying framework. Place loss "results in identity discontinuity, which nostalgia can repair by creating a shared generational identity to mend the lost one."[98]

Invisible exiles, however, face several challenges when trying to converge around lost place attachments. One challenge is that, although they often mourn specific objects and people, they are rarely nostalgic for the prior environment as a whole. On the contrary, the suffocation of homophobia, classism, and religious abuse rarely inspires a desire to return. These negative associations interfere with nostalgia-based healing because "it is only when individuals feel a connection to the fondly remembered past that their nostalgia will have positive consequences for well-being and ability to cope with challenges."[99] Without a fondly remembered past, the call to revisit and replicate the places and cultures left behind may feel triggering and spark avoidance.

Alongside these triggering effects, a second challenge is that, for many invisible exiles, the relative obscurity of their dislocation makes it difficult to locate similarly exiled peers. I agree that global war, poverty, and climate change have ushered in an age of mass immigration.[100] However, invisible exiles usually leave in ones or twos, not hundreds or thousands. Moreover, they often take steps to conceal their exile status, as Janet Mock did when deciding not to disclose her transgender status after moving to New York. In these atomized and private contexts, invisible exiles are not easy to find. As one author explained, "there were rebels before me . . . who broke the rules openly, and everyone talked about them. But where are they now, these rebels? No one knows."[101]

The challenge of locating invisible exiles, as opposed to other immigrants, is especially well expressed in a memoir written by a woman who experienced both forms of displacement simultaneously. In her post-exile city, she could easily locate other Somalian refugees through their restaurants and mosques. However, it was nearly impossible to locate other refugees who, like herself, had separated not only from their country of origin but also from its religion. "We were all very far from where we had been born, but only I had left behind that culture. They had brought their web of values with them, halfway across the world. I felt as though I was the only true nomad."[102]

These challenges make it difficult for invisible exiles to find each other. Difficult, however, is not impossible. Moreover, invisible exile life history writing suggests that, when travelers find or create spaces to connect, these spaces provide a much-needed place of collective healing. "All of us, when in deep trauma, find we hesitate, we stammer; there are long pauses in our speech. The thing is stuck."[103] The solution, it seems, is to converse with people with similar experiences. "We get our language back through the language of others. We can turn to the poem. We can open the book. Somebody has been there for us and deep-dived the words."[104]

In short, just as *leaving* by stepping into the Void is a fateful moment, a second fateful moment in invisible exile journeys involves disclosure, or making the decision to share risky stories. In environments that offer empathic reflections, invisible exiles—like other trauma survivors—can more easily separate their sense of self from the problematic but dominant narratives otherwise told about them. Hearing similar stories can also prompt travelers to imagine ways they might reframe their narratives. This mirroring process can make healing and empowerment feel more real. "It's not a story of recovery until you tell someone else. Until that happens, it is just a hope inside you."[105]

Creating Places for Co-narration

Travelers create these spaces of shared reflection anywhere and everywhere that accommodates filtered co-narration. This includes media spaces, work environments, and public spaces.

Starting with media spaces, travelers searching for a post-exile self-reflection often find useful elements within literature, art, and film. Written work allows people "to explore their lives and experiences with the published life stories of those who have already come to provisional answers to the question."[106] As one author observed, "writers are often exiles, outsiders, runaways and castaways. These writers were my friends. Every book was a message in a bottle. Open it."[107] One author found similar co-narrative support through a documentary "about gay Orthodox Jews struggling to reconcile their faith with their sexuality."[108] Another found it through imaginary conversations with Shakespearean characters, like Caliban from *The Tempest* who, like herself, was plagued by sexual anxieties and physical ailments. "'My body is my enemy,' I told him. 'It hurts; it breaks. It wants things I can't want.' Caliban nodded. 'Yes,' he said. 'I understand you.'"[109]

Spaces of indirect co-narration with absent others are useful, especially prior to exile. However, in a post-exile context where travelers have greater choice over their mobility, most authors also deeply value opportunities to connect with fellow travelers in person.

In some cases, professional workplaces assist with this goal. One author's work as a journalist enabled her to "set off on the road to spend a year with people like me, people who had at one time been labeled 'abnormal.'"[110]

Another author accepted an entry-level position with an adoption agency—a profession unrelated to her college degree—because the environment provided co-narrative support. "I had spent my entire life trying to help other people understand adoption so they would accept me and my [mixed-race] family. Perhaps now I could help address those gaps in knowledge on a much larger scale."[111]

Similarly, a third author's professional work as a public speaker and writing coach brought her to prisons where she could co-narrate with peers. "My story is a natural fit for the women, and I share what I've learned."[112]

In examples like these, professional endeavors gave invisible exiles a structured way to connect with strangers walking similar life paths. This professional role also provided some protection because travelers could feel out potential kindred spirits without leading with vulnerable self-disclosure.

Although work environments can be useful, more often, travelers find places for co-narration in less formal settings, for instance through leisure. A queer traveler found her reflection through underground parties where "the instructions are intentionally misleading to discourage straight people and their dangerous curiosity."[113]

An immigrant traveler found peer support in a certain public park where, on specific days of the week, "Iraqis, Burundis, Rwandans, Somalis, Latin Americans, and other people all [play] soccer together.... I had no idea all these people lived in Maine!"[114]

A third traveler found camaraderie with other expats at certain diners and restaurants. "I haven't met them, but ... I've seen them congregating in Doña Lina's restaurant for breakfast."[115] Asking to join them initially felt awkward, but after clearing that hurdle, "I'm in."[116]

Similarly, for countercultural exiles, Critical Mass bike rides were a crossroads where, on the last Friday of every month, "so many of us come to see our friends and feel the power of numbers."[117] These kindred spirits congregated around anarchist bookstores and infoshops as well. "It was a cool little scene I'd stumbled into made up almost entirely of people from other parts of the country who'd come together to create an enclave of radical culture."[118]

In rare cases, travelers have personal contacts with other exiles willing to serve as guides, for instance a parent who had also left Scientology or a friend in exile from the same Hindu-inspired cult. Conversations with these acquaintances raised awareness about religious trauma. "The more they told me, the more it confirmed what I already knew or suspected. This type of coercive behavior was widespread."[119] This mentoring also built confidence about the future. "I left ... and I'm fine. Safes don't drop on my head as I walk down the street.... Your soul isn't going to push you in front of a speeding bus."[120]

Most often, however, invisible exiles simply did not have former acquaintances who, like themselves, had also left. In these contexts, co-narrating with strangers was the only option. These strangers include fellow travelers walking similar paths and who, in places like Footsteps, provided validating reflections and co-narrative support.

Co-narrating with Fellow Travelers Can Facilitate Healing

Based on invisible exile travelogues, it appears that the primary attraction of places like Footsteps is that they flip the script. Instead of the traveler being the odd one out—the person expected to accommodate and conform—travelers are instead surrounded by people experiencing similar Othering. By connecting with fellow travelers in co-narrative spaces, travelers reduce isolation, build community, and model possible futures. As a caveat, there are reasons why invisible exiles sometimes avoid places like Footsteps. However, in general, most travelers appear to experience considerable relief from visiting these sheltered spaces of filtered narration.

Starting first with the benefits, places like Footsteps help travelers feel less alone. It was through a visit to a transgender support group that one author met "the first trans masculine person I had ever seen in real life."[121] It was through cross-country interviews that another met professionals who, like her, spoke with a stutter. "Having believed" as a child "that I was one of a small handful of stutterers, I wonder if I would have been appalled or comforted to find out that there were millions of us across the globe."[122] A third author struggling with mental health challenges knew exactly how to answer that question. "Knowing there were others out there who could relate to my thoughts was the most precious of lifelines."[123]

Finding people with shared experiences and embarking on similar journeys creates opportunities to build a sense of community around difference. In refugee studies, "the thing that unites us, even though we are from different countries is, sadly, our grief; it's knowing that you are looking a person in the eyes and that that other person understands exactly what you are saying."[124] Then, within such groups and at arm's length from judgmental onlookers, participants can articulate their lives and identities in new ways. In gender studies, "a female business executive will share certain aspects of the life script with her male colleagues that will lead to the voicing and silencing of particular life stories, and this will be different from the aspects of the life script shared with her working mothers' group."[125]

Similar dynamics of mutual reflection and alternative narration are evident within invisible exile travel writing. For the author working at the adoption agency, "after a lifetime of feeling isolated by my adoption, I began to think of myself as part of a broader culture of people affected by it."[126]

For the author playing pickup soccer with other racially diverse immigrants in the park, "as much as I loved my [white host] family . . . I decided I needed to be close to these people."[127]

For the author trying to build connections with expats at restaurants, "once I discover the travelers' network, I have no more problems about eating dinner alone. In fact, I'm almost never alone, unless I choose to be."[128]

For the epileptic author advised to conceal her condition, "when I read Tennyson," a fellow epileptic, "it seemed that I had found a friend."[129]

For Janet Mock, the transgender author who attended Chrysalis as a teenager, that support group "was a sanctuary of our own creation where we let our members know they were not alone."[130]

Similarly, for Shulem Deen, the ex-Orthodox author visiting Footsteps in Manhattan, his fellow Footsteppers became a surrogate family. "The sparks of a second generation would glow from the cracks of so many broken hearts."[131]

As these examples show, in whatever form Footsteps takes, it is a place where invisible exiles feel seen, validated, and connected. This sense of camaraderie is a precious resource given how much erasure these authors experience elsewhere.

Alongside this sense of connection, a second key benefit of places like Footsteps is that, in these environments, travelers find respite from the pressure to self-censor. This sense of release is especially well-captured in the account of the traveling journalist who, as part of her cross-country research into ableist culture, attended a conference on stuttering. "It is the first time that I've heard so many stutters in one place, and I'm transfixed by the cacophony."[132] She felt empowered when immersed in a hotel ballroom where everyone shared her speech pattern. "I feel myself gradually change. . . . I stop thinking about my speech, I stop listening out for my own stumbles."[133] In that ballroom, the trait that usually evoked shame instead felt normal and even playful. "I use more voluntary stuttering because I feel comfortable playing with my speech."[134]

Another invisible exile describes a similar sense of release when, instead of socializing with leisure hikers, she befriended the lifeguards and waitresses serving them. Priced out of the housing market, these low-wage workers lived together in an empty barn. In the company of people who, like herself, were living rough, the author felt "no need to lie" and instead announced, "We're homeless, lost our house, business, everything we've ever worked for all our lives, . . . so we thought: What the fuck, let's go for a walk."[135] Gone was the guardedness she felt around other hikers. In its place, "a beautiful haze of happiness filled the barn and I curled on the sofa in bliss."[136]

In my assessment, this sense of release arises when people in similar circumstances validate the exiled parts of self that do not find a reflection elsewhere. By contrast, in Footsteps-like spaces, invisible exiles "were not looked at as dysfunctional; the system was dysfunctional."[137] In these *places of our own,* people "complimented me, people who knew that I was trans and told me I was beautiful."[138]

Discovering this peer support could be deeply empowering. For one author, it changed her sense of racial identity. "I look in the mirror and allow myself to see not what whites *might* see or what they might *want* to see or what they might want *not* to see; not conforming to what *they* admire. To see my actual self."[139]

For another author, having access to a digital version of Footsteps created a platform where, instead of hiding her sexuality, she could embrace it in full vivid color. "My fetishist friends and I swap photos and stories about our adventures in gluteal perversion."[140]

In these conversations among people with shared experiences and away from ill-informed, judgmental observers, unexpressed experiences find a common voice. These affirmational reflections then create opportunities for travelers to develop more explicit, complicated, and multivocal narratives about who they are and how they wish to live.

This future-oriented aspect emerges because, alongside connection and empowerment, Footsteps is a place to find role models. "I wanted role models of what life was like for a trans man who had taken the transitional path that I needed to take. How successful had it been for them?"[141] These role models help travelers question internalized stigmas. "As a kid I believed that my life would be perfect if I didn't stutter. I never considered that my stutter might make me better."[142] Shedding stigma—whether about race, gender, or ability—facilitates healing. "Like climbing out of a deep depression, I hadn't known I was this afflicted until I wasn't."[143]

This healing allows invisible exiles to begin envisioning other futures. Instead of allowing other people's judgments to define their identities, "ours became two in a chorus of voices calling for change. . . . We wanted to rewrite the whole story of how we talked about ourselves and how others talked about us."[144] These conversations helped galvanize a sense of empowerment. "Up until then, it felt as though I and a few others had been fighting . . . with our backs to the wall. . . . To see a group of people rise up like this in defense of the many who had been wronged . . . was a huge testament to the kindness of the human race."[145]

This potential for social activism underscores that conversations beginning in places like Footsteps may then spill out into the larger public realm. Although self-representation is a useful first step, a more activist perspective is that deep and lasting healing requires people "to challenge and to change the narratives that dominate the places where they dwell."[146] This external focus links narration with justice, a concept that requires "turning to a wider public of initially disinterested people" and pushing for recognition and inclusion within that larger moral community.[147] "It is by claiming the moral truth that resistance narratives gain their power."[148] By transforming painful emotions into public testimony, marginalized groups "can channel their sorrow, anger, and fear about injustice into activities of social activism."[149]

Reaching this broader audience is often an outcome of prior organizing, including through places like Footsteps, rather than its precursor, and social transformation might be a long time coming. In the meantime, *places of our own* provide a place of reflection and a landscape for healing.

Spaces of Co-narration Include a Mix of Barriers and Possibilities

In short, shared but sheltered spaces of co-narration bring many potential benefits. However, there are also reasons why some travelers avoid them. Participating can feel triggering, as well as empowering, and not all travelers feel equally welcome. Although acknowledging these limitations is important, my general sense is that, despite these valid concerns, *places of our own* play an important role in postexile healing.

Starting first with questions of environmental triggers, one barrier is that the places and people associated with trauma can activate a survivor's fight-or-flight response, which can lead to aggression and avoidance. These dynamics help explain why, when one author tried to reconnect with an also-ostracized older brother, he refused to engage. "Look, I don't give a shit about my family. They don't mean anything to me."[150]

Another author likewise felt a split desire both to connect and to avoid after rediscovering her long-lost mother. She initiated contact with this fellow exile by sending flowers, but "I'm not ready to talk to her. . . . She calls me a few days later, but I don't pick up the phone."[151] Although the prospect of co-narrating felt enticing, it also felt triggering and emotionally overwhelming.

This triggering dynamic is likewise why a third author felt both invigorated and exhausted by the prison writing workshops that, for her, were a crucial venue for co-narration. "Each time I leave a prison it's as if I've left a war zone" filled with "hundreds of wounded souls. Afterward I need a power wash of my own so I can reconnect into my world a little less charred."[152]

Alongside these trauma triggers, a related barrier is that shared spaces may not feel equally welcoming to every new arrival. Walking a similar path does not make travelers the same. One barrier was age. "You can't camp all that way, you're like, well, too old."[153] Another barrier was race. "We talked to one another and endeavored to make each other feel less like strangers in a strange land. . . . But talking scripture was not powerful enough to erase the barriers created by racism that had taught us to fear and beware difference."[154] A third barrier involved variations in how comfortable travelers felt about being open. "You are so *out* that everybody is afraid to talk to you" for fear of being outed themselves.[155] In situations like these, Footsteps provided only partial acceptance.

This sense of partial acceptance is precisely what a transgender author experienced while attending an LGBT organizing event. When she said trans kids should use the bathroom of their choosing, a gay participant rebutted, "Well, you're stupid, because it's going to cause riots in schools, and gay kids will get a bad name."[156] When she explained her identity by saying, "I was born biologically a boy, but I was always a full woman," an older trans man replied, "Excuse me, but you need to shut your mouth . . . because everyone here is pissed off at what you're saying."[157] These examples are important reminders that being in the company of peers is no guarantee of acceptance, let alone consensus.

These caveats are important. However, finding or creating spaces where travelers can co-narrate—including by narrating stories that otherwise remain silenced—is nevertheless an important part of invisible exile recovery. As Janet Mock observed when trying to decide whether to disclose her transgender past to her potential new boyfriend, "living by other people's definitions and perceptions shrinks us to shells of ourselves, rather than complex people embodying multiple identities."[158] By contrast, discussing all aspects of her experience in safe and supportive environments helped Mock begin to heal from the shame-based identity she otherwise carried.

In conclusion, in these co-narrative processes, it often feels unsafe—at least initially, when travelers are vulnerable and narratives are raw—to share risky stories with the general public. Due to the audience's limited imagination, selective attention, and moral stance, those listeners often have limited capacity to hear and understand exile-specific information. By contrast, in places like Footsteps, travelers can co-narrate with each other at arm's length from uninformed and judgmental observers. This co-narration can then lead to the collective knowledge often required to move beyond assimilation-only thinking and to instead push against social silencing. For Janet Mock, "I believe that telling our stories, first to ourselves and then to one another and the world, is a revolutionary act."[159] This revolutionary act could, in theory, bring exile to some type of resolution. This question of whether and how invisible exile ends is the subject of the next chapter.

EIGHT

The Provisional End of Exile

Sorrowjoy

Stories often follow the narrative convention of having a beginning, middle, and end. The protagonist has a dream or goal and works tirelessly to make it happen facing various obstacles along the way, until finally she reaches a climactic moment, like breaking through the finishing line and going home with the trophy. All parts of the story are important, but it is this satisfying end moment that everything else builds up to. Endings like these provide a sense of closure. They tie up loose ends, reveal ultimate fates, and make the moral implications clear.

By contrast, stories that do not end in resolution may leave the audience feeling confused or unsatisfied. Nevertheless, invisible exile often concludes precisely in these places of partial irresolution. Journeys reach clear destinations by some measures, for instance as travelers climb out of poverty, come out of the closet, escape cults, transition genders, finish hikes, leave abusers, reassess racialization, and reclaim lost voices. However, on reaching these goalposts—the places that, at the beginning of a journey, seemed to symbolize resolution—these endings usually turn out to be provisional only, and the exile journey remains incomplete.

Journeys remain incomplete for several reasons. First, although invisible exiles have finishing lines in mind, reaching them concludes only some aspects of their narratives. Some conflicts are resolved, some struggles set aside, but other threads remain active and tug in different directions.

Second, on arrival, the finishing line that, from a distance, looks like a clear thin line may look different on closer inspection. Some lines turn out to be a mirage, while others widen and thicken into vast terrains requiring further exploration. Within these amorphous landscapes, journeys do not end so much as splinter, deepen, or even repeat.

A third reason why invisible exile often ends in partial irresolution is that, instead of making a clean transition from an old identity to a new one, the past and present remain commingled. Even after reaching supposed finishing lines, the past returns. Some returns are intrusive, such as the flashbacks associated with trauma. Other returns are voluntary, as when travelers explore the past to gain new perspectives on the present and future. In either situation, the end of exile looks less like leaving the past behind and more like learning how to manage returns without dissolving into old narrative threads.

A fourth reason why invisible exile's end remains incomplete is that, instead of reaching an arrival point, exiles often arrive in places of new construction. As travelers gain more confidence in the legitimacy of their claim to new spaces and identities, it may feel easier—and urgently necessary—to push back against some aspects of how those spaces and identities are defined. Instead of assimilation and deference, travelers might challenge the norms that otherwise re-silence them. This advocacy work can then construct new finishing lines both for the author and for future travelers making similar journeys.

Cumulatively, these observations suggest that invisible exile often reaches a *relative* ending only. This notion of a relative end contradicts the more doom-laden theories that, "once banished, the exile lives an anomalous and miserable life,"[1] is doomed to exist as "a permanent outcast,"[2] and that, "however intimate the newcomer becomes with place, he can never become a complete insider."[3] Conversely, these observations also differ from the rosy claims that the "opportunities and sociability of exile" give it an "upbeat tenor."[4] Instead, in my assessment, invisible exile narratives resonate more strongly with a third notion, which is that, eventually, exiles may find their way into new landscapes—ones they feel affectionately toward and personally connected with—which blunts the "endless comparisons of one landscape with another" and "in that sense . . . means the relative ending of exile."[5]

This chapter explores this sense of a relative ending by analyzing hybrid places of conclusion mixed with irresolution. To accomplish this goal, I begin by providing detailed examples of amorphous finishing lines as recounted within invisible exile travel writing. Next, I assess the importance that invisible exiles place on the notion of arrival, as well as the indicators they use to signal that they have, by some measures, reached their intended destinations. Then, I explore the reasons why these endings may feel incomplete. This includes challenging common misunderstandings about arrival, for instance that it is an either/or condition rather than a matter of degrees, and that it is a durable state rather than a fleeting event requiring ongoing construction. Similarly, I challenge common misunderstandings about how arrival relates to departure, for instance the assumption that the past ends and is left behind, as opposed to being a place that travelers continually spiral back through. I also challenge the misunderstanding that invisible exile ends because travelers find acceptance elsewhere, as opposed to constructing their own modified places to call home. Cumulatively, these characteristics help explain why invisible exile so often ends in a space of conclusion mixed with irresolution.

"Reconciliation Never Showed up at My Door"

Starting with detailed examples as recounted within life history writing, Deborah Jiang-Stein captures this notion of arrival mixed with irresolution in her narrative about being born inside a federal prison. As explained in her memoir *Prison Baby,* she discovered this secret about herself when, at twelve years old, she went snooping through her adoptive parents' bedroom and found a hidden letter describing the circumstances of her birth.

After reading the letter, Jiang-Stein's first response was denial. "Impossible. Read it again."[6] Next came self-loathing. "What's wrong with me? . . . Who loves anyone from prison?"[7] Then came the internal splintering of dissociative amnesia and the banishment of this knowledge from her consciousness. Or so she thought. It turns out, however, that "buried secrets live forever, glued to our insides like sticky rice."[8]

Tormented by her buried secret, Jiang-Stein spent her teenage and young adult years spiraling through a rage-fueled drug addiction before reaching her version of rock bottom and deciding to make a change. Making this change meant committing to counseling, building new social ties, and rediscovering things that brought her joy. On a personal level, she "switched from the addict outlaw to a hands-on mom" arranging playdates and trips to the park.[9] On a professional level, she won poetry awards and joined anti-prison advocacy work.

Importantly, to move forward through this journey, Jiang-Stein felt she needed to revisit her past. She started by contacting the prison where she was born and requesting her birth mother's file—a nine-hundred-page document that, among other things, chronicled the deceased inmate's numerous attempts to keep custody of her baby. Next, Jiang-Stein visited the prison and received a guided tour of the rooms she occupied as an infant. Although facing the prison felt overwhelming, she pushed forward and, "for the first time," the secret of her birth sparked "hope" instead of only panic.[10] Jiang-Stein then visited other prisons, as well, where she led writing workshops for incarcerated women and girls. "These prison workshops show how redemption is made possible by hope. Hope alone won't solve anything. Yet without hope, nothing's possible."[11]

These writing workshops wrapped in hope might seem like the tidy end to a painful journey. Stopping there, however, would omit the key detail that, even at this seemingly successful point where Jiang-Stein is in recovery from addiction and living a middle-class lifestyle, she remains haunted by the past. "I don't have words for the fury and sadness I can still feel at irregular times. . . . They puncture my heart."[12] Jiang-Stein's paternal lineage remains unknown, which leaves her racial identity ambiguous, nor can she say whether she was born of love, rape, or prostitution. She will never know whether her ongoing struggle with Hepatitis C is tied to her birth. Furthermore, no matter how much time passes, how many playdates she organizes, or how many awards she wins, the past still hurts. "I waited for the day when grief would heal, . . . but reconciliation never showed up at my door."[13]

Jiang-Stein eventually gave up waiting for her pain and confusion to ebb. "Identity is whatever we make for ourselves, and not everything ends in resolution."[14] Instead of resolution, Jiang-Stein's narrative emphasizes acceptance. On a personal level, this means learning how to live more freely. "A wall of fear and resentment, not a bricks-and-mortar prison, had constricted me, even though I was free."[15] On a professional level, it means looking for structural solutions. With the rate of female incarceration rising, "we need solutions because more and more inmates are pregnant at time of sentencing."[16]

In short, arriving at a place where Jiang-Stein could embrace her new identity was less about leaving her prison origin behind and more about letting it live within her in a less damaging way. "One thing I've reconciled at last and for certain: I do not reconcile my prison birth

and all its impacts."[17] In her new self-narrative, the past is both painful and nourishing. Being born in prison and everything that followed
"feeds my creativity, my love and joy for life . . . and my ability to endure uncertainty. All of which give my world beauty and power."[18]

Welcome to Sorrowjoy, an Untidy Space of Both/and Contradictions

In Jiang-Stein's account, her journey into and partially out of invisible
exile spans several decades, and it ends not in triumphal resolution
but with the acceptance of a version of freedom that remains provisional and infused with grief. Jiang-Stein names this place Sorrowjoy.
Sorrowjoy, as she describes it, is a space of contradictions and incomplete resolutions. It is a landscape of hope and despair where
opposing elements coexist not in some transcendental harmony
but as separate and often colliding narratives. She calls this place of
smashed-together realities "*Sorrowjoy,* because if we sit still inside and
let it in," sorrow and joy "live together and we thrive."[19]

This description of Sorrowjoy as a provisional end to exile resonates with other invisible exile narratives that similarly conclude in
spaces of achievement mixed with grief. For example, although Sarah
Smarsh does not use this word, her memoir *Heartland* certainly captures the sentiment. Smarsh's narrative describes her journey out of
rural poverty and into urban comfort. By the narrative's end, Smarsh
has a white-collar job and a beautiful house, and she expresses relief
at reaching this destination—"thank God"—but she also emphasizes
"how it hurt. I had done what I set out to do, and I was glad. . . . [But] I
cried in my bed" for all that was lost along the way.[20] "It was a separation born of class, that a child might lose a sense of belonging within
her own family for going to college."[21] Although she knew she'd made
the best choice for herself, this break with family and heritage remained painful. "I felt the separation from you in my bones."[22]

For many people, Smarsh's story, like Jiang-Stein's, is one of arrival.
They are stories of people pulling themselves up by the proverbial
bootstraps, recovering from addiction or getting out of poverty, and
then building stable homes for themselves as part of the American
middle class.

Smarsh, however, prefers a different story. Having been born into
rural poverty, "people have asked me many times, 'How did you get
out?' It is a deeply flawed question."[23] The problem is not that there is

no story to tell. On the contrary, "I needed to square where I was with the story about where I came from—a seemingly great distance to reconcile."[24] However, for Smarsh, the question's phrasing asked for the wrong story.

One reason Smarsh felt it was the wrong story is because the prompt *How did you get out?* presumes she was *out*. It presumes her relationship to poverty has in fact ended. But Smarsh doesn't see it that way. "Now I am in a different place. But have I really gotten out of those red places?"[25] Her environment suggests otherwise. "I've seen something of the world, but I still live in my home state. I have a good leather bag, but I love it most for the fact that it cost $3 at the Goodwill. I have a cell phone, but I get voice mail messages from collection agencies looking for my immediate family members. I have a graduate degree but a heap of debt acquired in obtaining it."[26] In other words, her experiences with rural poverty persist. "I did not leave one world and enter another. Today I hold them simultaneously."[27]

Another reason Smarsh felt the question *How did you get out?* was flawed was because it invited a narrative of individual accomplishment, as opposed to a critique of society's failings. "How can you talk about the poor child without addressing the country that let her be so?"[28] For her, the point of narrating her journey is not to explain how she changed her fate but rather to question why society is so divided, why rural lives are systematically devalued, and why upward economic mobility feels exquisitely painful. "Mine isn't a story about a destination that was reached but rather about sacrifices I don't believe anyone, certainly no child, should ever have to make."[29]

Reflecting on this pain while sobbing into her pillow, Smarsh found her version of Sorrowjoy. She had made it into the world of white-collar work, and her beautiful house reflected this success. However, this space of accomplishment was deeply infused not only with freedom but also with grief.

This sense of freedom blended with grief is ubiquitous within invisible exile travel writing. Importantly, as a landscape that contains joy—and not just pain—the provisional end of invisible exile is different from the experience of being stripped bare during exile's onset. Compared to the Void, even as pain persists, Sorrowjoy adds hope into the mix. "Sweet, sweet exile. . . . Blessed exile. . . . Sweet home, Chicago, my promised land, my Babylon, gained and lost. . . . I'm so, so happy, and so, so grief stricken all at once."[30] The Void persists, but as exile reaches a relative end, The Void is not *all* that persists, and it becomes comingled with joy.

Invisible exiles find this mix of grief and achievement in many locations. For some, Sorrowjoy is a physical location that marks a journey's conclusion. It is the final stop on a cross-continental trek or the new home that symbolically inverts the place left behind. Travelers find these physical locations in Galicia,[31] Patagonia,[32] Cambridge,[33] Park Avenue,[34] and on Oprah Winfrey's couch.[35] For other travelers, Sorrowjoy is a social space where the identity they have been cultivating—for example, secular, female, capable, or queer—finally receives external validation. Travelers experience these social dynamics in restaurants,[36] airports,[37] forests,[38] and coffee shops.[39] In other narratives, travelers construct Sorrowjoy through environmental symbolism—for instance through metaphorical references to Babylon,[40] watery mirrors,[41] haunted houses,[42] and fresh starts[43]—and the way these symbols inscribe places like Chicago or New York with new, personal meanings.

Although Sorrowjoy can take as many forms as there are travelers, what these places have in common is their mix of conclusion and irresolution. In my assessment, Sorrowjoy is anywhere travelers stabilize their future-oriented trajectories while simultaneously honoring their pasts and acknowledging their losses. These are landscapes of joy and pain, of successes and shortfalls, of visibility mixed with erasure. They are defined by arrivals moving in the wrong directions and by failures that provide a sense of reprieve. They are places where travelers feel at home in themselves and in their environments, even as these homes and selves remain partial and ever changing. In these spaces of contradiction, Sorrowjoy is the bittersweet place where dying and dancing meet.

Arriving at the Imagined Finishing Line

To understand these dynamics, it helps to first understand the role that arrival plays in invisible exile travel writing. An *arrival scene* is different from *the sense of having arrived*. In travel writing, arrival scenes come early in the expedition when a voyager disembarks from an airplane or crosses through border control and is suddenly bombarded by an overwhelming cacophony of unfamiliar sights and sounds in a foreign location.[44] In contrast, the sensation of having arrived emerges later in the journey. At this juncture, instead of feeling like a bewildered outsider, the traveler begins to perceive a clarity of purpose, a sense of accomplishment, and a diminishing impulse to wander.

By several measures, invisible exiles appear highly committed to the notion of having arrived. This embrace of finishing lines makes sense given the social pressure to craft stories with clear redeeming outcomes. However, this yearning for resolution appears to run deeper than mere narrative convention. Instead, like Jiang-Stein's long-standing wish for reconciliation to arrive at her door, my sense is that the search for a finishing line reflects the deeply held hope that, if only travelers could reach some definitive point on a map or some Zen-like emotional state, the pain of exile would end.

That being said, narrative convention certainly plays a role. Invisible exiles often write their stories not because they have reached an end but because they hope the act of storytelling will help them discover the resolutions they seek. Storytelling is useful in these endeavors because narrative is "a vehicle for imposing order on otherwise disconnected experiences."[45] Life is messy, and organizing that mess into a coherent sequence makes sense of the disarray by using "language or another symbolic system to imbue life events with a temporal and logical order," which can "demystify" those events and "establish coherence."[46] This coherence helps invisible exiles understand how their experiences might fit within a larger causal structure.

These causal structures include beginnings, middles, and endings, but endings are often afforded special significance. A central goal of the life history genre is to "depict a temporal transition from one state of affairs to another."[47] Indeed, in a well-told narrative, this end is what everything else builds up to, which is why writing instructors—including those specializing in life history writing—advise authors to cut all scenes or subplots that do not directly contribute to the narrative's climax and the protagonist's struggle to reach it.[48]

For invisible exiles, the allure of finding a tidy conclusion is understandable. Identifying a larger purpose within exile—even if this purpose only becomes clear through hindsight—helps travelers justify their journeys as more than aimless wanderings. Additionally, being able to claim success can retroactively signal that departing on the journey was reasonable, that the costs were worthwhile, and that the burden of traveling can finally be set down. For invisible exiles whose journeys involve such tremendous losses, the idea of finding a "concise, neat, teleological package" that moves "from crises to resolution"[49] offers a much-needed salve.

When viewed through this end-state lens, it is immediately clear that invisible exile narratives are filled with references to yearned-for finishing lines. Moreover, authors use a range of indicators to signal arrival, including physical characteristics, social interactions, psychological changes, performance capacities, and authorial voice.

Starting with physical indicators, one way to mark a journey's conclusion is to arrive at a destination that, in the traveler's mind, inversely mirrors the point of departure. Instead of living in the Pacific Northwest, an author peddles his bicycle into Patagonia.[50] Instead of being surrounded by rural poverty, an author marries her way into a Park Avenue apartment filled with bronze-and-silver vases, Georgian maps, leather armchairs, and Persian rugs.[51] Instead of bouncing between homelessness and foster care, the now adult traveler becomes financially secure with a home of her own.[52] Instead of reselling candy on a New York City subway, an author feels he has arrived when he stands in the kitchen of his very own restaurant.[53]

In examples like these, authors describe physical environments that seem to mark their journey's conclusion. For the chef, "all that hustling had paid off. Finally, I had made it."[54] For the author cycling into Patagonia, "like the last grain of sand dropping in an hourglass, my experiment in time ended without a sound."[55] For the author escaping foster care, "we created a whole generation of children that will never suffer intense poverty, homelessness, or abuse. Together, we stopped the cycle."[56] In all these examples, invisible exiles embrace the notion of arrival, and they use physical details to signify that they've arrived.

Alongside physical characteristics, another set of arrival indicators involves social interactions that signal the solidification of a new identity. For a transgender author, strangers in airports begin spontaneously calling her ma'am and directing her to the women's restrooms.[57] For an author whose family disowned her for enrolling in college, her new friends become "a kind of family, and I felt a sense of belonging with them that, for many years, had been absent."[58] Similarly, for a religious exile who once felt out of place in secular contexts, she cherishes the experience of being waited on "like royalty" when dining in an upscale New York City restaurant.[59]

In examples like these, social dynamics seem to provide evidence that travelers can finally stop *striving* because, in the eyes of others, they have *arrived*. For the religious exile who not only blends in but also embodies privilege, "I think it is ironic that he doesn't know that the two of us are outsiders. . . . I never thought this day would come."[60] These social interactions provide supposed evidence of having reached a finishing line.

Alongside physical and social indicators, a third benchmark of reaching a journey's imagined conclusion involves a psychological state where, instead of feeling denial and resistance, travelers find acceptance. Shame may give way to a sense of peace as an author discovers a sense of home within herself, despite still being houseless.[61] Instead of disavowing Blackness, an author may finally acknowledge, for the first time, how racism has affected her.[62] Similarly, instead of hiding sexual identity, an author may give it a name, speak it out loud, and write a book about it to try to spark a national debate.[63]

Invisible exile travel narratives are filled with spaces of acceptance. It's deciding, "I am not white . . . because I do not want to be."[64] It's announcing, "here's what I, for decades, was afraid to tell myself: . . . My fetish isn't something I do. It's something I am."[65] Accepting these core traits does not reverse exile losses. It does, however, soften the compulsion to continue the quest. It's proclaiming that "I was no longer striving, fighting to change the unchangeable. . . . A new season had crept into me, a softer season of acceptance."[66]

Next, a fourth indicator of having arrived involves the realization that, at this point in the journey, travelers can consistently perform in ways that seemed impossible when the journey began. Some performances are physical. "My strong body pushed me across the peaks of the High Sierra, I could survive violent hunger—find my way through, against all odds," whereas her pre-exile self "couldn't."[67]

Other performances are social. Instead of going to bed hungry rather than facing the shame of eating alone, "I walk into Mirna's Pancakes for breakfast and ask a young woman if I can join her. After more than a year of traveling alone . . . it has become easy for me to approach other tourists."[68]

Some performances are psychological, as when a transgender author felt secure enough in her female identity to draw a mascara mustache on her upper lip. "The more comfortable I was in my own gender, the more I found myself wanting to play around with it."[69]

In examples like these, the newfound capacity to perform differently marked the arrival of a new self. It's not that other people treated them differently, but rather that travelers felt at ease in a new embodiment that finally seemed to supplant their old one.

A fifth indicator of having reached a supposed finishing line involves the sense that, after so much silencing, travelers have finally found their voice. One voice came through poetry. "The poems came to me" while "searching for the voice that would remain when my own reflection ceased to be."[70]

Another voice came through song. "I have the entire 'stage' to myself. . . . It occurs to me: I'm not just a soldier anymore. I'm someone with a voice."[71]

A third author found her voice through self-employment. "I no longer needed to impress anybody. . . . As a result, I found myself inundated with ideas and with the words to express them."[72]

In other instances, voice came through stillness. "The silence roars loud and beautiful from my extended family. Sometimes, such silences are comforting. In it there is room to hear one's own voice."[73]

Finding these voices symbolized the end of feeling trapped by other people's narratives. "I had built a new life, and it was a happy one, but I felt a sense of loss . . . not by leaving but by leaving silently. I had retreated . . . and allowed my father to tell my story for me, to define me to everyone I had ever known. I had conceded too much ground—not just the mountain, but the entire province of our shared history."[74] Having made it to an arrival point, which for her was receiving a PhD, she decided it was time to speak out and reclaim her story.

In all these examples, whether travelers emphasize physical, social, psychological, performative, or authorial benchmarks, their statements define a measurable sense of arrival. By occupying a certain location, achieving a certain reflection, reaching a particular state of being, performing a specific action, or enacting a unique form of self-expression, travelers feel some long-pursued goal has been obtained. Once travelers reach these goals, they often expect their journeys to feel complete. The hope is that, by reaching these new states and places, the messiness of alienation, liminality, and exile can finally be set to rest.

Arrival Is More Fragmented than It First Appears

There are good reasons why travelers often want to tell stories that end with arrival. However, although some sense of arrival is clearly occurring, an arrivals-only framework would obscure the reality of ongoing journeys.

This quandary is not unique to invisible exile. "All narrative exhibits tension between the desire to construct an overarching storyline that ties events together in a seamless explanatory framework and the desire to capture the complexities of the events experienced, including haphazard details, uncertainties, and conflicting sensibilities among protagonists."[75] When faced with this tension, because uncertainty feels unsettling, narrators generally err on the side of coherence. This approach, however, sacrifices authenticity through oversimplification. "The plotting of psychic interiors on to comforting narrative frames is full of obstacles, not the least of which is the nagging sensation that one's life is more fragmented than the experiential world depicted in cultural stories."[76]

Building on these themes, invisible exile travelogues offer ample evidence that their hoped-for finishing lines are more complex and provisional than initially expected. Specifically, their narratives challenge the apparent coherence of arrival points in terms of their all-inclusiveness, durability, and visibility.

Starting with all-inclusiveness, although many invisible exiles embrace the idea of finishing lines—for instance by setting clear goals and identifying key moments when those goals are met—after reaching these points, travelers often feel as though the long-anticipated sense of conclusion does not materialize. For the cyclist peddling into Patagonia, "I had arrived. Now what? . . . At the end of the trip, I felt a dull melancholy. . . . I was excited, sure, but I was tired. I wondered if old age felt like this."[77]

Similarly, for a cyclist peddling into Vietnam, "Phan Thiet, the town of my birth, the end of my journey, lies only a few hours' ride away, but the marching drums that have driven me onward for a year now have abruptly quieted. An unexpected lull. The finishing line seems unimportant, secondary, symbolic."[78]

Part of the problem, it turns out, is that arriving at a prespecified destination concludes only one of many entangled storylines. Over the course of the journey, some activities bring travelers closer to their goals, but other experiences pull in different directions. These splintering threads, many of which remain unfinished, then complicate arrival with still-unanswered questions.

Some destinations remain partial because of the route taken to get there. For example, one author's arrival point—her hard-won embrace of her Black identity—felt complicated by her previous search for whiteness, including her decision to marry a white husband. Years later, when she felt ready to embrace Blackness, she found that having a light-skinned daughter "lessened my Blackness among Blacks," and her darker-skinned son had a father who "cannot teach him how to be a Black man in America."[79] Embracing Blackness marked the end of her racial dysphoria, but it could not undo the aspects of Blackness that, because of her life journey, felt "irretrievably lost."[80]

Other authors describe a similar sense of accomplishment mixed with irresolution, and for various reasons. For an author grappling with homophobia, "I suppose I'd worked through some things on the road. My faith had gotten rearranged, the puzzle pieces disassembled and spread across the table. Not put back together, but not a total mess either."[81]

For an author crossing class divides, "I preferred the family I had chosen to the one I had been given," but because this preference implied betrayal, "I felt damned for those feelings" as well.[82]

Similarly for a religious exile, despite becoming comfortable with secular culture, "there hasn't been that day, that day that I thought would come sooner, when I would wake up and think, *This is the day when I realize it was all worth it.* Everything I sacrificed, everything I endured, justified."[83]

Another author felt similarly haunted by a past that was both over and ongoing. In a previously published memoir, "I had tried to show that I had put the convent completely behind me, had erased the damage and completed the difficult rite of passage to a wholly secular existence."[84] However, as time passed, "at some inchoate, unconscious level, I felt that God and I had unfinished business—even though I didn't believe that he existed."[85] This unfinished business explains why she rewrote the memoir, this time emphasizing irresolution rather than certainty.

In examples like these, the sorrows and complications that linger even in the face of achievement illustrate invisible exile's provisional end. Travelers arrive at their destinations, which yields important benefits, but satisfaction is partial, grief persists, and new questions arise. In this way, exile ends, and it lingers, on parallel tracks.

"Happy Endings Are Only a Pause"

These unfinished narrative threads are one reason why arrival turns out to be less coherent than it initially appears. Alongside this inconclusiveness, a second reason is the lack of durability. Arrival is performative, rather than static. Travelers reach their destinations only to realize those finishing lines are not at all like stable coordinates on a map or inert chunks of clay. Instead, they are events, which, like all events, only persist if continually remade. Moreover, these events are moving targets. The act of arrival may encourage travelers to rethink or even abandon the happy endings they once envisioned to make space for other possible endings they only discover after arriving.

When thinking about arrival as an event, rather than a fixed point, invisible exiles are not alone in the struggle to reconcile life's contingencies with the desire for resolution. A similar tension exists within recovery narratives where the story of a life-altering illness or injury "attempts to restore an order that the interruption fragmented, but it must also tell the truth that interruptions will continue."[86] This sense of lingering uncertainty is evident in queer geographies, as well, where, in addition to pre-exile scouting trips, migrants pursue post-exile "moves—often within cities—that mediate the ongoing process of coming out after a destination has been reached."[87] Similarly, in immigrant life histories, "home might be multiple, fluid, provisional, a process; a verb. . . . A constant simultaneous making and re-making, dismantling and rebuilding, even as we might feel 'settled' and 'at home.'"[88]

Examples like these reinforce the point that there is no final state, no point where history stops. As with other forms of mobility, "migration is not a one-off move to a permanent destination, nor is it the final part of a journey. . . . We are all continually engaged in the pursuit of (an albeit vaguely defined) happiness. We might be seeking to live in utopia, but this is always just out of reach."[89] Because wins are ephemeral, arrival often feels less like a finishing line and more like settling into a still-to-be-charted terrain.

The inevitable ephemerality of everyday life, however, does not negate the significance of traveling in pursuit of asylum, rebirth, authenticity, or escape. On the contrary, "there is the additional sense that the good life is there, in their chosen destination, to be had if only they could learn how to get hold of it."[90]

For invisible exiles, this ongoing quest for self-actualization sometimes involves letting go of the goals they once worked to achieve. For one author, it meant walking away from the job that provided financial stability—an outcome that felt impossible at her journey's start—to make space for work that was less financially secure but more aligned with her values. "I felt in some strange way as though I were back on track. The bus was taking me away from my nice safe job, but it seemed to be going in the right direction."[91]

For another author, this moment of reassessment involved moving out of her husband's lavish Park Avenue apartment—the same one that initially signified post-exile arrival. After her impoverished childhood, she cherished the apartment's comforts, but eventually it began to feel less like a finale and more like playing house. "He was a good man, but not the right one for me. And Park Avenue was not where I belonged."[92] She got a smaller apartment with fewer perks, but it was hers, had elements she liked, and left her free to continue exploring.

Other authors describe similar experiences where imagined endpoints turned out to be stepping stones on the way to other, still-to-be-discovered futures. This was certainly the case for an author who, after becoming a Dutch citizen, earning a college degree, and winning a seat in national government, saw her achievements unravel. As part of her quest to find her voice, she coproduced a film criticizing religious misogyny, and then had to go into hiding when a religious terrorist began murdering the film's producers.[93] This visibility led to politically motivated allegations that her asylum paperwork was fraudulent, which led to the temporary revocation of her citizenship and, by extension, forced her resignation from parliament. Not long after, her neighbors won a court case to have her evicted from their apartment building on the grounds that the threats against her life put their lives at risk as well. At that point, stripped of nationality, job, and home, she decided it was time to find a new finishing line in another country. "I was a nomad once more."[94]

Examples like these demonstrate the shape-shifting nature of exile's provisional end. Time and again, travelers arrived exactly at the places they were aiming for, only to have those destinations dissolve. One author opened his own restaurant, but the business "lasted for all of twenty minutes."[95] Another author got married only to have her spouse abandon her just as her memoir entered production.[96] A third author reconnected with her birth mother, but almost immediately the relationship soured.[97] From these perspectives, arrival points are real, and invisible exiles value them, but arriving is not the same as ending. "Happy endings are only a pause."[98]

These dissolutions do not erase invisible exile journeys. Travelers do not start over, they are not back to square one, and their achievements still carry weight. Even so, these examples demonstrate that arrival is less like a fixed goalpost and more like an amorphous cloud. The state of arrival—the landscape that is Sorrowjoy—is vast, rugged, and unpredictable. It often requires considerable exploration before travelers can locate the precise spots that fit. Even then, those places can change rapidly. This ephemerality does not negate that arrival exists and is important, but it does help explain why the end of invisible exile remains relative only.

Arriving Does Not Stop Ongoing Erasure

Alongside unfinished narrative threads and amorphous finishing lines, a third reason why arrival lacks full coherence involves the challenge of visibility. Even after having *made it,* travelers continue to experience erasure. Although travelers may soothe the pain of erasure by co-narrating with peers in places of their own, until there is broad social understanding about where invisible exiles come from and how they define themselves, problems of re-erasure persist. This re-erasure makes it difficult to conclude that a traveler has *gotten out* of something when the people around them continually reconstruct one of the key experiences they were hoping to leave.

As an example, one author's on-campus rape was a significant factor driving her into exile, but a contributing factor was the college administration's refusal to acknowledge the attack. This lack of support motivated her to look elsewhere for healing, including by dropping out of school to become a long-distance hiker. Years later, after publishing a memoir about her experience, she was invited to return to her former campus to speak about the book. Even then, however, the promotional material misrepresented her perspective. "The college didn't mention I'd been raped there. Instead, they ambiguously said, 'a horrific trauma.' Instead of a dropout, I was now a successful 'alumna' enhancing the prestige of their institution. . . . They were obscuring me again."[99]

Invisible exiles describe many such instances of ongoing erasure. Some erasures are born of ableism, as when an impatient barista tries to quiet a stuttering customer by passing her pen and paper. "If there is any reaction more able to shatter my ecstasy, I'm hard-pressed to guess what it would be."[100]

Other erasures are linked to sexuality, as when an author finally names her desires out loud only to find that she still lacks a ready-made language to explain the details of her identity either to her "vanilla" boyfriend or to "people from other branches of the BDSM tree."[101]

Some erasures are connected to gender, as when an author finds acceptance within the cisgender community, but only because she is perceived as "the 'right' kind of trans woman (educated, able-bodied, attractive, articulate, heteronormative)."[102] Instead of comforting her, she wonders, "where does that leave the sisters I grew up with . . . who didn't 'make it'" in the same normative way?[103]

Other erasures are linked to religion, including the tendency within U.S. culture to minimize religious abuse or to dismiss it as "aberrant, a 'cultural thing.'"[104] Although news outlets sometimes report on such events, they also publish church leaders' denials and "outright lies," which can feel "like a spit in the face of everyone who had gone through hell."[105]

In cases like these, instead of feeling heard, invisible exiles may feel re-silenced and re-erased. This was Deborah Jiang-Stein's experience when, even after gaining respect for her prison-writing workshops, she was nevertheless treated as an anomaly, rather than an overlooked norm. When she shared her life history with psychologists attending a foster care fundraiser, an audience member raised her hand and asked, *How did you change?* Jiang-Stein felt confused by the question and asked the speaker to elaborate. "Today, if one of us called the Mayo Clinic to seek consultation about a child with the kind of behavior you describe, they'd refuse to treat you and your family. . . . 'What? Why?' I ask. Her answer shocks me. 'It's untreatable. . . . That's why I asked how you changed.'"[106]

These comments underscore the plight of invisible exiles. Travelers who by all appearances have *gotten out* of their past and *arrived* at some new identity nevertheless remain stigmatized, misunderstood, and erased by the same peers who allege to accept them. These experiences provide yet more evidence that exile's end is provisional only.

The Past Does Not Stay Put

Having shed some light on arrival points, this section shifts gears to consider evidence that challenges the apparent coherence of departure points. The question that frustrated Sarah Smarsh—the question *How did you get out?* where *out* means out of rural poverty—presumes

a duality between past and present, or between the places and circumstances left behind versus the new ones that supplant them. This
narrative framework prioritizes the present over the past while also
discursively relegating the past to the dustbin of things that are supposedly over and done with.

Invisible exile travel writing, however, tells a different story. In
these accounts, the past lingers. Sometimes it forcibly intrudes, like
tentacles reaching into the present and snatching travelers back to
elsewhere. Other times, travelers follow a spiraling path by choosing to revisit the past to facilitate forward motion. In both scenarios,
inhabiting Sorrowjoy is not so much about *getting out* of somewhere—
which travelers have technically already achieved—but rather is about
learning how to navigate returns without losing track of present-
day threads.

The first set of returns—involuntary returns—are often rooted
in trauma. Trauma geographies are often considered "fundamentally unmappable" because survivors do not fully process trauma in
the moment and instead carry traumatic embodiments with them to
other times and places.[107] These traveling embodiments explain the
subsequent blurring of past and present landscapes as "'flashes' of the
event are able to re-engage bodily senses" in other times and places.[108]
Once triggered, the traveler "becomes drawn into the drama of the attack itself, losing track of how the attack fits into a coherent storyline,
with a beginning, middle, and end."[109] Because of these dynamics,
even when travelers perceive themselves as occupying a place of arrival, the past may nevertheless surge into consciousness as though
history is repeating. This sense of repetition leaves journeys feeling
incomplete.

Some invisible exiles self-identify as experiencing post-traumatic
stress disorder, but even narratives lacking this clinical language are
filled with descriptions of intrusive thoughts, panic attacks, and traumatic dissociation. These intrusive memories are often triggered by
unexpected encounters with the objects, people, or images associated
with Plato's Cave. Importantly, trauma triggers are different from
nostalgic mementos. In nostalgic contexts, visual and material culture
helps people preserve a sense of attachment to lost or faraway places.
In immigration studies, family photographs, traditional clothing,
and religious iconography are "charged with memories that activate . . . connections to pre-migratory landscapes."[110] Invisible exiles

sometimes carry such totems, for instance a familiar rug,[111] a tattooed wrist,[112] a cherished book,[113] a rock collection,[114] or a set of braided tobacco leaves.[115] However, given the pain, abuse, and alienation of their exile-related experiences, my sense is that, instead of reminiscing, invisible exiles spend far more energy trying to *avoid* charged objects that might stimulate unwanted remembering.

One avoidance strategy involves steering clear of the places associated with Plato's Cave. For one author, this meant avoiding all of Suffolk County. "The smallest stimulus—a certain bar, an old gas station—triggers memories" of childhood trauma, including her mother's "torment, her smell, her constant reminders that nobody wanted me."[116]

For another author, it meant avoiding Williamsburg. "Every time I glimpsed the familiar Hasidic costume from across a busy street, I would cringe inside.... I couldn't bear to be reminded of my past."[117]

An added complication is that, although people living with trauma may wish to avoid triggering environments, place has the habit of not staying put. Contrary to the "popular but wholly mistaken assumption that to be exiled is to be totally cut off . . . from your place of origin, . . . the fact is that for most exiles," living in "today's world" means "living with the many reminders . . . that your home is not in fact so far away."[118] Some immigrants may welcome this ongoing sense of connection, but for invisible exiles these reminders can be highly triggering.

Some triggers arise because different locations share a common history. This shared history explains why one author got "the willies" when visiting Savannah, which was built around the same time and in a similar architectural style as his Cuban childhood home.[119] This resonance made Savannah "seemed as plagued by dark spirits as my deeply haunted Havana. . . . Slavery. Human beings bought and sold. . . . Too much cruelty mixed with gentility. . . . A lost war, and a lost cause. . . . More ghosts than living residents."[120] The weight of these architectural reminders felt so overwhelming that, instead of spending the day sightseeing, he turned around and drove away "at top speed" to Florida City, a less picturesque location that "had no such baggage . . . and I loved it for that."[121]

Other triggers arise not because of a shared past but because places share a common culture in the present. One author, for example, thought leaving the rural South would free her from the racism of her youth. Instead, "that fear followed me," and "I learned to recognize the myriad faces of racism, racial prejudice and hatred" operating nationwide.[122] This ongoing exposure to structural violence felt destabilizing. "Carrying the voices of my ancestors within me everywhere I called home, I carried remembered pain and allowed it to continually sweep me away. This sensation of being swept away was like spinning."[123]

In other examples, travelers encountered environmental triggers because new patterns of mobility were knitting formerly distant places closer together. This explains how an author exiting a London hospital suddenly found herself surrounded by women in hijabs, inhaling the aroma of spicy lamb sandwiches, and facing a large mosque. Despite having traveled across a continent to escape religious trauma, those sights and scents ignited "an instant sense of panic and suffocation. I was right back in the heart of it all."[124]

This tendency toward mobility also explains why, even after another author left her cult and enrolled in college, she still faced environmental reminders of her traumatic past. "I thought I was in a Guru-free zone, but soon enough, . . . I found posters for Guru's upcoming public concert as well as for the formation of a new meditation club on campus. I wanted them to go away—how dare they encroach on my space."[125]

It was the same for another author who, after moving five hundred miles to get away from her Appalachian childhood home, unexpectedly passed her homeless mother on a New York City sidewalk. With just one glimpse of this familiar figure, "I was overcome with panic that she'd see me and call out my name, and that someone . . . would spot us together . . . and my secret would be out."[126]

Similarly, for a queer author, an unexpected voice on his favorite radio program yanked him back into another time and place. "Here it is: This voice I've tried hard to forget reaching through the barriers I've erected."[127] At the sound of this voice, his awareness of the present splintered, "dots swimming in my eyes, orange and yellow streaks swirling."[128] The speaker, a former leader of the ex-gay conversion program the author once attended under duress, was publicly recanting his homophobia. The apologetic tone did not negate the author's panic, nor did it sate his instantly reignited rage. "As if this is all it takes—[his] admitting to the obvious lie he'd sold me and my family—to repair the damages inflicted on all of us."[129]

In examples like these, the past resurges because objects, scents, and voices travel to the places where invisible exiles went to escape. As a form of "haunting," these encounters transform "that which appears to be not there" into "a seething presence."[130] Sometimes all it takes is one sound, one face, or one aroma for the carefully constructed analytical boundaries separating here from there to shatter.

The intensity of these experiences reveals the stark misalignment between the question *How did you get out?* and the astute observation that, for many people, "The past is not dead. It is not even past."[131] Rather than experiencing the past as over, "I had a sense of myself as a haunted house. I never knew when the invisible thing would strike."[132] This uncertainty explains why another traveler "started believing in ghosts from watching myself and the way I haunt places from my past. . . . Something brings me back that might not exist anymore, something with its own map of the city carved into its graying eyes."[133]

Managing these intrusive memories can feel never-ending. "I have to remind myself that I am no longer dirt-poor, that there are no hands reaching out to do me harm, that I am no longer a child without resources."[134] Despite these reassurances, and despite the mounting physical evidence of professional successes—including one author's guest appearance on *The Oprah Winfrey Show*—her home environment revealed the lingering intrusion of old anxieties. "In my adult life I buy everything in bulk, and never let myself run out of anything, so I always have more than enough toilet paper, soap, and bread to keep a small army clean and fed."[135]

In examples like these, this sense of intrusion and haunting makes it impossible to tell a simple story about *getting out.* Instead, the coherence of arrival is endlessly recompromised by an ever-intruding past that refuses to stay put.

Moving Backward to Move Forward

These unexpected intrusions of the past into the present persist no matter that they are unwanted. Moreover, these intrusions help explain the second type of returns that travelers negotiate in Sorrowjoy. Alongside traumatic returns, invisible exiles often choose to partially revisit the places they once tried to leave behind. Travelers revisit for many reasons, including to make sense of what happened, to measure the distance traveled since leaving, and to mentally offer forgiveness. These visits are not like other homecomings—the ones involving warm welcomes or renewed social ties—nor do they resolve the past and present into one coherent harmony. However, when managed productively, selective returns can facilitate healing.

Within invisible exile travel narratives, authors often describe feeling a compulsion to return—and for reasons they may not initially understand—even while also feeling the desire to avoid. One author was astonished when her sister asked her to move back to Suffolk County. "*Where is this coming from?* I spent my childhood trying to get out of Suffolk County. . . . Of course, the people with whom I share the deepest connections all live there, but it is still the place where all the hurt in my life took place."[136] She eventually agreed, as did her siblings, and to her surprise, "healing came" through having "all five of us together again in one place."[137] The environment remained triggering, but in her new self-narrative—the one where she and her siblings were economically stable and safely housed—that landscape became more than just the crystalized stage set of past trauma. Instead, the environment now contained hope as well.

Another author felt similar trepidation when contemplating a possible visit to her former neighborhood. "When I finally did return to Williamsburg as my new self, I was wrapped in a scarf and sunglasses to avoid being recognized."[138] However, despite this trepidation, she felt compelled to return. She never stayed long, but her occasional visits allowed her to reconsider her past from a safe distance, which softened her sense of shame and heightened her sense of accomplishment. "I finally saw my life with estranged eyes, and suddenly my past struck me as wildly colorful and exotic."[139] These visits showed her how far she had traveled and how unusual her journey had been. "Even Roald Dahl," her favorite Girl Planet author, "could not have dreamed up a journey such as this. I have freed myself from my past, but I have not let go of it. I cherish the moments and experiences that formed me. I have lived the story."[140]

Other invisible exiles describe similar patterns of leaving and returning. "Every time I leave Miami, I tell myself I'm never coming back, only to end up right back where I started. I leave and come back again and again."[141] Some returns are for work, for instance to support "free creative writing summer camps taught by writers of color, a mission close to my heart."[142] Other returns are personal, for instance to attend a funeral. "Miami, like my family, is a place you learn to love and hate simultaneously. You can find yourself leaving it your whole life but never manage to leave, spend the rest of your life going back to it and never really get there."[143]

These spiraling patterns change how travelers understand not only their past but also their future. When stepping into the Void, most invisible exiles never expected to return. "Indeed, I feared that if I returned home to Kentucky I would be shattered, triggered in ways that would disrupt and fragment."[144] Instead, in Sorrowjoy, returning is sometimes what leads to a different future. "Resurrecting the memories of home, bringing the bits and pieces together was a movement back that enabled me to move forward."[145]

Cumulatively, these examples reinforce the claim that, instead of asking how travelers *get out,* it might make more sense to ask how travelers *return.* For invisible exiles, the true marker of Sorrowjoy is not separating from the past. Instead, settling into Sorrowjoy is about developing an aggregated-enough sense of self that travelers can engage in partial returns without dissolving into old pain.

One implication of this observation is that spiraling patterns are a defining feature of Sorrowjoy. Returning rarely leads to resolution, but finding ways to manage returns can make the past feel less haunting and more nourishing. For Deborah Jiang-Stein, since distance could not resolve the trauma of her prison birth, returning to prisons by leading writing workshops helped her origin story cohabitate more comfortably with her present self. "Maybe some experiences don't need to go away. Maybe we just need to metabolize and integrate them, to get a few stakes in the ground to navigate by."[146] For Jiang-Stein, that relative resolution felt like enough.

Another implication is that, in Sorrowjoy, these spiraling patterns, although painful, can facilitate healing. This is why, many years after one author's expulsion from his ultra-Orthodox village, he experimented with partial returns by attending events with new, non-Orthodox Jewish friends. After so much loss, he was "deeply and fundamentally suspicious of any hint of dogma or ideology," but he yearned for the soothing comfort he once found in "a time and place when ideas moved me, . . . a time when I allowed myself to be fired up with passion for something, anything, because it held a 'truth.'"[147] Although he was ultimately unwilling to reembrace faith, those partial returns helped him name his desires and more fully mourn his losses. "I let the stream of tears fall over the open pages of my prayer book."[148] Through the puncturing of those shards from elsewhere, grief and healing intermingled.

Voicing the Potential for Alternative Futures

Having presented evidence to challenge common misconceptions about arrival points and departure points, in this final subsection I explore the possibility of arriving at yet-to-be-determined futures. Asking the question *How did you get out?* implies that travelers have agency in departing, but it does not recognize their agency in shaping the places where they might go. Unlike other segments of the invisible exile journey, which involve considerable deference to external norms, Sorrowjoy has a different tone. In Sorrowjoy, as travelers become more confident in their new identities and more certain of being past the finishing line, it becomes easier to ask provocative questions. Instead of assimilating into social roles defined without reference to travelers' experiences, a more empowering sense of arrival occurs when travelers feel able to rework those subjectivities and mark them as their own. Measuring arrival from this perspective is not about making it to a predefined space. Instead, it's about using new capabilities to push toward a not-yet-existing but potentially more inclusive future.

Within travel writing, taking an environment and making it your own is sometimes called *stamping*. After a new arrival becomes familiar enough with a space to begin exploring it more intentionally, travelers then "stamp" personal meanings onto those places.[149] Instead of describing a place by parroting other people's narratives, these self-generated descriptions incorporate the traveler's personal details and lived experiences.

Stamping, in other words, is an expression of agency. It is about surveying the environment and making choices about which aspects to embrace, which to ignore, which to reject, and which to remake. This agency can feel defiant at times. In contrast to the blind assimilation of Basic Training, travelers in Sorrowjoy may become more like the exile who "cannot or, more to the point, will not make the adjustment, preferring instead to remain outside the mainstream, unaccommodated, uncoopted, resistant."[150] Other times, this agency is about co-construction. Instead of opting out of a larger moral community, travelers may push for an altered type of recognition based on "a process of reflection and sensitization to the suffering of others."[151]

In my assessment, invisible exiles are especially likely to stamp Sorrowjoy in one of two ways. The first is by speaking up to encourage change. One author, for example, began speaking publicly about her religious trauma because she wanted to challenge society's tolerance of religious abuse. "I feel that people should be warned about what the Church truly is, who its founder really was, what really goes on there, the lengths it is willing to go to, and what they are willing to sacrifice in the name of achieving their ends."[152] Without this information, she feared those abuses would "go on unchecked."[153]

Speaking up to promote change is likewise why another author decided to educate her partner—and, later, the general public—about what it means to have a kinky sexuality. As an alternative to acknowledging her sexuality but not practicing it, she decided to structure the conversation akin to a religious conversion class with the material presented simply, directly, and without justification. If anything, her partner reciprocated by making the process even more technical. "We were measuring the intensity of different strokes with scientific meticulousness."[154] This analytical framework felt somewhat contrived compared to her more intuitive understanding, but the process worked, her partner learned, and her arrival state changed as a result.

Although speaking up is one way to stamp an environment, a second option is to claim the privilege of remaining silent. This is why, even when one author began speaking publicly about her experience as a trans woman, she did not correct people in everyday contexts who assumed she was cisgender. "I'm not responsible for other people's perceptions. . . . It is not a woman's duty to disclose that she's trans to every person she meets."[155] Queer activists sometimes criticized her for this choice. They alleged that, by *passing,* she was somehow *in the closet.* She disagreed that she was *passing,* a term implying she was *pretending* to be a woman rather than truly being one. Additionally, by remaining silent, she implicitly transferred the responsibility for mistaken assumptions from her shoulders to those of society at large. "We must abolish the entitlement that deludes us into believing that we have the right to make assumptions about people's identities and project those assumptions onto their genders and bodies."[156]

This insistence that other people take responsibility for managing difference is likewise why another author refused either to tolerate racial microaggressions or to explain why those actions were hurtful. When white people pet her hair, "I say simply, 'Please don't. You shouldn't do that.'"[157] Similarly, after receiving a backhanded compliment from a white coworker, "I . . . remove the microphone clipped to my lapel, shake her hand while shaking my head, leave this small television studio, and walk confidently back to my office."[158] In both examples, her response signaled disapproval, but her refusal to explain or defend the nature of the injury left the responsibility for self-examination with her white peers.

Making these decisions about when to speak and when to remain silent is a political act. By voicing the taboo in some situations and by refusing to explain in others, travelers challenge the people around them to consider their own culpability when expectations do not align. In this way, a key characteristic of Sorrowjoy is that, instead of allowing other people to dictate the terms of belonging, travelers begin to claim authority to make that decision for themselves.

This goal of claiming agency both through voice and through silence helps explain why, in one author's personal campaign to assert her agency despite ableist culture, she insisted on placing her coffee order verbally. No matter how many times the barista guessed at her order or slid pen and paper across the counter, "I smile and I say, 'No thank you,'" then "I resume my request," stretching the stuttering to "semi-real" limits.[159] The point was to assert belonging not by silencing her stutter, which prioritized other people, but by urging other people to slow down, hear her voice, and accept her decision to use it. The cup of coffee that resulted was "beautiful. Not because I have found a cure but because . . . it holds the potential for everyday victories rather than everyday defeats. I am not going to be fluent. Who is?"[160]

These examples speak to the complicated nature of exile. Travelers may never be free from intruding bouts of "crippling sorrow" and feelings of "orphanhood,"[161] and yet, alongside this pain, Sorrowjoy includes "the pleasures of exile," including "the pleasure of being surprised, of never taking anything for granted."[162] Rather than following "a prescribed path," an invisible exile may find joy in "doing things according to your own pattern," which is itself "a unique pleasure."[163]

In conclusion, claiming agency over when to speak and when to remain silent is a key characteristic of Sorrowjoy. Invisible exile narratives demonstrate the many ways that the question *How did you get out?* misrepresents the exile journey. At this point in their quests, travelers express the sense of having built a solid foundation, and their new identities and relationships feel relatively stable. But this relative stability does not mean the past has ended, nor does it mean the past and present coexist in some tidy resolution. On the contrary, by revisiting the past, travelers gain new insights into their present and reconsider their possible future. This outcome does not end grief, but it adds an element of healing, which changes the feeling of exile. Reflections on how to interpret these larger journeys into, through, and partially out of invisible exile are the subject of the concluding chapter.

Conclusion

Travel is a powerful social governing tool. Ritual pilgrimages to religious and historical sites can deepen a traveler's commitment to the status quo. Conversely, exploratory journeys through socially foreign worlds can spark questions about identity and taken-for-granted worldviews. For these reasons, the normative policing surrounding travel, as well as the tales travelers tell, is deeply political.

This book asserts that excessively narrow definitions of who counts as a *traveler* and what counts as *travel writing* is a form of linguistic oppression. Many types of mobility contribute to self-transformation, and those transformations feed into contentious politics. By analyzing a range of narrative artifacts—including ones that may otherwise be excluded from the travel-writing genre—this book sheds light on the topography of invisible exile, as well as on the role travel plays in vulnerable acts of self-actualization.

Next, by mapping invisible exile—by giving the phenomenon a name and analyzing its contours—my hope is to sensitize readers to issues often engulfed in silence. Much of this silence arises through the environment, for instance through the construction of physical and social infrastructure that pulls identity in some directions while foreclosing other options. This silence also arises through the stories we tell—and don't tell—about place and identity, as well as the systems of belonging those stories represent.

One way to better understand the role of place and narration in identity construction is through acts of narrative resistance. The cultural artifacts analyzed within this book describe journeys that often felt impossible, unthinkable, or taboo. By organizing those experiences into a narrative form, these authors brought their journeys out of the chaos, out of the shadows, and into the spotlight for others to see.

Analyzing these acts of narrative resistance sheds light on the relationship between place and identity. It shows how movement through space relates to constructions of self. It also explains why such journeys might feel necessary, where travelers go, what helps them advance, what blocks their path, what price they pay, and what they hope their journeys will achieve.

By tracing the contours of these journeys, this book traces systems of belonging that operate beyond formal systems of law and citizenship. Although some exiles cross international borders, others experience exile closer to home. In both cases, exile includes the loss of cherished places, people, and identities, as well as the trauma of navigating socially foreign worlds without the benefit of prior socialization or adequate support. My hope is that, by building a unifying narrative around these journeys, this book might help fellow travelers—including those already deep into their journeys, as well as those who might be contemplating their first steps—to coalesce around a collective, empathic, and visible place of validation and resistance.

Invisible Exile Exists, and Its Hardships Should Be Acknowledged

One key takeaway of this book is simply that invisible exile exists. Many people for many reasons live as unacknowledged refugees dispossessed from their social worlds with or without crossing international borders. Their stories reveal that, despite the burgeoning literature on global cosmopolitanism and self-reflexivity, many people are *not* free to choose their own life paths. In oppressive contexts, travel can help people discover more empowering alternatives, but those journeys come with considerable costs in lost place attachment, revoked social support, and fractured identity coherence.

Moreover, many of these journeys are not included within the scholarship on travel writing. This exclusion implies that invisible exiles do not present as the right sort of travelers (i.e., adventurers, rather than refugees), that they do not visit the right sorts of destinations (i.e., far away and international, rather than physically close but culturally foreign), and that they do not embrace travel with the right sort of attitude (i.e., courageously, rather than in desperation). This book pushes against these biases by narrating a type of travel—invisible exile—that is ubiquitous, even if misunderstood. This travel typology incorporates diverse travel modes—such as imaginative travel, scouting trips, assimilation treks, and co-narrative journeys— all of which link travel to self-transformation and, potentially, to social change.

These findings shed light on the relationship between place and identity. Many social groups use environmental controls to stabilize the status quo, including by restricting opportunities for travel and by encouraging tectonic behaviors that blunt a journey's provocative potential. However, travel always remains possible, even if only through the imagination. Indeed, imaginative travel is a common first step in invisible exile quests. The supportive architecture of fantasy worlds that partially eludes repressive gatekeeping can motivate travelers to seek similarly validating environments in real life. However, because of the desire to maintain place attachment, instead of breaking free from oppressive spaces by permanently relocating, many travelers work desperately to remain embedded within their communities even when those places feel suffocating, and even when, through scouting trips, travelers identify other places that feel more authentic.

For travelers who, for the sake of their safety, are unable or unwilling to remain within the social worlds of their birth, the scale of rupture that follows underscores that exile does not need to involve international borders to be profound. On the contrary, in my assessment, exile includes any rupture in place attachment that exploits the link between social exclusion and capital punishment. Exile revokes the permission for and the capacity of travelers to continue identifying with the places, identities, and cultures anchoring their everyday lives. The liminal crisis that follows is not a temporary reprieve from everyday roles and drudgeries. Instead, invisible exiles are frequently thrust into the harsh, crisis-prone state of having no home to return to and no alternative place to land.

This crisis of nonbelonging is then coupled with another dynamic, which is that, even though assimilation culture is inherently exclusionary, assimilation work may nevertheless feature prominently in exile life histories, even in tales emphasizing resistance. However, the repetitive failure of assimilation to deliver belonging, even despite invisible exiles' eager embrace of assimilation projects, shows that societal gatekeeping remains alive and well, even in today's era of purported global cosmopolitanism. These findings challenge the notion that travelers can find meaningful post-exile healing by co-narrating their experiences with hosts. Instead, invisible exiles may recover best by constructing places of their own, not as nostalgic acts of heritage preservation, but as places for co-narration with fellow travelers and at arm's length from other groups. In these filtered spaces, exiles can begin to heal from the trauma of recurring exclusions.

Finally, these findings challenge the assumption either that exile ends, after which travelers have *made it,* or that exile persists indefinitely and traps travelers in perpetual pain. Instead, invisible exile often reaches a provisional end that straddles the past and the future, and that embraces a mix of accomplishment and mourning.

These findings are important because, without these critical perspectives, invisible exile is easily misread as a bootstrap narrative of moving to opportunity. On the contrary, invisible exile is first and foremost about the ongoing influence of social oppression. These insights push against the idea that the best way for exiles to resolve nonbelonging is either by assimilating into an imagined mainstream or by building a separate subcultural enclave. By contrast, invisible exile travel writing suggests that a better resolution would be for other social groups to take responsibility for ongoing exclusionary practices, including by doing the work required to build more inclusive environments. These findings also validate the often overlooked but profoundly painful experiences that often accompany journeys of supposed upward social mobility, which should spark deep questioning about why society constructs its supportive architecture in ways that make mobility so hurtful, as well as how those barriers could be addressed.

The Journey into, Through, and Partially out of Invisible Exile

To explain these dynamics, this book analyzed a collection of life history narratives that, in my assessment, not only link travel with self-transformation but also diversify the genre of travel writing. Literary geographers have long attended to stories of close-to-home trips, poor people's movements, and unresolved journeys, but these narratives are often dismissed as *not travely enough* to analyze through the more selective lens of travel writing. However, a defining feature of travel writing and a primary goal of travel-writing scholarship is to understand how travel contributes to self-change. Narratives of invisible exile fit that description perfectly. By including these narratives in travel-writing analysis, scholars can rethink how the concept of a *journey* is defined.

Moreover, this book has pushed against the tendency to analyze diverse experiences—for example, related to class, race, gender, sexuality, ability, religion, and trauma—separately within specialized subfields. In other scholarly work, instead of analyzing invisible exile life history writing as part of a shared phenomenon, gay cyclists would show up in queer studies, post-rape hikers would land in gender studies, cult survivors enrolling in higher education would appear in religious studies, and anti-ableist traveling reporters would appear in disability studies. However, by bringing these narratives together under the shared umbrella of travel writing, this book traces the topography of invisible exile that these narratives share.

Next, by giving coherence to these disparate journeys—while also acknowledging their nonteleological character—this book provides readers with a guided tour of invisible exile. By giving invisible exile a name, outlining its contours, and plotting its trajectory on a map, my hope is to give invisible exile a stronger environmental reflection, as well as to help non-exile readers gain greater awareness of and empathy for ongoing systems of exclusion.

To sum up, I started this book by analyzing environmental practices that limit identity development. Since encounters with difference can promote social change, one common tactic of social control is to shape environments in ways that limit exposure to other places and perspectives. However, since no environment is hermetically sealed, since change is always possible, and since border crossing is always possible, a second tactic of social control involves socializing people to adopt tectonic attitudes during encounter moments, including while traveling through socially foreign worlds where competing ideas are visible. These environmental practices reinforce the status quo by restricting travel that might facilitate change, as well as by weakening the interplay between travel and transformation.

These obstacles to physical travel help explain the importance of imaginative travel and its potentially generative effects. Through media and fantasy play, travelers transport themselves to other environments capable of sustaining different identities. In addition to offering a temporary reprieve from places that feel suffocating, these imagined journeys provide a replacement architecture that supports other modes of self-expression. By providing a safe-enough place to explore other worlds and other selves, these journeys play an important early role in invisible exile quests.

Imaginative journeys and their suggestion that travelers could live otherwise can then motivate people to take scouting trips. Scouting trips are short, exploratory journeys to physical locations where travelers temporarily shed their preexisting identities and test alternative performances in the company of strangers. When these journeys validate traits that feel authentic, despite being taboo at home, this validation could, in theory, encourage travelers to permanently relocate to these more supportive environments. However, instead of embracing these opportunities, invisible exiles often move in the opposite direction. To embrace these seemingly incommensurate places and selves, travelers are often given no choice except to simultaneously relinquish the places, resources, and identities they already possess. To avoid these devastating losses, travelers sometimes try to spatially splinter their identities by planting one foot in both worlds, but that process can be exhausting and rarely leads to fulfillment.

Instead, travelers often reach a breaking point where, despite their desire to remain in their communities, continuing to do so becomes unworkable or unsafe. At this fateful moment, travelers separate from their places and identities of origin. In some cases, travelers hope that, by shedding their old skin, they might discover a healthier, more authentic future. However, that's not why invisible exiles leave. Instead, as an extreme form of dispossession, exile is often imposed as a substitute for capital punishment, and travelers experience it first and foremost as a form of self-death. Through this exile, travelers lose access to the places, people, and social roles that previously anchored their identities and infused their lives with meaning, which can lead to profound feelings of existential erasure.

From this place of existential death, things usually get worse, at least for a while. After exile, travelers have no choice but to make their way through socially foreign worlds, and they usually do so without the benefit of prior socialization. Despite previous imaginative travel and scouting trips, invisible exiles usually come from environments that intentionally blocked access to the information needed to effectively navigate socially foreign spaces. This lack of socialization explains why new environments often feel confusing and why invisible exiles make so many mistakes. Through trial and error, travelers become more familiar with new norms, but those blunders also show them just how much they do not yet belong. Moreover, the confused and judgmental responses of onlookers usually reinforce this sense of incomplete transition.

To find a way out of this harsh liminal swamp, many travelers experiment with assimilation. Through various structured retraining programs, travelers try to erase the lingering markers of who they once were, and they work to acquire the technical skills and symbolic knowledge they associate with the groups they wish to join. The hope is that, by doing what hosts do, wearing what they wear, and thinking how they think, invisible exiles might find new belonging. Often, however, these strategies fall short because hosts have their own systems of privilege, which they defend through gatekeeping. Furthermore, learning to perform according to new expectations does not erase the memory of exile, and those unhealed wounds remain raw and hurting.

Instead, the healing that most often leads to invisible exile's provisional end comes less from blending in with an imagined mainstream and more from co-narrating with fellow travelers. Co-narration is a crucial tool for identity narration and trauma recovery. However, co-narrating with hosts is rarely effective because the limited imagination, selective attention, and moral stance of hosts interferes with the goal of mutual intelligibility and co-learning. By contrast, shared but sheltered places organized around exile provide a partial antidote to environmental silencing elsewhere. In these spaces of their own, travelers find a fuller reflection of their identities and life experiences, which facilitates healing.

Even then, however, the past lives on, and the future remains undetermined. This lack of closure or resolution is why, to the extent that exile ends, it is not because exiles leave the past behind or because their losses are offset by new gains, but rather because travelers find more effective ways to manage the commingling of past and present. Furthermore, as invisible exiles become more secure in their new environments and more confident in their new identities, they may become more vocal in issuing calls for action. These calls suggest that a more comprehensive end to invisible exile might arise through social change, not only by reducing the intolerance leading to exile, but also by constructing safer, more numerous, and more welcoming places to call home.

These Journeys Point Toward New Possible Futures

This potential for travel to facilitate transformation speaks to the question of why invisible exiles narrate their journeys in a public format. Invisible exiles traveled to remake their identities even when it meant resisting the status quo. However, sharing their histories with readers who may not understand their values or withhold their judgments can expose travelers to renewed exclusion. Given the risks associated with going public, why do travelers write about their journeys, and what changes do they hope their narratives will promote?

In my assessment, invisible exiles create narrative artifacts for many reasons. Some write as advocates for their communities, to advance activist causes, or to spark public debates.[1] Others write to find their voices, reclaim their stories, or give themselves permission to express difficult truths.[2] Some write to explain what they've endured, to correct dismissive or distorted records, and to challenge outright lies.[3] Travelers write to tame roiling emotions, grieve major life losses, and express unsaid goodbyes.[4] They write to provide other travelers with a reflection, to reach out and connect with kindred spirits, and to show strangers they are not alone.[5] They also write because narration is a tool for seeing the self and the world more clearly, with greater nuance, and as an integrated whole.[6]

Within this mix, one recurring theme involves the work that narration performs for the travelers themselves. These self-directed functions help authors make sense of their confusing journeys, which can empower travelers to keep moving forward, let go of old pain, and mourn the losses associated with success.

A second recurring theme involves the way travel narratives can benefit peers. Having made these invisible journeys and disclosed them to the general public, this heightened visibility can provide fellow travelers with a road map or guide. Although each journey is unique, by showing readers one possible path forward, other travelers might be better able to find similar paths. Additionally, since no journey is perfect, writing a narrative that includes honest portrayals of the pitfalls and perils of the journey can help invisible exiles learn from each other's missteps.

A third recurring theme involves the construction of camaraderie. By recording the journey, rather than simply stepping off the trail without a trace, travelers let each other know they are not alone.

Other people are walking similar paths. Although these travelers might be separated by time, place, and identity traits, their journeys nevertheless have several patterns in common. By adding their voices to the larger chorus of invisible exile, travelers get the benefit of journeying together, including with absent peers.

From this place of collaboration—a place born of narratives that are simultaneously personal and systemic—change becomes possible. The collective experience of invisible exile highlights the shared barriers facing all such travelers. By identifying these constraints, this book calls attention to the inhospitable aspects of invisible exiles' communities of origin. It also calls on other social groups to help diversify the not-yet-fully-welcoming places that travelers hope to call home. It is my hope that this book and the map of invisible exile it provides will assist with this work.

Acknowledgments

I would like to express my sincere appreciation to my University of Michigan colleague Scott Campbell for his close reading of the initial draft of this manuscript. Our informal conversations illuminated areas in writing and analysis that needed additional clarity.

I am deeply indebted to the three peer reviewers from the University of Minnesota Press, including Adam Morton, as well as the two anonymous reviewers. Their invaluable insights, suggestions, and contributions greatly enhanced the quality of this work.

Special thanks are due to Jason Weidemann and the dedicated staff at the University of Minnesota Press for their diligent efforts in shepherding this manuscript through the review and production process.

Above all, I am immensely grateful to the forty authors whose courage in sharing their stories made this project possible. As a fellow invisible exile, I found profound guidance—both professionally and personally—in your narratives. Your willingness to entrust your stories to strangers like me made an indelible mark on my life. This book is my tribute to you.

Appendix

Annotated Reading List

Ayaan Hirsi Ali, *Nomad*
This memoir recounts Ali's odyssey from her strict Islamic upbringing in Somalia to her eventual embrace of Western values, offering a narrative of clashing civilizations and the ongoing global struggle for women's rights and personal freedom.

Karen Armstrong, *The Spiral Staircase*
Armstrong's memoir offers an introspective exploration of her journey from a disillusioned Roman Catholic nun living with undiagnosed epilepsy to a scholar of comparative religion, providing insights into the complexities of faith, doubt, and ableism.

Howard Axelrod, *The Point of Vanishing*
Axelrod recounts his transformative experience of living in solitude for two years in rural Vermont following a life-altering accident that left him blind in one eye, delving into themes of isolation, identity, and the search for an inner voice.

Caspar Baldwin, *Not Just a Tomboy*
Baldwin's memoir shares a personal journey of self-discovery as a transgender man grappling with dysphoria, voicelessness, and eventual empowerment while navigating the process of undergoing a female-to-male gender transition.

Jennifer Finney Boylan, *She's Not There*
This memoir chronicles Boylan's journey of gender transition as a middle-aged adult, shedding light on her inner conflict between her desire to live an authentic life and the love and loyalty she feels toward her wife and children.

Regina Calcaterra, *Etched in Sand*

Calcaterra's narrative delves into themes of childhood poverty, parental abuse, and the foster care system in her coming-of-age story about overcoming trauma, navigating family court, and building safety for herself and her siblings.

Staceyann Chin, *The Other Side of Paradise*

This memoir chronicles Chin's journey from a childhood in Jamaica marked by poverty, violence, and familial abandonment to her emergence as a queer rights activist and spoken-word poet living in New York City.

Nicole Chung, *All You Can Ever Know*

Chung's memoir describes her experiences growing up as a racialized adoptee in a white family, as well as her experiences as an expectant mother preparing to start a family of her own, by exploring the complexities of family ties, cultural heritage, and the search for one's roots.

Garrard Conley, *Boy Erased*

This memoir describes the author's experience of being pushed into an anti-gay conversion therapy program as a young adult in the Evangelical South, exploring the power of family bonds, sexual assault, and religious trauma.

Shulem Deen, *All Who Go Do Not Return*

Deen's memoir chronicles his journey from being a devout Hasidic Jew to becoming an outsider in his own community whose pursuit of self-discovery and intellectual freedom leads to his abandonment by friends and family, as well as the heartbreaking loss of his children.

Jaquira Díaz, *Ordinary Girls*

Díaz offers a poignant account of her tumultuous coming-of-age experiences in Puerto Rico and Miami, navigating poverty, family dysfunction, and her identity as a queer woman of color, including her attempt to find belonging within the U.S. Navy.

Sascha Altman DuBrul, *Maps to the Other Side*

This narrative chronicles DuBrul's personal journey of navigating punk culture with bipolar disorder, offering an exploration of mental illness, political activism, and the challenges of remaining true to one's values despite the stigmas of Western medicine.

Carlos Eire, *Learning to Die in Miami*

Eire recounts his experiences as a Cuban refugee adjusting to life in Miami, offering a poignant and deeply personal reflection on the complexities of cultural assimilation and the enduring impact of political upheaval on personal identity.

Deborah Feldman, *Unorthodox*

Feldman's memoir details her journey of breaking away from her closed Hasidic community in Brooklyn, leading her readers through the complexities of family expectations, self-discovery, and educational aspirations in a strict religious setting.

Rita Golden Gelman, *Tales of a Female Nomad*

Gelman's narrative recounts her journey of leaving behind her comfortable, conventional life as a wife and mother in Los Angeles to embracing a nomadic existence exploring global culture as a single, middle-aged woman traveling solo.

Jenna Miscavige Hill, *Beyond Belief*

Hill's childhood memoir provides a firsthand account of her upbringing within Scientology, offering readers a compelling narrative of manipulation, control, and eventual escape from a coercive religious environment.

Katie Rain Hill, *Rethinking Normal*

Hill's coming-of-age memoir shares her journey of self-discovery as a high school and college student craving authenticity, openness, and friendship in a world where transgender people often struggle to find acceptance, even within the LGBTQ community.

bell hooks, "Kentucky Is My Fate"

In this essay, hooks, a prolific Black feminist scholar, reflects on her upbringing in rural Kentucky and its impact on her identity and intellectual pursuits while navigating the privileged white world of California's urban universities.

Abdi Nor Iftin, *Call Me American*

Iftin's memoir of life as a refugee recounts his journey from war-torn Somalia to the realization of his childhood dream—embracing American culture—in a context where his adopted country does not always conform to the images he adored on the silver screen.

Jedidiah Jenkins, *To Shake the Sleeping Self*

Jenkins recounts his transformative cycling journey from Oregon to Patagonia as a closeted gay man in his thirties torn between his loyalty to Christianity and his desire to live a more fulfilling life filled with love and without regrets.

Deborah Jiang-Stein, *Prison Baby*

In this memoir, Jiang-Stein chronicles her turbulent young adulthood as a mixed-race child who was born to an incarcerated mother and then adopted into a white Jewish family, offering insights into addiction, redemption, and the intergenerational impact of the criminal justice system.

Saeed Jones, *How We Fight for Our Lives*

This memoir describes Jones's experiences as a gay Black man coming of age in Texas and Kentucky, exploring themes of family loyalty, identity repression, and sexual trauma.

Jillian Keenan, *Sex with Shakespeare*

Keenan's narrative uses hypothetical conversations with Shakespearean characters to explore her personal experiences of sometimes repressing and sometimes embracing her kinky sexual orientation.

Julie Lythcott-Haims, *Real American*

Lythcott-Haims shares her personal journey as a biracial woman transitioning from initially embracing whiteness as the assumed marker of belonging in America to ultimately celebrating Blackness in a context where her acceptance into the Black community is complex and multifaceted.

Aspen Matis, *Girl in the Woods*

Matis narrates her transformative journey of hiking the Pacific Crest Trail following a sexual assault, offering readers an exploration of the process of healing from sexual trauma, as well as reclaiming agency following a disempowering childhood.

Janet Mock, *Redefining Realness*
Mock shares her intimate journey as a transgender woman of color, offering a compelling narrative of resilience, self-acceptance, and activism that critiques the exclusionary aspects of queer culture and the uneven access to medical care.

Liz Murray, *Breaking Night*
Murray shares her story of overcoming childhood adversity and homelessness to ultimately attend Harvard University, shedding light on the few but precious safe havens that helped her on her way.

Kwame Onwuachi, *Notes from a Young Black Chef*
This memoir chronicles Onwuachi's journey from troubled youth to acclaimed chef, offering reflections on the racial dynamics of being Black while navigating the white world of French cuisine.

Dan-El Padilla Peralta, *Undocumented*
Peralta shares his journey from being a homeless undocumented immigrant of color to becoming a college student in the Ivy League, shedding light on legal barriers to self-actualization and the complexities of inhabiting diverse social worlds.

Andrew Pham, *Catfish and Mandala*
Pham narrates his soul-searching bicycle journey from California to Vietnam, exploring his identity as a Vietnamese refugee struggling to find belonging within the racial mosaic of U.S. culture by revisiting his war-torn roots.

Katherine Preston, *Out with It*
Preston's description of her life journey as a person with a stutter challenges societal stigmas surrounding speech impediments and empowers readers to embrace vulnerability while striving to find independent, empowered voices.

Dorit Sasson, *Accidental Soldier*
Sasson recounts her journey of enlisting in the Israel Defense Forces

as an American immigrant, offering readers a narrative of personal growth by stepping outside one's comfort zone, in her case by navigating the complexities of foreign military service.

Sarah Smarsh, *Heartland*

Smarsh reflects on her journey from an impoverished Kansas farm to her life as an academic and journalist, presenting a powerful narrative that explores class, poverty, and devalued life in what is supposed to be the richest country on Earth.

Jayanti Tamm, *Cartwheels in a Sari*

Tamm recounts her upbringing as *the chosen one* in a Hindu-inspired cult in the New York metropolitan region, along with the shunning and alienation she experienced when leaving that cult to pursue the freedom to choose whom to love.

Jeannette Walls, *The Glass Castle*

This memoir describes Walls's struggle to make peace with her tumultuous upbringing in a dysfunctional family riddled with poverty while building a new life for herself as an author and journalist in New York City.

Ruth Wariner, *The Sound of Gravel*

Wariner's childhood memoir chronicles her upbringing in a polygamist cult and her determination, after the traumatic death of her mother and two brothers, to rescue her remaining siblings from a life of abject poverty, religious coercion, and sexual abuse.

Tara Westover, *Educated*

Westover recounts her journey from growing up in a survivalist family in rural Idaho where she was prohibited from attending public school to earning a PhD from Cambridge University, a journey that tore her family in half.

Chris Wilson, *The Master Plan*

Wilson's narrative details his journey from being sentenced to life in prison at age sixteen to constructing his own path toward redemption through hard work and self-education in defiance of the racial structures blocking Black access to self-actualization.

Raynor Winn, *The Salt Path*
This memoir recounts Winn's journey with her terminally ill husband while walking the South West Coast Path after a legal battle stripped them of their home and livelihood, shedding light on the social stigma of homelessness and the healing power of nature.

Jeanette Winterson, *Why Be Happy When You Could Be Normal?*
Winterson's memoir delves into her tumultuous upbringing by an adoptive mother who strictly adhered to religious and homophobic doctrine, providing poignant insights into the quest to find identity, belonging, and authenticity through life and literature.

Notes

Introduction

1. Bosangit et al., "'If I Was Going to Die'"; Craib, *Cartographic Mexico;* Galani-Moutafi, "Self and the Other"; Gregory, *Geographical Imaginations;* Heins, *Beyond Friend and Foe;* Hulme and Youngs, "Introduction"; McWha et al., "Travel Writers and the Nature"; Noy, "This Trip Really Changed Me"; Pratt, *Imperial Eyes.*

2. Galani-Moutafi, "Self and the Other"; Lisle, *Holidays in the Danger Zone;* Torkington, "Place and Lifestyle Migration."

3. Bosangit et al., "'If I Was Going to Die'"; Elsrud, "Time Creation in Travelling"; Noy, "This Trip Really Changed Me"; Lewis, "Remapping Disclosure."

4. Elsrud, "Time Creation in Travelling"; Gideon, "Gendering Activism, Exile and Wellbeing"; Hubbard and Wilkinson, "Walking a Lonely Path"; Hulme, "Travelling to Write"; Willis, "Re-storying Wilderness and Adventure Therapies."

5. Elsrud, "Risk Creation in Traveling"; Noy, "This Trip Really Changed Me"; Takacs, "Becoming Interesting."

6. Bosangit et al., "'If I Was Going to Die'"; Li and Wang, "China in the Eyes of Western Travelers"; Pan et al., "Travel Blogs"; Van Nuenen, "Here I Am."

7. Rak, *Boom!,* 9–11.

8. Wright, "Recognising the Political," 421.

9. Ellis et al., "Autoethnography."

10. Brosseau, "In, Of, Out, With, and Through."

11. Jenkins, *To Shake the Sleeping Self;* Pham, *Catfish and Mandala;* Sasson, *Accidental Soldier.*

12. Deen, *All Who Go Do Not Return.*

13. Jiang-Stein, *Prison Baby.*

14. Smarsh, *Heartland.*
15. Baldwin, *Not Just a Tomboy.*
16. Chung, *All You Can Ever Know.*
17. Preston, *Out with It.*
18. Chin, *Other Side of Paradise.*
19. Jones, *How We Fight for Our Lives;* Mock, *Redefining Realness.*
20. Calcaterra, *Etched in Sand;* Wilson, *Master Plan.*
21. Axelrod, *Point of Vanishing;* Eire, *Learning to Die in Miami;* hooks, "Kentucky Is My Fate"; Walls, *Glass Castle;* Wariner, *Sound of Gravel.*
22. Said, *Reflections on Exile,* 176.
23. Iftin, *Call Me American;* Peralta, *Undocumented.*
24. Davies, "Assemblage and Social Movements."
25. Hackl, "Key Figure of Mobility," 56.
26. Bowstead, "Women on the Move," 115.
27. Hobbs, *Chosen Exile,* 4–5.
28. Tamm, *Cartwheels in a Sari.*
29. Winn, *Salt Path.*
30. Feldman, *Unorthodox.*
31. DuBrul, *Maps to the Other Side;* Matis, *Girl in the Woods.*
32. Hill, *Rethinking Normal;* Keenan, *Sex with Shakespeare.*
33. Díaz, *Ordinary Girls;* Murray, *Breaking Night.*
34. Lythcott-Haims, *Real American;* Onwuachi, *Notes from a Young Black Chef.*
35. Conley, *Boy Erased;* Hill, *Beyond Belief.*
36. Gelman, *Female Nomad;* Winterson, *Why Be Happy.*
37. Ali, *Nomad;* Boylan, *She's Not There.*
38. Armstrong, *Spiral Staircase;* Westover, *Educated.*
39. Edwards, "Diaspora"; Ibrahim, "New Flâneur"; Leyshon and Bull, "Bricolage of the Here"; Nijman, "Locals, Exiles and Cosmopolitans"; Papadopoulos, "In the Ruins of Representation"; Yuval-Davis, "Theorizing Identity."
40. Bosangit et al., "'If I Was Going to Die'"; Llewellyn-Beardsley et al., "Characteristics of Mental Health Recovery."
41. Atkinson, "Anthony Giddens as Adversary," 538; Papadopoulos, "In the Ruins of Representation," 151; Yuval-Davis, "Theorizing Identity," 267.
42. Ochs and Capps, *Living Narrative,* 207.
43. Ochs and Capps, 207. See also Leyshon and Bull, "The Bricolage of the Here," 176.
44. Nurser et al., "Personal Storytelling in Mental Health," 31.
45. Beech, "Liminality and the Practices," 286, 288.

46. Yuval-Davis, "Theorizing Identity," 274.

47. Yuval-Davis, 275.

48. Toolis, "Theorizing Critical Placemaking," 187.

49. Ochs and Capps, *Living Narrative*, 252.

50. Yuval-Davis, "Theorizing Identity," 267.

51. Ochs and Capps, "Narrating the Self," 33.

52. Fivush, "Speaking Silence," 89.

53. Fivush, 96.

54. Ochs and Capps, *Living Narrative*, 145. See also Llewellyn-Beardsley et al., "Characteristics of Mental Health Recovery," 3.

55. Fivush, "Speaking Silence," 91.

56. Fivush, 91.

57. Ochs and Capps, *Living Narrative*, 146.

58. Ochs and Capps, "Narrating the Self," 37.

59. Ochs and Capps, 37.

60. Toolis, "Theorizing Critical Placemaking," 188–89.

61. Hauf, "Teaching World Cultures."

62. Denning, *Cultural Front*; Eichhorn, *Archival Turn in Feminism*; Hogan, *Feminist Bookstore Movement*.

63. Hauf, "Teaching World Cultures," 114.

64. Hones, *Literary Geography*, 11.

65. Hones, 78.

66. Seamon, "Newcomers, Existential Outsiders and Insiders," 85.

67. Brosseau, "In, Of, Out, With, and Through," 10.

68. Lisle, *Holidays in the Danger Zone*, 192.

69. Heins, *Beyond Friend and Foe*, 85, 90.

70. Heins, 79, 84, and 85.

71. Kaplan, *Questions of Travel*, 2.

72. Heins, *Beyond Friend and Foe*, 85–86.

73. Heins, 85.

74. Heins, 85–86.

75. Heins, 85–86.

76. Heins, 83.

77. Heins, 84.

78. White, *Flâneur*, 52.

79. Hubbard, *Cities and Sexualities*, 124.

80. White, *Flâneur*, 39.

81. Heins, *Beyond Friend and Foe*, 106; White, 51.

82. Heins, 83.

83. White, *Flâneur*, 47.

84. Chawla and Jones, "Introduction," xiv.

85. Said, *Reflections on Exile*, 185.

86. Heins, *Beyond Friend and Foe*, 99.

87. Heins, 93.

88. Aizura, *Mobile Subjects*, 3.

89. Hulme, "Travelling to Write," 90.

90. Hulme, 94.

91. Rubies, "Travelling to Write," 254–55.

92. Hopper, "Isles/Ireland," 188.

93. Youngs, "Africa/The Congo," 167.

94. Youngs, 193.

95. Carr, "Modernism and Travel (1880–1940)," 79–80.

96. Bassnett, "Travel Writing and Gender," 232.

97. Bassnett, 234, 238.

98. Teltscher, "India/Calcutta," 194.

99. Hulme, "Travelling to Write," 92.

100. Kist, "Life Moments in Texts"; Ross et al., "War Stories?"

101. Altier, "In Their Own Words?"; Herrmann, *Written in Red*.

102. El Refaie, *Autobiographical Comics*; Imamaliyeva, "Some Aspects in Azerbaijainian Memoir."

103. Willis, "Restorying the Self."

104. Calvillo, "Memoir and Autobiography"; Wallach, *Closer to the Truth*.

105. Mlakar, *Merely Being There Is Not Enough*; Taylor, "Problem of Women's Sociality."

106. Donohue-Smith, "Telling the Whole Story"; Radden and Somogy, "Epistemological Value of Depression Memoirs."

107. Brosseau, "In, Of, Out, With, and Through," 18.

108. Brosseau, 18.

109. Brosseau, 16.

110. Bosangit et al., "'If I Was Going to Die'"; Brosseau, "In, Of, Out, With, and Through"; Hones, *Literary Geography*; Zehrer et al., "Perceived Usefulness of Blog Postings."

111. Aronie, *Memoir as Medicine*; Llewellyn-Beardsley, "Characteristics of Mental Health Recovery"; Woods et al., "Recovery Narrative."

112. Eastmond, "Stories as Lived Experience," 259. See also Gupta et al., "Eyes on the Street," 3.

113. Goldberg, *Old Friend from Far Away*, xix. See also Rak, *Boom!*, 11.

114. Ellis et al., "Autoethnography," n.p.

115. Hones, *Literary Geography,* 124.
116. Brosseau, "In, Of, Out, With, and Through," 13.
117. Heins, *Beyond Friend and Foe,* 78. See also Johnson, "Writing Liminal Landscapes," 522.
118. Heins, 78.
119. Brosseau, "In, Of, Out, With, and Through," 13.
120. Brosseau, 15. See also Hones, *Literary Geography,* 122–23.
121. Kinney, *Beautiful Wasteland;* Safransky, "Greening the Urban Frontier."
122. Heins, *Beyond Friend and Foe,* 5.
123. Brosseau, "In, Of, Out, With, and Through," 14.
124. Brosseau, 14. See also Johnson, "Writing Liminal Landscapes."
125. Eastmond, "Stories as Lived Experience," 250. See also Brosseau, "In, Of, Out, With, and Through," 20.
126. Ochs and Capps, *Living Narrative,* 33.
127. O'Reilly and Benson, "Lifestyle Migration," 3–6; Bondi, "Understanding Feelings," 335; Llewellyn-Beardsley et al., "Characteristics of Mental Health Recovery," 3.
128. Howell and Prevenier, *From Reliable Sources;* Megill, *Historical Knowledge.*
129. Gardner, "Unreliable Memories and Other Contingencies"; Umemoto, "Walking in Another's Shoes"; Watson, "Unreliable Narrators?"
130. Pocock, "Introduction," 10.
131. Pocock, 10.
132. Hones, *Literary Geography,* 117.
133. Hones, 86.

ONE The Foundations of Belonging

1. Deen, *All Who Go Do Not Return,* 13.
2. Deen, 77.
3. Deen, 149.
4. Deen, 79.
5. Deen, 79.
6. Deen, 80.
7. Wilson, *Master Plan,* 13.
8. Wilson, 13–14.
9. Wilson, 14.
10. Wilson, 14.
11. Wilson, 16.
12. Wilson, 20.
13. Gustafson, "Place Attachment in an Age," 38.

14. Althusser, *Lenin and Philosophy,* 105, 117–18. See also Foucault, "Subject and Power"; Mauss, "Category of the Human Mind"; Taylor, *Sources of the Self.*
15. Elsrud, "Risk Creation in Traveling," 600.
16. Elsrud, 600.
17. Atkinson, "Anthony Giddens as Adversary," 538.
18. Lisle, *Holidays in the Danger Zone,* 240.
19. Heins, *Beyond Friend and Foe,* 83.
20. Thomassen, "Revisiting Liminality," 28.
21. Kwan and Schwanen, "Geographies of Mobility," 243.
22. Gustafson, "Place Attachment in an Age," 27.
23. Probyn, *Outside Belongings,* 9.
24. Duncan and Smith, "Individualisation Versus the Geography," 169; McCloud, "Liminal Subjectivities and Religious Change," 307; Torkington, "Place and Lifestyle Migration," 74.
25. Cresswell, "Mobilities I," 551.
26. Di Masso et al., "Between Fixities and Flows," 126.
27. Sheller, "Theorizing Mobility Justice," 24–25.
28. Yuval-Davis, "Theorizing Identity," 276.
29. Yuval-Davis, 277.
30. Yuval-Davis, 277.
31. Heins, *Beyond Friend and Foe,* 16.
32. Lisle, *Holidays in the Danger Zone,* 11.
33. Toolis, "Theorizing Critical Placemaking," 188.
34. Lisle, *Holidays in the Danger Zone,* 11.
35. Said, *Reflections on Exile,* 185.
36. Antonsich, "Searching for Belonging," 645.
37. Seamon, "Newcomers, Existential Outsiders and Insiders," 90.
38. Antonsich, "Searching for Belonging"; Mee and Wright, "Geographies of Belonging"; Probyn, *Outside Belongings;* Wright, "More-Than-Human, Emergent Belongings."
39. Wright, "More-Than-Human, Emergent Belongings," 395.
40. Heins, *Beyond Friend and Foe,* 83.
41. Said, "Intellectual Exile," 117.
42. Said, *Reflections on Exile,* 182.
43. O'Reilly and Benson, "Lifestyle Migration."
44. Seamon, "Newcomers, Existential Outsiders and Insiders," 86.
45. Wright, "More-Than-Human, Emergent Belongings," 399.
46. Young, "City Life and Difference," 337, 343.

47. Rose, "Spatialities of 'Community,' Power and Change," 3.

48. Deen, *All Who Go Do Not Return*, 13–14.

49. Wariner, *Sound of Gravel*, 26.

50. Hill, *Beyond Belief*, 13–14.

51. Valentine, "Living with Difference," 324. See also Jacobs, *Death and Life of Great American Cities*, 143–45; Young, "City Life and Difference," 337.

52. Tamm, *Cartwheels in a Sari*, 133.

53. Feldman, *Unorthodox*, 59; see also 97.

54. Ali, *Nomad*, xv, 136.

55. Hill, *Beyond Belief*, 120.

56. Armstrong, *Spiral Staircase*, 26.

57. Armstrong, 25.

58. Lythcott-Haims, *Real American*, 38.

59. Lythcott-Haims, 121.

60. Lythcott-Haims, 129–30.

61. Calcaterra, *Etched in Sand*, 95.

62. Walls, *Glass Castle*, 165.

63. Murray, *Breaking Night*, 111, 163.

64. Wilson, *Master Plan*, 170.

65. Wilson, 171.

66. Smarsh, *Heartland*, 39.

67. Smarsh, 125.

68. Smarsh, 273.

69. Smarsh, 3.

70. Jenkins, *To Shake the Sleeping Self*, 92.

71. Jenkins, 92.

72. Ochs and Capps, *Living Narrative*, 45.

73. Ochs and Capps, 253.

74. Toolis, "Theorizing Critical Placemaking," 187.

75. Díaz, *Ordinary Girls*, 179.

76. Keenan, *Sex with Shakespeare*, 219.

77. Hill, *Rethinking Normal*, 57.

78. Baldwin, *Not Just a Tomboy*, 132.

79. Armstrong, *Spiral Staircase*, 46.

80. Preston, *Out with It*, 66.

81. Murray, *Breaking Night*, 69.

82. Conley, *Boy Erased*, 133, 181.

83. Matis, *Girl in the Woods*, 38.

84. Massey, *For Space*.

85. Wilson, "On Geography and Encounter," 452, 454.

86. Wilson, 456.

87. O'Sullivan-Lago and Abreu, "Maintaining Continuity," 75.

88. McWha et al., "Travel Writers," 15.

89. Galani-Moutafi, "Self and the Other," 205.

90. Noy, "This Trip Really Changed Me," 81, 91.

91. Bosangit et al., "'If I Was Going to Die,'" 1.

92. Wilson, "On Geography and Encounter," 460.

93. Jackson and Butler, "Revisiting 'Social Tectonics,'" 2350.

94. Valentine, "Living with Difference," 325.

95. Leitner, "Spaces of Encounters," 830.

96. Wilson, "On Geography and Encounter," 456–57.

97. Heins, *Beyond Friend and Foe*, 80.

98. Wilson, *Master Plan*, 15.

99. Tamm, *Cartwheels in a Sari*, 34.

100. Jones, *How We Fight for Our Lives*, 60.

101. Peralta, *Undocumented*.

102. Feldman, *Unorthodox*, 58.

103. Conley, *Boy Erased*, 75–76.

104. Tamm, *Cartwheels in a Sari*, 46–47.

105. Westover, *Educated*, 51.

106. Baldwin, *Not Just a Tomboy*, 46.

107. Feldman, *Unorthodox*, 89.

108. Preston, *Out with It*, 10–11.

109. Jones, *How We Fight for Our Lives*, 60.

110. Jones, 60.

111. Feldman, *Unorthodox*, 59.

112. Tamm, *Cartwheels in a Sari*, 36.

113. Peralta, *Undocumented*.

114. Deen, *All Who Go Do Not Return*, 108.

115. Huard, *Plato's Political Philosophy*, 7.

116. Hill, *Rethinking Normal*, 38.

117. Jiang-Stein, *Prison Baby*, 38.

118. Tamm, *Cartwheels in a Sari*, 67–68.

119. Mock, *Redefining Realness*, xv.

120. Conley, *Boy Erased*, 6.

121. Díaz, *Ordinary Girls*, 80.

122. Lisle, *Holidays in the Danger Zone*, 240.

123. Goffman, *Presentation of Self in Everyday*; Joyce, *Rule of Freedom*.

124. Baldwin, *Not Just a Tomboy*, 145.

125. Deen, *All Who Go Do Not Return*.

126. Baldwin, *Not Just a Tomboy*, 121.

127. Winterson, *Why Be Happy*, 60.

128. Hill, *Beyond Belief*, 320.

129. Hill, 51; Tamm, *Cartwheels in a Sari*, 269.

130. Winterson, *Why Be Happy*, 109.

131. Deen, *All Who Go Do Not Return*, 56–57.

132. Feldman, *Unorthodox*, 18.

133. Hill, *Beyond Belief*, 51.

134. Deen, *All Who Go Do Not Return*; Feldman, *Unorthodox*; Mock, *Redefining Realness*; Murray, *Breaking Night*; Preston, *Out with It*.

135. Chung, *All You Can Ever Know*; Eire, *Learning to Die in Miami*; Jiang-Stein, *Prison Baby*; Lythcott-Haims, *Real American*.

136. Chin, *Other Side of Paradise*; Hill, *Rethinking Normal*; Jones, *How We Fight for Our Lives*; Mock, *Redefining Realness*.

137. Feldman, *Unorthodox*.

138. Smarsh, *Heartland*; Walls, *Glass Castle*.

139. Hill, *Beyond Belief*; Iftin, *Call Me American*; Tamm, *Cartwheels in a Sari*.

140. Armstrong, *Spiral Suitcase*; Conley, *Boy Erased*; DuBrul, *Maps to the Other Side*; Feldman, *Unorthodox*.

141. Hill, *Rethinking Normal*; Winterson, *Why Be Happy*.

142. Mock, *Redefining Realness*.

143. Wilson, *Master Plan*.

144. Mock, *Redefining Realness*; Walls, *Glass Castle*.

145. Tamm, *Cartwheels in a Sari*.

146. Winterson, *Why Be Happy*.

147. Deen, *All Who Go Do Not Return*; Iftin, *Call Me American*; Winterson, *Why Be Happy*.

148. Chin, *Other Side of Paradise*; Conley, *Boy Erased*.

149. Ali, *Nomad*; Feldman, *Unorthodox*; Keenan, *Sex with Shakespeare*.

150. Ali, *Nomad*; Calcaterra, *Etched in Sand*; Chin, *Other Side of Paradise*; Deen, *All Who Go Do Not Return*; Eire, *Learning to Die in Miami*; Matis, *Girl in the Woods*; Murray, *Breaking Night*; Wilson, *Master Plan*.

151. Deen, *All Who Go Do Not Return*, 117.

152. Hill, *Beyond Belief*, 150.

153. Hill, *Rethinking Normal*, 67.

154. Deen, *All Who Go Do Not Return*, 79.

155. Onwuachi, *Notes from a Young Black Chef*, 36.

156. Baldwin, *Not Just a Tomboy*, 23.
157. Baldwin, 23.
158. Smarsh, *Heartland*, 14.
159. Hill, *Beyond Belief*, 82.
160. Baldwin, *Not Just a Tomboy*, 143–44.
161. Jenkins, *To Shake the Sleeping Self*, 92.
162. Jiang-Stein, *Prison Baby*, 8.
163. DuBrul, *Maps to the Other Side*, 5.
164. Keenan, *Sex with Shakespeare*, 221.
165. Armstrong, *Spiral Staircase*, 22.
166. Hill, *Beyond Belief*, 340.
167. Preston, *Out with It*, 33.
168. Jenkins, *To Shake the Sleeping Self*, 94.

TWO The Power of Imagination

1. Hones, *Literary Geography*, 110, 120.
2. Hones, 115.
3. Brosseau, "In, Of, Out, With, and Through," 15.
4. Chung, *All You Can Ever Know*, 10.
5. Chung, 7.
6. Chung, 9.
7. Chung, 16.
8. Chung, 17.
9. Chung, 18.
10. Chung, 38.
11. Chung, 18.
12. Chung, 41.
13. Chung, 40–41.
14. Chung, 41.
15. Chung, 41.
16. Chung, 18.
17. Boylan, *She's Not There*, 20.
18. Boylan, 20.
19. Boylan, 20.
20. Boylan, 20.
21. March, "Queer and Trans* Geographies," 8.
22. March, 8.
23. Szerszynski and Urry, "Visuality, Mobility and the Cosmopolitan," 116. See also Di Masso et al., "Between Fixities and Flows," 130.

24. White, *Flâneur*, 34–35.
25. Said, *Reflections on Exile*, 436, 438.
26. Lisle, *Holidays in the Danger Zone*, 18.
27. Ward, "Danger Zones," 186.
28. Tamm, *Cartwheels in a Sari*, 19.
29. Jenkins, *To Shake the Sleeping Self*, 97.
30. Deen, *All Who Go Do Not Return*, 43.
31. Deen, 43–44.
32. Lisle, *Holidays in the Danger Zone*, 18.
33. Heins, *Beyond Friend and Foe*, 2.
34. Winterson, *Why Be Happy*, 40.
35. Heins, *Beyond Friend and Foe*, 78.
36. Heins, 79.
37. Winterson, *Why Be Happy*, 38.
38. Noxolo and Preziuso, "Postcolonial Imaginations," 165.
39. Collie, "Cities of the Imagination," 424.
40. Mathews, *Fantasy*, 1, 4.
41. Mathews, 3.
42. Mathews, 3.
43. Valli, "When Cultural Workers Become," 647.
44. Bondi, "Understanding Feelings," 45.
45. Rose, "Encountering Place," 1384.
46. Said, *Reflections on Exile*, 494.
47. Collie, "Cities of the Imagination," 425.
48. Groth, "Frameworks for Cultural Landscape Study," 1.
49. Davis, *City of Quartz*, 226.
50. Collie, "Cities of the Imagination," 424.
51. Collie, 424.
52. Wilson, *Master Plan*, 117.
53. Wilson, 117.
54. Wilson, 118.
55. Wilson, 117.
56. Jones, *How We Fight for Our Lives*, 92.
57. Baldwin, *Not Just a Tomboy*, 39.
58. Bondi, "Making Connections," 435; Davidson and Smith, "Emotional Geographies," 440.
59. Barbieri and Rossero, "'It Is Like Post-Traumatic Stress Disorder,'" 9.
60. Duff, "Atmospheres of Recovery," 64.
61. Power and Bartlett, "Self-Building Safe Havens," 347.

62. Hayes-Conroy and Hayes-Conroy, "Visceral Geographies"; Longhurst, "Visceral Approach."
63. Pagis, "Embodied Therapeutic Culture," 181.
64. Mountz, "Political Geography III," 759.
65. Maddrell, "Mapping Grief," 65.
66. Baldwin, *Not Just a Tomboy*, 110.
67. Conley, *Boy Erased*, 115.
68. Conley, 115.
69. Díaz, *Ordinary Girls*, 260.
70. Murray, *Breaking Night*, 243.
71. Jiang-Stein, *Prison Baby*, 44.
72. Tamm, *Cartwheels in a Sari*, 185.
73. Jenkins, *To Shake the Sleeping Self*, 92.
74. Preston, *Out with It*, 6.
75. Winterson, *Why Be Happy*, 40.
76. Deen, *All Who Go Do Not Return*, 122.
77. Deen, 122.
78. Jones, *How We Fight for Our Lives*, 18.
79. Jones, 16–17.
80. Jones, 18.
81. Preston, *Out with It*, 8.
82. Matis, *Girl in the Woods*, 15.
83. Baldwin, *Not Just a Tomboy*, 52, 54.
84. Mock, *Redefining Realness*, 48.
85. Keenan, *Sex with Shakespeare*, 35.
86. Preston, *Out with It*, 73.
87. Westover, *Educated*, 78–79.
88. Mock, *Redefining Realness*, 68–69.
89. Mock, 69.
90. Baldwin, *Not Just a Tomboy*, 59.
91. Hill, *Rethinking Normal*, 60.
92. Hill, 60.
93. Jones, *How We Fight for Our Lives*, 41.
94. Iftin, *Call Me American*, 75.
95. Matis, *Girl in the Woods*, 14.
96. Wilson, *Master Plan*, 131.
97. DuBrul, *Maps to the Other Side*, 109.
98. Calcaterra, *Etched in Sand*, 39.
99. Baldwin, *Not Just a Tomboy*, 24.

100. Iftin, *Call Me American*, 115.

101. Jones, *How We Fight for Our Lives*, 92.

102. Feldman, *Unorthodox*, 20–21.

103. Mock, *Redefining Realness*, 139.

104. Tamm, *Cartwheels in a Sari*, 185.

105. Baldwin, *Not Just a Tomboy*, 110.

106. Winterson, *Why Be Happy*, 33.

107. Windling, "Into the Woods," 36.

108. Von Benzon, "'I Fell,'" 332–33.

109. Keenan, *Sex with Shakespeare*, 35.

110. Keenan, 36.

111. Windling, "Into the Woods," 43.

112. Baldwin, *Not Just a Tomboy*, 38.

113. Mock, *Redefining Realness*, 70.

114. Boylan, *She's Not There*, 32.

115. Murray, *Breaking Night*, 271.

116. Preston, *Out with It*, 8.

117. Baldwin, *Not Just a Tomboy*, 54.

118. Jenkins, *To Shake the Sleeping Self*, 92.

119. Jiang-Stein, *Prison Baby*, 44.

120. Iftin, *Call Me American*, 91.

121. Feldman, *Unorthodox*, 21.

122. Murray, *Breaking Night*, 242–43.

123. Baldwin, *Not Just a Tomboy*, 99.

124. Baldwin, 54–55.

125. Keenan, *Sex with Shakespeare*, 36.

126. Conley, *Boy Erased*, 53.

127. Jiang-Stein, *Prison Baby*, 15.

128. Jones, *How We Fight for Our Lives*, 9.

129. Westover, *Educated*, 79.

130. Keenan, *Sex with Shakespeare*, 35.

131. Jones, *How We Fight for Our Lives*, 4.

132. Mock, *Redefining Realness*, 70.

133. Harris-Perry, *Sister Citizen*, 104.

134. Harris-Perry, 108.

135. Jones, *How We Fight for Our Lives*, 92–93.

136. Mock, *Redefining Realness*, 19–20.

137. Westover, *Educated*, 80.

138. Mock, *Redefining Realness*, 80–81.

139. Winterson, *Why Be Happy*, 41.

140. Iftin, *Call Me American*, 105.

141. Iftin, 105.

142. Hill, *Beyond Belief*, 113–14.

143. Tamm, *Cartwheels in a Sari*, 187.

144. Murray, *Breaking Night*, 107.

145. Eire, *Learning to Die in Miami*, 117.

146. Eire, 150–51.

147. Westover, *Educated*, 60.

148. Feldman, *Unorthodox*, 81.

149. Deen, *All Who Go Do Not Return*, 123.

THREE   The Process of Unbecoming

1. Boylan, *She's Not There*, 70.

2. Boylan, 115.

3. Boylan, 70.

4. Boylan, 70.

5. Boylan, 115.

6. Boylan, 79–80.

7. Boylan, 80.

8. Boylan, 83.

9. Boylan, 118.

10. Boylan, 122.

11. Boylan, 102.

12. Boylan, 103.

13. Keenan, *Sex with Shakespeare*, 66.

14. Keenan, 61.

15. Keenan, 60–61.

16. Keenan, 61.

17. Baker, "What We Found," 238.

18. Galani-Moutafi, "Self and the Other," 210.

19. Elsrud, "Time Creation in Travelling," 598.

20. Bosangit et al., "'If I Was Going to Die,'" 4.

21. Elsrud, "Time Creation in Travelling," 599.

22. Noy, "This Trip Really Changed Me," 85.

23. Lewis, "Remapping Disclosure," 217.

24. Lewis, 217, 219.

25. Keenan, *Sex with Shakespeare*, 60.

26. Maddern and Adey, "Editorial," 292.

27. Wylie, "Landscape, Absence, and the Geographies," 278–79.
28. Heins, *Beyond Friend and Foe*, 93, 98.
29. Heins, 84.
30. Heins, 81.
31. Elsrud, "Time Creation in Travelling," 604.
32. Seamon, "Newcomers, Existential Outsiders and Insiders," 89.
33. Elsrud, "Time Creation in Travelling," 605.
34. Seamon, "Newcomers, Existential Outsiders and Insiders," 89.
35. Jenkins, *To Shake the Sleeping Self*, 259–60.
36. Keenan, *Sex with Shakespeare*, 60.
37. Boylan, *She's Not There*, 21.
38. Keenan, *Sex with Shakespeare*, 122.
39. Heins, *Beyond Friend and Foe*, 83–84.
40. Gelman, *Tales of a Female Nomad*, 9.
41. Axelrod, *Point of Vanishing*, 94.
42. Jenkins, *To Shake the Sleeping Self*, 260.
43. Kinder, *Radical Bookstore*.
44. Mock, *Redefining Realness*, 134.
45. Jones, *How We Fight for Our Lives*, 67.
46. Murray, *Breaking Night*, 187–88.
47. Feldman, *Unorthodox*, 230.
48. Tamm, *Cartwheels in a Sari*, 161.
49. Jones, *How We Fight for Our Lives*, 67.
50. Feldman, *Unorthodox*, 232.
51. Ochs and Capps, *Living Narrative*, 50–51.
52. Jones, *How We Fight for Our Lives*, 66.
53. Deen, *All Who Go Do Not Return*, 216.
54. Deen, 217.
55. Feldman, *Unorthodox*, 116.
56. Feldman, 116.
57. Keenan, *Sex with Shakespeare*, 17.
58. Keenan, 17–18.
59. Keenan, 10.
60. Feldman, *Unorthodox*, 46.
61. Baldwin, *Not Just a Tomboy*, 47.
62. Baldwin, 46.
63. Baldwin, 47.
64. Keenan, *Sex with Shakespeare*, 221.
65. Hill, *Rethinking Normal*, 8.

66. Hill, 33–34.
67. Conley, *Boy Erased,* 223.
68. Baldwin, *Not Just a Tomboy,* 47.
69. Armstrong, *Spiral Staircase,* xvi.
70. Deen, *All Who Go Do Not Return,* 217.
71. Westover, *Educated,* 135.
72. Chin, *Other Side of Paradise,* 189.
73. Devine-Wright, "Think Global, Act Local?," 62.
74. Middleton, "Roots and Rootlessness," 101.
75. Logan and Molotch, *Urban Fortunes.*
76. Dudley, "Therapeutic Landscapes of Stillness"; Iyer and Jetten, "What's Left Behind"; Winterton and Warburton, "Ageing in the Bush."
77. Cresswell, "Mobilities I," 551.
78. Di Masso, "Between Fixities and Flows," 126.
79. Sheller, "Theorizing Mobility Justice."
80. Bowstead, "Women on the Move," 111.
81. Wright, "More-Than-Human, Emergent Belongings," 396.
82. Murray, *Breaking Night,* 235.
83. Murray, 235–36.
84. Conley, *Boy Erased,* 164.
85. Feldman, *Unorthodox,* 237.
86. Małecka, "Self Lost, the Self Adjusted," 157, 159.
87. Gelman, *Tales of a Female Nomad,* 4.
88. Feldman, *Unorthodox,* 234.
89. Conley, *Boy Erased,* 164.
90. Milligan, "Displacement and Identity Discontinuity," 383. See also Leyshon and Bull, "Bricolage of the Here."
91. Vandemark, "Promoting the Sense of Self," 242. See also Iyer and Jetten, "What's Left Behind"; O'Sullivan-Lago and Abreu, "Maintaining Continuity."
92. O'Sullivan-Lago and Abreu, "Maintaining Continuity," 75.
93. Milligan, "Displacement and Identity Discontinuity," 382.
94. Vandemark, "Promoting the Sense of Self," 244.
95. Stobbelaar and Pedroli, "Perspectives on Landscape Identity," 327; Vandemark, "Promoting the Sense of Self," 244.
96. Conley, *Boy Erased,* 135.
97. Armstrong, *Spiral Staircase,* xvi–xvii.
98. Hill, *Beyond Belief,* 328.
99. Boylan, *She's Not There,* 122.

100. Boylan, 122.
101. Feldman, *Unorthodox*, 81.
102. Armstrong, *Spiral Staircase*, 168.
103. Winterson, *Why Be Happy*, 36.
104. Feldman, *Unorthodox*, 182.
105. Tamm, *Cartwheels in a Sari*, 110.
106. Jones, *How We Fight for Our Lives*, 84.
107. Baldwin, *Not Just a Tomboy*, 48.
108. Ali, *Nomad*, xii.
109. Feldman, *Unorthodox*, 47.
110. Conley, *Boy Erased*, 165.
111. Jenkins, *To Shake the Sleeping Self*, 195.
112. Baldwin, *Not Just a Tomboy*, 137.
113. Elsrud, "Risk Creation in Traveling," 597–98.
114. Takacs, "Becoming Interesting," 1.
115. Fraser, "Unbecoming Place." See also Antonsich, "Searching for Belonging"; Larsen and Christensen, "Unstable Lives of Bicycles."
116. Feldman, *Unorthodox*, 241.
117. Tamm, *Cartwheels in a Sari*, 94.
118. Gelman, *Tales of a Female Nomad*, 4.
119. Critcher and Ferguson, "Cost of Keeping It Hidden," 722.
120. O'Brien and Linehan, "Problematizing the Authentic Self," 1531.
121. Critcher and Ferguson, "Cost of Keeping It Hidden"; O'Brien and Linehan, "Problematizing the Authentic Self."
122. Conley, *Boy Erased*, 82.
123. Westover, *Educated*, 89.
124. Keenan, *Sex with Shakespeare*, 182, 184.
125. Keenan, 184.
126. Mock, *Redefining Realness*, 98.
127. Feldman, *Unorthodox*, 239.
128. Preston, *Out with It*, 145.
129. Gelman, *Tales of a Female Nomad*, 3.
130. Keenan, *Sex with Shakespeare*, 185.
131. Deen, *All Who Go Do Not Return*, 129.
132. Hill, *Beyond Belief*, 212.
133. Jones, *How We Fight for Our Lives*, 49.
134. Bondi, "Feeling Insecure," 392.
135. Tamm, *Cartwheels in a Sari*, 159.
136. Tamm, 166.

137. Peralta, *Undocumented*, 4.
138. Westover, *Educated*, 174.
139. Feldman, *Unorthodox*, 117.
140. Feldman, 90.
141. Tamm, *Cartwheels in a Sari*, 166.
142. Ali, *Nomad*, 80.
143. Deen, *All Who Go Do Not Return*, 200.
144. Boylan, *She's Not There*, 70.
145. Tamm, *Cartwheels in a Sari*, 169.
146. Tamm, 160.
147. Wylie, "Spectral Geographies of WG Sebald," 172.
148. Wylie, 171.
149. Murray, *Breaking Night*, 77.
150. Feldman, *Unorthodox*, 229.
151. Ali, *Nomad*, xvi.
152. Deen, *All Who Go Do Not Return*, 14.
153. Westover, *Educated*, 159.
154. Conley, *Boy Erased*, 165.
155. Tamm, *Cartwheels in a Sari*, 230.

FOUR The Fateful Moment of Exile

1. Winn, *Salt Path*, 29.
2. Winn, 112.
3. Winn, 112–13.
4. Winn, 7.
5. Winn, 22.
6. Winn, 23.
7. Winn, 36.
8. Winn, 37.
9. Winn, 30.
10. Eire, *Learning to Die in Miami*, 1.
11. Eire, 1.
12. Eire, 13.
13. Eire, 13.
14. Ali, *Nomad*, xvi; Armstrong, *Spiral Staircase*, 26; Calcaterra, *Etched in Sand*, 196; Chin, *Other Side of Paradise*, 244–45; Conley, *Boy Erased*, 275; Díaz, *Ordinary Girls*, 250; Feldman, *Unorthodox*, 81, 245; Gelman, *Tales of a Female Nomad*, 43; hooks, "Kentucky Is My Fate," 17–18; Hill, *Beyond Belief*, 150; Iftin, *Call Me American*, 129; Murray, *Breaking Night*, 182.

15. Chin, *Other Side of Paradise*, 273; Calcaterra, *Etched in Sand*, 196; Díaz, *Ordinary Girls*, 250; Smarsh, *Heartland*, 259; Westover, *Educated*, 153.

16. Winn, *Salt Path*.

17. Deen, *All Who Go Do Not Return*, 9.

18. Murray, *Breaking Night*, 180–82; Winterson, *Why Be Happy*, 38.

19. Tamm, *Cartwheels in a Sari*, 238. See also Hill, *Beyond Belief*, 365.

20. Walls, *Glass Castle*, 221. See also Chung, *All You Can Ever Know*, 18; Matis, *Girl in the Woods*, 44; Wariner, *Sound of Gravel*, 327-28.

21. Gelman, *Tales of a Female Nomad*, 39.

22. Jones, *How We Fight for Our Lives*, 34.

23. Wariner, *Sound of Gravel*, 327.

24. Onwuachi, *Notes from a Young Black Chef*, 109.

25. Baldwin, *Not Just a Tomboy*, 158.

26. Smarsh, *Heartland*, 247.

27. Axelrod, *Point of Vanishing*, 13.

28. Tamm, *Cartwheels in a Sari*, 259. See also Armstrong, *Spiral Suitcase*, 28.

29. Feldman, *Unorthodox*, 244. See also Eire, *Learning to Die in Miami*, 163.

30. Hill, *Rethinking Normal*, 71. See also Boylan, *She's Not There*, 18.

31. Feldman, *Unorthodox*, 244.

32. Eire, *Learning to Die in Miami*, 65.

33. Giddens, *Modernity and Self Identity*, 113.

34. Giddens, 114.

35. Giddens, 114.

36. Giddens, 114.

37. Chin, *Other Side of Paradise*, 271.

38. Preston, *Out with It*, 138.

39. Preston, 138.

40. Jenkins, *To Shake the Sleeping Self*, 100.

41. Wariner, *Sound of Gravel*, 211.

42. Preston, *Out with It*, 122.

43. Baldwin, *Not Just a Tomboy*, 103-4.

44. Keenan, *Sex with Shakespeare*, 221.

45. Jenkins, *To Shake the Sleeping Self*, 7.

46. Boylan, *She's Not There*, 111.

47. Baldwin, *Not Just a Tomboy*, 154.

48. Tamm, *Cartwheels in a Sari*, 259.

49. Boylan, *She's Not There*, 80.

50. Tamm, *Cartwheels in a Sari*, 271-73.

51. Hill, *Beyond Belief*, 320.

52. Hill, *Rethinking Normal*, 111.

53. Hill, 111.

54. Hill, 100.

55. Deen, *All Who Go Do Not Return*, 196.

56. Deen, 214.

57. Deen, 214.

58. Smarsh, *Heartland*, 249–50.

59. Jenkins, *To Shake the Sleeping Self*, 7.

60. Jenkins, 9.

61. Matis, *Girl in the Woods*, 47.

62. Matis, 48.

63. Pham, *Catfish and Mandala*, 23.

64. Chin, *Other Side of Paradise*, 268.

65. Feldman, *Unorthodox*, 245.

66. Walls, *Glass Castle*, 221.

67. Walls, 229.

68. Conley, *Boy Erased*, 275.

69. Pham, *Catfish and Mandala*, 23.

70. Tamm, *Cartwheels in a Sari*, 227.

71. Tamm, 227.

72. Feldman, *Unorthodox*, 235.

73. Feldman, 236.

74. Feldman, 234.

75. Armstrong, *Spiral Staircase*, xvii.

76. Onwuachi, *Notes from a Young Black Chef*, 107.

77. Onwuachi, 109.

78. Onwuachi, 109.

79. Ali, *Nomad*, xi.

80. Iftin, *Call Me American*, 129.

81. Walls, *Glass Castle*, 221.

82. Wariner, *Sound of Gravel*, 320.

83. Feldman, *Unorthodox*, 242.

84. Feldman, 243–44.

85. Westover, *Educated*, 147–48.

86. Westover, 147.

87. Díaz, *Ordinary Girls*, 250.

88. Calcaterra, *Etched in Sand*, 196.

89. Winterson, *Why Be Happy*, 38.

90. Chin, *Other Side of Paradise*, 204.

91. Iftin, *Call Me American*, 119.
92. Murray, *Breaking Night*, 182.
93. Deen, *All Who Go Do Not Return*, 8.
94. Deen, 10.
95. Deen, 11.
96. Deen, 9.
97. Deen, 221.
98. Said, *Reflections on Exile*, 173–74.
99. McGregor, "Locating Exile," 62.
100. Murphy, "From Place to Exile," 473.
101. McGregor, "Locating Exile," 63.
102. McGregor, 63.
103. Murray, *Breaking Night*.
104. Armstrong, *Spiral Staircase*.
105. Wilson, *Master Plan*.
106. Winn, *Salt Path*, 169.
107. Eire, *Learning to Die in Miami*, 23.
108. Calcaterra, *Etched in Sand*, 199.
109. Sasson, *Accidental Soldier*, 53–54.
110. Baldwin, *Not Just a Tomboy*, 158.
111. Pham, *Catfish and Mandala*, 30.
112. Sasson, *Accidental Soldier*, 63.
113. Iftin, *Call Me American*, 121.
114. Armstrong, *Spiral Suitcase*, 6.
115. Chin, *Other Side of Paradise*, 267.
116. Preston, *Out with It*, 152–53.
117. Matis, *Girl in the Woods*, 47.
118. Matis, 47.
119. Matis, 49.
120. Murray, *Breaking Night*, 185–86.
121. Said, *Reflections on Exile*, 184.
122. Waitt and Gorman-Murray, "Journeys and Returns," 1242.
123. Deen, *All Who Go Do Not Return*, 9.
124. Winterson, *Why Be Happy*, 58.
125. Winn, *Salt Path*, 29–30.
126. Gustafson, "Place Attachment in an Age," 40.
127. Suárez-Orozco, "Right Moves?," 9.
128. Said, *Reflections on Exile*, 185.
129. Deen, *All Who Go Do Not Return*, 115.

130. Hobbs, *Chosen Exile*, 4.
131. Hobbs, 4.
132. Hobbs, 14–15.
133. Hobbs, 13.
134. Abbott, "Exile and Banishment."
135. Abbott.
136. Sundberg, "Reconfiguring North-South Solidarity," 149.
137. Leyshon and Bull, "Bricolage of the Here," 165.
138. Iyer and Jetten, "What's Left Behind," 95–96.
139. Said, *Reflections on Exile*, 175.
140. Vandemark, "Promoting the Sense of Self," 246.
141. Hackl, "Key Figure of Mobility," 62.
142. Said, *Reflections on Exile*, 174.
143. Armstrong, *Spiral Staircase*, 6.
144. Gelman, *Tales of a Female Nomad*, 38.
145. Wariner, *Sound of Gravel*, 327.
146. Ali, *Nomad*, xii.
147. Feldman, *Unorthodox*, 245.
148. Feldman, 245.
149. Westover, *Educated*, 211.
150. Jones, *How We Fight for Our Lives*, 34.
151. Jones, 35.
152. Murray, *Breaking Night*, 182.
153. Deen, *All Who Go Do Not Return*, 278.
154. Deen, 273.
155. Deen, 279.
156. Smarsh, *Heartland*, 261.
157. Smarsh, 285.
158. Smarsh, 285–86.
159. Tamm, *Cartwheels in a Sari*, 234.
160. Tamm, 279.
161. Tamm, 237.
162. Hill, *Rethinking Normal*, 101.
163. Hill, 101.
164. Winterson, *Why Be Happy*, 133.
165. Axelrod, *Point of Vanishing*, 13.
166. hooks, "Kentucky Is My Fate," 18.
167. Eire, *Learning to Die in Miami*, 65.
168. Feldman, *Unorthodox*, 244.
169. Armstrong, *Spiral Staircase*, 29.

170. Axelrod, *Point of Vanishing*, 13.

171. Eire, *Learning to Die in Miami*, 13.

172. Feldman, *Unorthodox*, 244.

173. Gelman, *Tales of a Female Nomad*, 37.

174. Eire, *Learning to Die in Miami*, 13.

175. Mitchell, "Pre-Black Futures," 240.

176. Eire, *Learning to Die in Miami*, 9.

FIVE The Swamp of Harsh Liminality

1. Torkington, "Place and Lifestyle Migration," 74. See also O'Reilly and Benson, "Lifestyle Migration," 9.

2. Armstrong, *Spiral Staircase*, 3–4.

3. Armstrong, 11.

4. Armstrong, 23.

5. Armstrong, 99.

6. Armstrong, 98–101.

7. Armstrong, 5.

8. Armstrong, 6.

9. Armstrong, 67.

10. Armstrong, 6.

11. Armstrong, 23.

12. Eire, *Learning to Die in Miami*, 9.

13. Eire, 50–51.

14. Eire, 34.

15. Eire, 33.

16. Eire, 8.

17. Armstrong, *Spiral Staircase*, 24.

18. Armstrong, 23.

19. Eire, *Learning to Die in Miami*, 5.

20. Jenkins, *To Shake the Sleeping Self*, 61.

21. Murray, *Breaking Night*, 248.

22. Deen, *All Who Go Do Not Return*, 269; Feldman, *Unorthodox*, 116; Hill, *Beyond Belief*, 50.

23. Gelman, *Tales of a Female Nomad*, 11; Sasson, *Accidental Soldier*, 160.

24. Winterson, *Why Be Happy*, 64.

25. Feldman, *Unorthodox*, 250.

26. Iftin, *Call Me American*, 213.

27. Jenkins, *To Shake the Sleeping Self*, 26.

28. Jenkins, 76.

29. Johnson, "Writing Liminal Landscapes," 507.

30. Atkinson, "Not All That Was Solid," 6.
31. Beech, "Liminality and the Practices," 287.
32. Beech, 287.
33. Beech, 287.
34. Elsrud, "Time Creation in Travelling," 312.
35. Beech, "Liminality and the Practices," 287.
36. Thomassen, "Revisiting Liminality," 28.
37. March, "Queer and Trans* Geographies," 10–11.
38. March, 1.
39. Bryant, "On Critical Times," 20. See also March, "Queer and Trans* Geographies," 3; Mee and Wright, "Geographies of Belonging," 776.
40. Heins, *Beyond Friend and Foe,* 84.
41. Heins, 85.
42. Elsrud, "Time Creation in Travelling," 312.
43. Bosangit et al., "'If I Was Going to Die'"; Elsrud, "Risk Creation in Traveling"; Galani-Moutafi, "Self and the Other"; McWha et al., "Travel Writers and the Nature"; Noy, "This Trip Really Changed Me"; O'Reilly and Benson, "Lifestyle Migration."
44. Bristow and Jenkins, "Spatial and Temporal Tourism," 221.
45. Ward, "Danger Zones," 185.
46. Beech, "Liminality and the Practices," 286.
47. Seamon, "Newcomers," 89–90.
48. White, *Flâneur,* 36.
49. Said, "Intellectual Exile," 113.
50. Said, 117.
51. Deen, *All Who Go Do Not Return,* 186.
52. Axelrod, *Point of Vanishing,* 13.
53. Ali, *Nomad,* 181.
54. Boylan, *She's Not There,* 126.
55. Jiang-Stein, *Prison Baby,* 66.
56. Gelman, *Tales of a Female Nomad,* 11.
57. Murray, *Breaking Night,* 249–50.
58. Ali, *Nomad,* 181.
59. Hill, *Beyond Belief,* 367–68.
60. Sasson, *Accidental Soldier,* 154.
61. Winn, *Salt Path,* 112.
62. Straughan, "Politics of Stuckness," 639.
63. Karlsen, "Waiting Out the Condition," 118.
64. Straughan, "Politics of Stuckness," 638.
65. Winn, *Salt Path,* 37.

66. Boeri, "Women After the Utopia," 345.

67. Seamon, "Newcomers, Existential Outsiders and Insiders," 91.

68. Seamon, 91.

69. Bondi, "Feeling Insecure," 332.

70. Boeri, "Women After the Utopia," 345.

71. Deen, *All Who Go Do Not Return*, 256–57.

72. Deen, 257.

73. O'Reilly and Benson, "Lifestyle Migration," 8.

74. Heins, *Beyond Friend and Foe*, 104.

75. O'Reilly and Benson, "Lifestyle Migration," 9.

76. Deen, *All Who Go Do Not Return*, 257.

77. Deen, 257.

78. Ali, *Nomad*, 155.

79. Boylan, *She's Not There*, 140.

80. Axelrod, *Point of Vanishing*, 43.

81. Jenkins, *To Shake the Sleeping Self*, 222.

82. Pham, *Catfish and Mandala*, 86.

83. Eire, *Learning to Die in Miami*, 2.

84. Westover, *Educated*, 202.

85. Ali, *Nomad*, 170.

86. Deen, *All Who Go Do Not Return*, 154.

87. Westover, *Educated*, xv.

88. Ali, *Nomad*, xvii, 158.

89. Westover, *Educated*, 161.

90. Westover, 165–66.

91. Bryant, "On Critical Times," 21.

92. Bryant, 20.

93. Lisle, *Holidays in the Danger Zone*, 22.

94. Heins, *Beyond Friend and Foe*, 90.

95. Bristow and Jenkins, "Spatial and Temporal Tourism"; Johnson, "Writing Liminal Landscapes"; O'Reilly and Benson, "Lifestyle Migration."

96. Gelman, *Tales of a Female Nomad*, 24, 26.

97. Matis, *Girl in the Woods*, 106, 209.

98. Sasson, *Accidental Soldier*, 159–60.

99. Winterson, *Why Be Happy*, 60–61.

100. Ali, *Nomad*, xvi.

101. Ali, 26.

102. Heins, *Beyond Friend and Foe*, 92.

103. Dewart, "Lugone's Metaphor of 'World Travelling,'" 370.

104. Coker, "Traveling Pains," 16.

105. Beech, "Liminality and the Practices," 287.

106. Coker, "Traveling Pains," 17.

107. Eastmond, "Stories as Lived Experience," 251.

108. Wylie, "Spectral Geographies of WG Sebald," 172.

109. Beech, "Liminality and the Practices," 287.

110. Said, "Intellectual Exile," 113.

111. Said, *Reflections on Exile*, 180.

112. Wylie, "Spectral Geographies of WG Sebald," 181.

113. Chin, *Other Side of Paradise*, 223.

114. Chin, 224.

115. Chin, 224.

116. Chin, 224.

117. Deen, *All Who Go Do Not Return*, 257.

118. Sasson, *Accidental Soldier*, 160.

119. Keenan, *Sex with Shakespeare*, 122.

120. Wilson, "On Geography and Encounter."

121. Smarsh, *Heartland*, 260.

122. Smarsh, 260.

123. Smarsh, 273.

124. Seamon, "Newcomers, Existential Outsiders and Insiders," 95.

125. Westover, *Educated*, 157.

126. Westover, 157.

127. Westover, 157.

128. Westover, 158.

129. Winn, *Salt Path*, 44.

130. Westover, *Educated*, 159.

131. Jenkins, *To Shake the Sleeping Self*, 76.

132. Pham, *Catfish and Mandala*, 172.

133. hooks, "Kentucky Is My Fate," 13–14.

134. Feldman, *Unorthodox*, 246.

135. Iftin, *Call Me American*, 271.

136. Chin, *Other Side of Paradise*, 224.

137. Westover, *Educated*, 166.

138. Westover, 166.

139. Deen, *All Who Go Do Not Return*, 257.

140. Feldman, *Unorthodox*, 250–51.

141. Pham, *Catfish and Mandala*, 183.

142. hooks, "Kentucky Is My Fate," 13.

143. Ali, *Nomad*, 39.

144. Smarsh, *Heartland*, 125.

145. Tamm, *Cartwheels in a Sari*, 282.

146. Tamm, 282.

147. Smarsh, *Heartland*, 261.

148. Smarsh, 261.

149. Smarsh, 262.

150. Axelrod, *Point of Vanishing*, 70.

151. Axelrod, 95.

152. Armstrong, *Spiral Staircase*, 11–12.

153. Armstrong, 12.

154. Pham, *Catfish and Mandala*, 43.

155. Pham, 43.

156. Axelrod, *Point of Vanishing*, 62.

157. Axelrod, 62.

158. Deen, *All Who Go Do Not Return*, 259.

159. Jenkins, *To Shake the Sleeping Self*, 87.

160. Mock, *Redefining Realness*, 150.

161. Pham, *Catfish and Mandala*, 50.

162. Armstrong, *Spiral Staircase*, 100–101.

163. Tamm, *Cartwheels in a Sari*, 246.

164. hooks, "Kentucky Is My Fate," 12.

165. Sasson, *Accidental Soldier*, 97.

166. Deen, *All Who Go Do Not Return*, 258.

167. Deen, 285.

168. Ali, *Nomad*, 39.

169. Axelrod, *Point of Vanishing*, 149.

170. Axelrod, 149.

171. Axelrod, 149.

172. Winterson, *Why Be Happy*, 63.

173. Winterson, 64.

174. Deen, *All Who Go Do Not Return*, 261.

175. Gelman, *Tales of a Female Nomad*, 14–15.

176. Jenkins, *To Shake the Sleeping Self*, 90.

177. Eire, *Learning to Die in Miami*, 4–5.

178. Winn, *Salt Path*, 88.

six The Project of Strategic Assimilation

1. Onwuachi, *Notes from a Young Black Chef*, 153.

2. Onwuachi, 156.

3. Onwuachi, 172.

4. Onwuachi, 172.

5. Onwuachi, 155.

6. Onwuachi, 164.

7. Onwuachi, 164.

8. Onwuachi, 192–93.

9. Onwuachi, 186.

10. Onwuachi, 186–87.

11. Onwuachi, 190.

12. Onwuachi, 8, 169.

13. Onwuachi, 222.

14. Onwuachi, 223.

15. Onwuachi, 175.

16. Onwuachi, 175.

17. Onwuachi, 175.

18. Díaz, *Ordinary Girls*, 214.

19. Díaz, 214.

20. Díaz, 214.

21. Díaz, 214.

22. Díaz, 230.

23. Díaz, 232.

24. Calcaterra, *Etched in Sand;* Eire, *Learning to Die in Miami;* Feldman, *Unorthodox;* hooks, "Kentucky Is My Fate"; Iftin, *Call Me American;* Peralta, *Undocumented;* Smarsh, *Heartland;* Tamm, *Cartwheels in a Sari;* Walls, *Glass Castle;* Westover, *Educated.*

25. Deen, *All Who Go Do Not Return;* Murray, *Breaking Night.*

26. Díaz, *Ordinary Girls;* Sasson, *Accidental Soldier.*

27. Lythcott-Haims, *Real American;* Westover, *Educated.*

28. Boylan, *She's Not There;* Preston, *Out with It.*

29. Chin, *Other Side of Paradise;* Deen, *All Who Go Do Not Return;* Feldman, *Unorthodox;* Iftin, *Call Me American.*

30. Boylan, *She's Not There;* DuBrul, *Maps to the Other Side;* Gelman, *Tales of a Female Nomad.*

31. Matis, *Girl in the Woods;* Winn, *Salt Path.*

32. Jenkins, *To Shake the Sleeping Self;* Pham, *Catfish and Mandala.*

33. Portes and Rumbaut, *Immigrant America,* 71.

34. Alba and Nee, "Rethinking Assimilation Theory," 35.

35. Suárez-Orozco, "Right Moves?," 15.

36. Suárez-Orozco, 15.

37. Suárez-Orozco, 9, 15.

38. Portes and Rumbaut, *Immigrant America,* 71.
39. Bhatia and Ram, "Theorizing Identity," 141.
40. Li, *Ethnoburb,* 12.
41. Alba and Nee, "Rethinking Assimilation Theory," 39.
42. Alba and Nee; Bhatia and Ram, "Theorizing Identity"; Mandaville, "Territory and Translocality"; Portes and Rumbaut, *Immigrant America;* Suárez-Orozco, "Right Moves?"; Suárez-Orozco, "Everything You Ever Wanted to Know."
43. O'Reilly and Benson, "Lifestyle Migration," 8.
44. Said, "Intellectual Exile," 123.
45. Said, *Reflections on Exile,* 177.
46. Heins, *Beyond Friend and Foe,* 103.
47. Said, "Intellectual Exile," 115.
48. Eire, *Learning to Die in Miami,* 33.
49. Sasson, *Accidental Soldier,* 199.
50. Wilson, *Master Plan,* 94.
51. Feldman, *Unorthodox,* 245.
52. Deen, *All Who Go Do Not Return,* 153.
53. Iftin, *Call Me American,* 217.
54. Iftin, 217.
55. Iftin, 217.
56. Iftin, 218.
57. Tamm, *Cartwheels in a Sari,* 281.
58. Winn, *Salt Path,* 39.
59. Jenkins, *To Shake the Sleeping Self,* 4.
60. Al-Sharif, *Daring to Drive,* 49.
61. Heins, *Beyond Friend and Foe,* 84; White, *Flâneur,* 16, 39.
62. Wilson, *Master Plan,* 111.
63. Wilson, 96.
64. Wilson, 111.
65. Westover, *Educated,* 171.
66. Westover, 171.
67. Díaz, *Ordinary Girls,* 250.
68. Díaz, 250–51.
69. Boylan, *She's Not There,* 122–25.
70. Sasson, *Accidental Soldier,* 182–83.
71. Calcaterra, *Etched in Sand,* 223.
72. Murray, *Breaking Night,* 270.
73. Feldman, *Unorthodox,* 241.

74. Hill, *Rethinking Normal*, 13.

75. Hill, 6.

76. Eire, *Learning to Die in Miami*, 160.

77. Eire, 163.

78. Ali, *Nomad*, 165.

79. Jenkins, *To Shake the Sleeping Self*, 9.

80. Gelman, *Tales of a Female Nomad*, 16.

81. Gelman, 16.

82. Eire, *Learning to Die in Miami*, 163.

83. Eire, 164.

84. Calcaterra, *Etched in Sand*, 235.

85. McDowell, "Thinking Through Work," 497.

86. McDowell, 497.

87. Mee and Wright, "Geographies of Belonging," 773.

88. Dudley, "Feeling at Home," 743.

89. Gelman, *Tales of a Female Nomad*, 25.

90. Gelman, 25.

91. Lythcott-Haims, *Real American*, 87.

92. Lythcott-Haims, 101.

93. Lythcott-Haims, 108.

94. Calcaterra, *Etched in Sand*, 176.

95. Wilson, *Master Plan*, 112.

96. Wilson, 112.

97. Wilson, 112.

98. Dewart, "Lugone's Metaphor of 'World Travelling,'" 370.

99. Boeri, "Women After the Utopia," 349.

100. Baldwin, *Not Just a Tomboy*, 85.

101. Antonsich, "Searching for Belonging," 650.

102. Probyn, *Outside Belongings*, 40.

103. O'Reilly and Benson, "Lifestyle Migration," 9.

104. Price, *How to Do Things with Books*; Spain, *Constructive Feminism*.

105. Peralta, *Undocumented*, 147.

106. Iftin, *Call Me American*, 237.

107. Westover, *Educated*, 20.

108. Deen, *All Who Go Do Not Return*, 150–51.

109. Peralta, *Undocumented*, 146–47.

110. Smarsh, *Heartland*, 256.

111. Smarsh, 257.

112. Mock, *Redefining Realness*, 119.

113. Mock, 213–14.

114. Jones, *How We Fight for Our Lives*, 62.

115. Westover, *Educated*, 204.

116. Smarsh, *Heartland*, 258.

117. Feldman, *Unorthodox*, 221.

118. Baldwin, *Not Just a Tomboy*, 163–64.

119. Baldwin, 164.

120. McDowell, "Thinking Through Work," 496.

121. Ong, "Cultural Citizenship as Subject-Making," 738.

122. Said, *Reflections on Exile*, 433.

123. Boylan, *She's Not There*, 155.

124. Boylan, 156.

125. Iftin, *Call Me American*, 259.

126. Eire, *Learning to Die in Miami*, 225.

127. Jiang-Stein, *Prison Baby*, 153–54.

128. DuBrul, *Maps to the Other Side*, 57.

129. Armstrong, *Spiral Staircase*, 91.

130. Armstrong, 92, 173.

131. Baldwin, *Not Just a Tomboy*, 215.

132. Antonsich, "Searching for Belonging," 650.

133. Portes and Zhou, *Immigrant America*, 82. See also Waters et al., "Segmented Assimilation Revisited."

134. Antonsich, "Searching for Belonging," 652.

135. Boylan, *She's Not There*.

136. Gelman, *Tales of a Female Nomad*, 89.

137. Matis, *Girl in the Woods*, 228.

138. Matis, 235.

139. Matis, 109.

140. Eire, *Learning to Die in Miami*, 101–2.

141. Eire, 51.

142. Wilson, *Master Plan*, 236.

143. Wilson, 255.

144. Wilson, 258.

145. Said, "Intellectual Exile," 123.

146. Baldwin, *Not Just a Tomboy*, 160.

SEVEN The Healing Potential of Co-narration

1. Mock, *Redefining Realness*, 247.

2. Mock, 247–48.

3. Mock, 3.
4. Mock, 7.
5. Mock, 9.
6. Mock, xvi.
7. Mock, 183.
8. Mock, 183.
9. Mock, 156.
10. Mock, 156.
11. Mock, 156.
12. Mock, 10.
13. Mock, 10–11.
14. Mock, xvi.
15. Deen, *All Who Go Do Not Return*, 267.
16. Deen, 267.
17. Deen, 267.
18. Deen, 269.
19. Deen, 269.
20. Kinder, *Radical Bookstore*, 201–30.
21. Lythcott-Haims, *Real American*.
22. Hill, *Rethinking Normal*.
23. DuBrul, *Maps to the Other Side*.
24. Chin, *Other Side of Paradise*.
25. Matis, *Girl in the Woods*; Gelman, *Tales of a Female Nomad*; Pham, *Catfish and Mandala*.
26. Deen, *All Who Go Do Not Return*; Matis, *Girl in the Woods*.
27. Armstrong, *Spiral Staircase*; DuBrul, *Maps to the Other Side*; Winterson, *Why Be Happy*.
28. Winterson, 119.
29. Bosangit et al., "'If I Was Going to Die,'" 4.
30. Fivush, "Speaking Silence," 90.
31. Heins, *Beyond Friend and Foe*, 15.
32. Heins, 31.
33. Van der Kolk, *Body Keeps the Score*, 43.
34. Jager et al., "Embodied Ways of Storying," n.p.
35. Sweet, *Politics of Surviving*, 104.
36. Bondi, "Making Connections," 444.
37. Bondi, 444.
38. Rimke, "Self-Help, Therapeutic Industries, and Neoliberalism," 45.
39. Rose, "Encountering Place," 1384–5.

40. Willis, "Re-storying Wilderness and Adventure Therapies," 101.

41. Rose, "Mainstreaming of Recovery," 217.

42. Davidson and Smith, "Emotional Geographies"; Rose, "Mainstreaming of Recovery"; Maddrell, "Mapping Grief"; Sweet, *Politics of Surviving*; Willis, "Re-storying Wilderness and Adventure Therapies."

43. Woods et al., "Recovery Narrative," 231.

44. Woods et al., 230.

45. De Leeuw, "Going Unscripted," 158.

46. Ochs and Capps, *Living Narratives*, 171.

47. Ochs and Capps, "Narrating the Self," 30.

48. Rippl et al., "Introduction," 9.

49. Davies, "Assemblage and Social Movements," 459.

50. Said, *Reflections on Exile*, 186.

51. Said, 186.

52. Said, 186.

53. Kirmayer, "Failures of Imagination," 167.

54. Kirmayer, 168.

55. Kirmayer, 167–68.

56. Said, *Reflections on Exile*, 173, 180.

57. hooks, "Kentucky Is My Fate," 17.

58. Armstrong, *Spiral Staircase*, 73.

59. Armstrong, 74–75.

60. Jones, *How We Fight for Our Lives*, 139.

61. Jones, 139–40.

62. Jones, 140.

63. McGregor, "Locating Exile," 65.

64. McGregor, 65.

65. Deen, *All Who Go Do Not Return*, 182.

66. Deen, 182–83.

67. Deen, 183.

68. Armstrong, *Spiral Staircase*, 166.

69. Armstrong, 166.

70. Armstrong, 166.

71. Deen, *All Who Go Do Not Return*, 183.

72. Fivush, "Speaking Silence," 96.

73. Spivak, "Can the Subaltern Speak?"

74. Fivush, "Speaking Silence," 96.

75. Fivush, 90–91.

76. Feldman, *Unorthodox*, 246.

77. DuBrul, *Maps to the Other Side,* 7.

78. Keenan, *Sex with Shakespeare,* 15.

79. Armstrong, *Spiral Staircase,* 199.

80. Peralta, *Undocumented,* 125–26.

81. hooks, "Kentucky Is My Fate," 14.

82. Fivush, "Speaking Silence"; Von Benzon, "I Fell Out of a Tree."

83. Winn, *Salt Path,* 101.

84. Winn, 101.

85. Westover, *Educated,* 273.

86. Westover, 273.

87. Hill, *Rethinking Normal,* 13.

88. Hill, 12.

89. Coddington, "Contagious Trauma," 67.

90. Nurser et al., "Personal Storytelling in Mental Health," 29.

91. Power and Bartlett, "Self-Building Safe Havens," 343.

92. Butterfield and Martin, "Affective Sanctuaries."

93. Doughty, "Therapeutic Landscapes of Stillness," 5.

94. Vanolo, "Shame, Guilt, and the Production," 768.

95. Schramm, "Introduction," 9.

96. Said, *Reflections on Exile,* 180, 183.

97. Lisle, *Holidays in the Danger Zone,* 194.

98. Milligan, "Displacement and Identity Discontinuity," 381.

99. Iyer and Jetten, "What's Left Behind," 94.

100. Said, *Reflections on Exile,* 174.

101. Feldman, *Unorthodox,* 238.

102. Ali, *Nomad,* 12.

103. Winterson, *Why Be Happy,* 9.

104. Winterson, 9.

105. Woods et al., "Recovery Narrative," 231.

106. Willis, "Re-storying Wilderness and Adventure Therapies," 101.

107. Winterson, *Why Be Happy,* 116.

108. Feldman, *Unorthodox,* 220.

109. Keenan, *Sex with Shakespeare,* 44.

110. Preston, *Out with It,* 12.

111. Chung, *All You Can Ever Know,* 60–61.

112. Jiang-Stein, *Prison Baby,* 123.

113. Chin, *Other Side of Paradise,* 270.

114. Iftin, *Call Me American,* 281.

115. Gelman, *Tales of a Female Nomad,* 47.

116. Gelman, 48.

117. DuBrul, *Maps to the Other Side,* 84.

118. DuBrul, 32.

119. Hill, *Beyond Belief,* 354.

120. Tamm, *Cartwheels in a Sari,* 235–36.

121. Baldwin, *Not Just a Tomboy,* 204.

122. Preston, *Out with It,* 12.

123. DuBrul, *Maps to the Other Side,* 6–7.

124. Sundberg, "Reconfiguring North-South Solidarity," 150.

125. Fivush, "Speaking Silence," 95.

126. Chung, *All You Can Ever Know,* 61.

127. Iftin, *Call Me American,* 281.

128. Gelman, *Tales of a Female Nomad,* 17.

129. Armstrong, *Spiral Staircase,* 92.

130. Mock, *Redefining Realness,* 183.

131. Deen, *All Who Go Do Not Return,* 270.

132. Preston, *Out with It,* 197.

133. Preston, 198.

134. Preston, 199.

135. Winn, *Salt Path,* 127.

136. Winn, 129.

137. Murray, *Breaking Night,* 254.

138. Hill, *Rethinking Normal,* 17.

139. Lythcott-Haims, *Real American,* 185.

140. Keenan, *Sex with Shakespeare,* 9.

141. Baldwin, *Not Just a Tomboy,* 189.

142. Preston, *Out with It,* 202–3.

143. Lythcott-Haims, *Real American,* 185.

144. DuBrul, *Maps to the Other Side,* 7.

145. Hill, *Beyond Belief,* 379.

146. Willis, "Restorying the Self, Restoring Place," 90.

147. Heins, *Beyond Friend and Foe,* 15, 21.

148. Fivush, "Speaking Silence," 92.

149. Gupta et al., "Eyes on the Street," 3.

150. Hill, *Beyond Belief,* 246.

151. Feldman, *Unorthodox,* 221.

152. Jiang-Stein, *Prison Baby,* 151.

153. Winn, *Salt Path,* 38.

154. hooks, "Kentucky Is My Fate," 14.

155. Chin, *Other Side of Paradise,* 269.
156. Hill, *Rethinking Normal,* 199.
157. Hill, 201.
158. Mock, *Redefining Realness,* 249.
159. Mock, xviii.

EIGHT The Provisional End of Exile

1. Said, *Reflections on Exile,* 181.
2. Said, "Intellectual Exile," 113.
3. Seamon, "Newcomers, Existential Outsiders and Insiders," 96.
4. McGregor, "Locating Exile," 62, 74.
5. Bunkše, "Feeling Is Believing," 227.
6. Jiang-Stein, *Prison Baby,* 3.
7. Jiang-Stein, 4.
8. Jiang-Stein, 5.
9. Jiang-Stein, 143.
10. Jiang-Stein, 98.
11. Jiang-Stein, 125.
12. Jiang-Stein, 166–67.
13. Jiang-Stein, 169.
14. Jiang-Stein, 169.
15. Jiang-Stein, 152.
16. Jiang-Stein, 150.
17. Jiang-Stein, 169.
18. Jiang-Stein, 169.
19. Jiang-Stein, 155.
20. Smarsh, *Heartland,* 285.
21. Smarsh, 264–65.
22. Smarsh, 286.
23. Smarsh, 280.
24. Smarsh, 284.
25. Smarsh, 281.
26. Smarsh, 281.
27. Smarsh, 281.
28. Smarsh, 3.
29. Smarsh, 281–82.
30. Eire, *Learning to Die in Miami,* 30–31.
31. Eire, *Learning to Die in Miami.*
32. Jenkins, *To Shake the Sleeping Self.*

33. Westover, *Educated*.
34. Walls, *Glass Castle*.
35. Chin, *Other Side of Paradise*.
36. Feldman, *Unorthodox*.
37. Boylan, *She's Not There*.
38. Deen, *All Who Go Do Not Return*.
39. Preston, *Out with It*.
40. Eire, *Learning to Die in Miami*.
41. Axelrod, *Point of Vanishing*.
42. DuBrul, *Maps to the Other Side*.
43. Armstrong, *Spiral Staircase*.
44. Johnson, *How We Fight for Our Lives*.
45. Ochs and Capps, "Narrating the Self," 24.
46. Ochs and Capps, *Living Narrative*, 2.
47. Ochs and Capps, "Narrating the Self," 23.
48. Aronie, *Memoir as Medicine*; Lourey, *Rewrite Your Life*; Smith, *Memoir Project*.
49. Waitt and Gorman-Murray, "Journeys and Returns," 1245–46.
50. Jenkins, *To Shake the Sleeping Self*, 298.
51. Walls, *Glass Castle*, 3–4.
52. Calcaterra, *Etched in Sand*, 300.
53. Onwuachi, *Notes from a Young Black Chef*, 246.
54. Onwuachi, 246.
55. Jenkins, *To Shake the Sleeping Self*, 298.
56. Calcaterra, *Etched in Sand*, 300.
57. Boylan, *She's Not There*, 137.
58. Westover, *Educated*, 280.
59. Feldman, *Unorthodox*, 1.
60. Feldman, 1.
61. Winn, *Salt Path*, 182–83.
62. Lythcott-Haims, *Real American*, 255.
63. Keenan, *Sex with Shakespeare*, 8–9.
64. Lythcott-Haims, *Real American*, 255.
65. Keenan, *Sex with Shakespeare*, 8–9.
66. Winn, *Salt Path*, 182–83.
67. Matis, *Girl in the Woods*, 230.
68. Gelman, *Tales of a Female Nomad*, 68.
69. Hill, *Rethinking Normal*, 194.
70. Axelrod, *Point of Vanishing*, 189–90.

71. Sasson, *Accidental Soldier*, 207–8.

72. Armstrong, *Spiral Staircase*, 176–77.

73. Chin, *Other Side of Paradise*, 280.

74. Westover, *Educated*, 319.

75. Ochs and Capps, *Living Narrative*, 4.

76. Ochs and Capps, 207. See also Eastmond, "Stories as Lived Experience"; Leyshon and Bull, "Bricolage of Here."

77. Jenkins, *To Shake the Sleeping Self*, 300–301.

78. Pham, *Catfish and Mandala*, 337.

79. Lythcott-Haims, *Real American*, 211, 172, 227.

80. Lythcott-Haims, 211.

81. Jenkins, *To Shake the Sleeping Self*, 300.

82. Westover, *Educated*, 280.

83. Feldman, *Unorthodox*, 251.

84. Armstrong, *Spiral Staircase*, xvii–xviiii.

85. Armstrong, 267.

86. Ochs and Capps, *Living Narrative*, 223.

87. Lewis, "Remapping Disclosure," 217.

88. Wyatt and Wyatt, "(Be)Coming Home," 32.

89. O'Reilly and Benson, "Lifestyle Migration," 10.

90. O'Reilly and Benson, 11.

91. Armstrong, *Spiral Staircase*, 223.

92. Walls, *Glass Castle*, 280.

93. Ali, *Nomad*, 5.

94. Ali, 107.

95. Onwuachi, *Notes from a Young Black Chef*, 246.

96. Matis, *Your Blue Is Not My Blue*.

97. Chung, *All You Can Ever Know*, 126.

98. Winterson, *Why Be Happy*, 225.

99. Matis, *Girl in the Woods*, 361.

100. Preston, *Out with It*, 177.

101. Keenan, *Sex with Shakespeare*, 174, 293.

102. Mock, *Redefining Realness*, xvii.

103. Mock, xvii.

104. Ali, *Nomad*, 130–31.

105. Hill, *Beyond Belief*, 376.

106. Jiang-Stein, *Prison Baby*, 148.

107. Coddington and Micieli-Voutsinas, "On Trauma, Geography, and Mobility," 52.

108. Adams-Hutcheson, "Spatialising Skin," 105.

109. Ochs and Capps, *Living Narrative*, 43.

110. Tolia-Kelly, "Locating Processes of Identification," 314.

111. Winterson, *Why Be Happy*, 63.

112. DuBrul, *Maps to the Other Side*, 85.

113. Jenkins, *To Shake the Sleeping Self*, 143.

114. Walls, *Glass Castle*, 89.

115. hooks, "Kentucky Is My Fate," 16.

116. Calcaterra, *Etched in Sand*, 287.

117. Feldman, *Unorthodox*, 246.

118. Said, "Intellectual Exile," 114.

119. Eire, *Learning to Die in Miami*, 23.

120. Eire, 23.

121. Eire, 23.

122. hooks, "Kentucky Is My Fate," 12.

123. hooks, 18.

124. Ali, *Nomad*, 12.

125. Tamm, *Cartwheels in a Sari*, 283.

126. Walls, *Glass Castle*, 3.

127. Conley, *Boy Erased*, 332.

128. Conley, 332.

129. Conley, 332–33.

130. Gordon, *Ghostly Matters*, 8.

131. Pred, *Past Is Not Dead*.

132. Winterson, *Why Be Happy*, 165–66.

133. DuBrul, *Maps to the Other Side*, 88.

134. Chin, *Other Side of Paradise*, 277.

135. Chin, 277.

136. Calcaterra, *Etched in Sand*, 287.

137. Calcaterra, 300.

138. Feldman, *Unorthodox*, 246.

139. Feldman, 246.

140. Feldman, 247.

141. Díaz, *Ordinary Girls*, 267.

142. Díaz, 307.

143. Díaz, 267.

144. hooks, "Kentucky Is My Fate," 18.

145. hooks, 18.

146. Jiang-Stein, *Prison Baby*, 169.

147. Deen, *All Who Go Do Not Return*, 298–99.
148. Deen, 300.
149. Bosangit et al., "'If I Was Going to Die,'" 3.
150. Said, "Intellectual Exile," 116.
151. Heins, *Beyond Friend and Foe*, 23.
152. Hill, *Beyond Belief*, 392–93.
153. Hill, 392.
154. Keenan, *Sex with Shakespeare*, 299.
155. Mock, *Redefining Realness*, 257.
156. Mock, 257.
157. Lythcott-Haims, *Real American*, 191.
158. Lythcott-Haims, 199.
159. Preston, *Out with It*, 177–78.
160. Preston, 178.
161. Said, *Reflections on Exile*, 173, 182.
162. Said, "Intellectual Exile," 121.
163. Said, 123.

Conclusion

1. Ali, *Nomad*; Jiang-Stein, *Prison Baby*; Keenan, *Sex with Shakespeare*; Mock, *Redefining Realness*; Smarsh, *Heartland*.
2. Axelrod, *Point of Vanishing*; Keenan, *Sex with Shakespeare*; Lythcott-Haims, *Real American*; Westover, *Educated*.
3. Gelman, *Tales of a Female Nomad*; Hill, *Beyond Belief*; Peralta, *Undocumented*; Pham, *Catfish and Mandala*; Preston, *Out with It*; Tamm, *Cartwheels in a Sari*.
4. Deen, *All Who Go Do Not Return*; Feldman, *Unorthodox*; Jones, *How We Fight for Our Lives*.
5. Baldwin, *Not Just a Tomboy*; DuBrul, *Maps to the Other Side*; Díaz, *Ordinary Girls*; Winterson, *Why Be Happy*.
6. Armstrong, *Spiral Staircase*; Boylan, *She's Not There*; Chin, *Other Side of Paradise*; Jenkins, *To Shake the Sleeping Self*.

Bibliography

Abbott, Geoffrey. "Exile and Banishment." *Britannica Academic*, 2024. https://www.britannica.com/topic/exile-law.

Adams-Hutcheson, Gail. "Spatialising Skin: Pushing the Boundaries of Trauma Geographies." *Emotion, Space and Society* 24 (2017): 105–12.

Aizura, Aren Z. *Mobile Subjects: Transnational Imaginaries of Gender Reassignment.* Duke University Press, 2018.

Al-Sharif, Manal. *Daring to Drive: A Saudi Woman's Awakening.* Simon & Schuster, 2017.

Alba, Richard, and Victor Nee. "Rethinking Assimilation Theory for a New Era of Immigration." In *The New Immigration: An Interdisciplinary Reader,* edited by Suárez-Orozco, Marcelo M., Carola Suárez-Orozco, and Desirée Qin-Hilliard. Psychology Press, 2005.

Ali, Ayaan Hirsi. *Nomad: From Islam to America, a Personal Journey through the Clash of Civilizations.* Free Press, 2010.

Althusser, Louis. *Lenin and Philosophy and Other Essays.* Monthly Review Press, 1971.

Altier, Mary Beth, John Horgan, and Christian Thoroughgood. "In Their Own Words? Methodological Considerations in the Analysis of Terrorist Autobiographies." *Journal of Strategic Security* 5, no. 4 (2012): 85–98.

Antonsich, Marco. "Searching for Belonging: An Analytical Framework." *Geography Compass* 4, no. 6 (2010): 644–59.

Armstrong, Karen. *The Spiral Staircase: My Climb out of Darkness.* Alfred A. Knopf, 2004.

Aronie, Nancy S. *Memoir as Medicine: The Healing Power of Writing Your Messy, Imperfect, Unruly (but Gorgeously Yours) Life Story.* New World Library, 2022.

Atkinson, Will. "Anthony Giddens as Adversary of Class Analysis." *Sociology* 41, no. 3 (2007): 533–49.

Atkinson, Will. "Not All That Was Solid Has Melted Into Air (or Liquid): A Critique of Bauman on Individualization and Class in Liquid Modernity." *The Sociological Review* 56, no. 1 (2008): 1–17.

Axelrod, Howard. *The Point of Vanishing: A Memoir of Two Years in Solitude.* Beacon Press, 2015.

Baker, Deirdre F. "What We Found on Our Journey Through Fantasy Land." *Children's Literature in Education* 37, no. 3 (2006): 237–51.

Baldwin, Caspar. *Not Just a Tomboy: A Trans Masculine Memoir.* Jessica Kingsley Publishers, 2018.

Barbieri, Andrea, and Eleonora Rossero. "'It Is Like Post-Traumatic Stress Disorder, but in a Positive Sense!': New Territories of the Self as Inner Therapeutic Landscapes for Youth Experiencing Mental Ill-Health." *Health & Place* 85 (2024): 103157.

Bassnett, Susan. "Travel Writing and Gender." In *The Cambridge Companion to Travel Writing,* edited by Peter Hulme. Cambridge University Press, 2002.

Beech, Nic. "Liminality and the Practices of Identity Reconstruction." *Human Relations* 64, no. 2 (2011): 285–302.

Bhatia, Sunil, and Anjali Ram. "Theorizing Identity in Transnational and Diaspora Cultures: A Critical Approach to Acculturation." *International Journal of Intercultural Relations* 33, no. 2 (2009): 140–49.

Boeri, Miriam Williams. "Women After the Utopia: The Gendered Lives of Former Cult Members." *Journal of Contemporary Ethnography* 31, no. 3 (2002): 323–60.

Bondi, Liz. "Making Connections and Thinking through Emotions: Between Geography and Psychotherapy." *Transactions of the Institute of British Geographers* 30, no. 4 (2005): 433–48.

Bondi, Liz. "Feeling Insecure: A Personal Account in a Psychoanalytic Voice." *Social & Cultural Geography* 15, no. 3 (2014a): 332–50.

Bondi, Liz. "Understanding Feelings: Engaging with Unconscious Communication and Embodied Knowledge." *Emotion, Space and Society* 10 (2014b): 44–54.

Bosangit, Carmela, Sally Hibbert, and Scott McCabe. "'If I Was Going to Die I Should at Least Be Having Fun': Travel Blogs, Meaning and Tourist Experience." *Annals of Tourism Research* 55 (2015): 1–14.

Bowstead, Janet C. "Women on the Move: Theorising the Geographies of Domestic Violence Journeys in England." *Gender, Place & Culture* 24, no. 1 (2017): 108–21.

Boylan, Jennifer Finney. *She's Not There: A Life in Two Genders.* Broadway Books, 2003.

Brosseau, Marc. "In, Of, Out, With, and Through: New Perspectives in Literary Geography." In *The Routledge Handbook of Literature and Space*, edited by Robert T Tally Jr. Routledge, 2017.

Bryant, Rebecca. "On Critical Times: Return, Repetition, and the Uncanny Present." *History and Anthropology* 27, no. 1 (2016): 19–31.

Bunkše, Edmunds Valdemārs. "Feeling Is Believing, or Landscape as a Way of Being in the World." *Geografiska Annaler: Series B, Human Geography* 89, no. 3 (2007): 219–31.

Butterfield, Angie, and Daryl Martin. "Affective Sanctuaries: Understanding Maggie's as Therapeutic Landscapes." *Landscape Research* 41, no. 6 (2016): 695–706.

Calcaterra, Regina. *Etched in Sand: A True Story of Five Siblings who Survived an Unspeakable Childhood on Long Island.* William Morrow, 2013.

Calvillo, Caroline M. "Memoir and Autobiography: Pathways to Examining the Multicultural Self." *Multicultural Education* 1 (2003): 51–54.

Carr, Helen. "Modernism and Travel (1880–1940)." In *The Cambridge Companion to Travel Writing,* edited by Peter Hulme. Cambridge University Press, 2002.

Chawla, Devika, and Stacy Holman Jones. "Introduction." In *Stories of Home: Place, Identity, Exile,* edited by Devika Chawla and Stacy Holman Jones. Lexington Books, 2015.

Chin, Staceyann. *The Other Side of Paradise: A Memoir.* Scribner, 2009.

Chung, Nicole. *All You Can Ever Know: A Memoir.* Catapult, 2018.

Coddington, Kate. "Contagious Trauma: Reframing the Spatial Mobility of Trauma within Advocacy Work." *Emotion, Space and Society* 24 (2017): 66–73.

Coddington, Kate, and Jacque Micieli-Voutsinas. "On Trauma, Geography, and Mobility: Towards Geographies of Trauma." *Emotion, Space and Society* 24 (2017): 52–56.

Coker, Elizabeth Marie. "'Traveling Pains': Embodied Metaphors of Suffering among Southern Sudanese Refugees in Cairo." *Culture, Medicine, and Psychiatry* 28, no. 1 (2004): 15–39.

Collie, Natalie. "Cities of the Imagination: Science Fiction, Urban Space, and Community Engagement in Urban Planning." *Futures* 43, no. 4 (2011): 424–31.

Conley, Garrard. *Boy Erased: A Memoir of Identity, Faith, and Family.* Riverhead Books, 2016.

Craib, Raymond B. *Cartographic Mexico: A History of State Fixations and Fugitive Landscapes.* Duke University Press, 2004.

Cresswell, Tim. "Mobilities I: Catching Up." *Progress in Human Geography* 35 no. 4 (2011): 550–58.

Critcher, Clayton R., and Melissa J. Ferguson. "The Cost of Keeping It Hidden: Decomposing Concealment Reveals What Makes It Depleting." *Journal of Experimental Psychology: General* 143, no. 2 (2014): 721–35.

Davidson, Joyce and Mick R. Smith. "Emotional Geographies." In *International Encyclopedia of Human Geography,* edited by Nigel Thrift and Rob Kitchen. Elsevier, 2009.

Davies, Andrew D. "Assemblage and Social Movements: Tibet Support Groups and the Spatialities of Political Organisation." *Transactions of the Institute of British Geographers* 37, no. 2 (2012): 273–86.

Davis, Mike. *City of Quartz: Excavating the Future in Los Angeles.* Verso Books, 2006.

De Leeuw, Sarah, Margot W. Parkes, Vanessa Sloan Morgan, Julia Christensen, Nicole Lindsay, Kendra Mitchell-Foster, and Julia Russell Jozkow. "Going Unscripted: A Call to Critically Engage Storytelling Methods and Methodologies in Geography and the Medical-Health Sciences." *Canadian Geographies / Géographies Canadiennes* 61, no. 2 (2017): 152–64.

Deen, Shulem. *All Who Go Do Not Return: A Memoir.* Graywolf Press, 2015.

Denning, Michael. *The Cultural Front: The Laboring of American Culture in the Twentieth Century.* Verso, 1998.

Devine-Wright, Patrick. "Think Global, Act Local? The Relevance of Place Attachments and Place Identities in a Climate Changed World." *Global Environmental Change* 23, no. 1 (2013): 61–69.

Dewart, Georgia, Hiroko Kubota, Charlotte Berendonk, Jean Clandinin, and Vera Caine. "Lugones's Metaphor of 'World Travelling' in Narrative Inquiry." *Qualitative Inquiry* 26, no. 3–4 (2020): 369–78.

Di Masso, Andrés, Daniel R. Williams, Christopher M. Raymond, Matthias Buchecker, Barbara Degenhardt, Patrick Devine-Wright, Alice Hertzog et al. "Between Fixities and Flows: Navigating Place Attachments in an Increasingly Mobile World." *Journal of Environmental Psychology* 61 (2019): 125–33.

Díaz, Jaquira. *Ordinary Girls: A Memoir.* Algonquin Books of Chapel Hill, 2019.

Donohue-Smith, Maureen. "Telling the Whole Story: A Conceptual Model for Analysing the Mental Illness Memoir." *Mental Health Review Journal* 16, no. 3 (2011): 138–46.

Doughty, Karolina. "Therapeutic Landscapes of Stillness: Creating Affective Sanctuary Through Practices of Cocooning and Immersing." *Geografiska Annaler: Series B, Human Geography* (2023): 1–15.

DuBrul, Sascha Altman. *Maps to the Other Side: The Adventures of a Bipolar Cartographer*. Microcosm, 2013.

Dudley, Sandra. "Feeling at Home: Producing and Consuming Things in Karenni Refugee Camps on the Thai-Burma Border." *Population, Space and Place* 17, no. 6 (2011): 742–55.

Duff, Cameron. "Atmospheres of Recovery: Assemblages of Health." *Environment and Planning A: Economy and Space* 48, no. 1 (2016): 58–74.

Duncan, Simon, and Darren Smith. "Individualisation Versus the Geography of 'New' Families." *Twenty-First Century Society* 1, no. 2 (2006): 167–89.

Eastmond, Marita. "Stories as Lived Experience: Narratives in Forced Migration Research." *Journal of Refugee Studies* 20, no. 2 (2007): 248–64.

Edwards, Brent Hayes. "Diaspora." In *Keywords for American Cultural Studies*, edited by Bruce Burgett and Glenn Hendler. New York University Press, 2007.

Eichhorn, Kate. *The Archival Turn in Feminism: Outrage in Order*. Temple University Press, 2013.

Eire, Carlos. *Learning to Die in Miami: Confessions of a Refugee Boy*. Free Press, 2010.

El Refaie, Elisabeth. *Autobiographical Comics: Life Writing in Pictures*. University Press of Mississippi, 2012.

Ellis, Carolyn, Tony E. Adams, and Arthur P. Bochner. "Autoethnography: An Overview." *Historical Social Research/Historische Sozialforschung* 12, no. 1 (2011): 273–90.

Elsrud, Torun. "Risk Creation in Traveling: Backpacker Adventure Narration." *Annals of Tourism Research* 28, no. 3 (2001): 597–617.

Elsrud, Torun. "Time Creation in Travelling: The Taking and Making of Time Among Women Backpackers." *Time & Society* 7, no. 2–3 (1998): 309–34.

Feldman, Deborah. *Unorthodox: The Scandalous Rejection of My Hasidic Roots*. Simon & Schuster, 2012.

Fivush, Robyn. "Speaking Silence: The Social Construction of Silence in Autobiographical and Cultural Narratives." *Memory* 18, no. 2 (2010): 88–98.

Foucault, Michel. "The Subject and Power." In *Power: Essential Works of Foucault 1954–1984 Volume 3*, edited by James D. Faubion. The New Press, 1982.

Fraser, Emma. "Unbecoming Place: Urban Imaginaries in Transition in Detroit." *Cultural Geographies* 25, no. 3 (2018): 441–58.

Galani-Moutafi, Vasiliki. "The Self and the Other: Traveler, Ethnographer, Tourist." *Annals of Tourism Research* 27, no. 1 (2000): 203–24.

Gardner, Graham. "Unreliable Memories and Other Contingencies: Problems with Biographical Knowledge." *Qualitative Research* 1, no. 2 (2001): 185–204.

Gelman, Rita Golden. *Tales of a Female Nomad: Living at Large in the World.* Random House, 2001.

Giddens, Anthony. *Modernity and Self Identity: Self and Society in the Late Modern Age.* Polity, 1991.

Gideon, Jasmine. "Gendering Activism, Exile and Wellbeing: Chilean Exiles in the UK." *Gender, Place & Culture* 25, no. 2 (2018): 228–47.

Goffman, Erving. *The Presentation of Self in Everyday Life.* Doubleday, 1959.

Goldberg, Natalie. *Old Friend from Far Away: The Practice of Writing Memoir.* Free Press, 2007.

Gordon, Avery. *Ghostly Matters: Haunting and the Sociological Imagination.* University of Minnesota Press, 1997.

Gregory, Derek. *Geographical Imaginations.* Wiley-Blackwell, 1994.

Groth, Paul. "Frameworks for Cultural Landscape Study." In *Understanding Ordinary Landscapes,* edited by Paul Groth and Todd Bessi. Yale University Press, 1997.

Gupta, Nisha, Eva-Maria Simms, and Aaron Dougherty. "Eyes on the Street: Photovoice, Liberation Psychotherapy, and the Emotional Landscapes of Urban Children." *Emotion, Space and Society* 33 (2019): 100627.

Gustafson, Per. "Place Attachment in an Age of Mobility." In *Place Attachment: Advances in Theory, Methods and Applications,* edited by Lynne Manzo and Patrick Devine-Wright. Routledge, 2014.

Hackl, Andreas. "Key Figure of Mobility: The Exile." *Social Anthropology* 25 no. 1 (2017): 55–68.

Harris-Perry, Melissa V. *Sister Citizen: Shame, Stereotypes, and Black Women in America.* Yale University Press, 2011.

Hauf, James E. "Teaching World Cultures Through Artifacts." *Journal of Geography* 109, no. 3 (2010): 113–23.

Hayes-Conroy, Jessica, and Allison Hayes-Conroy. "Visceral Geographies: Mattering, Relating, and Defying." *Geography Compass* 4, no. 9 (2010): 1273–83.

Heins, Volker. *Beyond Friend and Foe: The Politics of Critical Theory.* Brill, 2011.

Herrmann, Gina. *Written in Red: The Communist Memoir in Spain.* University of Illinois Press, 2010.

Hill, Jenna Miscavige. *Beyond Belief: My Secret Life Inside Scientology and My Harrowing Escape.* HarperCollins, 2013.

Hill, Katie Rain. *Rethinking Normal: A Memoir in Transition.* Simon & Schuster, 2014.

Hobbs, Allyson. *A Chosen Exile: A History of Racial Passing in American Life.* Harvard University Press, 2019.

Hogan, Kristen. *The Feminist Bookstore Movement: Lesbian Antiracism and Feminist Accountability.* Duke University Press, 2016.

Hones, Sheila. *Literary Geography.* Routledge, 2022.

hooks, bell. "Kentucky Is My Fate." In *Belonging: A Culture of Place.* Routledge, 2009.

Hopper, Glenn. "The Isles/Ireland: The Wilder Shore." In *The Cambridge Companion to Travel Writing,* edited by Peter Hulme. Cambridge University Press, 2002.

Howell, Martha C., and Walter Prevenier. *From Reliable Sources: An Introduction to Historical Methods.* Cornell University Press, 2001.

Huard, Roger L. *Plato's Political Philosophy: The Cave.* Algora Publishing, 2007.

Hubbard, Phil. *Cities and Sexualities.* Routledge, 2013.

Hubbard, Phil, and Eleanor Wilkinson. "Walking a Lonely Path: Gender, Landscape and 'New Nature Writing.'" *Cultural Geographies* 26, no. 2 (2019): 253–61.

Hulme, Peter. "Travelling to Write (1940–2000)." In *The Cambridge Companion to Travel Writing,* edited by Peter Hulme. Cambridge University Press, 2002.

Hulme, Peter, and Tim Youngs. "Introduction." In *The Cambridge Companion to Travel Writing,* edited by Peter Hulme. Cambridge University Press, 2002.

Ibrahim, Awad. "The New Flâneur: Subaltern Cultural Studies, African Youth in Canada and the Semiology of In-Betweenness." *Cultural Studies* 22, no. 2 (2008): 234–53.

Iftin, Abdi Nor. *Call Me American: A Memoir.* Alfred A. Knopf, 2018.

Imamaliyeva, Leyla Majid. "Some Aspects in Azerbaijanian Memoir Literature." *Amazonia Investiga* 11, no. 54 (2022): 109–20.

Iyer, Aarti, and Jolanda Jetten. "What's Left Behind: Identity Continuity Moderates the Effect of Nostalgia on Well-Being and Life Choices." *Journal of Personality and Social Psychology* 101, no. 1 (2011): 94–108.

Jackson, Emma, and Tim Butler. "Revisiting 'Social Tectonics': The Middle Classes and Social Mix in Gentrifying Neighbourhoods." *Urban Studies* 52, no. 13 (2015): 2349–65.

Jacobs, Jane. *The Death and Life of Great American Cities.* Random House, 1961.

Jager, Adèle de, Anna Tewson, Bryn Ludlow, and Katherine Boydell. "Embodied Ways of Storying the Self: A Systematic Review of Body-Mapping." *Forum Qualitative Sozialforschung / Forum: Qualitative Social Research* 17 no. 2 (2016): Art. 22.

Jenkins, Jedidiah. *To Shake the Sleeping Self: A Journey from Oregon to Patagonia, and a Quest for a Life with No Regret.* Convergent Books, 2018.

Jiang-Stein, Deborah. *Prison Baby: A Memoir.* Beacon Press, 2014.

Johnson, Patricia Claudette. "Writing Liminal Landscapes: The Cosmopolitical Gaze." *Tourism Geographies* 12, no. 4 (2010): 505–24.

Jones, Saeed. *How We Fight for Our Lives: A Memoir.* Simon & Schuster, 2019.

Joyce, Patrick. *The Rule of Freedom: Liberalism and the Modern City.* Verso, 2003.

Kaplan, Caren. *Questions of Travel: Postmodern Discourses of Displacement.* Duke University Press, 1996.

Karlsen, Marry-Anne. "Waiting Out the Condition of Illegality in Norway." In *Waiting and the Temporalities of Irregular Migration,* edited by Christine M. Jacobsen, Marry-Anne Karlsen, and Shahram Khosravi. Routledge, 2020.

Keenan, Jillian. *Sex with Shakespeare: Here's Much to Do with Pain, but More to Do with Love.* HarperCollins, 2016.

Kinder, Kimberley. *The Radical Bookstore: Counterspace for Social Movements.* University of Minnesota Press, 2021.

Kinney, Rebecca J. *Beautiful Wasteland: The Rise of Detroit as America's Postindustrial Frontier.* University of Minnesota Press, 2016.

Kirmayer, Laurence J. "Failures of Imagination: The Refugee's Narrative in Psychiatry." *Anthropology & Medicine* 10, no. 2 (2003): 167–85.

Kist, William. "Life Moments in Texts: Analyzing Multimodal Memoirs of Preservice Teachers." *English Journal* 106, no. 3 (2017): 63–68.

Kwan, Mei-Po, and Tim Schwanen. "Geographies of Mobility." *Annals of the American Association of Geographers* 106, no. 2 (2016): 1–14.

Larsen, Jonas, and Mathilde Dissing Christensen. "The Unstable Lives of Bicycles: The 'Unbecoming' of Design Objects." *Environment and Planning A: Economy and Space* 47, no. 4 (2015): 922–38.

Leitner, Helga. "Spaces of Encounters: Immigration, Race, Class, and the Politics of Belonging in Small-Town America." *Annals of the Association of American Geographers* 102, no. 4 (2012): 828–46.

Lewis, Nathaniel M. "Remapping Disclosure: Gay Men's Segmented Journeys of Moving Out and Coming Out." *Social & Cultural Geography* 13, no. 3 (2012): 211–31.

Leyshon, Michael, and Jacob Bull. "The Bricolage of the Here: Young People's Narratives of Identity in the Countryside." *Social & Cultural Geography* 12, no. 2 (2011): 159–80.

Li, Xu, and Youcheng Wang. "China in the Eyes of Western Travelers as Represented in Travel Blogs." *Journal of Travel & Tourism Marketing* 28, no. 7 (2011): 689–719.

Li, Wei. *Ethnoburb: The New Ethnic Community in Urban America.* University of Hawai'i Press, 2008.

Lisle, Debbie. *Holidays in the Danger Zone: Entanglements of War and Tourism.* University of Minnesota Press, 2016.

Llewellyn-Beardsley, Joy, Stefan Rennick-Egglestone, Felicity Callard, Paul Crawford, Marianne Farkas, Ada Hui, David Manley, et al. "Characteristics of Mental Health Recovery Narratives: Systematic Review and Narrative Synthesis." *PLOS ONE* 14, no. 3 (2019): e0214678.

Logan, John R., and Harvey Molotch. *Urban Fortunes: The Political Economy of Place.* University of California Press, 2007.

Longhurst, Robyn, Lynda Johnston, and Elsie Ho. "A Visceral Approach: Cooking 'at Home' with Migrant Women in Hamilton, New Zealand." *Transactions of the Institute of British Geographers* 34, no. 3 (2009): 333–45.

Lourey, Jessica. *Rewrite Your Life: Discover Your Truth Through the Healing Power of Fiction.* Red Wheel/Weiser, 2017.

Lythcott-Haims, Julie. *Real American: A Memoir.* Henry Holt and Company, 2017.

Maddern, Jo Frances, and Peter Adey. "Editorial: Spectro-Geographies." *Cultural Geographies* 15, no. 3 (2008): 291–95.

Maddrell, Avril. "Mapping Grief. A Conceptual Framework for Understanding the Spatial Dimensions of Bereavement, Mourning and Remembrance." *Social & Cultural Geography* 17, no. 2 (2016): 166–88.

Malecka, Katarzyna. "The Self Lost, the Self Adjusted: Forming a New Identity in Bereavement Memoirs by American Women." *Studia Anglica Posnaniensia* 50, no. 2–3 (2015): 155–74.

Mandaville, Peter. "Territory and Translocality: Discrepant Idioms of Political Identity." *Millenium: Journal of International Studies* 28, no. 3 (1999): 653–73.

March, Loren. "Queer and Trans* Geographies of Liminality: A Literature Review." *Progress in Human Geography* 45, no. 3 (2021): 455–71.

Massey, Doreen. *For Space.* Sage Publications, 2005.

Mathews, Richard. *Fantasy: The Liberation of Imagination.* Psychology Press, 2002.

Matis, Aspen. *Girl in the Woods: A Memoir.* HarperCollins, 2015.

Matis, Aspen. *Your Blue Is Not My Blue: A Missing Person Memoir.* Little A, 2020.

Mauss, Marcel. "A Category of the Human Mind: The Notion of Person, the Notion of Self." In *The Category of the Person: Anthropology, Philosophy, History,* edited by Michael Carrithers, Steve Collins, and Steve Lukes. Cambridge University Press, 1985.

McCloud, Sean. "Liminal Subjectivities and Religious Change: Circumscribing Giddens for the Study of Contemporary American Religion." *Journal of Contemporary Religion* 22, no. 3 (2007): 295–309.

McDowell, Linda. "Thinking Through Work: Complex Inequalities, Constructions of Difference and Trans-National Migrants." *Progress in Human Geography* 32, no. 4 (2008): 491–507.

McGregor, JoAnn. "Locating Exile: Decolonization, Anti-Imperial Spaces and Zimbabwean Students in Britain, 1965–1980." *Journal of Historical Geography* 57 (2017): 62–75.

McWha, Madelene, Warwick Frost, and Jennifer Laing. "Travel Writers and the Nature of Self: Essentialism, Transformation and (Online) Construction." *Annals of Tourism Research* 70 (2018): 14–24.

Mee, Kathleen, and Sarah Wright. "Geographies of Belonging." *Environment and Planning A* 41, no. 4 (2009): 772–79.

Megill, Allan. *Historical Knowledge, Historical Error: A Contemporary Guide to Practice.* University of Chicago Press, 2007.

Middleton, Catherine A. "Roots and Rootlessness: An Exploration of the Concept in the Life and Novels of George Eliot." In *Humanistic Geography and Literature: Essays on the Experience of Place,* edited by Douglas Pocock. Routledge, 2014.

Milligan, Melinda J. "Displacement and Identity Discontinuity: The Role of Nostalgia in Establishing New Identity Categories." *Symbolic Interaction* 26, no. 3 (2003): 381–403.

Mitchell, Katharyne. "Pre-Black Futures." *Antipode* 41, no. S1 (2010): 239–61.

Mlakar, Heike. *Merely Being There Is Not Enough: Women's Roles in Autobiographical Texts by Female Beat Writers.* Universal Publishers, 2008.

Mock, Janet. *Redefining Realness: My Path to Womanhood, Identity, Love & So Much More.* Atria, 2014.

Mountz, Alison. "Political Geography III: Bodies." *Progress in Human Geography* 42, no. 5 (2018): 759–69.

Murphy, Joseph. "From Place to Exile." *Transactions of the Institute of British Geographers* 36, no. 4 (2011): 473–78.

Murray, Liz. *Breaking Night: A Memoir of Forgiveness, Survival, and My Journey from Homeless to Harvard.* Hachette Books, 2010.

Nijman, Jan. "Locals, Exiles and Cosmopolitans: A Theoretical Argument about Identity and Place in Miami." *Tijdschrift voor Economische en Sociale Geografie* 98, no. 2 (2007): 176–87.

Noxolo, Patricia, and Marika Preziuso. "Postcolonial Imaginations: Approaching a 'Fictionable' World Through the Novels of Maryse Condé and Wilson Harris." *Annals of the Association of American Geographers* 103, no. 1 (2013): 163–79.

Noy, Chaim. "This Trip Really Changed Me: Backpackers' Narratives of Self-Change." *Annals of Tourism Research* 31, no. 1 (2004): 78–102.

Nurser, Kate P., Imogen Rushworth, Tom Shakespeare, and Deirdre Williams. "Personal Storytelling in Mental Health Recovery." *Mental Health Review Journal* 23, no. 1 (2018): 25–36.

O'Brien, Elaine, and Carol Linehan. "Problematizing the Authentic Self in Conceptualizations of Emotional Dissonance." *Human Relations* 72, no. 9 (2019): 1530–56.

O'Reilly, Karen, and Michaela Benson. "Lifestyle Migration: Escaping to the Good Life?" In *Lifestyle Migration,* edited by Michaela Benson and Karen O'Reilly. Routledge, 2009.

O'Sullivan-Lago, Ria, and Guida de Abreu. "Maintaining Continuity in a Cultural Contact Zone: Identification Strategies in the Dialogical Self." *Culture & Psychology* 16, no. 1 (2010): 73–92.

Ochs, Elinor, and Lisa Capps. "Narrating the Self." *Annual Review of Anthropology* 25, no. 1 (1996): 19–43.

Ochs, Elinor, and Lisa Capps. *Living Narrative: Creating Lives in Everyday Storytelling.* Harvard University Press, 2001.

Ong, Aihwa. "Cultural Citizenship as Subject-Making: Immigrants Negotiate Racial and Cultural Boundaries in the US." *Current Anthropology* 37, no. 5 (1996): 737–62.

Onwuachi, Kwame, with Joshua David Stein. *Notes from a Young Black Chef: A Memoir.* Alfred A. Knopf, 2019.

Pagis, Michal. "Embodied Therapeutic Culture." In *The Routledge International Handbook of Global Therapeutic Cultures,* edited by Daniel Nehring, Ole Jacob Madsen, Edgar Cabanas, China Mills, and Dylan Kerrigan. Routledge, 2020.

Pan, Bing, Tanya MacLaurin, and John C. Crotts. "Travel Blogs and the Implications for Destination Marketing." *Journal of Travel Research* 46, no. 1 (2007): 35–45.

Papadopoulos, Dimitris. "In the Ruins of Representation: Identity, Individuality, Subjectification." *British Journal of Social Psychology* 47, no. 1 (2008): 139–65.

Peralta, Dan-el Padilla. *Undocumented: A Dominican Boy's Odyssey from a Homeless Shelter to the Ivy League.* Penguin, 2015.

Pham, Andrew. *Catfish and Mandala: A Two-Wheeled Voyage through the Landscape and Memory of Vietnam.* Farrar, Straus and Giroux, 1999.

Pocock, Douglas. "Introduction: Imaginative Literature and the Geographer." In *Humanistic Geography and Literature: Essays on the Experience of Place,* edited by Douglas Pocock. Routledge, 2014.

Portes, Alejandro, and Ruben G. Rumbaut. *Immigrant America.* University of California Press, 1990.

Portes, Alejandro, and Min Zhou. "The New Second Generation: Segmented Assimilation and Its Variants." *The Annals of the American Academy of Political and Social Science* 530, no. 1 (1993): 74–96.

Power, Andrew, and Ruth Bartlett. "Self-Building Safe Havens in a Post-Service Landscape: How Adults with Learning Disabilities Are Reclaiming the Welcoming Communities Agenda." *Social & Cultural Geography* 19, no. 3 (2018): 336–56.

Pratt, Mary Louise. *Imperial Eyes: Travel Writing and Transculturation.* Routledge, 2007.

Pred, Allen. *The Past Is Not Dead: Facts, Fictions, and Enduring Racial Stereotypes.* University of Minnesota Press, 2004.

Preston, Katherine. *Out with It: How Stuttering Helped Me Find My Voice.* Atria, 2014.

Price, Leah. *How to Do Things with Books in Victorian Britain.* Princeton University Press, 2012.

Probyn, Elspeth. *Outside Belongings.* Routledge, 1996.

Radden, Jennifer, and Somogy Varga. "The Epistemological Value of Depression Memoirs: A Meta-Analysis." In *The Oxford Handbook of Philosophy and Psychiatry,* edited by K. W. M. Fulford, Martin Davies, Richard G. T. Gipps, George Graham, John Z. Sadler, Giovanni Stanghellini, and Tim Thorton. Oxford University Press, 2013.

Rak, Julie. *Boom!: Manufacturing Memoir for the Popular Market.* Wilfrid Laurier University Press, 2013.

Rimke, Heidi. "Self-Help, Therapeutic Industries, and Neoliberalism." In *The Routledge International Handbook of Global Therapeutic Cultures,* edited by Daniel Nehring, Ole Jacob Madsen, Edgar Cabanas, China Mills, and Dylan Kerrigan. Routledge, 2020.

Rippl, Gabriele, Philipp Schweighauser, and Therese Steffen. "Introduction: Life Writing in an Age of Trauma." In *Haunted Narratives: Life Writing in an Age of Trauma,* edited by Gabriele Rippl, Philipp Schweighauser, Tina Kirss, Margit Sutrop, and Therese Steffen. University of Toronto Press, 2013.

Rose, Diana. "The Mainstreaming of Recovery." *Journal of Mental Health* 23, no. 5 (2014): 217–18.

Rose, Emma. "Encountering Place: A Psychoanalytic Approach for Understanding How Therapeutic Landscapes Benefit Health and Wellbeing." *Health & Place* 18, no. 6 (2012): 1381–87.

Rose, Gillian. "Spatialities of 'Community', Power and Change: The Imagined Geographies of Community Arts Projects." *Cultural Studies* 11, no. 1 (1997): 1–16.

Ross, Jeffrey Ian, Richard Tewksbury, Lauren Samuelson, and Tiara Caneff. "War Stories? Analyzing Memoirs and Autobiographical Treatments Written by American Correctional Professionals." *Criminology, Criminal Justice, Law & Society* 22, no. 3 (2021): 1–13.

Rubies, Joan Pau. "Travelling to Write (1940–2000)." In *The Cambridge Companion to Travel Writing,* edited by Peter Hulme. Cambridge University Press, 2002.

Safransky, Sara. "Greening the Urban Frontier: Race, Property, and Resettlement in Detroit." *Geoforum* 56 (2014): 237–48.

Said, Edward W. "Intellectual Exile: Expatriates and Marginals." *Grand Street* 12, no. 3 (1993): 112–24.

Said, Edward W. *Reflections on Exile and Other Essays.* Harvard University Press, 2000.

Sasson, Dorit. *Accidental Soldier: A Memoir of Service and Sacrifice in the Israel Defense Forces.* She Writes Press, 2016.

Schramm, Katharina. "Introduction: Landscapes of Violence: Memory and Sacred Space." *History and Memory* 23, no. 1 (2011): 5–22.

Seamon, David. "Newcomers, Existential Outsiders and Insiders: Their Portrayal in Two Books by Doris Lessing." In *Humanistic Geography and Literature: Essays on the Experience of Place,* edited by Douglas Pocock. Routledge, 2014.

Sheller, Mimi. "Theorizing Mobility Justice." In *Mobilities, Mobility Justice, and Social Justice,* edited by Nancy Cook and David Butz. Routledge, 2019.

Smarsh, Sarah. *Heartland: A Memoir of Working Hard and Being Broke in the Richest Country on Earth.* Scribner, 2018.

Smith, Marion R. *The Memoir Project: A Thoroughly Non-standardized Text for Writing & Life.* Grand Central Publishing, 2011.

Spain, Daphne. *Constructive Feminism: Women's Spaces and Women's Rights in the American City.* Cornell University Press, 2016.

Spivak, Gayatri. "Can the Subaltern Speak?" In *Marxism and the Interpretation of Culture,* edited by Cary Nelson and Lawrence Grossberg. University of Illinois Press, 1988.

Stobbelaar, Derk Jan, and Bas Pedroli. "Perspectives on Landscape Identity: A Conceptual Challenge." *Landscape Research* 36, no. 3 (2011): 321–39.

Straughan, Elizabeth, David Bissell, and Andrew Gorman-Murray. "The Politics of Stuckness: Waiting Lives in Mobile Worlds." *Environment and Planning C: Politics and Space* 38, no. 4 (2020): 636–55.

Suárez-Orozco, Marcelo M. "Right Moves? Immigration, Globalization, Utopia, and Dystopia." In *The New Immigration: An Interdisciplinary Reader,* edited by Marcelo M. Suárez-Orozco, Carola Suárez-Orozco, and Desirée Qin-Hilliard. Psychology Press, 2005.

Suárez-Orozco, Marcelo M. "Everything You Ever Wanted to Know About Assimilation but Were Afraid to Ask." In *The New Immigration: An Interdisciplinary Reader,* edited by Marcelo M. Suárez-Orozco, Carola Suárez-Orozco, and Desirée Qin-Hilliard. Psychology Press, 2005.

Sundberg, Juanita. "Reconfiguring North–South Solidarity: Critical Reflections on Experiences of Transnational Resistance." *Antipode* 39, no. 1 (2007): 144–66.

Sweet, Paige. *The Politics of Surviving: How Women Navigate Domestic Violence and Its Aftermath.* University of California Press, 2021.

Szerszynski, Bronislaw, and John Urry. "Visuality, Mobility and the Cosmopolitan: Inhabiting the World from Afar." *The British Journal of Sociology* 57, no. 1 (2006): 113–31.

Takacs, Christopher George. "Becoming Interesting: Narrative Capital Development at Elite Colleges." *Qualitative Sociology* 43, no. 2 (2020): 1–16.

Tamm, Jayanti. *Cartwheels in a Sari: A Memoir of Growing Up in a Cult.* Harmony Books, 2009.

Taylor, Charles. *Sources of the Self: Making of Modern Identity.* Harvard University Press, 1989.

Taylor, Judith. "The Problem of Women's Sociality in Contemporary North American Feminist Memoir." *Gender & Society* 22, no. 6 (2008): 705–27.

Teltscher, Kate. "India/Calcutta: City of Palaces and Dreadful Night." In *The Cambridge Companion to Travel Writing,* edited by Peter Hulme. Cambridge University Press, 2002.

Thomassen, Bjørn. "Revisiting Liminality: The Danger of Empty Spaces." In *Liminal Landscapes: Travel, Experience and Spaces In-Between,* edited by Hazel Andrews and Les Roberts. Routledge, 2012.

Tolia-Kelly, Divya P. "Locating Processes of Identification: Studying the Precipitates of Re-Memory Through Artefacts in the British Asian Home." *Transactions of the Institute of British Geographers* 29, no. 3 (2004): 314–29.

Toolis, Erin E. "Theorizing Critical Placemaking as a Tool for Reclaiming Public Space." *American Journal of Community Psychology* 59, no. 1–2 (2017): 184–99.

Torkington, Kate. "Place and Lifestyle Migration: The Discursive Construction of 'Glocal' Place-Identity." *Mobilities* 7, no. 1 (2012): 71–92.

Umemoto, Karen. "Walking in Another's Shoes: Epistemological Challenges in Participatory Planning." *Journal of Planning Education and Research* 21, no. 1 (2001): 17–31.

Valentine, Gill. "Living with Difference: Reflections on Geographies of Encounter." *Progress in Human Geography* 32, no. 3 (2008): 323–37.

Valli, Chiara. "When Cultural Workers Become an Urban Social Movement: Political Subjectification and Alternative Cultural Production in the Macao Movement, Milan." *Environment and Planning A* 47, no. 3 (2015): 643–59.

Van der Kolk, Bessel. *The Body Keeps the Score: Brain, Mind, and Body in the Healing of Trauma.* Penguin Books, 2014.

Van Nuenen, Tom. "Here I Am: Authenticity and Self-Branding on Travel Blogs." *Tourist Studies* 16, no. 2 (2016): 192–212.

Vandemark, Lisa M. "Promoting the Sense of Self, Place, and Belonging in Displaced Persons: The Example of Homelessness." *Archives of Psychiatric Nursing* 21, no. 5 (2007): 241–48.

Von Benzon, Nadia. "'I Fell Out of a Tree and Broke My Neck': Acknowledging Fantasy in Children's Research Contributions." *Children's Geographies* 13, no. 3 (2015): 330–42.

Vanolo, Alberto. "Shame, Guilt, and the Production of Urban Space." *Progress in Human Geography* 45 no. 4 (2021): 758–75.

Waitt, Gordon, and Andrew Gorman-Murray. "Journeys and Returns: Home, Life Narratives and Remapping Sexuality in a Regional City." *International Journal of Urban and Regional Research* 35, no. 6 (2011): 1239–55.

Wallach, Jennifer Jensen. *Closer to the Truth than Any Fact: Memoir, Memory, and Jim Crow.* University of Georgia Press, 2010.

Walls, Jeannette. *The Glass Castle: A Memoir.* Scribner, 2005.

Ward, Simon. "'Danger Zones': The British 'Road Movie' and the Liminal Landscape." In *Liminal Landscapes: Travel, Experience and Spaces In-Between,* edited by Hazel Andrews and Les Roberts. Routledge, 2012.

Wariner, Ruth. *The Sound of Gravel: A Memoir.* Flatiron Books, 2015.

Waters, Mary C., Van C. Tran, Philip Kasinitz, and John H. Mollenkopf. "Segmented Assimilation Revisited: Types of Acculturation and Socioeconomic Mobility in Young Adulthood." *Ethnic and Racial Studies* 33, no. 7 (2010): 1168–93.

Watson, Cate. "Unreliable Narrators?: 'Inconsistency' (and Some Inconstancy) in Interviews." *Qualitative Research* 6, no. 3 (2006): 367–84.

Westover, Tara. *Educated: A Memoir.* Random House, 2018.

White, Edmund. *The Flâneur: A Stroll Through the Paradoxes of Paris.* Bloomsbury, 2001.

Willis, Alette. "Restorying the Self, Restoring Place: Healing Through Grief in Everyday Places." *Emotion, Space and Society* 2, no. 2 (2009): 86–91.

Willis, Alette. "Re-storying Wilderness and Adventure Therapies: Healing Places and Selves in an Era of Environmental Crises." *Journal of Adventure Education & Outdoor Learning* 11, no. 2 (2011): 91–108.

Wilson, Chris. *The Master Plan: My Journey from Life in Prison to a Life of Purpose.* G. P. Putnam's Sons, 2019.

Wilson, Helen F. "On Geography and Encounter: Bodies, Borders, and Difference." *Progress in Human Geography* 41, no. 4 (2017): 451–71.

Windling, Terri. "Into the Woods: A Writer's Journey through Fairy Tales and Fantasy." *Journal of the Fantastic in the Arts* 28, no. 1 (2017): 33–45.

Winn, Raynor. *The Salt Path: A Memoir.* Penguin, 2018.

Winterson, Jeanette. *Why Be Happy When You Could Be Normal?* Grove Press, 2011.

Winterton, Rachel, and Jeni Warburton. "Ageing in the Bush: The Role of Rural Places in Maintaining Identity for Long Term Rural Residents and Retirement Migrants in North-East Victoria, Australia." *Journal of Rural Studies* 28, no. 4 (2012): 329–37.

Woods, Angela, Akiko Hart, and Helen Spandler. "The Recovery Narrative: Politics and Possibilities of a Genre." *Culture, Medicine, and Psychiatry* 46, no. 2 (2022): 221–47.

Wright, Katie. "Recognising the Political in the Therapeutic." In *The Routledge International Handbook of Global Therapeutic Cultures,* edited by Daniel Nehring, Ole Jacob Madsen, Edgar Cabanas, China Mills, and Dylan Kerrigan. Routledge, 2020.

Wright, Sarah. "More-Than-Human, Emergent Belongings: A Weak Theory Approach." *Progress in Human Geography* 39, no. 4 (2015): 391–411.

Wyatt, Jonathan, and Tessa Wyatt. "(Be)Coming Home." In *Stories of Home: Place, Identity, Exile,* edited by Devika Chawla and Stacy Holman Jones. Lexington Books, 2015.

Wylie, John. "Landscape, Absence and the Geographies of Love." *Transactions of the Institute of British Geographers* 34, no. 3 (2009): 275–89.

Wylie, John. "The Spectral Geographies of WG Sebald." *Cultural Geographies* 14, no. 2 (2007): 171–88.

Young, Iris Marion. "City Life and Difference." In *Readings in Planning Theory,* 2nd ed., edited by Scott Campbell and Susan Fainstein. Blackwell Publishing, 2003.

Youngs, Tim. "Africa/The Congo: The Politics of Darkness." In *The Cambridge Companion to Travel Writing,* edited by Peter Hulme. Cambridge University Press, 2002.

Yuval-Davis, Nira. "Theorizing Identity: Beyond the 'Us' and 'Them' Dichotomy." *Patterns of Prejudice* 44, no. 3 (2010): 261–80.

Zehrer, Anita, John C. Crotts, and Vincent P. Magnini. "The Perceived Usefulness of Blog Postings: An Extension of the Expectancy-Disconfirmation Paradigm." *Tourism Management* 32 (2011): 106–13.

Index

KIMBERLEY KINDER is associate professor of urban and regional planning at the University of Michigan. She is author of *The Radical Bookstore: Counterspace for Social Movements* (Minnesota, 2021), *DIY Detroit: Making Do in a City without Services* (Minnesota, 2016), and *The Politics of Urban Water: Changing Waterscapes in Amsterdam*.